SELF, WAR, & SOCIETY

SELF, WAR, & SOCIETY

George Herbert Mead's Macrosociology

Mary Jo Deegan

Transaction Publishers
New Brunswick (U.S.A.) and London (U.K.)

First paperback printing 2012
Copyright © 2008 by Transaction Publishers, New Brunswick, New Jersey.

This book is printed on acid-free paper that meets the American National Standard for Permanence of Paper for Printed Library Materials.

Library of Congress Catalog Number: 2008014817
ISBN: 978-0-7658-0392-4 (cloth); 978-1-4128-4757-5 (paper)
Printed in the United States of America

Library of Congress Cataloging-in-Publication Data

Deegan, Mary Jo, 1946-
   Self, war, and society : George Herbert Mead's macrosociology / Mary Jo
Deegan.
      p. cm.
   Includes bibliographical references and index.
   ISBN 978-0-7658-0392-4 (alk. paper)
      1. Macrosociology. 2. Mead, George Herbert, 1863-1931. 3. World
War, 1914-1918--Psychological aspects. 4. Social psychology--United states-
-History. I. Title.

HM490.D44 2008
301.092--dc22
                                                        2008014817

This book is dedicated

to the good friends I met in Trento, Italy, 1992 —

Luigi Tomasi

Tony Blasi

Barbara Lal

Thomas Keil

and

The late Jeffrey Crane

Contents

Preface

Many, many people helped me to prepare and understand this unique stage in Mead's life and ideas which I have been studying for thirty-five years. I can acknowledge only a few of them here but everyone's help is greatly appreciated. The late Irene Tufts Mead, in particular, was an enthusiastic and insightful person to interview and consult about Mead as a political activist, philosopher, and family man. I am grateful for her interest spanning a number of years and several periods of inquiries. The late Gregory Stone was an early supporter who saw the complicated implications of my work better than I did in 1974 and 1975. The marvelous symbolic interactionists whom I met at Trento, Italy in October 1992 changed my life. Luigi Tomasi organized the meetings and invitation, and we have met numerous times over the intervening years. We read each others works and have presented papers on shared panels on numerous occasions. Anthony Blasi, who introduced me to Luigi, has helped me repeatedly and greatly expanded my ideas. Barbara Lal is a delightful friend even though she likes Robert E. Park much more than I do. The late Jeffrey Crane subsequently invited me to Hawaii where he was a most gracious colleague and host. Thomas Keil was part of this circle of friends although our paths have crossed only a few times since those two momentous conferences. The late Edward Shils also participated at these events, and as a former faculty member at the University of Chicago when I was a graduate student there, we exchanged many friendly words at dinners and receptions. Shils and I, however, disagreed on almost every epistemological assumption in the world, so we avoided disciplinary discussions whenever possible.

I have been most fortunate in having talented and congenial help in the physical preparation of this manuscript. Joleen Deats has been skillful, cheerful, and a good friend over the many years of our association, as has Lori Ratzlaff who provided significant help in preparing the original Mead writings.

My thanks to the archivists and staff at the University of Chicago. Daniel Meyer of the Special Collections Research Center at the University of Chicago aided me in this project as he has done in so many others. Jay Satterfield, a curator in this same center, and Barbara Gilbert were also helpful.

Michael R. Hill provided constant support and much deserved criticism of all drafts. Because of some physical limitations, my reliance on his time and energy is particularly demanding yet his strength has been unwavering.

Mary Jo Deegan
Spring 2006
Benton Harbor, Michigan

Part 1

Introduction

1

George Herbert Mead on Self, War, and Society: The Genesis of the International Self and a World Community

> *"War fever is a virulent disease, and people fired by propaganda may do things and say things foreign alike to character and to principles." (Wald 1933, 287)*

> *"Revolution has been incorporated into the constituted form of government itself. And this has involved a revolution itself, for such an institution-alizing of revolution has been no less revolution-ary with reference to revolution itself than it has been with reference to fixed forms of government." (Mead 1915a, reading 3C here)*

> *"Warfare is an utterly stupid method of settling differences of interest between different nations." (Mead 1929b, reading 10D here)*

George Herbert Mead created a profound and unique American theory that analyzed society and the individual as social objects. Both society and the individual emerged from cooperative, democratic processes between the self, the other, and the community. Both were learned and the ideal process of learning, especially for children and youth, was education which should be available to everyone. Mead employed scientific theory in order to improve society through the generation of "working hypotheses" (Mead 1899b) or the more sweeping process of "social reconstruction," a major theme in Mead's writings on war (see also Campbell 1992, 23-37). His writings, especially the essays published during his lifetime, are permeated with the development of theoretical concepts, such as the "self" and the "generalized other," which have direct impact on histori-cally based, politically engaged, human behavior. In this book, I examine the close relationship between Mead's work and writings on democracy, the self, international mindedness, peace, the citizen, war, and society.

3

Most sociological textbooks categorize Mead as a "microsociologist," a theorist definitively concerned with face-to-face and small group interactions. Mead's writings and political commitments that focused on the meaning of war, peace, citizenship, and democracy unequivocally refute such interpretations (See also Mead 1999, 2001). Mead is both a "micro" and "macro" sociologist, fundamentally committed to the avoidance of dichotomized analyses. Some sociologists (especially Deegan 1988, 1992, 1999, 2001; Deegan and Burger 1978; Habermas 1985/c. 1987; Shalin 1987, 1988) have long recognized Mead's large-scale, international approach, but this is a minority perspective within the discipline of sociology.

Mead was a "classical theorist in sociology" who started publishing and teaching in the early 1890s and his life was affected profoundly by World War I (hereafter referred to as WWI). Because of the posthumous publications of four of his books in the 1930s (Mead 1932, 1934, 1936, and 1938), and sociologists' emphasis on *Mind, Self, and Society* published in 1934,[1] Mead is misclassified, again, as a theorist who emerged during that decade. He is labeled a "contemporary theorist," therefore, and he is often compared to theorists of the 1930s or 1940s, such as Robert E. Merton, Talcott Parsons, and Alfred Schutz who worked and taught in the generations after his death. These more contemporary theorists asked questions that did not exist for Mead. The emergence of pragmatism, and Mead's role in it and his ideas should be compared instead to those of his contemporaries: Jane Addams, John Dewey, Émile Durkheim, Charlotte Perkins Gilman, and Max Weber.

Mead devoted a considerable portion of his life to the analysis of conflict and cooperation, and their connection to democracy, social reconstruction, and international relations. The study of war and peace loomed so large in his social thought that he should be considered one of the most significant American male sociologists in this area. He frequently discussed these topics in Chicago, particularly from 1915 until 1920, a period immediately before the United States entered WWI in 1917 and two years after the war ended in 1918.

America's entry into the Great War fundamentally challenged Mead's social thought, as it did that of his friends and colleagues John Dewey and Jane Addams. Prior to the war the three friends created an extraordinary American theory of human action and meaning. The men's ideas were called "Chicago pragmatism" (James, 1904) and Addams' approach is called "feminist pragmatism" (Deegan 1988, 1999; Siegfried 1991). Before the war there was a different emphasis on gender and political action in these two approaches, but the fundamental definitions of the self, the other, democracy, and education were held in common (Deegan 1999).

During the war, however, their commonality was fractured and strained. Mead and Dewey became noted speakers and authors in defense of the war; they supported the power of the state to use violence. Addams became a noted speaker and author in opposition to the war: she repeatedly challenged the power and wisdom of the state to use violence. She actively resisted the war and advocated non-violence, arbitration, and co-operation between nations. She became the most famous, international leader of women who opposed the war. She based this activity on a number of American positions: on William Lloyd Garrison's non-resistance, her family's heritage as Hicksite Quakers, and most importantly, women's values and culture. In the 1920s, and the cool aftermath of a return to rational thought, Mead and Dewey came to accept Addams' position, but only after a deep and painful struggle to understand war's impact on their thought and practices (Deegan 1988, 1991, 1999, 2001; Rucker 1969, Seigfried 1998).

Dewey's war-time arguments, usually shared with Mead, are the subject of great controversy (e. g., Bourne 1964; Chatfield 1970; Diggins 1981; Ryan 1995). Mead's ideas, in stark contrast, are virtually unexamined. Mead's ideal model for social change during these years closely followed the one institutionalized by most Europeans in their national welfare states, particularly by the Fabian socialists who were popular in England between 1890 and 1930. This model was shared with most of the early[2] men and women of the Chicago school of sociology, established at the University of Chicago; and the Hull-House school of sociology, established at the social settlement of that name, and with his colleagues in philosophy, especially Dewey, with whom he co-founded Chicago pragmatism (Deegan 1988, 1999, 2002b; James 1904; Rucker 1969). By documenting and emphasizing Mead's pragmatic theory and action on worldwide issues, I reveal the macrosociological dimensions of Mead's theory and thereby open discussion and debate on the importance of these Meadian perspectives today when Americans are once more in the throes of war and state-sponsored violence.

Mead's writings on war and peace include his critiques of other theorists of the state, such as Thomas Hobbes, Jean-Jacques Rousseau, and Karl Marx. Mead directly connects their analyses with his theory of democracy. A large segment of this book, chapters 6-8, contains Mead's unpublished essays written during the war. I believe he delivered these often lengthy pieces as lectures in his course on "The Intellectual Background to the War" which he offered in the spring of 1918. He often typed his classroom lectures, and these formal notes became the basis for much of his posthumous books and articles. Occasionally he wrote his war lectures by hand and parts of them are illegible. I indicate problems in deciphering these notes by the use of bracketed words that are my best estimates of the meaning of the passages. These previously unpublished essays, then, comprise a significant, working manuscript where he developed his ideas on self, war, and society during war-time, the most volatile period for any citizen writing on war and peace (Addams 1922/1960). Mead's passions ran high and his emotional response permeates his writings. He stepped away from this fervor in the postwar years when he struggled to articulate what he firmly believed in the aftermath of state aggression.

Mead's corpus spans almost five decades, from the late 1880s until his last posthumous book based primarily on his work in the classroom in the late 1920s. The "early Mead" writings prior to 1921 have been systematically under-studied; and when this early work has been studied, it has been misinterpreted usually as "fragmented" and "less serious" than his posthumous books. As I have documented in five other books, however, including three books discussing Addams and pragmatism (Deegan 1987b, 1988, 2002b) and two books comprised primarily of Mead's (1999, 2001a) writings, Mead was an engaged political activist with a complicated theory of democracy and applied sociology. "Early Mead" is an exciting classical theorist of macro-sociology whose writings directly address issues surrounding many contemporary problems and their amelioration.

This book, therefore, is my third book focusing on the writings of the "early Mead," and it complements David L. Miller's (1982) edited book on *The Individual and the Social Self* which also draws heavily from Mead's work during this era. There are, therefore, four books on "early Mead" that should be combined with the four posthumous books on "late Mead" to invigorate new research and social thought about the impact of a major intellectual. Most contemporary sociological analyses of Mead interpret him as an abstract, apolitical, small-group theorist whose ideas emerged after the classical era of sociological theory. Their work needs serious revision.

Not only was Mead an "expert" on war and peace, especially during and immediately after WWI, but his personal and professional life was shaped dramatically by the war. His family and friends were intrinsically part of the world at war. The greatest personal sacrifice emerged from his family situation: his only son Henry served in the military and was wounded and his daughter-in-law Irene Tufts Mead served as a caretaker for French children orphaned by the violence ("5 Women Sent by Chicago Will Save War Babies" 1917). Professionally, Mead focused his philosophy and views of society on war and state violence. The meaning of war and its impact on his social thought is the core topic of this book. This work is in many ways unique to the period of war, because these analyses broke with many of his prewar and postwar ideas about international peace. To employ a Meadian explanation, his theory emerged in response to the war. But in many other ways, there is a deep continuity in his ideas before and after the war. Ironically, his emphasis on many of these continuous themes was muted often in his posthumous books finished by his philosophy students. Examining his ideas on self, war, and society restores the balance of concerns shaping his social thought and practices and his serious attendance to national and international processes.

Mead's life and thought were surrounded by "the world of Chicago pragmatism," a large network of academicians, students, activists, family, friends, and the community and educational organizations in which they implemented their ideas. This vast interconnecting group and associated institutions were anchored at the University of Chicago but included other people, cities, and academic institutions such as William James at Harvard University in Cambridge and Charles H. Cooley at the University of Michigan in Ann Arbor. This complex network sometimes supported and sometimes challenged his work on war and peace. Mead's theory of the self and the other was the foundation for his unique contribution to Chicago pragmatism as an intellectual enterprise and is the beginning of our entree into his world and, more specifically, his approach to war and peace. This story does not begin in Chicago, however, but in Boston and Germany.

Mead's Formative Experiences in Germany, 1888-1891

In 1887, Mead entered Harvard University as a graduate student where he studied for a year with Josiah Royce, the Christian neo–Hegelian. He then switched from a philosophy major to the study of physiological psychology influenced by the work of William James (1907), a former student of Wilhelm Wundt. Gary Cook argues that Mead left Harvard before completing his studies because of a summer infatuation with William James' sister-in-law, an insightful invalid who spent her life in a sickroom (A. James 1934). James thought this relationship was unsuitable, and he strongly suggested that Mead begin his doctoral studies in Germany (Cook 1993, 15-19). James' (1910/1991) analysis of the need to channel aggression into a "moral substitute for war" inspired Mead to ask similar questions during and after WWI (see chapters 3 and 10 here).

Mead followed his mentor's advice and moved to Leipzig, Germany to study under Wilhelm Wundt in the winter of 1888–1889. He transferred after one semester to the University of Berlin where he studied under the psychologists Wilhelm Dilthey, J. Ebbinghaus, and F. Paulsen, and under the socialist Gustav Schmoller. With Dilthey as his doctoral advisor, Mead asserted that the psychology of the child's early moral development was the most important field of research, and he planned to translate a volume of articles on this subject (Joas 1985, 19). Although Mead did not complete this project, his commitment to the study of play and early childhood is evident. The young scholar also built strong ties with German life and education; he combined both scientific and romantic values which drew on this culture. Mead's strong attraction to German life and ideas and his familiarity with its faults provided an emotional dimension to his dramatic and aggressive response to WWI decades later.

Henry Northrup Castle, Mead's best friend and undergraduate roommate at Oberlin College, joined Mead in Germany, deepening their already intense tie. Henry's sister and George's future bride, Helen Castle, was studying in Germany as well, and the three friends roomed with a woman named Frau Steckner. Henry fell in love with Frieda Steckner, their landlady's daughter, and they married in 1889. Henry's young wife Frieda, then the mother of their infant daughter Dorothy, died tragically in 1891 when she was thrown from her carriage by a runaway horse. Henry and Helen experienced profound grief following Frieda's death, and Helen later claimed that George "saved her life or reason" in the aftermath of the tragedy (H. C. A. Mead, Henry 1938, lxxix). On 1 October 1891 George and Helen were married in Berlin. Germany was the incubator for this welding of family, mind, and heart.

Mead had been depressed by Frieda's death, too. He immediately left Berlin after his wedding, without completing his doctorate, after receiving an offer from Dewey to join the faculty at the University of Michigan. From 1891 to 1894, Mead taught at the University of Michigan, alongside Dewey, who had been a student of G. Stanley Hall, who was, in turn, a former student of James and Wundt. Thus both Mead and Dewey were influenced by German scholarship through James and Wundt. German philosophy, therefore, was Mead's intellectual home at the start of his professional life. He continued this international allegiance until 1917 when he became an advocate for the American participation in WWI and a strong critic of German values and institutions.

Chicago and the Emergence of Pragmatism

The vast and complex connections between Chicago pragmatists created a world emerging from intellectual and emotional bonds; including men and women, home and academy, children and adults, politics and ideas, community ritual and everyday life. Chicago pragmatism arose in a distinctive American setting and era; in the city of Chicago at the dawn of the twentieth century. Chicago was booming then, industrially and commercially, in the middle of the Midwestern prairie at the southern terminus of Lake Michigan. Immigrants from Europe poured into this exploding metropolis seeking new life, employment, and the promise of social equality. Immediately prior to, during, and after WWI, African Americans moved from the South to Chicago in large numbers, drawn by its promise of jobs, racial tolerance, and education. Chicago's social scientists were amazed and impressed by the city's dynamic growth and by the opportunity to develop a new profession in the midst of such changes. They were enthused by the abundant opportunities to create new communities and new definitions of behavior. They literally saw humans create a new society as a result of their rapidly changing, emerging city. [3]

They needed new ideas to explain this new reality. They rejected earlier theories of biological and/or economical determinism, and they started from the assumption that *people* generate other people. The biological basis for human action emerged from flexible impulses. Although aggression and self-defense were important primal impulses, parenting, sociality, neighborliness, and cooperation with others were strong and usually dominant impulses drawing individuals into peaceful social actions and interactions. Consequently, Chicago pragmatists held that people control human action and behavior, and the primary mechanism creating their control resides in socially constructed meanings. Chicago's early sociologists assumed that people are flexible in their values and attitudes. Thus these scholars and activists hypothesized that changing the definition of a given behavior could generate a new social pattern of behavior (e. g., Mead 1899b, 1934; Addams 1907, 1909, 1910; Thomas 1923). Their theory of human behavior is called Chicago pragmatism, and it is related directly to feminist pragmatism, the theory I employ here which places a primary emphasis on women's freedom, their values, social justice, and the welfare state.[4]

The World of Chicago Pragmatism, 1894-1920

Mead's entrance into the world of Chicago pragmatism emerged primarily from the core people in Chicago surrounding him: his family — his wife Helen, his sisters-in-law Harriet Castle and Mabel Wing Castle; his best friend and brother-in-law Henry Northrup Castle, and his son Henry and his daughter-in-law Irene Tufts Mead. It also included his friendships with John Dewey, his closest colleague and friend, and his wife Alice Chipman Dewey, who co-founded the Laboratory Schools at the University of Chicago (Deegan 1999). John Dewey's pragmatic writings and the application of these ideas during his years in Chicago are integral to Mead's work on war. Together they built intellectual and personal ties with other faculty and students at the university. These academic women and men blended interests in science, social reconstruction, social justice, and democracy to generate "Chicago pragmatism" (Rucker 1969).

Finally, Mead was also close to many of the remarkable women based at Hull-House, the social settlement, especially Jane Addams who headed Hull-House and Mary McDowell who was an early resident there and later headed the University of Chicago Social Settlement (Wilson 1928). These women blended interests in sociology, social work, public policy, kindergartens, play-grounds, social settlements, and education to generate a theory I call "feminist pragmatism." They were close friends with all the people mentioned above (Deegan 1988, 1999).

The Chicago pragmatists are the subject of hundreds of books and articles (e.g., Diner 1980; Faris 1967; Kurtz 1984; Rucker 1969), but this literature is usually gender segregated, divorced from private and family life, and focused on the male faculty and their ideas but rarely their politics (this is changing, e.g., Shalin 1986). Dewey receives the most attention, followed by Mead. Thus most scholars study the Chicago pragmatists by violating the epistemology of the theory: it cannot be stated too strongly that pragmatism opposes the dichotomization of action and ideas; public vs. private; mind vs. body; male vs. female; home vs. marketplace, etc.

There is a lengthy letter (typed, double-spaced, with narrow margins, set in a pica font, and eleven pages long) from George Mead to Helen Castle Mead on 1 July 1906 (Mead papers, box 1, folder 5, Department of Special Collections and Social Research, Regenstein Library, University of Chicago; hereafter referred to as "Mead papers") that illustrates this amazing world. I analyzed it in depth elsewhere (Deegan 1999, xxv-xxxi) and summarize that analysis here.

Mead's loving letter to Helen shares the enthusiasm, criticism, politics, and ideas that made this community so remarkable. Food, talk, arguments, work, men, women, children, parents, and homes are themes that flow throughout the missive. It is the unity, not each part, that created this lifeworld. Although one concept, like play, and one relationship, like Mead's and Addams', can be examined, the complexity and multidimensionality of this world provides the context generating the parts. This holistic approach is, of course, a dramatic example of the philosophy of Chicago pragmatism. Mead gave another peak into this world through his war-time correspondence with his soldier son, Henry, and Henrys wife, Irene Tufts Mead. At first he shared his anxiety over Henry with Irene. After she volunteered to serve in an orphanage in France he was both proud and anxious over her decision and work which was sponsored by the "American Fund for French Wounded" ("5 Women Sent by Chicago Will Save War Babies" 1917; see chapter 4 here).

This world was directly connected to the epistemology and practice of Chicago pragmatism. It helps explain how and why it originated in Chicago during the particular era when it appeared. A bi-gendered, intellectual world comparable to this intellectual and emotional powerhouse has never been explored before, and it was changed fundamentally by the Great War.

The World of Chicago Pragmatism and World War I, 1914-1920

The global conflagration began on 28 June 1914 with the assassination of Archduke Franz Ferdinand, but the United States did not declare war until 6 April 1917. Until the United States entered the fray, Mead continued to elaborate his co-operative, scientific, rational model of the self and society: A model wherein play, not war, held a central place (Mead 1999). International cooperation and life flourished in this perspective. Mead's ideas were compatible with and strengthened by his ties to Addams, a Quaker and pacifist, although Mead did not share these religious and political commitments. Mead, moreover, experienced and loved Germany during his personally and intellectually formative years as a graduate student as noted above. Thus he was drawn to Germany because he received postgraduate training in Germany, was fluent in German, and had family members who were German (Deegan 1999, 2001; Joas 1985).

From his student days until approximately 1910, Mead continued many of the questions explored by Wundt and the study of comparative psychology (see Mead 2001). After 1910 Mead increasingly explored the importance of democracy, education, and the American tradition of pragmatism, although he never abandoned his ties with Wundt (see Mead 1919a, 1934). Mead's belief in rationality, although rooted in Enlightenment values, was grounded also in a Germanic emphasis on the mind over emotions (e.g., Weber 1947).

Once the U. S. entered the war, Mead abandoned his international pacifism: his ideas and world underwent a dramatic change. As already noted, in terms of his family, Mead made pain-wracked sacrifices during the war because of his son and his beloved daughter-in-law, Irene Tufts Mead. I. T. Mead was also the daughter of his friend and another Chicago pragmatist James Hayden Tufts, an interconnection of personal and professional ties typical of this world. In addition, his wife and several of his female relatives were active members of the Women's International League of Peace and Freedom (WILPF), founded by Addams and McDowell (Deegan 1999, 2003), that Mead did not support in war-time.

In terms of his professional colleagues and friends he was torn by seismic shifts in their understanding of the best, ethical actions during war-time. Thus

- His closest female colleagues, Jane Addams, the Peace Nobelist, and Mary McDowell, were pacifists, and he broke with their ideas and practices;
- His closest male colleague, John Dewey, struggled with the meaning of war and peace and his friendships with pacifists were strained and sometimes broken. This became part of a national debate, especially between Dewey and his former student and friend Randolph Bourne. Ultimately Mead and Dewey held similar positions during the war, but Dewey was in the center of more visible, national debates.
- His mentor William James struggled with the meaning of war and peace and also shared his friendships with pacifists, especially with Addams. James argued that men needed a moral substitute for war because men were naturally aggressive, and Mead sided with James.
- In addition to McDowell and Addams, Mead critiqued other pacifists and their approach to war, especially the work of William James and Thorstein Veblen.
- And during war-time, Mead's approach to war was gendered as male, if not patriarchal, and more similar to German patterns of aggression than he ever acknowledged in his writings.

All these facts and forces turned the world of Chicago pragmatism inside out. Mead was pushed to the wall to respond to his most basic beliefs about violence, the failure of rationality, the meaning of democracy, and the beloved world of his youth, Germany. His emotionally uninvolved, rational work was undermined when his son and daughter-in-law were endangered and on the war front. Mead had dedicated his life to a vision of progress, rationality, education, co-operation, and growing internationalism. This vision was sundered and undermined by war which flourished in destruction, irrationality, ignorance, fear, conflict, and unreflective nativism. WWI revealed several flaws in the epistemology of Chicago pragmatism.

The world of Chicago pragmatism was anchored for the men in a number of volunteer organizations, many of them founded by pragmatists, men and women, who applied pragmatist assumptions through their leadership positions. Mead, for example, was active in garment workers strikes in Chicago alongside the women of Hull-House and women strikers in 1910, 1912, and 1915 (Deegan 1988; Deegan and Wahl 2003). He participated in the Immigrants Protective League to help young women entering the city alone and disoriented by the transitions from the Old World to the New World. His major male-only club, the Chicago City Club (CCC), often made friendly alliances with women-only groups before the war. After war began, however, the former friends split into the aggressive, male, patriots of the CCC and the radical, female pacifists. The men, moreover, rarely invited the women to speak before the group between 1916 and 1920. When Addams (1917, 1922) did address the group in 1917 on her volatile topic of "Pacifists in War-Time," Mead (1917a) stood by her side, an act that must have elicited considerable criticism for him. As Addams (1922, 111) recalled:

> It was a distinct shock to me to learn that it had been difficult to secure a chairman to preside over the City Club meeting at which I spoke, and that even my old friends were afraid that the performance of this simple office would commit them to my pacifist position.

This is the same period when Dewey (1917b) sharply opposed pacifists, too, so Mead's loyalty to Addams is even more remarkable in light of the men's friendship. Mead played the most important role in this city-wide club from 1918 to 1920 when he served two terms as president of the CCC, the topic of chapter nine here.

The World of Chicago Pragmatism, the University of Chicago, and World War I, 1914-1921

During this tumutuous time, the University of Chicago became a center for research, expertise, and teaching about this specific war and wars in general. Mead was part of this campus-wide expertise.

- He helped organize and support public lectures on war and peace in Chicago.
- He developed a sophisticated, albeit flawed, critique of Marxist conflict theory to explain the class unrest in Germany and not in the United States.
- He developed an analysis and critique of aggressive instincts and impulses.
- He supported Fabian socialism, or extensive government programs to guarantee minimal standards of living for the disabled, unemployed, ill, homeless, and poor.
- He helped establish the American welfare state in his role as a pragmatist, citizen, and leader of social change, including his understanding of social reconstruction emerging from war-time.

- He taught an entire course on the topic of war in the spring of 1918.
- His theory and practices emerged from his historical location, and as this changed his work changed: During peace-time he was an international pacifist and during war-time he was an advocate of "the war to end wars."
- His theory and practices remained stable, nonetheless, concerning his support of internationalism, anti-militarism, and arbitration. His model of the self also stayed the same.
- He changed his understanding of German values and ideas from one of appreciation to one of criticism.
- His theory and practices changed in reference to the definitions of democracy; the dichotomization of the enemy; his understanding of hostility, both nationally and personally, and cooperation. He also became more emotional in his observations of society.
- And his theory and practices were shaken by his professional and personal definitions of democracy and cooperation during war-time.

These professional issues are examined in depth here. A large segment of his unpublished writings written during war-time is included as readings in chapters four to eight and chapter ten. His understanding of the nation-state, Germany as the "enemy," and unreflective trust in the American government's definitions of the need for self-defense, democracy, and social justice reveal both weaknesses and strengths in his theory which he never exposed so dramatically again.

The theory and praxis surrounding pacifism, conflict, cooperation, and war demarcate a significant dividing line between the feminist pragmatists and the male-defined Chicago pragmatists.[5] As I examine in detail here and as Mead reveals in his writings, the women decided in favor of cultural pluralism, pragmatism, feminism, pacifism, and a cooperative model after 1915. Between 1916 and 1918 the men defined war as part of defending democracy; men needed to protect and obey the orders of the state and the military; male values of competition, belligerence, and violence were sometimes necessary and sometimes the basis of values such as courage and community. The men often articulated sweeping generalizations about the enemy, particularly Germans, Germany, and the Germanic culture. The men, including Mead and Dewey, often built on the work of William James as he articulated it in "The Moral Equivalent of War" (1910). This world view was less open, flexible, cooperative, pacifist, and feminist than the women who supported and developed feminist pragmatism (Schott 1993). The Great War massively challenged the ideas and work of both groups.

Mead maintained a position during the war that was closer to Addams than Dewey did. Thus Mead tried to understand and reflect on the conscientious objector (see chapter 3 here); he physically and symbolically stood with Addams when she delivered a controversial speech on pacifists during war-time (Mead 1917f; Addams 1917); and there is no record of a break in their friendship, unlike the situation between Dewey and Addams (see Addams 1929a, 1929b; Dewey 1930, 1945a, b, c). Mead also continued to believe in internationalism during the war. He was committed to a peaceful arbitration process through the League to Enforce Peace (LTEP), a group in which Addams briefly served as a vice president, but found to be increasingly supportive of war.

At the end of the war, both Mead and Dewey regretted much of their war-time fervor and ultimately came closer to the view of the feminist pragmatists. Mead had a shorter path to follow than Dewey did, but both men abandoned the vitriolic and aggressive rhetoric that they had adopted during war-time. Ironically, Dewey (Dewey 1945, 1946) became a pacifist after the war and wholeheartedly adopted this position even during World War II, but Mead never adopted this position on non-violence as clearly as Dewey did. The women's values, analyses, and culture pointed to a new way to conceptualize co-opera-tion, the unity of people around the world, and the need for more peacemaking. In fact, this analysis emerges from my earlier work that focuses on women's cultural feminism, a major theory and practice that interacted with pragmatism and created a new branch of thought, feminist pragmatism (e.g., Deegan 1987b, 1988, 1991, 1996, 1999). It emerged from a shared community based on the interaction of cultural feminism, nonviolence, and pragmatism.

The Chicago Female World of Love and Ritual

In a previous study of the correspondence shared by two feminist pragmatists, Marion Talbot and Sophonisba Breckinridge, I (Deegan 1996a) documented how their work emerged from what I called "the Chicago female world of love and ritual" and its union of activism, feminism, intellectual labor, and emo-tions. I drew upon the work of Carroll Smith-Rosenberg (1975, 1) who studied "the female friendship of the nineteenth century, the long-lived, intimate, lov-ing friendship between two women...[these] deeply felt, same-sex friendship were casually accepted in American society...from at least the late eighteenth century through the mid-nineteenth century." She called the pattern of such friendships "the female world of love and ritual." Supportive networks "were institutionalized in social conventions or rituals which accompanied virtually every important event in a woman's life, from birth to death" (Smith-Rosenberg 1975, 9). This world was emotionally dense and complex including devotion to and love of other women.

Smith-Rosenberg's subjects led relatively obscure lives, married, and lived in patriarchal families mainly in the Northeastern and Southern U. S. In con-trast, the female feminist pragmatists typically: (1) were unmarried; (2) lived in Chicago; (3) were longtime intimate friends; (4) lived together in female-headed homes, social settlements, or in college/university dormitories; (5) were powerful political and intellectual leaders; and (6) were part of the world of Chicago pragmatism.

The Chicago women created a new model of friendship that creatively extended the earlier, much less public and less publicly powerful friendship patterns of the eighteenth and nineteenth centuries described by Smith-Rosenberg. The Chicago female world of love and ritual is a distinctive American ritual based on the liminal status of professional women from the 1890s to the 1930s (Deegan 1989, 1995, 1998). It was based institutionally in the academy and social settlement and was integral to the formation of sociology as a profession.

This world was not only gendered but composed of international pacifists opposed to militarism. As a cooperative theory, strongly influenced by Quaker thought, especially through Addams, Kelley, the Abbott sisters, and Emily Green Balch, the Chicago female world of love and ritual is the foundation for WILPF and the growing worldwide resistance to state violence (Addams 1907, 1922, 1930; Addams, Balch, and Hamilton 1915/2003; Deegan 2003).

Comparing the Chicago Female World of Love and Ritual to the World of Chicago Pragmatism

The male Chicago pragmatists lived in a dense emotional and intellectual world that sometimes overlapped with the female world of love and ritual and sometimes differed from it. In contrast to the women, the male Chicago pragmatists, especially Mead and Dewey, typically: (1) married highly educated, often feminist, wives; (2) fathered children; (3) were longtime intimate friends with each other, their extended families, and female professionals and intellectuals; (4) lived in private homes in which they frequently visited each other and others in the community, especially those in social settlements, politics, or other academies; and (5) were powerful political and intellectual leaders who helped build a major school of thought and action: Chicago pragmatism.

Although the world of Chicago pragmatism and the Chicago female world of love and ritual interacted, their distinct spheres remained. The women in their own institutions were critical of academia and the capitalists who financed these universities, while the married men and women in their homes and at the University of Chicago supported primarily male careers, elite education, and the use of capitalist money from John D. Rockefeller. Another example of their differences is their emphasis on the mind and its connection to action. Intellectual labor was more highly prized in the academy than at Hull-House which more directly combined ideas and social actions. The most divisive issue, defining the boundaries between Chicago pragmatism and feminist pragmatism, was their position on war and peace especially from 1917 to 1920. The men more aggressively defended the American participation in WWI while the women opposed it and led a worldwide effort for peace.

Addams, Mead, and Pacifism, 1914-1918

Before the war, Addams, Mead, and Dewey shared an international pacifism, albeit the men were more restricted in their approaches than Addams although these differences did not seem to be apparent to them at that time. The three scholars and friends, for example, were invited "To Act As Correspondents of the Neutral Conference for Continuous Mediation" in 1915 (See JAM, reel 10, frame 0017) before the United States entered the war.

A year earlier, Addams had invited Mead to participate in a major issue of the *Survey*, which both of them supported as associates and authors, on peaceful ends to the War in Europe (See discussion in chapter 2 here). Once the United States entered the fray, however, the two friends parted in a fundamental way, although less decisively than the break between Addams and Dewey. Addams' position on war and peace must be understood to see the dimensions of their conversations on this topic, and this becomes a common thread throughout this book.

The World of Chicago Pragmatism in the Immediate Aftermath of World War I, 1918-1921

After the end of the war, both Mead and Dewey developed a new appreciation of the women's values, analyses, and culture. The women pointed to a new way to conceptualize co-operation, the unity of people around the world, and the need for more peace-making. Both Mead and Dewey reassessed their commitments to democracy, internationalism, world unity (especially with Germany and other former "enemy states") the role of war fever to rationalize state violence, and their understanding of human values and value-neutral science. Mead, in particular, wrote differently during the war about impulses, Marxism, and social reconstruction and this set of war-time ideas confronted his postwar theory and praxis. In many ways he was restored to his prewar international pacifism. But he was shocked that the Versailles Treaty was harsh and unfair, a punitive pact that could never end wars. WWI was not a war for democracy, and his behavior during the war was neither wholly rational nor logical. Dewey changed his ideas and practices even before the war ended, but Mead continued to struggle with his war-time ideas until 1920. Dewey (e.g., 1945a, b) became more radical politically and adopted a very strong pacifist commitment, especially to Addams' feminist pragmatism. Mead became more abstract, less oriented to political discussions, and less active in social settlement work.

The Outline of the Chapters

Mead's writings on self, war, and society changed according to the historical events of war and peace: an emergent theory of war and peace. I present his fundamental theory in chapter 2 drawing on his corpus as it developed over his lifetime. This baseline for his peacetime concepts is mixed-up chronologically in his publications. Thus many of his writings in 1914, available in Miller (1972), are compatible with his posthumous publications, especially *Mind, Self, and Society* (1934), but some of his writings in 1917 and 1918 are not. I attend to the historical development of his theory and behaviors in relation to WWI throughout the remaining chapters of this book.

After I establish his basic pragmatist concepts and assumption, I develop a chronological analysis of his thought between 1907 and 1929 to understand his changing ideas and their response to the community. Three different stages order these events: before, during, and after the American entry into World War I. These times of war and peace pose a number of challenges to Mead's ideas and practices: moving from an active engagement and promotion of a cooperative, democratic society, to an active engagement and promotion of a cooperative, democratic society under attack that calls out the use of world-wide violence and its attendant carnage and destruction; and then to a sober, reflective Mead who teaches and writes a theory of a cooperative, democratic society governed by a rational, educated public. These major, chronological categories organize the rest of the book. Mead's writings, largely unpublished, augment this analysis and allow me to use this own words and thoughts to unfold as they progressed through time and initiated different macro conversations on self, war, and society, between Mead, his colleagues, and the larger society.

Throughout this process, Mead is surrounded by the world of Chicago pragmatism and its connection to the international pacifism of the Chicago female world of love and ritual. These two worlds meet in his family where his son is on the front line and his daughter-in-law is in the medical corps. At some point, his wife and sister-in-law joined WILPF. Within the world of Chicago pragmatism, his best friend John Dewey was a national figure justifying, articulating, and rationalizing a militant support of war. Other Chicago institutions also anchored his life: especially the University of Chicago and the Chicago City Club.

In my conclusion, I bring Mead's theory of self, war, and society into a few contemporary debates. I then connect Meadian thought to various theories articulating a cooperative, democratic, and rational world while the United States once more engages in world conflicts. This time, the American nation-state uses slogans like "pre-emptive strikes" and the language of a battle between "good and evil nations" to rationalize its irrational, illegitimate violence, and state-sponsored mayhem.

Notes

1. Almost every introductory and theory textbook in sociology presents this view of Meadian thought. Herbert Blumer (1969) popularized this interpretation and many sociologists who call themselves "symbolic interactionists" support it. Many others, however, do not and their macrosociological interpretations are ignored systematically in textbooks and sociological journals. This latter analysis of Mead can be found in the work of Joe R. Feagin (2001); Feagin and Vera 2001); Kathy

Ferguson (1980); Jurgen Habermas (1992); Hans Joas (1985); Dimitri N. Shalin (1987, 1988); and my colleagues and myself (e. g. Burger and Deegan 1981; Deegan 1988, 1999, 2002b; Deegan and Burger 1978; Deegan and Hill 1987).

2.   By "early" I mean the years between 1892 and 1920. See discussion in Deegan 1988, 2002b.

3.   Dorothy Ross (1989) is a historian who does not use the same categories of groups, ideas, and networks that sociologists employ. She rejects the idea that American theory was unique in its origins, actions, and impact.

4.   The "Chicago school of symbolic interaction," the term used by many sociologists, is a particular type of theory generally attributed to men who worked at the University of Chicago, including George Herbert Mead, William Isaac Thomas, Robert E. Park, and Louis Wirth (Kurtz 1984). "Symbolic interaction" is seen as part of the Chicago school of sociology. Philosophers call this same approach "Chicago pragmatism," (Rucker 1969) and several feminists, particularly Charlene Haddock Seigfried (1991, 1996, 1999) and myself, refer to "feminist pragmatism."

All these Chicago sociologists comprise a complex and encompassing group, including people in cities other than Chicago. Thus Charles H Cooley, who worked at the University of Michigan, is still considered part of the Chicago School. I, and a few other contemporary scholars (e.g., Seigfried 1996; Lengermann and Niebrugge-Brantley 1998) include many Hull-House women in this school (Deegan 1988, 1991, 1995, 1996).

The early situation is clearer, however, than the contemporary one. A later school based on the Chicago school that used quantitative measures (instead of qualitative or descriptive data) of the self is called the "Iowa school of symbolic interactionism." In the 1960s, many symbolic interactionists were located in California and Michigan, and at Brandeis University in Boston making Chicago sociology more national (Fine 1995). The dominant approach, found in this paper, is the Chicago school which includes Chicago pragmatism and feminist pragmatism that is both qualitative and quantitative and it emphasizes the writings of Mead, Dewey, Veblen, Thomas, Addams, and McDowell. See also fn. 1.

5.   Ella Flagg Young was a founder of Chicago pragmatism and her role needs more extended analysis, a topic beyond the intent of this book.

2

Mead's Concepts of Self, War, and Society

*"Our economic organization is getting more and
more worked out, so that the goods we sell in South
America, in India, in China, are definitely affecting
our lives." (Mead 1934, 271)*

Mead was an "international pacifist" before and after WWI. He defined co-
operation, or "peace," between the "self," the "other," the "community," and the
"nation" as in interconnected process that was the most common, desirable, and
beneficial relationship between the parts creating "society." In the United States,
this harmony was recreated continuously through "democratic processes," emergent from shared "liberal values," the use of "the scientific method," equality in
citizenship, "public education," and "community leaders." He believed the U. S.
Constitution, Bill of Rights, and Declaration of Independence best articulated
these values which, in turn, were the basis of law, social justice, and social
goals (see reading 3B here). They "universally" defined meanings for social
actions within this particular society, or nation-state. Before the war, he believed
an international model of such co-operation operated in the arts, sciences, and
finances. This worldview led to his support of international pacifism.

Citizens played a fundamental role in the maintenance and creation of a
democratic society. They learned to interpret shared "meanings," "attitudes,"
"behaviors," and "symbols." They could articulate and rationally communicate
through "language," defined by shared significant gestures," and "social institutions,"
especially through "liberal institutions" guided by the liberal meanings for conduct
and interaction. Social justice and liberal rights also emerged from this process
and affected the definition of citizenship. Mead, as a highly educated, community
leader, and citizen, had a public responsibility to articulate rational plans and policies to achieve democratic goals. He rejected the use of violence or the military
to maintain the peace process between citizens who were "rational," "intelligent,"
and able to engage in "conversations of gestures" to settle their differences. In
order to become a citizen, each individual developed a "self" "emergent from
the society," embodied in the other located within a community.

The Genesis of the Self and Society

Mead discusses the genesis of the self as a process dependent on one's ability to call out a response to the behavior of others. This response allows each self to understand and cherish his/her own society and to develop the ability to appreciate different cultures and communities. Both the self and the other employ a mind, intelligence, and reflexivity to create a shared understanding of everyday life. The Meadian concepts of "international-mindedness" (Mead 1915a, 1929b) and "the genesis of the self" (Mead 1934) create a model of cooperative relations between the self and the other, first in one's community of birth and potentially in other communities after the emergence of a stable, rational self (Deegan 1992).

Social Interaction and the Genesis of the Self

Mead defines the "self" as a social structure that emerges from human interaction and the meanings assigned to it. Each person is taught the meanings for behavior, and each person, in turn, teaches it to others. This process involves more than simply learning behavior. It involves the entire person in the process of becoming human. Being a member of society is an ongoing social process. Actors have the capacity to learn and create new meanings for behavior throughout their lives.

The infant develops into a social being in the following sequence. Initially copying others' "gestures," the infant progresses through "play," which is not goal-oriented, and "games," which are rule-oriented and coordinated interactions, until a "mind" with the rational ability to understand symbolic gestures, with shared meaning between the self and the other, emerges. This mind allows the child to become an object to itself with the capacity to make moral judgments and decisions on courses of action. Each child develops in this way a "self" that is reflective and capable of viewing actions from both its own point of view and that of "others." The self is "that which can be an object to itself, (it) is essentially a social structure, and it arises in social experience (Mead 1934, 204). The self is historically located in the "community" which is the source of symbols and interaction (Mead, 1934, 1999).

The self has the capacity to "take of the role of the other." The ability to call out a response in the self that is like that aroused in the other is due to the existence of shared social groups in the human environment that are collectively called "the generalized other." "In abstract thought the individual takes the attitude of the generalized other" (Mead 1934, 155) enabling the self to take the role of the other. The "generalized other" allows the community to become a factor in human development and reflection. Different selves that emerge from the same community share similar responses due to their similar attitudes, values, and definitions of the situation (see also Thomas and Znaniecki 1918-1920).

Social Interaction and the Continual Creation of the Community

The "community," like the "self," is socially generated and maintained. It exists as a product of collective selves. Considerable continuity therefore exists between the individual and social institutions. Individuals create and sustain "institutions," or habitual ways of defining action and meaning through the use of symbolic gestures. "Optimal development of the self involves the increasing capacity to understand larger and more complex groups of others, from the small group, to the community, to national-mindedness" (Mead, 1929b, 1934). "Social disorganization" occurs when the self and the community disagree about the meaning of behaviors and the definitions of situations (Thomas 1923; [Thomas,] Park and Miller 1921; Thomas and Znaniecki 1918-1920). One individually based source of social disorganization is the self's limited ability to take the role of the other, especially if the other emerged from a very different group. Learning a new language reshapes the self to such an extent that Mead viewed it as the creation of "a new soul" (Mead 1934, 283).

In times of social disorganization, the self can be tied more closely to the generalized other through the process of defining specific "others" as enemies or "outsiders." Group solidarity, therefore, can be grounded on disliking and hating an "enemy." Individual differences are obliterated in the common attack upon the enemy. Temporary relief from these social frictions is found in this way as well in gossip, scandal, patriotism, mobs, and warfare (see discussion in Burger and Deegan 1981). This alleviation from everyday divisiveness is manipulated by those in power, especially in times of social upheaval (Mead 1929b, 386).

An optimal community depends upon the actions of all members, however. Thus all the members are needed to define the community. The nation-state is a community in an ideal democracy. For Mead, this ideal community is the goal of WWI. The community, moreover, like the self, is reflexive. It has the ability to identify with others. As this collective ability to take the role of other communities increases, the community expands until it encompasses the world. Mead wrote: "We must think of ourselves in terms of the great community to which we belong" (Mead 1929, 400). Mead asked, for example, "Can we carry on a conversation in international terms?" He continued: "The question is largely a question of social organization. The necessary responses have become more definitely a part of our experience because we are getting closer to other people than before" (Mead 1934, 271).

Social Interaction and the International Society

Western society had become international before the war started. Science, art, industry, the economy — these institutions were international and not bounded by the laws and borders of nation states. Addams also advanced this argument in 1915 (p. 114 in Addams, Balch, and Hamilton 1915/2003), as did Balch (p. 39 in Addams, Balch, and Hamilton 1915/2003), who noted the worldwide foundation for "medicine, reform, labor, [and] religion." In 1915 and 1917 Mead called upon an existing international society to once again reassert its rational interests and goals.

Another way to end intergroup conflict is to appeal to shared self-interests and thereby replace conflict with cooperation. This process is directly related to Mead's support of liberal values and his belief in the common good. Freedom of speech was necessary to hear the opinions (Mead 1938) of various populations as well as a vital component in the conversation of gestures between the individual in the community and within the individual self. Anti-militarism and internationalism are consistent assumptions and themes in Mead's view of the American nation-state. This framework for understanding the other through an international community is the basis for the genesis of new selves.

The Genesis of the Self and Nation

Mead argued that the nation and the self followed similar processes in their development. Thus the nation had a "mind," "intelligence," "consciousness," and international corollaries to self concepts, such as "international-mindedness" and "international rights" in an "international community." As I discuss elsewhere, this process lead to the development of a "national self" which precedes the possibility of an emerging "international self" (Deegan 1992).

Following this logic, a "democratic self" emerging from the democratic state incorporates the liberal values found in core documents that define the American state: the U. S. Constitution, Bill of Rights, and the Declaration of Independence. Beliefs in freedom of the press, speech, and religion become incorporated within the self and the community. Equality of opportunity and social justice for all similarly become part of the genesis of the self.

A major role in the creation of the democratic self is "the citizen" and its corollary "citizenship." Voting, petitioning, lobbying, and discussing issues are all part of this role. The expectations accompanying it are part of citizenship. Mead took his role as a citizen seriously and spoke on the state, war, and peace in his writings and as a professor in the classroom. Citizenship was integral to both his own democratic self and the general role expectations between the self and the nation-state.

Developing Liberal Institutions

Democracy and education, and the liberal institutions dedicated to maintaining these social processes, needed to emerge rationally, consciously, and as a result of working hypotheses. Before the war this new type of social reconstruction had a few institutions in place. His theory of liberal institutions can be inferred from these working models of socially reconstructed community habits. Social settlements and universities were often the incubators for such experiments, and Mead frequently used the liberal institutions of the Juvenile Court and the Laboratory School as examples of viable models. In addition, he supported arbitration to settle labor conflicts (Deegan 1988, Deegan and Wahl 2003) and the World Court to settle international conflicts. Probably he saw the Labor Museum, instigated in 1902 through the joint efforts of Addams and Dewey, in this light, too (Deegan and Wahl 2003). The Labor Museum taught the importance of work in everyday life and its connection to the myriad patterns of constructing a home, self, and society (Addams [1902]). Progressive education was another new type of liberal institution. Thus the "Laboratory School" at the University of Chicago followed the nature of the child. It was not guided by business interests but trusted in the curiosity and co-operative spirit of children. The Juvenile Court acted on the beliefs that children and youth could be taught new habits and learn to become part of communities. It avoided the punitive punishment integrated into older forms of incarceration and notions of justice (Neeley and Deegan 2005).

He also dedicated a large segment of his time and community efforts to the Chicago City Club (CCC) which he must have viewed as a new form of liberal institution (see chapter 9 here). Mead joined the CCC from its inception in 1907. He spoke on school and education and served for years on its education committee (Deegan 1988). He supported the development of the public library and its promise of free access to books and other forms of knowledge (Deegan 1988, 115), a liberal institution supported by John Ruskin and by Addams. In fact, Hull-House actively created the art-lending program of public libraries, and a branch of the Chicago Public Library was located at Hull-House for years (Deegan and Wahl 2003).

Mead consistently lauded the international liberal institutions developed by scientists and artists throughout his writings before, during, and after the war. The war proved how fragile these institutions could be, however. Elites, the military, and politicians could control the nation state and could rend such associations into powerless pieces.

Mead wanted more liberal institutions to be formed. He criticized England and France for failing to make more liberal institutions, and argued that this failure led to wars and their continuation. During WWI he believed Wilson's "Fourteen Points" supported liberal institutions and he did not foresee their failure to be implemented at home or abroad. Organizations such as the LTEP provided another such mechanism. The League of Nations was yet another model for future arbitration, communication, and international co-operation. When all of these liberal institutions were not supported by the American people, Wilson, and the U. S. Congress after the war, Mead's wartime hopes for an end to all future wars and a victory for democracy were crushed.

The failure to develop liberal institutions in the nations comprising Old Europe, especially in the nations comprising the Central Powers, argued Mead, led to social conflict because the masses demanded more community participation while the aristocracy and the military maintained a tight control over the people. This led to the rise of socialism in Europe.

Marxist Socialism

Mead was a sophisticated critic of conflict theory. As a democratic, cooperative theorist, Mead believed that the workers in aristocratic, feudally organized states needed socialism to oppose the birth-based, or ascriptive, privileges of class. Socialism also opposed tyrants and dictatorships which, by definition, are anti-democratic and oppress the will of the people. Socialism in these states was rational and necessary to form a new government representing the people. "It has logically pitted against the privileged classes the laboring masses. It has undertaken to give them a class consciousness and a class program with which to fight the dominant classes." It is, in these cases, a "democratic fighting formation" (1917f, reading 4E here).

Mead supported the rights of the working class to unionize, and he became involved in garment workers' strikes in Chicago in 1910, 1912, and 1915. He felt that this liberal institution — labor unions — was only possible in a nation and community that were democratic. Aristocratic nations did not believe in the rights of workers and this oppression resulted in conflict and a dichotomized class society. Thus Mead did not view this conflict as one between "proletariat" and "bourgeoisie" but between "aristocrats" and "commoners." Democracies created members and citizens who shared a common good, language, and fundamental equality which allowed for nonviolent arbitration.

This type of democratic struggle, however, did not represent the attitude of societies with hierarchies, such as Germany and Russia with their strong aristocracies and militaries. These divisive communities were unable to develop cooperative organizations for the whole society. Such nations cannot develop cultural pluralism with a spirit of unity, and they cannot achieve national self-consciousness. Mead's ability to create a new theory and praxis, a striking contrast to most European theories, emerged from his community composed of intellectuals, family, friends, social activists, and institutions in the city of Chicago.

A Meadian Theory of War: 1915-1918

WWI profoundly affected all Americans, but Mead's particular perturbation arose from its direct challenge to his philosophical understanding of the self and society. Mead believed that the individual and society were emergents of each other and that sociability and harmony were their mutual goal. War was direct evidence to the contrary. There is but one acceptable rationale for killing which nations or individuals are willing to accept: self-defense. This point was established also by Julia Grace Wales at the international peace conference organized by women and led by Addams in 1915 (see Wales cited in Addams,

Balch, and Hamilton 1915/2003, 138). "The function of social organization is to build up and enlarge the personality of nations as truly as that of individuals, and this cannot include the deliberate destruction of the very members of international society, the consciousness of whom is essential to national self-consciousness" (Mead 1915a, reading 3C here). Nonetheless, Mead viewed patriotism as ultimately a destructive element of social consciousness. Bonds within an "international" community were the most desirable ones for a modern nation-state, echoing Addams' (1907) support for "newer ideals of peace."

Despite his criticisms of war, Mead (1918) initially viewed the outcome of WWI positively. He saw new government organizations that were adopted during wartime as the basis for a more socialist, and just, society. Optimistically, he saw WWI as the generator of a series of international rights and organizations, pointing to a saner and more secure future. Clearly, he was wrong. His positions that were compatible with Addams' pacifism were his partial defense of the conscientious objector, particularly for those with religious convictions opposed to all wars, his defense of internationalism, and his opposition to militarism. Otherwise, Mead (1918b) defended the American participation in WWI and accepted the then-popular view of it as necessary to protect democracy. For Mead this defense arose from his key commitment to democratic values and government.

The World of Chicago Pragmatists and the Genesis of a Community Self

The Chicago world of pragmatism has many androgynous characteristics, despite its coexistence with separate spheres for men and women. This group and ideology were on the forefront of generating new ways for men and women to live together harmoniously. This model emerged in part from the important father-daughter relation in the lives of many Hull-House women including Addams, Talbot, Breckinridge, and Edith Abbott. The Chicago women forged a new, woman-centered, intimate relationship that merged women's traditional values with the formerly male worlds of ideas and public service. The wives of male pragmatists participated in this same-sex community, and echoed this pattern with traditional ties to their families. Mead and Dewey's wives enacted this pattern.

The men in this world were often close to intellectual mothers, especially Mead whose mother was the first president of Mount Holyoke College (Deegan 1999). They had family-centered lives with access to the male-dominated world of the university and to the female-dominated world within that academy and in social settlements. They lived in a way that allowed for different patterns of friendship, family, and intimacy that invigorated the group with its variety and complexity.

The self generated in this context was dependent on a number of social movements that they, male and female, led in Chicago (Taft 1915). It emerged in a social context built on reflexivity, a feminist, activist consciousness, and the philosophical perspective generated by many Chicago theorists. Thorstein Veblen, Thomas, and Mead, for example, elaborated a worldview stressing the social origins of behavior, inequality, and the self (Deegan 1988; Deegan and Hill 1987; Hill and Deegan 2004).

The male pragmatists' "professional self" (Taft 1942; Deegan and Hill 1991) combined elements from the Chicago women's world of love and ritual with a male socialization in which women often played significant roles. Although the philosophy department never hired a woman before 1920 as a full-time faculty member, they trained many remarkable female theorists such as Jessie Taft (Deegan 1991), Helen Bradford Thompson Woolley (Rosenberg 1982), and Anna Louise Strong (1908) who gained fame as a radical journalist. The powerful Chicago women in sociology established role models for professional life combining emotional and intellectual labor, and this influenced women in all the social sciences and humanities at the University of Chicago.

The Chicago pragmatists formed a "community" or "world" that used their collective skills as writers, speakers, lobbyists, teachers, lawyers, and community leaders to alter their own minds and selves. These new "social selves" (Mead 1913), in turn, changed the larger society. They did this through years of conversations of gestures that blended formal writings, everyday life, symbols, and emotions (Addams 1910a, 1930a; Mead 1934). This community was ultimately international in intent and reality (Addams 1930a; Deegan 1992, 1996b, 2003) and shared a unique, worldwide memory (Addams 1916), uniting the pragmatists across divisions of race, class and nation (Deegan 2002b; West 1989). This working relationship did not erase the differences, nonetheless. It provided a living model of cooperation without assimilation. Although these men and women went "beyond separate spheres" (Rosenberg 1982) in the world of Chicago pragmatism, they made this journey firmly based in distinct communities and cultures. This made a unique foundation for the praxis of Chicago pragmatism. Further analysis of the world of Chicago pragmatism will provide us with information about the intersection of the personal and the public, the role of gender in the creation of Chicago pragmatism, the relationship between home, school, family, social settlement and academy; and the mechanisms generating pragmatism as a major school of thought that changed a city, a nation, and, ultimately, the world. Chicago, the harsh and exciting city they shared, was tied uniquely to the Old World and its violence through the millions of immigrants to the New World (Thomas and Znaniecki 1918-1920).

Addams on War

Addams believed women's culture was an international and trans-historical phenomenon. This culture was not biologically based beyond the fact that women bore and nursed children. The culture emerged from social behaviors and meanings: from women's caring for children and dependent adults, preparing food, making art, and tending to the hearth. She followed the archaeological arguments of cultural feminists, particularly the work of Otis Tufts Mason (1894; Deegan 1988, 2003). Lillian Wald (1933, 287), Addams' close friend and colleague in social settlements and pacifism, aptly summarized their shared view: "It is tragic to remember how soon the natural resentment to war by women formulated long ago in *The Trojan Women*, was dissipated by the clamore of the patrioteers, and how their treasured spiritual and reasoning convictions were made objects of dislike, and sometimes of persecution."

William James was Mead's mentor and a friend of Addams. This pragmatist alliance is understudied with the notable exception of Linda Schott (1993, 1997), and to a lesser degree by Seigfried (1996), Davis (1973), and me (Deegan 1988). Schott analyzed the gendered division between the ideas of William James and his "moral equivalent of war" and Addams' pacifist ideology and praxis. Schott (1993, 246) shows the core of similar activities and beliefs between them, including their dislike of philosophical abstraction and preference for concrete behavior and experiences; their shared commitment to cultural pluralism; and their strong criticism of imperialism. Addams and James argued that war was psychologically attractive, but their response to this passion was gendered. James argued that "the possibility of war" should remain an option for men while women could meet this need through marriage (Schott 1993, 248). Impulses to aggression, domination, and "bellicosity" were part of human nature to James and to Mead, or an essentialist argument (Schott 1997). Addams argued that human nature was more flexible than this. She believed human passions could be met with substitutions involving a moral community and fighting for the common good.

Addams directly confronts James' position in her *Newer Ideals of Peace* (1907). Taking on his phrase "the moral equivalent of war" as her starting point, Addams (1907, 24-30) argues this is an outdated view neglecting the changes in warfare that invite mass destruction on an unknown scale. This book is a critique of James and his gendered view of community and human nature as warlike. "Newer ideals," "newer humanitarianism," newer social processes can draw on the desire to struggle and create new social institutions and challenge infringements on civil rights. The modern city was the location for these new battles. Women were central to this new society and filling new roles. They were not restricted to the marriage that James defended (Addams 1907, 180-208). "War virtues" were dangerous ideals to defend while new, more encompassing and less bellicose behaviors needed to be established. She attacked patriotism that called for violence. She rejected the colonialism of the British which oppressed people of other nations under the guise of helping the subjugated. Addams (1907) substituted the ideals of Leo Tolstoy and non-resistance for those of James. Tolstoy was forward looking and fought against imperialism, colonialism, nativism, and narrow national interests.

This gendered argument is crucial here, because Addams and her hundreds of female allies around the world acted on this view of human society and action while Mead, Dewey, and James joined the millions of men around the world who defended the destructive war virtues. Mead displays this allegiance, and mistakes, through his writings during wartime. Of course, Mead was a leader in the university, the city, and pragmatism during the war while Addams was ostracized; verbally and intellectually attacked; and hunted and persecuted by the government for her beliefs (Davis 1973; Deegan 1988). James had died before the war began, but Mead and Dewey continued his arguments into this next era.

Addams and Mead were initially largely compatible on their positions on war. Thus in 1907 Mead favorably reviewed her book *Newer Ideals of Peace* (see chapter 3, reading 3A here) although he did not believe it was her best book. The two friends shared a joint interest in arbitration in 1910 as they both worked to settle the Garment Workers' Strike (Deegan 1988, 115-16). They were hard-working allies who advanced cooperative models for social change (e.g., Mead 1899b, 1999), internationalism (Addams 1930; Mead 1915a), immigrant rights, and public education (Deegan 1988).

Addams expected this kind of friendly alliance with Chicago pragmatists. Thus in 1915 Addams gave the Meads (and the Deweys and Harriet and W. I. Thomas)[1] a complimentary copy of *Women at the Hague* ("List of People to Receive Copies of *Women at the Hague*, SCPC, JA, Series 1), the book that discusses the founding of WILPF and women's international work for peace (see discussion on WILPF and Mead's family below).

Although Mead and Addams shared a variety of pragmatic assumptions, especially about anti-militarism and internationalism, they did not share her belief in cultural feminism or women's learned, traditional values. At some point, however, Mead's wife and her sister-in-law Mabel Castle did share Addams' views and they became active in WILPF. When they joined this group, however, is unknown (Deegan 1999). Mead (see reading 5A here) also publicly supported Quakers' right to conscientious objection to war, and he shared a speaking platform with Addams at least twice after her work had been rejected vigorously by other former allies (see especially Mead 1917a, 1918a; Addams 1917a, 1918). During the war, the friends briefly shared an interest in the LTEF, discussed at greater length later in this book.

Many years after the war, Mead (1929a/1999, 76-77) documented his support of another pacifist and WILPF stalwart in another format: in his convocation address at the University of Chicago where he introduced Mary E. McDowell as the keynote speaker. Here Mead honored her spirituality and inspiring soul that was a necessary balance to the overly rational academy controlled by white men. He loves her, literally, documenting the passion beneath the demeanor that still presents his closest friends as "Mr. Dewey" and "Miss Addams." The centrality of this close community changed each member.

Dewey and War

John Dewey, like Mead and Addams, opposed Wilson's warlike and aggressive policies prior to America's entry into WWI. The friends and colleagues were part of a significant and well-recognized group called "internationalists" or "progressive liberals" (Chatfield 1970). On 17 October 1916, however, Dewey joined a number of other "progressive liberals" who published a statement reversing their former opposition to Wilson's pro-war statements. Their signed statement appeared in the *New York Times* (Knock 1992, 94, 303 n. 31). Mead was not listed as a petitioner on this document. After Wilson declared war, Dewey quickly became a national figure who represented a supportive war position among the internationalists. Mead shared the majority of Dewey's positions at this time, and both men split with those opposing the war within this formerly united group. Thus in July 1917 Dewey wrote (1917c/1991, 21):

> we are fighting for democracy.... It seems certain that the Allies will be victorious.... We are fighting to do away with the rule of kings and Kaisers. When we have finished the job we may find that we have done away with the rule of money and trade.

Dewey foretold positive changes in capitalism, marriage, the family, and women's roles in society. A year later, Dewey (1918) was arguing that a victory was needed to secure American liberal ideals. Mead (see reading 5E here) expected similar sweeping and positive social processes, basing his argument in 1918 on changes in the welfare state in England and the United States.

John Patrick Diggins (1981, 214) aptly noted that "the outbreak of World War I confronted John Dewey's Pragmatism with its great challenges." This applies to Mead as well. Randolph S. Bourne, Dewey's prewar friend and a liberal pacifist, was shocked and betrayed by Dewey's militant, pro-war positions. Bourne (1917/1964) wrote in October 1917 a passionate, widely read article on the "Twilight of Idols." Here he articulated his disillusionment with Dewey and those who supported him. Dewey and Bourne engaged in public debates in the *Nation* and the *New Republic* and their differing views were widely considered and discussed. During the virulent flu pandemic in 1918, however, Bourne rapidly declined and died. His tragic passing ended their personal confrontations, but not their debates (Bourne 1964).

The liberals were uneasy about their split and would rejoin their former international pacifist allies on a few occasions. Thus, in April of 1918, Max Eastman, another staunch ally and former student of Dewey, was tried for his anti-war positions that he published and popularized in his journal the *Masses*. His trial ended in a hung jury, and a second trial appeared likely. Liberals, radicals, and socialists, however, united to successfully protest against another trial (Knock 1992, 158).

Mead and Dewey and Pacifism during Wartime, 1914-1918

Alan Cywar (1969) has analyzed Dewey's combination of patriotism and international progressivism," and Cywar's work clarifies Mead's perspective, too. This position exhibited a belief that good would emerge from the violence and this specifically meant that bureaucracy, rationality, and efficiency would increase. Class conflict in Europe would result and be succeeded by socialist welfare states. The socialist goals would be accomplished as a result of WWI (Cywar 1969, 580-581; Mead, see reading 5E here). Dewey, however, underestimated the irrationality of war, and the unintended consequences of efficiency serving the goals of war. Dewey started pulling back from many of these positions in 1918 and before the end of the war: but Mead did not. Mead's son and daughter-in-law were still in Europe and Mead was leading the CCC as a wartime leader at the university and in the city.

Both Dewey and Mead argued that German *Kultur* was dualistic. They supported its achievements in religion, music, and science, but not its nativism, sentimentality, arrogance, and domination (Cywar 1969, 584). Both men favored American ways and government, especially America's commitment to democracy. They saw a new economic and pacifist international order, but they underestimated the forces of destruction, animosity, and control that had been set in motion. (See Mead's discussion of this problem in reading 10B here.)

Dewey's widely recognized and often discussed position is echoed in the life and writings of Mead during wartime. For both men, their patriotic nativism broke with their ideas and practices both prewar and postwar. Dewey's views have been widely examined (especially in Chatfield 1970; Diggins 1981; Ryan 1995), while Mead's have not.

Although both Mead and Dewey split with the feminist pacifists during WWI, the differences in their approaches are examined throughout this book. This fundamental division on a major issue strained but did not break their ties and friendships. Mead and Dewey later modified their support of war, with Dewey (1945) becoming an ardent pacifist and Mead condemning the deceptive practices of President Wilson (see reading 10D here).

Dewey's Emotional Upheavals in Wartime

Dewey is portrayed frequently as an unusually even-tempered, somewhat boring person in terms of his affect. The notion of an upright and repressed New Englander is evoked, especially in descriptions of his sleep-inducing lectures. During the war, however, Dewey's demeanor was far from this staid image. Two indicators of his emotional turmoil are his poetry and his emotional attraction to a talented and volatile Polish immigrant, Anzia Yezierska (1932), Dewey (1977) wrote poetry privately for many years, but he captured his emotional upheaval associated with Yezierska in his poetry which is now published. JoAnne Boydston (1977) ably recounts the bizarre stories of intrigue over collecting and publishing these poems in her introduction to the volume of his poetry.

Helen Castle Mead and Feminist Pragmatism

Mead's family life is a largely unexplored area of study, and a full biography of him has not been written. Although I pieced together segments of it earlier (Deegan 1988, 1999, 2001) and here, a fuller examination is needed. Helen Castle Mead was independently wealthy and sometimes exhibited more political daring than George Herbert. At some point she and other women in her maternal family, the Castles, supported WILPF, worldwide pacifism, and women's particular contributions to it. As I noted earlier, WILPF emerged from the Women's Congress at The Hague in 1915 and this international, feminist, pacifist movement is discussed by Addams, Balch, and Hamilton (1915) during wartime. Addams sent a copy of the book to the Meads *gratis*. It contains positions on war that Mead objected to in his own writings during 1917 and 1918. Perhaps Helen did not act on her pacifist interests until after the war, or perhaps she acted on them during the war, reflecting a gendered split within the Mead's home which would have been difficult to manage. We do know, however, that such a split dramatically occurred with disastrous consequences within the home and career of W. I. Thomas, Mead's former student, friend, and colleague, discussed below.

Harriet Thomas and Feminist Pragmatism

Harriet Thomas, the first wife of W. I. Thomas, was an even more outspoken peace activist than Helen Castle Mead, her friend and Hull-House ally. The Thomases, like the Meads, were sent a copy of *Women at the Hague* as part of Addams' circle of Chicago allies and pragmatists. Harriet Thomas, however, was nationally known as the secretary to the Women's International Congress for Peace (which subsequently became WILPF after WWI), and she was a lecturer and organizer for them as well. Morris Janowitz (1966) argued that this work for peace was so controversial that it led to the arrest of W. I. Thomas for adultery with a soldier's wife. Thomas lost his position at the University of Chicago and his career was destroyed for many years. Only philanthropic and collegial support from Hull-House allies allowed him to recover partially from this vicious attack (see Deegan 1988 for a more in-depth discussion). Helen Castle and Mead's work with feminist pragmatists during wartime seems relatively mild in comparison to her friend's debacle ending in the destruction of W. I. Thomas' career, their move from Chicago into separate domiciles, and ultimately their divorce. In contrast, Mead continued his lifework at the University of Chicago until his death in 1931.

Conclusion

Mead's intellectual apparatus was profoundly changed by WWI and his allegiance to male values held by male pragmatists becomes clear. The differences between men and women, including husbands and wives as well as the women of Hull-House and the women faculty at the University of Chicago, split the formerly compatible ideas and practices of Chicago pragmatism and feminist pragmatism. Mead's continuing interest in internationalism, the arts, sciences, liberal institutions, democracy, arbitration, and the welfare state, nonetheless, reveals a stable basis for his thought. His jarring support of WWI, however, made war an arm of democracy and frayed his former friendships with German and international pacifists. Documenting Mead's theory and praxis as a function of war reveals not only his macrosociology and its emergence from its social situation, but also Mead's difficulty in addressing these fundamental shifts in his perspectives.

Note

1.   Also the sociologists Edith Abbott, Sophonisba Breckinridge, Kelley, McDowell, Anna Garlin Spencer, W. I. and Harriet Thomas, Mrs. Booker T. Washington, and Young.

Part 2

Mead's Writings before America Entered World War I

3

Mead's International Pacifism before World War I

> *"The war in Europe has paid certain great spiritual*
> *dividends. From Germany, from France, from*
> *England, and from Russia have come accounts of*
> *the fusing of people and peoples into self-conscious*
> *nations. Men and women and children passed*
> *under the spell of the great experience. They felt, if*
> *they did not think it out, that these overwhelming*
> *moments of emotion were theirs because of their*
> *complete identification with each other in the whole*
> *community. It was only because of this flood-tide*
> *of national consciousness that they could be swept*
> *up to these ultimate heights of human experience."*
> *(Mead 1915/reading 3C)*

Between 1894 and 1916, Mead, Dewey, and Addams built a remarkable theory of the unity of theory and behavior; the mind and body; peace and society; and the expert and the citizen, particularly from the perspectives of urban and rural life in America. Although Addams is the most feminist, radical, pacifist, and political actor of the three friends during this period, all shared a co-operative, global worldview called "international pacifism" or "progressive internationalism" (Kloppenberg 1998). They drew others into their work and created a unique American theory and praxis. This approach is documented in Mead's writings in this chapter.

Mead and Addams as International Pacifists Pre-World War I, 1907-1916

The world of Chicago pragmatism and international pacifism is revealed in a list of colleagues that Addams sent to her publisher in 1907. (See discussion in chapter 4 on a similar list for *Women at the Hague*.) Each person was to receive a complimentary copy of her new book *Newer Ideals of Peace*. These names included the following Chicago sociologists/pragmatists: Dewey, Charles R. Henderson, G. H. Mead, Edward A. Steiner, James Tufts, W. I. Thomas, George E. Vincent, Ella Flagg Young, and Charles Zueblin; and their colleague at the University of Michigan, Charles Horton Cooley (Addams to A. H. Nelson, 11 January 1907, p. 3, SCPC, JA, Series 1). It also included several Fabian sociologists and socialists including John A. Hobson, Sidney Webb, and L. T. Hobhouse. In addition, she sent a copy to the Harvard pragmatists, William James and Josiah Royce (loc. cit.), thereby documenting the broad academic circle of pragmatists and English sociologists who advocated Addams' and Mead's position on war and peace at this time (Deegan 1988; Deegan and Wahl 2003).

Mead's alliance with Addams, especially in terms of world peace and co-operation, resulted in his important review of this book, the *Newer Ideals of Peace*, in the *American Journal of Sociology* (see reading 3A here). Here he supported her view of a new consciousness and corresponding concepts to show how the community increasingly questioned the need for war. He also endorsed her opposition to militarism; her belief in immigrants as a source of change that required a larger voice in social, economic, and political processes, her international standpoint, and the need for new government programs to respond to these new social situations. Although he mildly criticized her book, he generally shared her emphasis on social reconstruction and change.

Mead, however, had a more hidden agenda, one of which he might not have been aware: his support for William James' arguments in favor of the war virtues, so-called human (i.e., male) aggressiveness, and the importance of social bonds created in wartime. James had presented this view first in 1904 when he and Addams presented their pacifist ideas at an internal peace conference (Schott 1993). At that time James called for "an alternative to war." (This major thesis was developed in several papers which reached their highest expression in 1910; James 1910/1991. See reading 10D here). Addams specifically criticized James' argument in her book that provided a different "alternative" or "substitute" to war. She did not believe war was noble and necessary, but outdated and primitive. Her challenging fight was for democracy and social justice, conducted without violence and destruction. These were the newer ideals of peace.

Both Addams and James continued to develop their ideas over the next few years. It is only in retrospect — especially in light of Mead's positions during and after WWI — that the latter's support for James becomes more significant and clarified. Mead does not openly call for James' arguments in this review, but he vaguely criticized Addams' "organization" and asserted that the book is "less logical" than others. I believe he was uneasy about her arguments without fully understanding why. William James, the target of Addams' critique, ironically did not share Mead's hesitations about Addams' book.

William James and *Newer Ideals of Peace*

Despite Addams' disagreement with James' argument for moral equivalents to war, he enthusiastically responded to her book. Thus on 12 February 1907 (pp. 1-3; Jane Addams papers, series 1, Swarthmore College Peace Collection, hereafter referred to as SCPC) James wrote that he had spent two weeks in New York city where he

> soothed myself by the perusal of your book. I find it hard to express the good it has done me in opening new points of view and annihilating old ones. New perspectives of hope! I don't care about this detail or that — it is the new *setting of questions*. Yours is a deeply original mind, and all is great and boundless! yet revolutionary in the extreme, and I should suspect that this very work would act as a fervent theme long years to come. I read precious little sociological literature, and my *opinions* in that field are worth nothing — but I am willing to *bet* on you.

Again in an ironic twist, James recognized the sociological import of Addams' writings, but many sociologists today are considerably more accepting of James as a sociologist, than Addams (e.g., Stone and Farberman 1970). James, additionally, was inspired and persuaded more by this book than Mead was.

James recommended sending the book to the English Fabians — notably, G. K. Chesterton, H. G. Wells, and George Bernard Shaw. [1] In fact, James had received two copies of the book (one sent by Addams and one sent by the publisher), and he was sending the second copy to Shaw himself. It is interesting to speculate if this book influenced James in his 1909 and 1910 revisions of "The Moral Equivalents of War."

Mead on Natural Rights and Political Institutions

Mead linked "Natural Rights and the Theory of the Political Institutions" in a liberal society (see reading 3B here). He viewed American democracy and its accompanying values as connecting the individual and the state, a continuing theme in his work on self, war, and society. This essay is part of the "liberal pacifism" characterizing his work before America entered the war. Mead interpreted human nature as flexible, optimistic, rational, and protected through the American political system. Mead advanced a similar argument on 29 December 1914 in a discussion held in Chicago at a joint session between members of the American and Western Philosophical Associations, the American Political Science Association, and the Conference on Legal and Social Philosophy. This discussion was summarized in 1915 in the *Journal of Philosophy, Psychology and Scientific Methods* and praised by William F. Dodd (1915) in the *Philosophical Review*.

This article explains Mead's adherence during the war to the ideals of liberal institutions that he defends in England, France, and the United States. His argument explains his support of these nation states and their joint opposition to the military and hierarchy found in Germany (see readings 7E, 8C here). Here Mead traced the historical development of Western democracy and liberal rights, and he argued persuasively against the notion of rights residing in an individual. This interpretation, fundamental to classical economics and the contemporary theory of rational choice (e.g., Coleman and Ferraro 1992), violated Mead's approach. The society created the self, and the self has rights insofar as they reflect the rights of all. The common good directs the development of political institutions and the interpretation of the abstract rights developed during the American and French Revolutions. Thus when an individual fights to protect a liberal right, they do so to protect everyone. Mead (1936) connected the political institutions in the United States, France, and England to a "movement of thought" which changes behavior, institutions, and the law. He immediately continued this international pacifism in an important article on war.

War and Social Reconstruction

By 1915, Mead was an "associate" of the *Survey*, a journal of applied sociology, and he wrote a major article for Addams, who was an editor there, as part of a symposium on "War and Social Reconstruction." Addams wrote a "Foreword" to the issue and gathered all the articles. Her introductory page was illustrated by Hull-House symbols visually announcing her central role in the issue. She collected these papers immediately after the Woman's Peace Party had met in December 1914 in Washington D.C. and just before she led the first International Congress of Women at The Hague in May (Addams, Balch, and Hamilton 1915; Deegan 2003).

Mead wrote here that nations, like individuals, develop "consciousness" and "self-consciousness." He discussed the links between these societal processes and the individual experiencing the first responses to a call for war: "for the time being they lived up to the enlargement of self-consciousness which is the inner side of the consciousness of a nation." Thus the nation state emerges from "psychological" processes that can be extended to a consciousness of other states and other people. His analysis of "The Psychological Bases of Internationalism" (see reading 3C here) examined how the state is supported by individuals who feel they are threatened as a people. This dangerous situation calls out both the individual's self and the nation's self to respond to a call for self-defense. Many social institutions, for example , labor, art, and science, reach their full potential only when they are coordinated with the processes, meanings, individuals, and resources that are found in various nations. He relied on a then-popular concept, "the international mind" to discuss the relation between self, war, and society.

War and the International Mind

Mead drew on the concept of "the international mind" advanced by Nicholas Murray Butler, who was a co-recipient with Addams of the Nobel Prize for Peace in 1931. Butler presented a speech on this general topic almost every year from 1907 until 1912 at the Lake Mohonk Conference on International Arbitration. On 15 May 1912, he argued for the judicial settlement of international disputes by applying the specific standard of the "international mind" (this definition is also the subtitle of his book on the subject in 1913). Justice would take the place of coercion: this plan for "practical politics" (Butler 1913, vii) appealed to pragmatic sensibilities like Mead's.

In 1907, this conference had occurred a month after the National Arbitration and Peace Congress where Addams and James had presented their ideas on peace, discussed in Addams' *New Ideals of Peace* and reviewed by Mead (see reading 3A here). Butler (1913, 10) enthused that the 1907 Lake Mohonk Conference had "carried us forward half a century." Mead followed this international pacifism literature and attendant conferences. He personally knew James and Butler, and probably many of the participants at both conferences. Mead adopted many of Butler's arguments, outlined below, when the former wrote his article for the *Survey*.

Butler (1913, 5) assumed, for example: "Like an individual, a nation has a mind and a conscience, and it has them in a very real sense." Mead echoed this belief when he wrote that this mind could be educated (Mead 1915, 6) and "evolve" into a higher stage (p. 7). Unlike Addams who supported immediate disarmament, Butler (1913, 12) argued that it would follow peace automatically and could not be pursued before that time. Mead and Butler (pp. 21-44), like Addams, opposed "militarism."

Butler (1913, 56) was skeptical of "patriotism": "What is needed is to leave off deluding ourselves with phrases, with shams, and with false historical analogies and to look the facts as they are in the face." He was also suspicious of the "war virtues" defended by James and Mead. Butler (1913, 60) called it "rattling rhetoric" and thought keeping peace was a challenge, as did Addams. Mead, however, supported patriotism and the war virtues even long after the war ended (see reading 10D here).

Although WWI did not start until late in 1914, the international arena was in turmoil by 1912. Thus by 1912 Butler had begun to temper his earlier enthusiasm and optimism for a peaceful future. He considered the international mind a "habit," a pragmatist term popularized by Dewey (1899), for constructing cooperative world relationships. It could be deliberately fostered by "developing commerce and industry, and in spreading enlightenment and culture throughout the world" (Butler 1913, 102). No stealing of land should occur; Butler (1913, 103) did not want to swing "sticks either big or little," clearly announcing a change from Teddy Roosevelt's presidential policy. People needed to understand the point of view of other nations (Butler 1913, 103-104), a restatement of Mead's "taking the role of the other." Butler advocated a commitment to peace that could resist minority pressures, national hysteria, and insults. Internal affairs needed to be ordered and enabled such that calm steps could be instituted for external affairs with other nations. A democratic citizenry able to communicate with each other was required to accomplish these goals. Given these proscriptions, Mead's adoption of the concept of "the international mind" is entirely understandable and logical and links his thought in 1915 to major pacifist arguments. John Haynes Holmes (1912/1972), a friend of Addams and Gandhi and a noted pacifist, also wrote a book on "the international mind," again echoing the circle of international pacifists that were united prior to the world at war.

Thus Mead's use of the concept of "the international mind" was one recognized by the readers of the *Survey* who generally supported international pacifism.

The Other Authors and Papers in the Symposium on War and Social Reconstruction

Mead's article was the first one in the issue, followed by that of Addams' close ally and sister Peace Nobelist, Emily Green Balch (1915; Deegan 1983, 1991, 1996b). Here Balch (1915, 610) adopted a cultural pluralism argument, supporting interracial contacts as factors in "the unconstrained fabric of a world at peace." Balch noted that the differences between races, including African Americans and whites, can divide people as well as unite them. These are cultural, not biological, differences and they are important, vital social processes. "The tendency to fuse, and to obliterate differences, appears to need the counterpoise of the other force which creates new unlikenesses, fresh types; and this in turn needs the growth of the power of mutual comprehension, appreciation, and sympathy to prevent divergence from meaning dissention" (ibid.) The pseudo-science of racial superiority is a curse and divisive. National vanity, greed, colonialism, and imperialism are evil. She (Balch 1915, 611) eloquently closed: "If we would end war, let us enlarge our hearts and rejoice in the otherness of others."

Simon N. Patton (1915), the political economist, showed that German aggression and economic exploitation were both wrong, but Americans could understand and condemn the former more easily than the latter. "Economic zones" resulted in new alignments of national sentiment, and such a change became particularly problematic for socialists. Frederic C. Howe (1915), the political bureaucrat and analyst, argued that the unequal distribution of wealth was "a cause of war" and a "reservoir of strife." George W. Nasmyth (1915) presented a complex chart and overview of "Constructive Mediation: An Interpretation of the Ten Foremost Proposals." These proposals for conflict resolution came from England, France, Holland, as well as from cities and groups throughout the United States, including the Woman's Peace Party that Addams headed. Chicago, in particular, was organized through the Emergency Federation of Peace Forces. The proposals called for armament reductions; often an international peace; no territorial changes resulting from war; the establishment of democratic governments; and usually the elimination of the economic causes of war. Mead supported such settlements in 1915. Mead's lack of an economic analysis, moreover, was offset by other authors in the symposium — Patton, Howe, and Nasmyth — who focused on the topic. Although this made the journal issue thorough, Mead's lack of an economic interpretation of the relation between capitalism and war was a gap in his theory which he never filled.

The last article, by August Shvan (1915), a Swedish politician then residing in England, discussed mechanisms for "Permanent Peace." He argued that international life eliminated old conceptions of the state and its need for military apparatus to defend itself against other states, two arguments Mead also advanced. All previous institutions and the concepts that justified them needed to be overturned. Universal free trade, world citizenship, the end of racial prejudice, and an international supreme court were methods to create this new institutional order.

This magazine issue was oriented toward a nation whose "international mind" was rational and outside the building war fever. The inhabitants of Chicago, however, were involved in a growing anger and debate over war between 1914 and 1916.

Chicago and WWI, 1914-1916

In 1914, Chicago's large German-speaking population consisted of 399,977 Germans and 58,843 Austrians, including immigrants and their children. The Germans were the largest immigrant group in the city and able to tap into significant money, cultural institutions, and leadership positions (Holli 1981, 262). Early in the war, many of these immigrants supported their former homelands.

The *Abendpost*, a German-language paper based in Chicago, had widespread appeal throughout the Midwest. On 14 August 1914, they published a chauvinist editorial proclaiming Germans' superior values and culture in comparison to that of their enemies in Europe (and their descendants in the United States). This inflammatory item was widely reprinted and said in part:

> What have the Russians, Poles, Bulgarians, and Serbs ever done for civilization? They have never made an invention, they have developed no political system, nor given us any new ideas (cited in Holli 1981, 260).

Calling Slavs "ignorant" and "barbarian," the editorial stated that a victory for them "means the obliteration of four centuries of European culture" (ibid). The Chicago immigrant groups attacked in this editorial, of course, quickly initiated counter-insults about the Germanic people.

The animosity between these groups heightened in early February 1916 after a bizarre local event which involved a German-born anarchist who tried to assassinate the Roman Catholic leader, Archbishop Mundelein, at an elegant dinner.

Chicago Hysteria and Archbishop George W. Mundelein, 10 February 1916

In early 1916, Archbishop (later Cardinal) Mundelein was appointed to the Diocese of Chicago, then one of the largest dioceses in the country. Mundelein was of German extraction and one of the youngest archbishops appointed to such an important position in the United States. He was greeted on 9 February 1916 by a boisterous and sometimes unruly crowd in a dramatic entry into his new home ("Chicago Bids Wild Welcome to Mundelein," 1916, p. 1, col. 5). He immediately identified himself as representing all Catholics, including immigrants who identified with various groups at war with each other in Europe. He stated: "I shall not speak to the Germans as Germans, or the Italians as Italians, or any other class of people. My simple message will be to all Catholics of whatever nationality" ("Chicago Bids Wild Welcome to Mundelein," 1916, p. 1, col. 5). He was initiated into his new position at the cathedral on the following day, 10 February, which ended in an elaborate banquet at the University Club[2] ("Becoming an Archbishop," 1916, p. 5, cols. 1-5).

A local anarchist, Jean Crones, violently opposed to Germans, Catholics, and the wealthy, secretly poisoned the soup for the dinner thereby attacking all his enemies simultaneously. The next morning's screaming headline in the *Chicago Tribune* read: "100 Poisoned At Banquet" (1916, p. 1) and ptomaine poisoning was suspected. The descriptions were graphic and frightening: first guests "toppled over," and an uproar ensued as more and more people were overcome. An "emergency field hospital" was erected and some victims were taken by ambulance to the hospital. Understandably few people wanted to continue the meal, although it was served in its entirety. Some people suggested that tobacco smoke or poor ventilation were at fault. The next day's news was "University Club Soup to Be Tried on Guinea Pigs" and Edward O. Jordan, a chemist from the University of Chicago, took samples of the soup to determine their contents and the cause of the illnesses.

On Valentine's Day, however, the huge headline was "Poisoner's Arrest Near" (1916, p. 1). The horrifying news was that authorities had determined that a cook had put "ARSENIC FOR DEATH OF 200 PUT IN SOUP. 96 Extra Guests Diluted Potion and Saved the Lives of All" (sub-headlines). This gruesome news named the anarchist as the poisoner and revealed that a friend of Crones, John Allegrini, had intended to bomb several other places and events. Other bombings and poisonings that had occurred in Chicago were being reevaluated and suspected of being caused by anarchists ("Huge Bomb Plot Exposed," 1916). This was the aura of fright, fear, and suspicion in Chicago in 1916.

Although Mead was not immune to this increasing urban terror, his publications on self, war, and society prior to WWI do not exhibit any of this war hysteria as we see in the readings that follow.

Conclusion

Mead's international pacifism is clear in his published writings on war and the nature of the state prior to 1916. Dewey, Addams, and Mead wove a powerful argument in support of a co-operative and peaceful society based on democracy and education. The world of Chicago pragmatism began to splinter in 1915 as Addams became a world leader for women's pacifism, but the friends did not separate until 1916 when Dewey began to push for America's entry into WWI.

READING 3A

REVIEW OF *THE NEWER IDEALS OF PEACE*, BY JANE ADDAMS[3]

The congestion of our great cities has been generally regarded as an unmitigated evil. We condemn the movement of population from the country to the city. Especially we condemn the perversity of the immigrant which leads him to herd with his kind in the city slums while the great harvest of our western plains are crying for labor; and condemnation passes over into indignation when the inevitable appeal is made to charity and conscience to cope with the suffering and vice that seem to be the sole fruit of these "plague spots" in our municipalities. This attitude has become fixed and almost traditional, because it is entrenched behind what we regard as the most admirable responses of human nature — its charity and conscience. We accept as our interpreters either the interested politician or the moral reformer, and the actual human experience that exists in these proscribed localities is separated from our vision by spiritual distances which dwarf the physical stretches these immigrants have covered to reach America.

Pre-eminent among those who have traversed these distances and have come into understanding contact with these social groups stands Miss Jane Addams, whose interpretation of the men and women who live in the congested districts of our cities, and of the conditions out of which they have arisen, and of the conditions of the whole social life which they determine, is again presented [to] us in *The Newer Ideals of Peace*.

The immediate theme of the book is the inadequacy of a governmental order that has arisen out of, and is still unconsciously dominated by, military ideals to express the democracy of an industrial community. For these military ideals Miss Addams substitutes those springing from actual human relationships, which do in fact surreptitiously dominate the government of the slums by its police and aldermen. The political corruption and protection of vice that ensue

Miss Addams traces to the helplessness of outworn political conceptions and the worse practice they involve. And finally the author affirms that our highest form of social emotion — patriotism — because it is dominated by warlike impulses and tradition is quite unable to sweep into itself the "finer spirit of courage and detachment" belonging to modern industrial struggles, although we defend warfare because it engenders these very qualities.

> To seek our patriotism in some age other than our own is to accept a code that is totally inadequate to help us through the problems which current life develops. We continue to found our patriotism upon war and to contrast conquest with nurture, militarism with industrialism, calling the latter passive, and inert, and the former active and aggressive, without really facing the situation as it exists. We tremble before our own convictions, and are afraid to find newer manifestations of courage and daring lest we thereby lose the virtues bequeathed to us by war. It is a pitiful acknowledgment that we have lost them already, and that we shall have to give up the ways of war, if for no other reason than to preserve the finer spirit of courage and detachment which it has engendered and developed. (p. 217)

The movement which would slough off warfare and usher in universal peace is perhaps more aggressively international than any other, unless it is the socialistic labor movement. It is then natural that a contribution to that movement should find its immediate motive in the international complex of our great city population, and of the laboring force of our great industries. Still, when the reader of Miss Addams' book recognizes the wide range of topic there considered, not simply the third chapter on the failure to utilize immigrants in city government, but the others ranging over the survivals of militarism in city government, militarism and industrial legislation, group morality and the labor movement, protection of children for industrial efficiency, utilization of women in city government, and the passing of the war virtues, one is struck by the constant appearance of the immigrant at the center of the author's treatment of nearly all these subjects. The conflict between the doctrinaire eighteenth-century ideals of government and present conditions,[4] and the consequent reversion to the repressive measures of a military community, is illustrated by the immigration problem. While immigration began in response to political impulses, and these still play some part, it has become in the main an industrial movement. The immigrant is imported to provide that fund of unskilled labor upon which our industries may draw at will. He comes ignorant and helpless before the system of exploitation which enwraps him before he leaves the old country and may last for two generations after he enters our gates. Our government has nothing to offer him by way of protection but the doctrine of the abstract rights of man, a vote he cannot intelligently exercise, and the police to hold him in his place. But in the cosmopolitan mass of which he becomes a part he enters into human relations with neighbors in the same uncomprehended struggle, with the alderman who can use his human needs and response to kindness, with the policemen who depend upon this alderman and have some comprehension of his daily life. All this social organization lies hopelessly outside of the governmental ideas and institutions. The so-called intelligent community, in its pity as well as its prudence, takes necessarily the attitude of the conqueror toward the conquered, because its government is purely repressive and legal. Our unconsciously military attitude prevents us from making any use of the actual social organization that is going on, and in fact this healthful process leads by its very human vitality to connivance with legal wrong, to protection of vice and municipal corruption.

The author does not, however, rest with this negative phase of the immigrants' condition. She sees the great positive losses to the community which its lack of comprehension of him entails. Just because the immigrant has torn himself loose from the old soil and comes with hope and fear to the new land, he brings with him a fund of emotion which is the precious material out of which social values and ends are built up. There are in addition the valuable habits, representing often the selective development of many centuries that our external repressive government is utterly unable to utilize. There is no encouragement for the combination of community life with agricultural occupations, which exists among Italian peasant groups. The Doukhobors[5] have occasioned endless complications with the Canadian government because its fixed and inflexible legal and property concepts could not adapt themselves to the common ownership of land that represents the inherited morale of these people. Apart from the organized habits of these immigrants, there is their native readiness to assist each other, to cooperate in human fashion in meeting the exigencies that surround them, that would be of enormous value if an intelligent government could recognize these possibilities and use the social materials already there. But our municipal governments offer only repression, or the extra-legal or illegal assistance of the politician who finds in the human situation his stock-in-trade. What might be done toward building up, out of social habits already there and their human social instincts and susceptibility, a deeper and more organic community control, if our government had other ideas and methods than those of police to repress crime and courts to protect vested rights! Even the more frankly military governments of Europe have made longer strides in this direction than we. Their legislation not only protects, where ours ignores, but takes positive steps toward better housing, toward health, and insurance, that our democratic community is helpless as yet to imitate.

In discussing militarism and industrial legislation, Miss Addams gathers her argument about two recent strikes-that in the anthracite coal-fields[6] and the Chicago Stock Yards strike. [7] She shows that a purely repressive government which is unable to reinterpret its legal conceptions from a larger industrial point of view, is quite outside the real struggle for social control. [8] The actual process of government takes place in the two camps of the employers and the employed. Representation, legislation, and executive administration, even the referendum, appear in these groups. And here the real issues appear — the issues of the standard of life, of economic efficiency — and actually control conduct. When, as in the anthracite coal-fields strike, the deadlock between the contending forces became unendurable, when the central government was forced to intervene and bring the issues before competent judges, the questions that were discussed were not simply those with which the military and legal type of government has concerned itself. On the contrary, the real questions, that everybody knew underlay the controversy, inevitably appeared in court:[9]

> Did the union encourage violence against non-union men, or did it really do everything to suppress violence? Did it live up to its creed, which was to maintain a standard of living, that families might be properly housed and protected from debilitating toil and disease, and that children might be nurtured into American citizenship? Did the operators protect their men as far as possible from mine damp, from length of hours proven by experience to be exhausting? Did they pay a wage to the mine laborer sufficient to allow him to send his children to school? Questions such as these, a study in the human problem, invaded the commission day after day during the sitting. One felt for the moment the first wave of a rising tide of humanitarianism, until the normal ideals of the laborer to secure food and shelter for his family, a security for his own old age, and a larger opportunity for his children, became the ideals of democratic government. (Pp. 98-99)

In the case of the Stock Yards strike in Chicago,[10] the issue was found in the reduction of the wage of the unskilled and unorganized labor. Organized skilled labor attempted to fight the battle, with the mixed motives that always arise — the fight against a movement to reduce wages which would inevitably reach them, and a fight for the weak and socially less effective by the stronger and better organized. False steps early in the contest, the unwieldy body of men to be controlled, endangered the hold which the labor-union strike managers had upon their men. The contest was a genuine one; the issue in terms of humanity took hold upon the Stock Yards community. The politician who understands dealing in human issues as the basis for his City Hall pull, tried to get possession of this struggle for the betterment of the condition of the underpaid unskilled labor. The real issue in terms of actual human conditions came to the surface, confronted the policemen on duty, the political leaders who controlled the repressive function[11] of government. It was so real, this issue, that the strike managers almost lost it, so eagerly did the politician want to make his use of it.

The moral is evident that as long as the government remains within its military attitude, as long as the policeman, its soldier, is its sole executive, and its arbiter courts which will admit to consideration only the abstract and property rights which hide the vital issues, its legislation cannot deal with the actual social forces out of which social control must arise. It cannot identify with itself the social organization which arises in the labor union, nor draw out in patriotism the devotion with which the laborer responds to its call. Actual social control and social emotion are lost to this government.

Again, it is the immigrant that forces this problem upon us. The anthracite coal field strike was but the climax of the long-drawn-out fight between the employers' power to import unskilled cheap labor, and the employees' power to assimilate him and identify him with the interests of his American fellows. In the Stock Yards strike, skilled organized labor found the lower unskilled positions being given to the immigrants from among the most oppressed peasantry of Europe. Identification of their interests with those of these Slovaks and Lithuanians was the price of their position. It is the immigrant who comes in response to the call of our feverish industry and our innumerable machines, that is forcing the deepest problems of social organization and evaluation upon us. It is the humblest and the stupidest among our foreign-born citizens that are forcing upon us the problems of our industrial, non-military community. And those who meet them in their real human form are not the legislators nor the executives nor the judiciary of our government. They have in a large degree isolated themselves in outworn categories, though they are still powers to be used by those who are face to face with the real problems. The employer to whom the immigrant is an economic possibility, and the laborer to whom he is a threat of a lower wage, and a different and often a lower standard of life — they are face to face with the problem. The problem grows rapidly with its human content. It involves the whole question of wage, standard of life, education, and insurance against sickness and old age. It involves protected machinery, control of dangerous callings, hygiene in the factory and home and city. All these pressing questions come in the train of the immigrant.

In dealing with group-morality in the labor movement, Miss Addams emphasizes the shortcomings of the unions which arise from their own isolated character. They are as handicapped in meeting the social exigencies as is any small group within a larger one, which must still maintain itself over against the larger whole of which it is a part. Thus the labor union arrays itself as the enemy of the employers' association, and their contacts naturally become those of warfare until common interests bring them close enough to each other to force to the surface the principle of common action, until the employer backs up his control by the judgments of the industrial expert, and the union comes forward with the consistent demand for collective bargaining in their commodity — labor and skill. Meanwhile the very human interests and impulses which make the labor union possible compel its earlier history to be that of effervescence and conflict. Because our outworn governmental conceptions make it impossible to the community to recognize and frankly deal with the human problems that face the laborer, he must attack them from the limited point of view of his group. Thus the machine is a social product for which no individual can claim complete responsibility. Its economic efficiency is as dependent on the presence of the laborer and the market for its products as mechanical structure is dependent upon the inventor, and its exploitation upon the capitalist. But the group-morality under which the community suffers, recognizes no responsibility of the exploiter to the laborer, but leaves him free to exhaust and even maim the operator, as if the community had placed a sword in his hand with which to subjugate. On the other hand, the laborer turns upon the machine with a hostility which assumes that there are no interests involved beyond his own which he is bound to recognize.

It is but natural that we should feel the loss, which a merely crime-preventing and contract-enforcing government entails upon society, most vividly in the case of the children; but the situation is rendered absurd as well as horrible by the fact that the community claims the right to give a certain education to the child, but regards itself as perfectly helpless over against the exploitation of the same child the moment he steps from the school. The very form of the machine has been adapted to this exploitation of the child as well as of the immigrant. This exploitation leaves the child worn out, and deprives not only him, but the community, of his inheritance of play, of imagination, and in so far of the great spiritual products of the play-impulses — art and aesthetic appreciation, with the life that depends upon them [Mead 1999].

An equal inconsequence Miss Addams brings to light in the attitude of the state toward woman. Because our more or less unconscious definition of citizenship includes only the warrior who will defend the community on the battlefield, woman is politically irresponsible; and yet the whole industrial nature of the community relates her and her interests as closely to the process of social control as the man. Indeed, the fields within which municipal inefficiency is most pronounced and corruption most rank are those whose functions have been the province of woman from the beginning of society. [12]

Over against the outworn conceptions of government which date from the military organization of society, Miss Addams places these ideals of social control[13] arising out of the industrial nature of our community. It is the contrast of nurture with repression; of the living social relation with the abstract formula; the instinct for workmanship [Veblen 1899] with the drudgery of unrelieved factory toil; the standard of life with an economic wage; the value of the child to the community with his legal right to freedom of contract; the intelligence born of social function with the use of doctrinaire concepts in the service of special interests. These ideals spring from the very industrial character of the community. To recognize them is to come socially to consciousness. On the other hand, the whole process and paraphernalia of warfare are outworn and antiquated means of interpreting the social situation.

One does not feel, in reading Miss Addams, the advance of an argument with measured tread. I think in logical organization this book suffers more than her earlier writing. On the other hand, perhaps, nowhere can one find the social point of view, which we must assume, presented with so much inherent necessity as here. It is not the necessity of a deduction, but the necessity of immediate reality. It is not burdened with a creed nor with socialistic dogma. It is the expression of enlightened social intelligence in sympathetic contact with men, women, and children whose reality is all the more impressive because our eyes have been holden from them by economic and political abstractions. The thesis of the book is that social control, that government, must arise out of these immediate human relations.

READING 3B

NATURAL RIGHTS AND THE THEORY OF THE POLITICAL INSTITUTION[14]

The term ["]natural rights["] suggests the political speculations of the seventeenth and eighteenth centuries in Europe, and the various revolutions that took them in some sense as their slogans. These revolutionary movements were one after the other increasingly forward-looking, constructive undertakings, until we may fairly say that as their results we find in representative government and growing democracy, revolution incorporated in the institution of government itself. That is, the form of government has become such that in its own operation the people can by legislation and amendment change it into any form they desire and still will have acted in a strictly legal and constitutional fashion. Furthermore, in the interplay of legislation and the execution and judicial interpretation of the legislation there arise not only the opportunities, but also the legally recognized occasions for the continual reconstruction of governmental institutions, so that a constant growth may take place in the form of institutions, and government may become in its own operation something entirely different from what it was, without any break or overthrow of constituted authority. Revolution has been incorporated into the constituted form of government itself.

And this has involved a revolution itself, for such an institutionalizing of revolution has been no less revolutionary with reference to revolution itself than it has been with reference to fixed forms of government. The tendency of each revolutionary movement had been to fix itself in relatively unchangeable governmental structure, that the successes it has spent and fought for might be preserved and entrenched, and thus had prepared the appropriate situation for the next revolution that sought in its turn to build its achievements into a new structure that should hold out against the wreckful siege of battering days.

In fact, the form of government in democratic countries has responded more completely to the demand for the opportunity for continual change than have the customs and attitudes of the community itself. The embedded structure of society has become more conservative than its more external forms and machinery. The possible revolutions, in the old sense, which we can envisage to-day are supposed to be directed against this inner structure such as the very producing and holding of wealth, or the procreating and nurture of children, and it is quite on the cards that these revolutions might be carried out by methods which would be strictly constitutional and legal.

It is not remarkable, then, that rights which looked very definite to the gentlemen who drew up the American Declaration of Independence, or those who formulated the bills of rights that were to justify the French revolutions, should have an entirely different aspect and meaning to-day. Life, liberty, security, property, and even the pursuit of happiness took on a definite connotation from the dangers and hindrances men sought to eliminate, the dangers and hindrances which an autocratic government could put in the way of the enjoyment of these imprescriptible rights. And when these dangers and hindrances had been removed the definitions of the rights which had been given in terms of what threatened them lost their bearings and at the same time their content. How simple and self-evident are the following definitions, taken from the declaration of rights and duties prefixed to the French constitution of September 23, 1795:

"The rights of man in society are liberty, equality, security, property."

"Liberty consists in the power to do that which does not injure the rights of others."

"Equality consists in this, that the law is the same for all, whether it protects, or whether it punishes."

"Equality does not admit any distinction of birth, or any inheritance of power."

"Security results from the cooperation of all to assure the rights of each."

"Property is the right to enjoy and dispose of one's goods, one's revenues, of the fruit of one's labor, and of one's industry."

"The law is the general will expressed by the majority of all the citizens or of their representatives."

"That which is not forbidden by law may not be prohibited. No one may be constrained to do that which the law does not ordain."

"No one may be summoned before court, accused, arrested, or detained, except in cases determined by law, according to the forms prescribed by law."

"Those who incite, give legal form to, sign, execute, or have executed arbitrary acts are culpable and are to be punished."

"All unnecessary severity in securing the person of the accused is to be severely repressed by law."

"No man may be judged until he has been heard or legally summoned."

"The law may only judge such penalties as are strictly necessary and proportioned to the offense."

"All treatment which aggravates the penalty set by the law is a crime."

"No law either criminal or civil may be applied retroactively."

"Every individual may dispose of his time and his services, but he may not offer himself for sale or be sold. His person is not alienable property."

"All taxes are established for the common good. It should be divided among those contributing to it, according to their abilities."

"The sovereignty resides essentially in the entirety of the citizens."

"No individual and no group of citizens may take to himself or itself sovereignty."

"No one without legal commission may exercise any authority or fill any public office."

"Every one has the right to take equal part in the formation of the law, in the nomination of the representatives of the people, and of public officers."

"Public offices may not become the property of those who hold them."

"Social security can not exist if the division of powers has not been established, if their limits have not been fixed, and if the responsibility of public officers has not been assured."

Here we find liberty defined in terms of taking away liberty and other rights to be defined, equality in terms of the absence of legal distinctions, security in terms of its source, property in terms of the absence of interference with its use, whatever it may be. But to the minds of men of the year four, these definitions had definite contents, because they were undertaking to determine the conditions under which certain powers which it did not even occur to them to define might be exercised.

Now that these conditions are in large measure assured, that the danger of inherited dynastic autocratic power has largely disappeared, these same powers lack the definition which the outlining of certain conditions of their exercise gave to them, and with Taine[15] we may criticize the working conceptions of the French Revolution as abstract.

It is to be remembered, however, that a working conception[16] can be abstract only in so far as that to which it refers for its functioning, needs only to be designated, not to be analytically defined. The abstract political individual of the seventeenth and eighteenth centuries and the abstract economic individual of the nineteenth century were quite concrete, every-day persons. They were pointed out by the negative definitions of those who speculated about them, and the negative definitions had reference to the hindrances to their activities which most interested the individuals. Thus [Baruch] Spinoza[17] was interested in a community in which the inherent reason of the individual should find its natural expression, and the passions should be relegated to their proper place. Such a state would be founded by and through a *libera multitudo* [liberated masses/public], free in the Spinozistic sense that it would be conscious of its essentially rational nature. It is from the standpoint of Spinoza's theory of the passions as passive and privation, that he is led to regard man as the embodiment of an abstract *potentia*, which by his definition comes to consciousness and so to freedom by the very disappearance of those privations which are our passions. It is the irony of Spinoza's speculation that for conduct it was the passions, the negations, which were after all defined as to their content, while the *potentia* which was to exist in positive consciousness is defined only in terms of the cessation of the passions, and the conditions under which this may take place. The positive content of reason to which Spinoza arises in the denouement of his "Ethics" [1677] is a mystical emotion. But in his own struggle and in that which he predicated of all human conduct it was through the definition of what he had to overcome that he designated the individual which was to rise triumphant. This potential has the right to express itself, but the right is defined in terms of the obstacles to its expression.

The timorous [Thomas] Hobbes[18] facing the disturbances of the Puritan revolution and the worse conditions which were likely to ensue defined the individual in terms of those hostile impulses which must lead to a *bellum omnium contra omnes* [all out war against all others]. It was this human being, lifted through Hobbes's fear out of all human relationship, whose rights, recognized only in a state of nature, must be entirely surrendered to an autocratic sovereign, who is defined entirely in terms of what he must surrender to be safely admitted within a human society. There could and can be no doubt to whom Hobbes referred in his abstract definition of the individual, nor can there be any question that the definition indicates the hindrances which keep the individual out of the social state to which he belongs. In the case of Hobbes the rights — so-called — of man are positive. They are the concrete satisfaction of every desire, just in so far as the man is able to attain that satisfaction. The individual who surrenders these rights, on the contrary, is entirely empty as a social being. He is the mere creature of the absolute sovereign.

The revolution of 1688 found its philosopher in John Locke[19] (1699/1967), and its theory in his treatise on "Civil Government." Building on the very foundations which had seemed so abhorrent to Hobbes, the party that dethroned James and brought in by act of Parliament William and Mary, appealed to a certain common interest which they felt to be the interest of the individual. Thus we find in Locke's account of the state of nature the whole content of social existence which, according to Hobbes, was possible only under the absolute autocrat. There is lacking only a settled statement of law, received by common consent, an indifferent judge to administer it, and an executive to enforce the decisions. But this legislation, justice, and execution is only the carrying out of actions with reference to common ends which are already in the natures and conduct of men, before the government is constituted. The government comes in only to give adequate expression and effect to natural social attitudes and conduct of men in a state of nature. There is to be found property, the family, and neighborly interest in one another. Was ever human nature so quickly regenerated as between the publications of the *Leviathan* (Hobbes 1651/1929) and the *Treatise on Civil Government* (Locke 1699/1967)? With such a human nature, so admirable in its native state, the emphasis must now be laid upon the restrictions to be placed upon government, not those to be placed upon the individual. The laws must be free from the influence of private interest, they must have in view alone the public good. The taxes raised must be by common consent, and the original power of the people to fashion its own government for its own ends must not be placed in any other hands or power.

Here we have a statement of rights of the people against any usurping, misgoverning government. And they again are negative, and yet they are the issues of the revolution of 1688, the elimination of court and dynastic interests in legislation, the vigor of parliament, and, in especial, its unquestioned hold upon the purse strings. But none of these human rights which Locke affirms over against a dethroned monarch is stated in positive form. There is no definition of the common good, nor of the purposes for which taxes should be raised and expended, nor what is the essential function of parliament. And for the purposes of presenting the case of the revolutionary party the statement was far more effective than one which had undertaken to state what the common good of the community was or in what lay the authority of the supreme legislative body.

With [Jean-Jacques] Rousseau[20] the affirmation of the social character of human nature is still more emphatic. There is not only a common good that exists, and can be recognized by all, there is also a common will by which it can be affirmed and enforced. The government which Locke calls out to carry out the social nature of men is but the expression of Rousseau's *volonto generale* [social contract] which, it is true, constructs a government as an instrument to carry out its purposes. This government, however, is but a means to accomplish a definite common purpose, commonly conceived, and the execution of which is commonly determined. Over against such a mere instrument, such a servant of the common interest and will, the rights of the men who make up the state are the more sharply defined, but for that very purpose negatively stated. A statement of them was given in the form of the preamble to the Constitution of the year four.

The rights of man, especially those which have been called natural rights, have been the expression of certain negative conditions under which men in society and under government could express themselves. And they have been formulated with reference to definite hindrances which have brought to consciousness the powers which were seeking expression, but only in terms of the obstacles themselves. In the *Areopagitica* (1904), in the whole eloquent plea for freedom of publication, [John] Milton undertakes no definition of what is good to print, and we are in the same case to-day. After all we are legally free to say and to print what a jury of twelve talesmen think it proper for us to say and print. If this legal situation were the actual situation and the determination of what we might say or publish did lie with any twelve theoretically good men and true, picked by the sheriff, and not with what we call public sentiment, the situation would be ludicrously absurd. However, public sentiment does not undertake to define what it is proper to print except over against the dictum of a legislature or a judge, and then it does not speak positively as to what is the nature of what may be said or printed. It approves or disapproves of the particular law or decision that is applied in the particular case, and if you undertake to formulate a right out of this, you find that you have only an abstraction.

The natural right to liberty may be rendered by the pregnant phrase that there is no freedom except under the law, which is another way of saying that nothing may be forbidden to you which must not, by the same act, be forbidden to every one else under the same conditions, although this is not all that this phrase implies; but it will tell you nothing of what you are at liberty to do. It has always been for the crushing out of exceptional privileges that our wars of freedom have been fought. Not even the statement that a man must be an end and never a means can be made a positive content, *i.e.*, can be made into a positive statement of what responsible personality consists in. In general no man is free who has not the means of expressing himself, but just what is necessary to that self-expression can not be made clear. It is probable that Epictetus was far freer than was his master, and at the present time millions of men are expressing their freedom in exposing their bodies to torture and death. I do not say that we can not formulate a fairly comprehensive statement of what has come to be the stature and measure of what the citizen should be in our minds at the present moment. We would give him undoubtedly economic freedom, an education, an association with his fellow citizens and fellow workmen that would ensure him the means of control over situations affecting his physical, social, and intellectual well-being. But of one thing we may be sure that the next struggle for liberty, or our liberties, will arise out of some infraction that will not have reference to the definition which we have formulated of what the man should be and, consequently, of what constitute his liberties. On the contrary, we will find in all probability that the struggle will lead to a quite different definition from the one with which we started. No more illuminating instance of such a struggle can be found than in the fight of laborers for liberty to combine. The contests have always been over concrete restrictions, and every victory and defeat has left the question of what is the right to liberty of combination still undecided, though it has settled possibly for long periods to come a certain class of cases. The contents of our so-called natural rights have always been formulated negatively, with reference to restrictions to be overcome. When these restrictions have been overcome they represent a positive content of what we call for the time being our liberties. Thus we claim freedom of conscience in religious conduct. Slavery has gone by the board. Popular education, freedom of laborers to combine, *etc.*, are mile-stones in our progress, and at each struggle we have added something to the fundamental rights of the man who is a part of the modern community. But we have also discovered that we never fight our battles over again. It is never the same question that arises again, and over against the new situation we find ourselves as unable satisfactorily to define the content of what our liberties are as our forefathers have been before us. We feel the narrow walls and brace ourselves to burst open the doors of opportunity that we find shut, but we can never apply the keys by which former doors were locked.

Historians of the theory of natural rights take pains to point out that the questions of the inherent character of these rights has been confused with that of their priority to the society within which they find their expression. The most glaring instance of this error is to be found in the common assumption of the contract theorists of society, that we can conceive of the individual citizen existing before the community, in the possession of the rights which afterwards the society undertakes to protect. On the contrary, it is pointed out that a right implies a recognition, and that this is a recognition which can not be found outside of an organized social group. Thus they deny the possibility of rights inhering in the men in the state of nature as presented by Spinoza[21] and Hobbes, for these men have only powers, such as have the beasts of the field, but no rights. On the other hand, the state of nature which upon Locke's hypothesis precedes the compact forming the state is already a society, however deficient it may have been in governmental institutions. Had Locke had the acquaintance of our anthropologists with primitive groups he would have recognized that his precontract men would have possessed an organized group of social habits out of which indeed governmental institutions were to arise, but which already performed the functions of government as definitely as the later institutions were destined to do. Rousseau of course is subject to the same error of supposing that his socially endowed men with their recognition of each other's personalities could have existed without some form of social organization that must have fulfilled the function in some way of social control. If we are to correct their history we would substitute, for the coming together of these Lockean and Rousseauian precontract-men, the situations in which tribes that include a number of clans find the blood-feuds so costly in life and tribe strength, that they get together to formulate a graduated set of fines and primitive courts to enforce these penalties. Here governmental institutions arise out of communities that have been controlled largely by customs that needed no institutional instruments for the exercise of their function. Here the rights that are formulated and enforced have already existed and hence have been already recognized in another form, and indeed in a true sense have been already enforced.

If we rob the term natural right of this implication of nature — that the right existed in a previous state of nature — can the term still be retained! We find that the term natural right is bound up with another very important conception in the history of political theory, that of natural law. Here the reference to nature does not imply a prior existence, but points rather to the fundamental character of the law, or in the other case to the fundamental character of the right. Here the emphasis upon natural sets it off against what is felt to be unnatural. Thus there is supposed to be a natural law of propinquity in marriage which throws into sharp contrast instances of unnatural marriages. And there are in the same sense the natural rights which may be contrasted with the unnatural rights which have been conferred upon privileged classes or individuals. Thus equality has been asserted as natural to man, and freedom of movement in the satisfaction of his wants. And the term may have either a backward or a forward look.

When Adam dug and Eve span.

Who was then the gentleman?[22]

looked backward for the typical expression of human nature. Nature as Aristotle conceived it, on the other hand, reached its typical expression at the end of a period of growth or realization. And a modern evolutionist, Herbert Spencer,[23] has presented the hypothesis of a human society that is to be the result of a process of evolution, within which there is to be complete adaptation, so that finally there will arise a human nature that is as yet only in embryo [Mead 2001].

This conception of a right that belongs to the nature of society and that of the men who constitute that society brings us finally to the question, what beyond its recognition is involved in a right. We have seen that it comes to consciousness through some infraction, but this does not reveal its essential character. It can only exist in a society. Is it, then, conferred upon the individual by the group or society? From the standpoint of [Jeremy] Bentham and [John] Austin[24] there are no natural rights, all rights being conferred, unless we accept [Herbert] Spencer's[24] criticism on Benthamism that there must be assumed an original right to the enjoyment of pleasure. In any case it is the common interest on the part of society or those who constitute society in that which is the right of the individual which gives that right its recognition, and gives the ground for the enforcement of the right.

The attitude of the individual and of society may, however, be quite different, depending upon the point of view we adopt as to the character of the object which the individual sets before himself as his end. Is he pursuing a private end which chances to have the approval of the rest of the community? Or is his object one that is to him also a common good? Even [John Stuart] Mill has sought to show that through indissoluble association the private end may become the common end in the view of the individual himself. [Immanuel] Kant sought, approaching the problem from the opposite pole, to reach a like goal through substituting the good will itself for the universal form of the act, advancing then from the good will as an end to a society of good wills as a kingdom of ends. It remained for post-Kantian philosophy to find in the doctrine of the universality of the end of the individual's act, and the fact that that end must be social, being an objectification of the self, the starting-point for a theory of the state. I have no intention of discussing this theory. I wish simply to point out that Kant, Hegel, and Mill (1963-1991) all assume that the individual in society in large measure pursues ends which are not private, but are in his own mind public goods and his own good because they are public goods. Here we have a basis for a doctrine of rights which can be natural rights without the assumption of the existence of the individual and his right prior to society. The right is arbitrary from the standpoint of neither the individual nor the community. In so far as the end is a common good, the community recognizes the individual's end as a right because it is also the good of all, and will enforce that right in the interest of all. An evident illustration is found in property. The individual seeks property in a form which at the same time recognizes the property of others. In the same fashion the community in recognizing property as a common social object, which is yet the end of the individual, enforces the right of the individual to his own possession. This character certainly inheres in all so-called natural rights. In all of them we recognize that the individual in asserting his own right is also asserting that of all other members of the community, and that the community can only exist in so far as it recognizes and enforces these common ends, in which both the individual and the community are expressed.

It follows from this conception that the number of natural rights will be limited and in some sense defined at any time, depending upon the meaning we give to the term enforce. If by that we imply the exercise of *force majeure* [greater force] through the judicial and executive institutions of the community, the number of kinds of rights which can be enforced at any one time in a community will be necessarily limited. If by enforcement we imply as well the action of custom, public opinion, and sympathetic response, and indeed these are the chief forces that enforce the will of the community, then the number of natural rights which men may possess will be practically unlimited, for their common objects may not be counted. Even the most selfish end must have the form of a public good, to have any value to the private individual, otherwise it can not be his to have and to hold. It is evident that in one sense we have boxed the compass. We started with life, liberty, security, equality, pursuit of happiness, as natural rights. They were recognized as present in happiness, as natural rights. They were recognized as present in consciousness only when they were in some manner touched upon. They were found to be incapable of definition as to their content. From the point of view just suggested, every object that is pursued in a common or social form, implies a common good, that may demand recognition and the enforcement of the right of the individual. Here there is no limit to the number of such goods, and hence no limit to such rights. They seem to be definable in terms of contents, for they are all the common interests of men and mankind, and we have them as contents ever in mind, as they are prizes of our effort, and the solace of our hours of relaxation.

This anomalous situation repeats itself when we look to the nature of human rights and to their guaranties in our political and judicial institutions. What is evident at once is the difficulty of formulating fundamental rights which are to be distinguished from the multitudinous objects, the ends of actions, that are sought through our government and courts. The problem is that of determining the distinction that is to be made between the private right which must take its chances against other demands of a like sort and the specific common good which is endangered and calls for the special protection of our institutions. I think I shall not be subject to contradiction if I assert that in this country at least, where we have gone further than men have gone in other countries in the attempt to formulate fundamental rights in our written constitutions, and in the use of the courts in their protection, we have not succeeded in rendering definite what the rights are which should receive these guaranties, and that behind the effort to state and defend these rights have always loomed other issues, which theoretically should be kept out of the question, but which come to be the deciding influences in the action of the courts.

It is evident that we do not assume that in other cases than those especially protected human rights are to be sacrificed. On the contrary, we assume that they are protected in the ordinary process of social conduct, both within and without the courts. Nor do we or should we assume that the rights which are so protected are less precious than those which call for the unusual action provided by our state and federal constitutions. On the contrary, must we not assume that issues which arise under the application of these guaranties are those leading to the formulation of new objects and the rights which attach to them. It is largely under the doctrine of the police power, that such new objects and rights are emerging in our kingdom of ends, and here what is demanded is not an exact definition of abstract human liberties, of the right to the due process of law, but that these new interests which have been what we have been pleased to call private interests in the past, should have the opportunity to appear as common goods. It is evident that categories which are to serve all these purposes must be abstract and empty of content and that they should get their content through the struggle which arises on the bare floor and between their distant walls.

It is not for me to discuss the architecture, curious and at times fascinating in its archeological interest, of the staircases and corridors and doorways by which these modern throbbing issues reach these halls, nor the strange garbs that they have to assume to be presented at court. It is important to recognize what is going on, and to distinguish between that part of the process which merely holds the issue back from making its plea, and that which allows it to become gradually formulated. And it is important that we should realize the relation between these two phases of the process. This can be recognized in the instances which are most in evidence in the courts, those having to do with the protection of rights involved in property. In the social legislation which is appearing in such volume in all our states, rights which have in the past inhered in property are seriously affected. Now it is not of importance that these earlier rights should be protected if some common good which they have failed to recognize is at stake, nor should there be obstacles placed in the way of the appearance of this common good involved, in the interest of the ancient right. What is of importance is that all the interests which are involved should come to expression. For this purpose it is of importance that no hasty action should take place. And from this standpoint it is clear that political guaranties which delay action in the legislatures and constitutional provisions which are enforced in the courts have the same function.

On the face of it the former method, that of political guaranties, is the more logical, for it is in the legislature that it is possible to present more fully the human interests that are involved. Especially in a legislature such as the English, in which the responsibility for the execution of the laws is and must be felt. And in England the political guaranties are practically the only ones in existence. But I can not discuss the relative value of these two types of guaranties, I can only insist that we should recognize that the drag which we put by means of both of them upon the changes in the structure in our society serves only the purpose of enabling all the interests that are involved in the issue at stake to come to the surface and be adequately estimated. Let us labor under no delusion; while we do not want hasty or ill-considered action, there is after all no right that must not eventually get its formulation in terms of a common good so universal that even those most opposed in the struggle will accept and acclaim it. And such a formulation must eventually take place in terms of concrete living interests.

In other words, we must recognize that the most concrete and most fully realized society is not that which is presented in institutions as such, but that which is found in the interplay of social habits and customs, in the readjustments of personal interests that have come into conflict and which take place outside of court, in the change of social attitude that is not dependent upon an act of legislature. In the society which is closest to that of the primitive man we find the reality of all that is prefigured and set out in the institutions, and while problems that are not and can not be solved through the readjustments of the individual's habit and the immediate change in social attitudes have to be dealt with in the halls of legislature and the rooms of our high courts, they are only brought there to enable men to envisage them more clearly and especially to become conscious of interests which could not appear immediately in their reactions to each other. When, however, this has taken place and the essential meaning of the problem has been grasped, its solution lies in the action of common citizens with reference to the common goods which our institutions have brought to their view and so analyzed that they can react to these new interests as they have to those to which they are already adjusted.

In these days of discussion over the meaning of *Kultur* [culture/civilization], we may entertain a false view of institutions. They are the tools and implements of the community; they are not civilization itself. Society has progressed by a process of integration which has gradually brought men and women who have been separated by physical and social distances so close together that they have come to react to those who have been afar off as to those with whom they have been in immediate sympathetic relation, and political institutions have held people together in these as yet not fully integrated groups and in part have helped them to get still closer together and in part have kept them still farther apart. The political institution has especially held men together because it has represented and in some sense undertaken to make good, what was lacking through the absence of immediate social interrelationship. Thus through military activity men of different groups and different localities have been brought into a relationship which could be but the shadow of a real human community. And yet the relation of those thus socially and geographically at a distance could be mediated by the direct connection to the monarch. Here was a common bond, though it did not run from man to man directly, but from each to the sovereign. It became, of course, a basis for direct relationship in war through the attitude toward the common leader. But it also served other purposes. It gave in the first place a sense of the larger social whole to which men belonged. In the second place, the subjection to the monarch carried with it the theory at least of his protection. Thus the relation to the king could serve to replace in some degree the complete socialization of the whole realm. The king was the guarantee for all the rights that were not respected because men belonged to so many different groups and classes and districts instead of to one self-conscious community. Not only military activity has thus brought men of different groups together and held them together by means of a political institution till social integration could take place. Religion has served the same purpose. In Europe Pope and Emperor were together the institutional figures which in the Holy Roman Empire drew the shadowy outlines of Christendom and made it possible for men to realize that theoretically they belonged to a single society. But even more compelling than the influence of arms and religious faiths has been the influence of barter and trade and the wealth which they have procreated. Exchange of goods does not wait upon the decision of the clanging fight nor the acceptance of the prophets' message. It has undistanced the Alexanders and the Gregorys,[25] and has set up a tenuous society of economic men from which no accessible member of the human race is excluded. Thus has money, that root of all evil, set the most grandiose problem to human kind of achieving the completed society which wealth-in-exchange has sketched. But if men that are otherwise hostile to each other will trade together there must be some guarantee that the human rights which neither is bound to respect in the other shall be regarded at least in so far as they continue to trade and barter. Let these same economic processes within a community force men from different classes together into relations which do not carry with them their own social organization and hence their own guarantee of mutual rights, and again some outside institution must arise to act as a surrogate for the control which a completely organized group would exercise directly. In a word, the political institution presupposes first, relations set up between those at an effective distance from each other, distance which may be measured in miles and days, or in unsurmounted barriers of social classes and castes; and second, that the social control over the conduct of men in this relationship, which would arise through the other social relations if these distances were overcome, must in the interest of the whole be exercised by some compelling social force within the radius of whose action the distant individuals fall; and third, that with the completion of the socialization of those who lie within this relationship the function of the institution, its guarantee of rights, ceases. Most of our quarrels are settled out of court, and except at the street corners within the loop district few of our actions are governed by the police, nor are human rights the less carefully guarded; they are indefinitely better protected than the most vigilant police administration or system of courts could guard them. Human rights are never in such danger as when their only defenders are political institutions and their officers.

If this is in any sense a true account of the situation, every right that comes up for protection by our courts or other constitutional institution is confessedly in a form which is incomplete and inadequate, because it represents a social situation which is incomplete and inadequate. Until that situation can change the right may demand such defense as an institution can give it. But to stereotype the incomplete social situation even in the interest of action which should be neither hasty nor inconsiderate is not the proper function of the institution. It is true that until the human interests involved can be brought to public consciousness action should halt. But is it wise to have one organ to halt action and quite others or perhaps none at all for bringing these issues to the surface when the actual right is being safeguarded?

Furthermore, whatever confidence we may have in the brakes and drags which we put upon the wheels of popular action, we should not forget that the ultimate guarantee must be found in the reaction of men and women to a human situation so fully presented that their whole natures respond. However lacking in rigidity and solidity this may seem, it is at bottom the only guarantee of a human right to which we can finally appeal. Our other appeals are to institutions which delay the action in this highest court, and are legitimate when they make possible the complete presentation of the case. But is it wise to put our faith entirely in the valiant delayer of action, rather than in the agencies which will lead to the final social readjustments through their adequate presentation of the issues involved? Is it not true that our confidence in our courts has worked in no small degree with other causes to weaken the responsibility of our legislatures on the one hand, and on the other, to lead many of us to face social problems by turning our backs upon them, and approach them only when we have exhausted every delay the constitution provides?

READING 3C

THE PSYCHOLOGICAL BASIS OF INTERNATIONALISM[26]

I[27]

The war in Europe has paid certain great spiritual dividends. From Germany, from France, from England, and from Russia have come accounts of the fusing of people and peoples into self-conscious nations. Men and women and children passed under the spell of the great experience. They felt, if they did not think it out, that these overwhelming moments of emotion were theirs because of their complete identification with each other in the whole community. It was only because of this flood-tide of national consciousness that they could be swept up to these ultimate heights of human experience. It was not so much that they were willing to sacrifice themselves for their country, as that for the time being they lived up to the enlargement of self-consciousness which is the inner side of the consciousness of a nation.

The most impressive accounts of these experiences come not so much from the outburst of great masses in the cities, as from the letters and reported incidents in the lives of families and individuals scattered throughout these countries.

Now, these are types of the highest experiences that human nature has attained. They are the same in nature with those of saints and martyrs, and while they persist in full emotional throb, they make possible what men and women have regarded as the greatest moments in their lives. From the standpoint of the observer the man may be sacrificing himself for others; from his own, he is realizing the meaning of his identity with his whole group.

We cannot remain long on these emotional heights. Devotion passes quite naturally into hatred of the enemy. This attitude in the presence of actual danger to oneself and to all that has been precious, can be kept vivid and effective much longer than devotion. It is part of the almost instinctive technique of the community and the government to stimulate and play upon this hatred because it provides another mechanism for the sense of social identity after the exalted feeling of devotion has ebbed.

It does not necessarily detract from the lofty quality of the experiences that there was nothing in the attitudes of the peoples of Europe toward each other to account for the war itself.

There was, to be sure among the people of France, Russia, and England, a sense of dread of the military power of Germany; and in Germany there was a widespread dread of the military power of Russia and France threatening Germany on both flanks, and of England upon the sea. But the actual populations of these different countries carried on without clash or hatred an international life of commerce, industry, and intellectual interchange in social ideas in litera-ture, science, education, and even sport, which was beyond comparison more vivid and intimate than the national life in any country of Europe one hundred years ago. There never has been, within a shorter period than a century, so highly organized an intra-national life and consciousness in any country of the Western world as the international life of Europe before the first of last August. There was, of course, one exception to this statement. Between the Serbs and Austrians existed a racial hatred of long standing that in Austria-Hungary, at least, called loudly for war.

II

With this exception, there was nothing in the minds of the peoples, in their attitudes toward each other, or in profound popular movements, that demanded or suggested war. Slavs in hundreds of thousands came every year into Germany to labor, not only in the harvest fields but even in manufacturing industry. The steady friendly invasion of France and England by Germans, took place without racial friction. The movement which was most profoundly popular, the labor movement, was international. Science was international. There was hardly a field of interest, within which there did not exist some international organization defining and asserting international standards.

There was not a social issue, an idea dear to the hearts of the European community, that could by any possibility be identified with any one nation or its peculiar institutions. There was far greater unanimity of the masses of the whole European population against the economic and social domination of the upper groups than of the mass of any nation against another people. In fact, with the exception of the Austrian government in its attack upon Serbia, no government has dared present to its people any issue except that of self-defense; and the whole effort of the publicity department of every chancellery among the powers at war, has been to present a case at home and abroad of a nation or a group of nations attacked without warrant and defending itself against unjustified aggression.

It would require the satire of a [Jonathan] Swift[28] or a Voltaire[29] to do justice to the present situation, in which the greatest powers in Europe are engaged in the most terrible struggle the world has ever seen, while each is professedly occupied merely in self-defense. There is, of course, abundant reason for this identical formulation of the causes of the war. It is first of all an appeal to a public sentiment that is to be voiced by neutral nations; but, in the life and death grapple that is on, it is still more a mobilization of the moral forces at home. Nor are these two purposes distinct. Nations, like individuals, can become objects to themselves only as they see themselves through the eyes of others. Every appeal to public sentiment is an effort to justify oneself to oneself.

I doubt if we have fully realized the importance of this identical formulation of the causes of the war. Whatever else it means, it indicates clearly that for the masses of the European communities there is no justifiable cause of war except self-defense. There has arisen among the militaristic groups a revival of the cult of Napoleon with the appeal to the glory of combat and triumph. But not a military leader in Europe dares voice this appeal to slaughter and conquest.

Out of the warlike birth of the modern Prussian state and the German Empire under its hegemony, there has arisen a cult of the strong-armed state that finds justification for warfare in its own fortunes and in its own morale. But today there is not a German who can catch the public ear, who will recognize that the cult of Treitschke and von Bernhardi[30] has an echo in the German nation. Throughout the Western world there is now but one cause which can give rise to that entire national unity that constitutes the moral fitness for a life and death struggle — and that is, self-defense.

Unfortunately the theory of warfare demands offense as the most effective form of defense, and the logic of offense carries with it capture and subjection, devastation and terror. To defend successfully their own, men must get down to the primitive instincts from which spring battle-fury, the lust of carnage, rape and rapine. But whatever may be said in justification of such offense from the standpoint of the sadistic psychologist, or of the [Friedrich] Nietzschean (1901) counsel "to live dangerously," it is impossible to organize the moral sentiment of the fighting nations for a campaign of offensive warfare, and each government feels the compulsion upon it to suppress reports of that terror which is the logic of offensive fighting. An accepted and avowed policy of terrorism would be more dangerous to the administration at home than to the conquered people. And this is true not because a womanish sympathy[31] has weakened the fiber of the peoples, but because the sense of social solidarity inevitably sweeps in the very people who are to be terrorized. The international fabric of European life could not be tossed aside when war was declared. Purely national cultures could not be substituted for the international culture of the Western world, and no more convincing evidence of this could be given than the attempt which certain German scientists made in their letters to their American colleagues to prove that English science was entirely negligible. It was psychologically impossible for these men to hate the English as enemies of the fatherland as they wish to hate them, and still be on terms of international amity and cooperation within the field even of abstract science.

There is but one justification for killing which nations or individuals are willing to consciously accept, that of self-defense. The function of social organization is to build up and enlarge the personality of nations as truly as that of individuals, and this cannot include the deliberate destruction of the very members of international society, the consciousness of whom is essential to national self-consciousness.

III

But while it is true that it is psychologically impossible to mobilize a modern Western nation for any but a defensive war, we cannot push aside the fact that these nations have been willing to accept military preparedness as an essential part of their rational lives. The knowledge that the nation is prepared to fight has given it the feeling of self-respect that the knowledge of the art of self-defense and physical fitness give to the well-mannered man.

There has been a great deal of superficial justification of this military preparation for self-defense. Up to the first of last August, men could still maintain that preparation for war is the best guaranty of peace. Prince [Petr] Kropotkin [1868][32] was the first to recognize publicly that the events which followed that date finally and utterly disproved this doctrine.

It has been stated that a nation in arms will not lightly go to war, and the phrase "a nation in arms" has been so pleasant on the tongue that men have stopped thinking when they have uttered it. A nation under arms is in fact a nation bound to the unthinking obedience of the soldier to his commander. It is not and cannot be a nation in conscious control of its own policies and its own fortunes. Could there be better evidence of this than the fact of the five great nations fighting with each other for national existence, while the people of all five believe that the war is one purely of self-defense? The government of each has assured them that this is the case.

Theirs not to reason why;

Theirs but to do and die. [33]

It is further maintained that in the relations of nations with each other, military power and readiness inspires international respect and enables a nation to enforce its rights without the final proof of the battlefield. In the words of our own militarist [Theodore Roosevelt], a nation with the big stick may speak softly. And here again the picture is so agreeable that we are loath to look to the history of diplomacy. There it stands very plainly written that as soon as military force is admitted into the argument it as inevitably crowds out considerations of right, as a file of soldiers introduced into a convention or a court silences every claim except that supported by the bayonet.

Lord Grey[34] stretched his diplomats' imagination nearly to the breaking point when he conceived of England as approaching Germany's situation from the standpoint of national right as distinct from national might and appealed to the seemingly unrealizable ideal formulated by Gladstone,[35] of a public right governing European nations.

We have been living largely in diplomatic papers, and have sat with statesmen and monarchs agonizing over the terror that they foresaw and could not forfend even when they hesitatingly suggested the impossible, an international right, that might conceivably be put into the scales over against orders of mobilizations and dates and provisions of ultimata. The monstrous puerility of it all!

Because of the pomp and circumstance of diplomatic intercourse and the terrible consequences it implies, we overlook the fact that there is at present no situation short of a street fight or a small boys' squabble in which the actual procedure is the same as that of our ministers plenipotentiary and embassadors extraordinary. And there is but one explanation: When there is an armed force behind every proposal, the only convincing counter argument is a *force majeure* [greater force]; and when this argument has been displayed any other is a work of supererogation. There is but one possible justification for the situation, and it is the one offered — the necessity of it.

"There is no international right that anyone needs to respect. Between nations, except in moments of exaltation, might is the only right."

While we are reading governmental papers we may accept it. We are back in the age of the Hohenstaufens,[36] when the only guardian of international rights was the Lord of Hosts, the God of Battles.

The curious thing is that while we agree with the diplomatist and the war lord behind him that there is no international right, we would have sent any man not a diplomat to an insane asylum who acted upon that theory. A Frenchman or Englishman who made a contract with a German and refused to keep it, an Italian scientist who laid claim to the achievements of a Russian physiologist, an Englishman who outraged a Belgian peasant girl, on the theory that there was no international right, would all have realized, not only in the country in which the offense was committed, but also in their own countries, that there is an international right that is quite indistinguishable from national right.

In any case, the fellow-countrymen of that grandson of a Scotchman who was born in Koenigsberg, Germany, and who is so loudly acclaimed by that Teutonized Englishman Houston Chamberlain,[37] — the fellow-countrymen of Immanuel Kant,[38] at least, might recognize that the only reason there is any right at all in any nation or country is because there is a right that is recognized as international and more than international.

IV

We know from some expensive experience that there is no such thing as national finance that is not founded upon international finance. We know there never has been a national science that has not been the outgrowth of an international science. We know not only that there never has been a civilized race that is not a mingling of many bloods, but that no self-conscious civilization has ever arisen except out of the intercourse of ideas which have been actually internationalized and have thus become universal. A standard of any sort could not be merely national unless it were willing to be a contradiction in terms.

In a word, no nation could come to consciousness as a nation except within an international society, and there is no capacity or right or achievement of any nation for which it is not as dependent upon the international society that has made the nation possible, as is any German or Englishman or Russian dependent upon his own society for his capacities and rights and achievements.

Now it is true that human rights, being social growths have been slow growths, and that their growth has been marked by the same sort of violence as that which now on a Brobdignagian scale is devastating Europe. It is, then, easy to assume that international right is a plant of still slower growth, and that we must have the divine patience for which a thousand years is as one day, and one day is as a thousand years. We must assume, according to this doctrine, that when our war lords and foreign secretaries and militaristic leaders address us we are still in the age of the Hohenstaufens and their shining armors, while words addressed to the world by the Pasteurs, the Kochs, the Mendelieffs, the Ibsens, the Anatole Frances, the Darwins, the Sir Henry Maines, the great industrialists, educators, and financiers reach their fellow-countrymen because a twentieth century international society gave them both their social equipment and their equally essential audience.

V

We know the doctrine is a false one. We know that we have not only all the mechanisms necessary for expressing international rights of which we are vividly conscious, but also for enforcing them. We know that it is only the unwillingness of the peoples of our so-called Christendom to surrender that peculiar egoistic consciousness which each one of us experiences when his own nation stands up and shakes its fist in the face of another nation, together with the more profound experiences of self-devotion which go with it, that has kept Europe from working out and presenting for enactment international legislation that at a stroke would have replaced nations submissively bowing before their under officers and drill sergeants, and quite at the mercy of their foreign offices, by a Hague or other tribunal and a small international police.

We know that it is not because the rights of people and peoples can be affirmed and protected only by the procedure of the Hohenstaufens or the more modern street ruffians, that we have refused to permit international institutions to formulate those rights and an international public opinion to enforce them.

What we are afraid to lose is this peculiar national self-consciousness, the sense of superiority to people of other nations, and the patriotism and lofty devotion which seems to be dependent upon national egotisms. We will not surrender these nor the occasions out of which they arise. There must be some things we are unwilling to arbitrate, otherwise we are craven people with dead souls.

It is of importance that men should realize that the problem of war is on the one hand ethical and on the other, psychological. It is not a problem of institutional mechanisms, nor of an apparatus of universal ideas, nor of means of international communication and acquaintanceship. It is not a question, in other words, of creating an international society. All of these exist. It is a question of relative values. Are the spiritual experiences, both the egoistical and those of self-surrender, both the contemptible and the heroic, which seem to us to presuppose war, — are these so valuable that we can afford to purchase them at the expense of Armageddon?

The problem is an ethical problem because it is a conflict of values. The Western world has now a definite bill of costs for its procedure in checking and cutting back the growth of the institutions and public sentiments which could without difficulty have settled the quarrel that was the occasion of Europe's holocaust. And on the other side, it has experienced the values for the sake of which it has exposed itself to this loss.

There have been those moments of priceless emotional experience, in which men and women realized that they were all one when the nation was in danger. With many, this elevated emotional tone will continue. With most, it has ebbed into the compelling routine of the group of habits we call discipline, in very many, into the hatred of the enemy by which one can still get that sense of solidarity that under other conditions we call mob consciousness.

These are enormously valuable experiences — even those which must be called ignoble in comparison with the sense of entire self-devotion. They pervade the whole consciousness, giving even insignificant objects and experiences a vicarious import. There have been periods in former struggles for human liberty when these moments stood out not only as worthwhile in themselves, but with the added value of the issues for which men were fighting. Today, men are fighting for no ideas. No nation is fighting for a better order of society. The international order of society is better than that of any nation which reserves to itself the right of fighting for any issue it chooses to call vital to its own interests.

VI

This war has taken place because the nations have maintained the right to carry arms and thus have made a relatively insignificant incident the occasion for a European catastrophe.

It is of importance that the relative values should stand out clearly. It is probable that in the aftermath of the war, these values will come with ever greater definiteness to men's minds. Unless men are so circumstanced that they cannot reflect, they must gradually recognize that as nations — apart from small interested groups — they were fighting simply because they demanded as their highest privilege the right to fight on any occasion, and at any time.

It is an ethical question, then, because, perhaps for the first time in human history, the value of war as a social institution existing for its own exercise, for its use in social organization, in physical training, in heightened national self-feeling, in opportunities for limitless hatreds and self-devotions, has been put sharply in contrast with the costs and losses of warfare.

It is a psychological question because the values of war, and the preparation for it, have to be stated more and more completely in terms of attitudes and states of mind. The objective human interests for which men have fought in the past are now so embodied in the institutions of civilized states, and in the habits and customs of communities, that they are there vastly better safeguarded than they could be by armies and navies. It is the feeling of enlarged personality, of the national *amour propre* [self-love], a feeling not so much of what a people have or want as of what they are, that militarism supports in national life.

VII

If the ethical problem arises out of the conflict between values which a national military attitude and training maintains and those which war destroys, the psychological question is whether the military attitude and training are essential for the self-respect of a nation; whether this antiquated, medieval method of giving every man the sense of being at one with the rest of the community must be preserved for the lack of better mechanism.

If the ethical problem is solved as we hope that it will be solved, if militarism is cashiered because it is too hideously expensive in human values, the question as to the way in which nations will arouse their patriotisms is likely to be left to answer itself. But though men are not likely to consider what form patriotisms will take in the future, it is true that because the problem has become so largely psychological, the ethical problem of war stands out so clearly.

It is because in the relations of Western nations with each other we have nothing left to fight for except the right to fight for the sake of fighting, that we can squarely assess the value of this so-called national right. If bloodless revolution had not been embodied in the constitution of most of our Western states, war would be still necessary to bring men to the common consciousness of their rights and their willingness to die for them. At present, any war is apt to be more dangerous than helpful to interests of those in our communities who need protection. In these days of scientific warfare, the disciplined populace who make up the army become the bulwark of economic and social privilege. No. At present, war, as an institution, cannot be cast in the role of Greatheart who goes forth to protect the weak. It must find alone in the consciousness of fighting and being ready to fight, all the values with which to offset the losses it entails.

Instinctively all those who were interested in social reform felt that this war must set back the clock of social betterment unless it accomplished the feat of destroying militarism itself. And here the militarist stiffens the sinews, throws out his chest, and contrasts his red-blooded virility with the feminist, philanthropic social reform, and asks us whether we are willing to exchange the fighting man for the milksop.

We will not stop to consider the childish assumption that we must pull down amid fire and slaughter the whole structure of the Western world to secure bulging sinews, deep chests, and red blood corpuscles. The real question is: Why should anyone consider the work with which these reforms are occupied as white-blooded and feministic? They are the identical interests — though vastly more intelligently conceived — for which our forefathers fought, bled, and died. They are attempted concrete definitions of the life, the liberty, and the pursuit of happiness of the great mass of the community. We cannot fight for them any longer at least after the fashion of the modern fighting state, because the militaristic state must look upon itself as the potential enemy of all other states while most of the social structure within which growth is taking place, is international. The state as the instrument of the separate community is the organ through which these changes get formulated in that nation. But as long as it is necessarily hostile to internationalism, it cannot become properly responsive to the labor movement, to social science, or even to industry. It follows that these movements of social reform and integration within the separate states are deformed, are allowed to advance only so far as the interests of the state in its separation permits them to go.

The result is that the so-called reformer is always on the begging hand over against the self-sufficient state. How far may the reform go without weakening the fixed order of society? There is certainly no process more definitely international than industry and commerce. But industry is divided up from the governmental standpoint into industries of the different nations, and barriers are set up to bring in a national net income by industries that are conceived of as if they could stand alone. There can be no adequate standard of social control of an essentially international industry, from the point of view of a national budget. *The reformer stands in the position of the man urging concessions in the interests of humanity, and at the expense of the state.*

Now, there are restricted fields, such as that of hygiene, in which national and international interest palpably coincide. Here the trained man speaks with authority and does not present a pathetic plea. Even here, of course, there are limits to state action.

The German militaristic state has more intelligently than any other, recognized the common grounds of international social growth and national state interests. Within these fields militarism has even advanced these reforms. The German bureaucracy has gained a certain detachment from the military standpoint of its government, which has enabled it to introduce industrial insurance, community care for infants, the fostering of vocational education, and better housing, among other reforms. The privileged interests, which have opposed these reforms in other countries have been summarily pushed one side by a purposeful government that has undertaken to make its people more effective, more powerful, more masterful than any other nation in the world.

Such a state can have only persecution for an international labor movement, whereas it will welcome an international hygiene. It will welcome an international physical science which puts nature under the control of a national industry, where it will frown upon Hague tribunals which would deal with conflicts of nations from the international standpoint instead of the national standpoint.

Even in Germany the social reformer brings his program to a government that has other interests besides those of international society, and asks somewhat humbly how much of his program may be accepted. If science, and hygiene, and education, and art, and industry, and commerce, were as narrowly national as are armament and warfare in their interests, the social reformer would speak with authority and not as something of a milksop who is after all only trying to get a little good done.

Militarism is not simply an evil in itself. It is typical and conservative of a state that is narrowly national in its attitude and that refuses to recognize the international society, that after all has made the self-conscious state possible. The problem is then largely a psychological problem, for it has to do with the change of attitude, the willingness to accept the whole international fabric of society, and to regard the states and the communities of which they are the instruments, as subject to and controlled by the life of the whole, not as potential enemies for whose assault each state must be forever on the watch.

Notes

1. Addams did send the book to other Fabians — Hon. John Burns, John Graham Brooks, L. T. Hobhouse, John A. Hobson, Sydney Webb, but not to Wells, Shaw, or Carpenter (Addams to A. H. Nelson, 11 January 1907, p. 3, SCPC, JA, Series 1).
2. This was a private club in downtown Chicago.
3. *American Journal of Sociology* 13 (July 1907): 121-128. *The Newer Ideals of Peace*, by Jane Addams (New York: The Macmillan Co. , 1907), Pp. xviii+243. $1.25. The pages cited by Mead match this edition of the book.
4. Mead's posthumously published book *Movements of Thought in the Nineteenth Century* (1936) parallels this discussion.
5. The Doukhobors were a group of pacifists following the ideals of Leo Tolstoy. See Addams (1910) for a brief discussion of Tolstoy and this group.
6. In 1902 the coal miners, supported by the United Mine Workers of America, fought for increased wages, union recognition, and an eight-hour day. The workers won a pay increase and a shorter day, but not union recognition, an end to child labor, nor safer working conditions after President Theodore Roosevelt acted to end the strike. For a discussion of Mead's interests in the stockyards neighborhood see Deegan (1999, xcv-cxi).
7. The 1902 Stockyards Strike was a violent and important labor protest. McDowell, of the University of Chicago Social Settlement, played a significant role in it. See Mead (1929/1999, 76-77) for his view of McDowell and Wilson (1928) on McDowell.
8. Mead uses "social control" in its formal, sociological meaning, to refer to social rules and not to the popular meaning of trying to control and repress a group. See Ross (1901).
9. Mead ultimately suggested industrial arbitration after the 1910 Garment Workers Strike. See Deegan (1988a, 115-117). See Deegan and Wahl (2003) for Mead's continuing interest in garment workers.
10. The 1902 Stock Yard Strike was central to unionization of that industry in Chicago and brought McDowell closer to her neighbors. Mead was active in this settlement, its neighborhood, and labor unions. See also ftn. 7.

11. Mead used "function" to refer to specific activities reflected in human behavior and the formation of consciousness. See Mead (2001).
12. Mead's argument is similar to that of Addams who drew upon the work of Otis Tufton Mason (1894) on this subject.
13. See ftn. 9.
14. *Journal of Philosophy, Psychology and Scientific Methods* 12 (18 March 1915): 141-155. This article was summarized as "Constitutional and Political Guarantees," by William F. Dodd in *Philosophical Review* 24 (March 1915): 193-194. This general topic was discussed at a joint session between members of the American and Western Philosophical Associations, the American Political Science Association, and the Conference on Legal and Social Philosophy, in Chicago, December 29, 1914.
15. Hippolyte Adolphe Taine (1828-1893) was a French critic and historian. He supported French naturalism, sociological positivism, and pessimism. He was also an influential art critic.
16. A "working conception" is a term similar to Mead's (1899) concept of "working hypothesis."
17. Baruch Spinoza (1632-1677) was a Dutch rationalist and ethicist. He helped establish arguments that led to the Enlightenment.
18. Thomas Hobbes (1588-1679) was an English philosopher who perceived human nature as self-interested cooperation.
19. Mead (1882-1883) wrote an essay on Locke while a student at Oberlin College.
20. Jean-Jacques Rousseau (1712-1778) tried to grasp emotion and passion in his thought. He argued that the state and society were corrupt and artificial. Humans were good by nature, "noble savages," but they banded together by creating a "social contract" for collective success. He attacked "private property" and influenced socialism, communism, and the French Revolution.
21. See ftn. 17.
22. These lines were written by John Ball (d. 15 July 1831), an English priest, in approximately 1381. He rebelled against the control of the church and the aristocracy in England.
23. Herbert Spencer (1820-1903) was a sociologist who argued that utilitarianism needed to be made "authentically liberal by infusing it with a demanding principal of liberty and robust moral rights."
24. Jeremy Bentham (1748-1832) was a moral philosopher who developed the "principle of utilitarianism which evaluates actions based upon their consequences, in particular the overall happiness created for everyone affected by the action."
25. The Russian dynasty of tsars of included Alexanders I, II, and III and the Gregorys.
26. *Survey* 33 (6 March 1915): 604-607. See also Box 3, folder 1, Mead Papers Addenda, Special Collections Research Center, Regenstein Library, University of Chicago (Hereafter referred to as "Mead Addenda.")
27. This paper is divided into unnamed sections indicated here by Roman numerals.
28. Jonathan Swift (1667-1745), Irish satirist best known for writing *Gulliver's Travels* first published in 1726.
29. François-Marie Arouet (1694-1778), under the pen name of Voltaire, was a witty author, philosopher, and defender of civil liberties.
30. Heinrich von Treitschke (1834-1896) and General Friedrich von Bernhardi (1849-1930) were German Generals and military writers. There were extreme nationalists of Pan-Germany and believed war was a right and a duty.
31. Mead equates sympathy here with a weak position of women. In this article he uses gendered language in several places.

32. Kropotkin visited Hull-House on several occasions and was a good friend of Addams (Deegan 1988, 262-63).
33. These lines are from the famous poem "Charge of the Light Brigade" by Alfred Lord Tennyson. This lost brigade made a heroic effort in the Crimean War, a disastrous military foray. See Deegan (2005c).
34. Lord Edward Grey (1862-1933) was an English politician and ornithologist. He was a Liberal, and served as Foreign Secretary from 1905 until 1916, when Lloyd George became Prime Minister. Grey played a key role in having the English enter WWI and in several treaty negotiations during the war.
35. William Ewart Gladstone (1809-1898) was a British Liberal Party member and served several terms as Prime Minister (1868-1874; 1880-1885; 1886, and 1892-1894). He was noted for his social reform ideas and policies.
36. This was the dynasty that ruled the Austro-Hungarian Empire but its power ended before WWI.
37. Houston Stewart Chamberlain (1855-1927) was born in Britain but became a naturalized German. He wrote about the so-called superiority of the Aryan race.
38. Mead taught a course on Immanuel Kant and connected him to the Germanic tradition of war in chapter 6, reading 6A here.

Part 3

Mead's Published Writings
after America Entered World War I

4

Articles in Chicago Newspapers during the Heat of the War: The Public Citizen as Expert, 1915-1918

> *"We were constantly told by our friends that to stand aside from the war mood of the country was to surrender all possibility of future influence, that we were committing intellectual suicide." (Addams 1922, 142)*

> *"To abolish war as a necessary condition of national safety is by the same stroke to abolish autocracy. War is essential to the existence of autocracy. It is unnecessary in a democratic world." (reading 4E here)*

The Great War started on 28 July 1914 when Austria-Hungary declared war on Serbia, and an increasing number of nations entered the war until 1917, when the United States also became a combatant state. Mead began speaking publicly as a citizen expert and writing professionally about the war and decrying its destructive response to internationalism in 1915.

Thus he helped to organize a series of six public lectures in 1915 on "The Great War Today" with the money from the sale of the tickets contributed to the University of Chicago Social Settlement (UCSS). The 1915 series was sponsored by the Chicago Lectures Association with lectures on 8, 15, 22, and 29 February; and 7 and 14 March, at a time when Mead served on the Executive Committee of the association. Mary McDowell, the head of the UCSS, would be sailing shortly to The Hague to meet with the International Congress of Women to plead for world peace, so I am unsure how much she would have supported this series (broadside program in file 231, Ethel Sturgess Dummer Papers, Schlesinger Library, Radcliffe College, hereafter referred to as "Dummer papers").

This same year the Meads served as patrons for another series, "The Present European War," offered by professors from the University of Chicago. These lectures were held on 9, 16, 23, and 30 January; and 6 and 13 February and the proceeds again went to the UCSS (lecture program in file 231, Dummer papers). Thomas spoke in this series on 9 January on "Racial Traits Underlying the War" (ibid.). If Mead had attended all these events, he would have heard twelve lectures in two and a half months, an intense experience and a considerable investment of time. Mead notes in his correspondence to his daughter-in-law in 1918 that he did attend various lectures on the war on campus. Mead was increasingly recognized as a spokesperson in defense of WWI between 1917 and 1920. For example, on 11 November 1917 he spoke to the Chicago Woman's City Club on the topic of "Children in Industry in War Time" ("News of the Chicago Women's Clubs" 1917). Mead also had several forums for writing about war as a war-time expert: newspaper articles, a pamphlet, and journals in the academy and in municipal life. Mead even wrote a series of newspaper articles on the meaning and cause of war that were published in the *Chicago Tribune* in 1918. These are reprinted here and discussed in this section on his war-time writings.

He also offered solutions for social reconstruction which became an organizing theme throughout the war. Mead repeatedly advocated the growth of the welfare state following the model used in England, and this is discussed more in his article on "Social Work, Standards of Living and the War" (1918; see reading 5E here). Before proceeding to this specific topic, however, I present the context for his newspaper articles. Some of it was private, but for many references in the articles he correctly assumed that the public was aware of the issues, names, and battles he discussed. I first present his personal context that fueled his intense response, and then discuss the University of Chicago's very strong involvement as a faculty. Finally I analyze the more public war situation.

Mead and His Family's Involvement in WWI: His Soldier Son, His Daughter-in-Law in the Medical Corps, and Family Letters About the War, 1917-1918

True to his pragmatic perspective, Mead's public and private lives were entwined. For example, his son Henry studied in Germany, as his parents and uncle had done. He spent part or all of his junior year in Berlin in 1914-1915. He witnessed the growing impact of the conflict on the city and the somewhat frenetic normality that the populace tried to enact. The fallen German soldiers were posted daily in the *Kriegsakademie*:

And up the gray stone steps and through the dark doors; into the dark room beyond there is an incessant stream, slow and silent — on the one hand going and on the other coming. Men go in there with fear in their eyes and come out again with the expressions of men who have seen beyond this life. The women often find relief in tears here — often they are more terribly dry eyed than the men (H. C. A. Mead, '16 1915, 175).

Thus Henry knew the cost of the war and the push and pull his family experienced in relation to that nation.

As noted earlier, Henry served in the Army, nonetheless, and was wounded in action. Mead was proud of his son and naturally deeply concerned over his fate. He expresses these feelings on 7 March 1918, when he writes Henry of his support and passionate involvement:

> I have never felt so strongly the necessity of America's fighting as I do now. The democratic issue that we fight for should be made clear not only by the president [sic] but also by the people. We should have a labor party that would put out the type of program[s] which the English labor party have issued. Barring the revolution there is nothing but America that can save the world from German domination, imperialistic commerce, and international politics and a more hideous war to succeed this. It may be a problem still whether we can fashion as efficient an army as we should. It can of course only be fashioned by using what we have, the traditional officers of the Regular Army and the political ones of the National Guard and the brand new ones of the National Army (G. H. Mead to Henry Mead, 7 March 1918, p. 2, Mead papers, box 1, folder 9).

These are his private views that he articulates more circumspectly for the public in his paper on "Social Work, Standards of Living and the War" (see reading 5E here). Mead also indicates his support for many of the goals of the Bolshevik Revolution but deplores its lack of practical steps for social change (Mead 1918, 637; see reading 5E here). Significantly, he understood that the Russian enterprise was establishing a new self as well as a new economic order.

Again in this letter Mead sympathizes with the flawed military apparatus in which his son risks his life: "There is, is there? no way of avoiding this use of what we have with its defects. I think the government at Washington has probably done about as well as an American government could." In this same letter he commented on the painful restrictions and human error attendant to military life:

> I suppose that one of the things that you and the others who are preparing to make supreme sacrifices have to face, the unnecessary restrictions, the bungling and stupidities that are among the human inevitables of getting a great army together. I imagine that they are harder to endure that [sic] the risks of the battle field. But the cause is as great as any cause can be, and I think it will become more evidently so as the days go by (*loc cit*).

When Henry wrote his father of a desire for universal military training, however, Mead forcibly decried such a program. In this answer to his son he clearly stated his views on education and democracy:

Military life calls for such an acceptance of caste distinction and restriction of individual freedom, that no democracy has ever adopted it, except in the face of threatening danger. Assuming that America can be brought to it, it will be reduced to the barest minimum. This has been eloquently supported by the attitude of the Universities and Colleges on the S.A.T.C. The latter (?) has been an utter and complete failure, fundamentally because of the entire opposition, which your friend Professor Bardeen pointed [out] with much warmth a month ago, between military discipline which trains a man to let some one else think for him, and then do what he is told, and University discipline which trains a man to think for himself, and question as far as he can the findings of others, especially his superiors, and to prove his points and stick by them if he can. I also recall (sic) the comment one of the privates made to me at Camp Green, that to appreciate liberty, one had only to enter the American Army and then get out of it (G. H. Mead to Henry Mead, 1 February 1919, Mead Papers, box 1, folder 9).

Mead opposed rigid lines between people, in this case those arising from the military hierarchy. For Mead, moreover, war was caused by a lack of international-mindedness. Methods of shaping the "generalized other" of all individuals would require training in critical thinking, democracy, and international world views so that each person's interests and those of others would be unified. Mead's attitudes in this area were consistent in his writings both before and after the war, and reflected his contributions as a citizen and as a family member. Thus here he represents an important continuity in his views on peace and society.

Later, on 10 October 1918, Mead wrote his niece, Elinor Nef, of his patriotic trust in the rightness of the war and for Wilson.

The onward movement of the Allies leaves no respite to the Germans and things of a serious character may be happening at home. Wilson's reply was consummate in its skill. It has I think deprived the German military party of the chance of saying that the Allies [sic] — or at least America — is undertaking to simply crush Germany, under a pretense [sic] of seeking a democratic peace. So far there has been no crisis to which Wilson has not successfully risen (G. H. Mead to Elinor Nef, 10 October 1918, Mead papers, box 4, folder 4).

Mead hopes that when the war ends that America will negotiate fairly with the defeated people and that they would understand the Allies' position. A few days later his optimism and faith in Wilson is again evident:

I think Wilson will demand that the government must be responsible to the German people in a political sense.... I am doubtful whether the English and French governments will be entirely governed by the Wilson fourteen points in the sense in which Wilson understands them (G. H. Mead to Elinor Nef, 13 October 1918, Mead Papers, box 4, folder 4).

Mead noted his disenchantment with England and France and their break with their own liberal institutions in a third letter to Nef a few days later: "There may be a definite break in which Wilson will be the representative of the masses over against the financially dominant interests, a division which would of course be found here also: (Mead to Elinor Nef, 17 October 1918, Mead papers, box 4, folder 5). Mead's expression of good will towards the people of Germany does not carry consciously over to its state institutions: the government and army. He continues to be in the thrall of war-time thinking and he wants revenge and suffering to be visited on the German people, despite his attempt to limit his primal feelings to institutions and not wish them on people: "I get a fresh accession of satisfaction every time that I think that they have been beaten at their own military game, out-generaled, out fought, and left without an alleviating circumstance for their ruthlessness" (Mead to Elinor Nef, 17 October 1918, box 4, folder 5, Mead papers). Mead's own bloodthirstiness is not apparent to him at this time.

He analyzed the events that called out this primitive and vicious response in his newspaper articles, although his public voice is less vindictive than the private family comments noted here. The newspaper articles, in turn, exhibit a more hostile tone than his academic ones.

President Wilson and the League to Enforce Peace, 1915-1921

Wilson strongly advocated that the Americans should stay out of the war between 1914 and early 1917. Addams (1922) outlined her faith in him during this period and her growing disillusionment, as well. One of Wilson's efforts for peace was the organization "the League to Enforce Peace" (LTEP), founded in 1915 by the former president William Howard Taft. At first, Addams believed this was a mechanism to work for peace, and she was listed as an officer in the group. She quickly withdrew from the organization, however, when she realized it was a mechanism to coerce nation states to adopt policies that Americans preferred. Mead, in contrast, never perceived the LTEP in this way prior to 1920. He repeatedly uses the group as a standard for peace negotiations and the flourishing of an international society. For example, he wrote that the group stood for:

the right of self-determination of nations, the demand for full security of the small nations, all of these are part of the *magna charta*[1] of an international society. But they approach the form of this international society from the outside, and by their structure they do not consider the inner nature of communities which may belong to such a society. The demand that diplomacy shall be open, that it shall be under the control of the people, is, to be sure, a step toward a reconstruction of inner order; but these measures also look toward the outer relations of nations with each other (Mead 5E, reading here).

In his newspaper articles Mead assumes the reader is familiar with the LTEP and shares his view of it.

Mead and the University of Chicago's Involvement in WWI

The University of Chicago was a deep resource for expertise on war. Albion Small, the chair of sociology, for example, "harshly denounced Germany and its political culture" (Boyer 2004, 4). Mead's newspaper articles fit into a series of similar ones published irregularly on the same page in the *Chicago Tribune*. For example, Shailer Matthews (1917), the noted minister from the Divinity School and sometimes viewed as a sociologist, authored a popular newspaper article in this series. Thus Mead was part of an institutional response by faculty at the university.

But more importantly, the men at the university served in the government as advisors on the war. They honed their academic training and turned it to the use of the state (Boyer 2004). On-campus and in the city, the university offered numerous public lectures, "war courses," and programs. Mead was in the center of this activity (see *Official Publication of the University of Chicago, 1917 — University Lecture Association in Cooperation with the University of Chicago, 1917-1918; War Courses. Official Publication of the University of Chicago, 1918 — University Lecture Association in Cooperation with the University of Chicago, 1918-1919; Patriotic Service; Training of Women for National Community Service.*)

John W. Boyer (2004) wrote a fascinating and detailed analysis of "Judson's War and Hutchins's Peace: The University of Chicago and War in the Twentieth Century." He noted that "By January 1918, seventy faculty members were involved in war service" (p. 3) and Mead was part of this community. Small (1917a, b) urged Americans to fight and depicted Germans harshly and President "Judson embraced the Great War" (Boyer 2004, 7). In 1918 Judson even revoked an honorary degree for the German ambassador to the United States, Count Johann von Bernstorff, bestowed upon him in 1911[2] (Boyer 2004, 7). Judson, like many of his colleagues, later reflected upon his enthusiastic nativism with some misgivings. Thus the university and the world of Chicago pragmatism both suffered from war fever and Mead was influenced by this, his community.

Mead's Newspaper Articles on War:
Analyzing the Worker and the State

Mead's five newspaper articles in the *Chicago Tribune*, published in the summer of 1918, advanced the argument that the role of German values, attitudes, and behaviors demanded a violent response by the United States. Ironically, he called upon the need for "self-defense," a reason he noted in 1915 that all nations used to justify war to their citizens even when it is not a legitimate reason. The essays' titles reveal their major points: "Germany's Crisis — Its Effect on Labor — Part I" (reading 4A); "Germany's Crisis — Its Effect on Labor — Part II" (reading 4B); "America's Ideals and the War" (reading 4C); "Democracy's Issues in the World War" (reading 4D); and "War Issue to U. S. Forced by Kaiser" (reading 4E).

In a two part article (see readings 4A and 4B here) Mead examined WWI from the German laborers' points of view. European socialism, to Mead, was a type of democracy where the working classes were struggling to gain a voice in government (see reading 4A here). Mead argued that European nations were fighting to obtain democracy while, in contrast, Americans fought to keep their democracy. "Germany's crisis," therefore, is linked intrinsically to a "labor crisis" precipitated by worker's demands for "government by the people." In "Germany's Crisis — Its Effect on Labor — Part II" (see reading 4B here) Mead averred that the common person wanted democratic representation, an end of militarism, imperialism, colonialism, and the aristocratic system of classes and government. In other words, the German was fighting for ideals that Americans already had institutionalized. Russia was also fighting for this type of government, albeit through a Russian Revolution. Both German and Russian workers used Marxist arguments because they must fight against an unjust ruling class, especially the aristocracy. The American Revolution overthrew the British aristocracy and other countries needed to "catch up" with the United States. Americans must join these struggles: "These are issues for which democracies can fight. They are issues for which democracies must fight when challenged by a military autocracy that finds the masses of its own people subservient to the control over national policy by a sovereign monarch" (see reading 4B here).

Although Mead's position on aristocracy was logical, he failed to grasp the intrinsic inequality and injustice of capitalism. Of course he did advocate Fabian socialism and this mitigates these injustices, but he did not anticipate the ultimate patchwork coverage of the feminist pragmatist welfare state which was unsuccessful in protecting male laborers and men in poverty.

American ideals (see reading 4C here) were lodged in liberal rights and rationality. Mead argued that the Monroe Doctrine and a lack of invasions within America made the people of the United States isolationists. Despite American's desire to avoid war, he believed America and Americans were being true to their ideals by fighting in WWI: "No country can put through successfully any undertaking of supreme importance which is not an expression of its fundamental subconscious habits." Mead also re-interpreted his beliefs in anti-militarism and internationalism by applying Wilson's war slogans[3] defining WWI as "a war to end all wars" and "a war for democracy." Mead translated these slogans into his theory as follows:

> our democracy is built upon the attitude of government with the consent of the governed, and warfare, even undertaken in self-defense or for idealistic motives, has always opened the door to domination over others through force, in other words to imperialism.

Thus Mead saw this war as a war for democracy, and the last one that would ever be needed. He was more cautious in this regard than Dewey was.

Mead recognized even in his war passion that war was fundamentally a path to disaster.

Finally, Mead saw the "War Issue to U. S. Forced by Kaiser" (reading 4E). Americans were peace-loving but must abandon these values to respond to the uncontrollable aggression of the German head of state and the aristocrats supporting him. Mead was not opposed to the Russian Revolution and his support of this earth-shattering event continued after the war. This was a period when such support was a controversial stand in the U. S. when a "Red scare" and witch-hunt against the feminist pragmatists shortly ensued. Mead, however, was not caught in the net of government persecution.

Conclusion

Mead's newspaper writings are important in revealing his position on Marx. Mead supported many of the goals of a free and just society that Marxists advocated, but Mead did not support most of their assumptions about the path to such a world. Mead believed that society was not based on materialism, or capital, or ownership of the means of production. Marx's dichotomies between owners and laborers were unacceptable to Mead. Mead did not believe in a historical dialectic, or any dialectic, because it dichotomized a more complex reality. Mead, moreover, did not believe in a conflict model but a cooperative model. He did not foresee class warfare because all classes were part of a democracy. Although he acknowledged that workers' problems were real, he argued that they could be solved through the government and welfare state; unionization, arbitration, and input from community representatives. Mead firmly believed that democracy is built on votes emergent from the whole community.

Thus Mead understood why European workers would become Marxists, not because Marx was correct for all workers but because they fought an aristocracy. German workers, in particular, were not part of a democratic community, but were oppressed by the military and the structures of a feudal society. Only conflict answered these workers' demands because they did not have access to the tools of full citizens. These newspaper articles, therefore, explicate several important ideas of Mead's view of Marxism, war, and the state.

Mead cast the German nation state as an aggressive, militaristic, anti-democratic nation that was attacking the innocent, democratic United States. Citizens in the United States and Germany were fighting for democracy and an end to war and state aggression. The future international community would be victorious.

READING 4A

GERMANY'S CRISIS — ITS EFFECT ON LABOR: PART I[4]

The present crisis in German politics is important from the point of view of labor. Indeed labor has perhaps more at stake in the war than any other element of society.

There seems to be a change of policy in the relations of social democrats and the German government. The democratizing of Germany is impossible so long as the present German government is free to pursue its policy of militarism by throwing its sop of social reform to the laboring men. The interests of American laboring men are wholly in the energetic pushing of the war in order to counteract the policy of the present German government. For unless the German people are made to feel that the present autocracy has failed, the war will leave democracy in Germany about where it found it.

* * *

It is too early to form a judgment upon the course of popular movement in Germany. A majority bloc in the *Reichstag* [German parliament] is demanding a peace close enough to that of the Russian formula to be regarded almost as a German translation of the new Slavic democracy. It is demanding such a parliamentary government in the empire as would give the German people the commanding voice in the determination of war and peace. The popular movement has been so pronounced that even the emperor himself revised his former project of electoral reform in Prussia and directed the chancellor to present to the Prussian Diet the outline of a law giving equal secret suffrage in place of the present three-class system which misrepresents the people of Prussia in its legislature today. This is the most fundamental attack yet delivered upon that Prussianism which all Europe and all the world are fighting.

* * *

Nor do these popular expressions fail to answer to the most characteristic note which America has given, viz., that demanding a plan for the settlement of disputes between nations by an international agency backed by the force of the organized nations of the world. This is a new attitude among the German people which must be carefully distinguished from the program of the social democrats early in the war.

If the German government would accept renunciation of annexation, the popularization of her government along the lines indicated both in the Prussian *Diet* and the imperial *Reichstag*, there would still remain the rehabilitation of Belgium and Serbia as the necessary preconditions to the discussion of the other great category of issues, the national aspirations of subject peoples and those caught in the maelstrom of the war, those of the Balkan communities, of the Poles, of Alsace and Lorraine and of the subject populations in Austria-Hungary itself.

However, the expressions of the leading statesmen of all the Allied Powers have without exception placed popular control within the German government as the most important goal to be sought in this war. If this could be attained the other conditions of peace are felt to be likely to follow as logical corollaries. It is insurance against the recurrence of the hideous struggle through which Europe has been fighting during these three dark years that is the deepest prayer of the peoples that are fighting the war, and with one consent it is recognized that only in the people's control of their governments can that insurance be sought.

*   *   *

This issue has been slowly fashioning itself in the development of the great conflict. Two great factors have been responsible for its sharper outline as the struggle has advanced. The first has been the reflection of the men in the trenches and the peoples that have sent them there, the reflection that such an enormous sacrifice must demand the result of terminating war itself. Never has the common soldier been so capable of reflection as he is today, and as the needle of his judgment has come to a rest it has been found in all the countries pointing toward the popular control of the issues of life and death in the conduct of the nation.

The second factor has been the formulations given by Russian and American democracies as they entered the war. For democratic Russia has come into the war as a new factor, with a new point of view and a new goal. She could not fight the war of her discarded autocracy. She was compelled to fight a democracy's fight. She had no imperialistic aims. She could not make conventional national prestige a justification of slaughter. The invasion of the right of self-conscious peoples to live their own lives could be the only *causus belli* [cause of war]. Annexations are national murders, and punitive indemnities differ from them only in seeking to enfeeble where forcible annexations kill.

*   *   *

That the people of Russia have had the power and the right to put their formula for peace authoritatively before the world has had a profound influence on the German people. And America has come with her declaration of the rights of the governed to determine their government and especially with their demand that out of the war must come an organized method of dealing with international disputes to forfend wars.

These are issues for which democracies can fight. They are issues for which democracies must fight when challenged by a military autocracy that finds the masses of its own people subservient to the control over national policy by a sovereign monarch.

READING 4B

GERMANY'S CRISIS — ITS EFFECT ON LABOR: PART II[5]

As long as the control in Germany is in the hands of its war lord there can be no compromise with safety to democracies, for not only do the armies of the

Central Powers threaten their neighbors, but the demands of Germany's far-flung commerce are to be made with the backing of Krupp's guns. [6] Germany has so explicitly affirmed that her own interpretation of what constitutes her own military necessity will transcend every international obligation, that no nation can sit down with Germany's present government at any council board without having provided herself with the military argument with which to argue her case if Germany conceives her own interests are in any degree at stake.

*   *   *

If we accept the only conclusion any other nation dared draw from what we know and what we must infer of Germany's internal history earlier in the war we must assume that a compact had been made between Germany's government and the majority group of the social democrats by which the advantages and profits of the war should redound also to the working classes, and that with these gains might go greater control in local government, while the military organization of the nation and the command over war and peace should remain with the monarch and the ministers he chose.

The increase in welfare and home-power of the masses in Germany was planned so that it would bring no added sense of assurance to the world against the treated of the mailed fist. The compromise which the major faction of the social democrats made in Germany and which led them to seek influence in the interest of Germany's socialist parties in other countries undoubtedly carried agreements from the military bureaucracy to still more improved conditions for the constituents of the social democratic members of the Reichstag.

*   *   *

If the German laborer could profit by the industry and commerce which a profitable war was meant to foster[,] the social democracy in Germany of that period had no interest in making the world a safe place for other democracies. The only conclusion which the rest of the world could draw from the attitude of socialist and liberal parties in Germany was that, in event of success in the war, there would have been no force at home to keep the Pan-German party from reaping the whole harvest of their program. The world that emerged after a German victory would have been subject to Germany or bound to arm itself against German commercial and military aggression.

The battle of the Marne[7] saved not only the world but Germany from the disastrous effects of the undertaking in which even the social democrats had concurred. The long war, with its heart-breaking experiences and terrible sufferings, has brought another frame of mind to men in all the ranks, and the men in the trenches have realized that in their hands lies, and can alone lie, the power to make such a war an impossibility. But most of all the Russian and the American formulas have represented a program which awakens a different type of democratic response in Germany from that which actuated the social democracy of Suedekum and Scheideman[8] in 1914. [9] It is a democracy that recognizes a society of nations whose principles and imperatives outrank those of the egotism of any nation, however great its military power.

*   *   *

The change is not alone one that has taken place in Germany. In all the nations there has been the same growth of reflection. The formulation of this democratic issue has been the result of a war which was made possible by other national egotisms beside that of Germany, but there is no question that when the issues was formulated it was Germany which accepted the role of military autocracy against a democracy which has found its ideals and the determination to save and re-enforce them among the Allies.

It is of the utmost importance to recognize that against this issue, when clearly stated and consistently supported, the people of Germany cannot oppose their spirit nor their social conscience. Just in so far as the war can be fought upon the level of these principles; that the right of peoples to determine their own government, and the right of the peoples of the society of nations to so organize and to so develop international institutions that international disputes may be settled by methods of arbitration and adjudication, just in so far as we are bound to have an ever increasing force of German popular sentiment upon the side which the Allies have taken.

*   *   *

It is for this reason that it is of supreme importance that the war should have the sort of democratic support with the group of the Allied peoples which these principles are bound to call out, when sharply stated and consistently held to. This means first of all that the laborers, organized and unorganized, should make this formulation of the issues of the war very consciously their own and hold to these principles whatever interests in the midst of the Allied nations may be willing to utilize militarism for other ends than these.

The masses of the Allied nations must make this war their own, and the American workingmen who have been spared as yet the martyrdom of the trenches are bound to recognize that only by the ending of the war in the interests of democracy can they be freed from the evils of militarism in America.

READING 4C

WAR ISSUE TO U. S. FORCED BY KAISER[10]

[Edmund] Burke has said that he did not know how to frame an indictment against a nation. [11] There is a like difficulty in giving praise to most acts of any nation. For nations as a rule do what they do without consciously determining it.

America is not to be blamed nor for that matter as a nation to be greatly commended for entering the war. She wanted to keep out of it. At the polls Wilson's election bore eloquent testimony to this attitude. The approval which followed his not always consistent state papers, that on the one hand demanded the recognition and maintenance of international law, while upon the other hand they maintained America's neutrality, this popular approval demonstrated how entirely the country felt that President Wilson expressed its own attitude. And the like unquestionable approval that has followed, without enthusiasm and without hesitation, upon the President's formulation of the case, for the recognition of a state of war between us and Germany, proves as clearly that the country has felt its inevitability.

The only alternative to war was to cease to have any international relations, to cease commerce, to abandon the high seas, to accept the proposition that the tissue of the society of nations had been rent in twain and that we had no responsibility for reconstructing it, to occupy an entirely isolated position till war was over, to remain the innocent bystander after our international relations and activities had been ruthlessly trodden upon.

* * *

Whether the country would have accepted this course had it been recommended by the President is, but for one consideration, a question whose answer is in doubt. That consideration is this, that, had America taken this attitude of isolation and withdrawn its ships from the high seas and agreed to sever its commercial relations with those countries with which our merchants and manufacturers wished to deal, it would have decided the war itself. For this would have brought with it the collapse of the Allies and victory of the Central Powers. If America shrank from the abyss of the war, America shrank still more from the responsibility of surrendering the world to the hegemony of the autocracies of Prussia and Hungary.

Even the pacifists,[12] in their arguments against the justice of America's going to war, had argued upon the unconscious presupposition that France and England would not succumb and that their peoples' governments would not cease from the earth with their precious import for humanity. Failure to adopt the cause of the Allies meant becoming the unwilling and ignominious allies of Germany and Austria.[13] There would probably have been no instance in the recorded history of the world in which the very failure to act would have been such decided action, and an action so contrary to the intent of the agents.

* * *

This was perhaps the one issue upon which American [sic] could go into the war, and Germany took pains to create it in the form in which America could not avoid it. The triumph of the U-boat meant the surrender of international relations by every neutral nation, just in so far as Germany saw fit to decree it and, therefore, made every neutral nation so challenged, in so far the unwilling ally of Germany. Germany announced to the United States that the triumph of the U-boat demanded the self-effacement of the United States as a member of the society of nations. The triumph of the U-boat meant the defeat of the allies. Thus Germany called not only for our self-surrender, but by the same act compelled the nation to take sides with one party or the other in the struggle, upon our own estimate of what those two parties represented, both for the United States and for the world to which the United States belonged.

As if to remove any question as to this issue, Russian democracy overturned its autocratic government by refusing to accept the formula of no annexations and no punitive indemnities.

*   *   *

Thus Germany said to us, surrender the international rights you have consistently affirmed and bring about the defeat of democratic peoples in their struggles with autocracy, or else go to war against us on the side of France, England and Russia.

Never was an issue more sharply drawn for America, and that by a government which professed to desire our neutrality. We accepted the issue which the German government had formulated and went into this war because, being the nation that we are, we could not do otherwise.

It is vastly important that we should now realize these issues and make them our own for the sake of our determined prosecution of the fight and for the sake of the determination of the terms upon which the war may be concluded.

READING 4D

AMERICA'S IDEALS AND THE WAR[14]

That which is most unique in President Wilson's deliverances upon the war is his emphasis upon the relation of American democracy to the international society which this war has embroiled.

Our geographical position, our history, our institutions have been such that we have not needed alliances with foreign nations to defend our borders or our institutions, or our interests in the world beyond our borders. Our fundamental political habits of feeling, thought and action have been such necessary outgrowths of the doctrine that government must be with the consent of the governed that we could never associate ourselves with the imperialistic aims which have so largely dominated the alliances and hostilities of European nations.

This has been most conclusively proved by the exceptions to the rule. After our war with Spain we found ourselves in military possession of Cuba and the Philippines. To the one we gave independence, and in our administration of the Philippines we have uniformly placed their independence as the goal of our occupation. Our recent legislation for these islands has placed that goal in the near future.

* * *

Still the rapidly growing intimacy of our industrial, commercial and other social relations with the rest of the world has brought us into uneasy recognition that the isolation that was our protection has largely disappeared. In the problems that have arisen out of the presence of Japanese on the Western coast, the defense of the Philippines, our policy with reference to the Panama Canal, but most especially in the problems arising out of the Monroe doctrine the possibility of war has arisen more than once on our national horizon, and yet we have never been willing to accept these threats of war as real dangers for which we were willing seriously to prepare ourselves.

This has been due partly to our dislike of the militarism which an efficient army entails, but the more profound disinclination has been rooted in the belief that readiness to fight is a powerful incentive to the use of the weight of our guns and the number of our bayonets in diplomatic dealings, with the imminent likelihood of making our threats good when the country had no wish for war.

The only definite response on the part of the government at Washington to this disquieting situation has been found in the numerous treaties of arbitration by which we have sought to prepare for disagreements with other nations and our vigorous support of The Hague tribunals and their promise of the adjudication of international disputes. But the uneasiness had not been allayed. We were at the parting of ways and we did not know in which direction to turn and, quite characteristically, left events to determine our future course for us.

* * *

It is with this background that we have found ourselves in this war, from which there was no escape which we were willing to accept, and it is this background of political attitudes and habits that America must use if the country is to fight it with whole-heartedness and express itself in the undertaking. No country can put through successfully any undertaking of supreme importance which is not an expression of its fundamental subconscious habits. A nation that by disposition is not imperialistic, that has deliberately put the temptation of imperial rule and dominion behind it, that has no world aim to enforce by a mailfisted diplomacy, that has no international policy to which it has been committed, except that of excluding European imperialism from this hemisphere: that has not sought consciousness of self in the fear it inspires in other peoples, and yet a nation that finds itself so essentially a part of the society of nations that it must enter the struggle contrary to its own traditions, such a nation can fight with grim determination and willingness to exhaust all its resources of lives and treasure only if its aim is to be done with war as the arbiter of international life. If that is clearly the goal of the war, America will fight it to the finish.

This issue is in a peculiar sense American, because our democracy is build upon the attitude of government with the consent of the governed, and warfare, even undertaken in self-defense or for idealistic motives, has always opened the door to domination over others through force, in other words to imperialism.

*   *   *

The people of the United States are the only people in the modern world who have turned their backs upon this will to power[15] when the vision of the kingdoms of this world was spread before them. The seeming renunciation has not been a deliberate sacrifice of an appetite for domination. It has been the expression of their own profound demand for home rule and self-government, which motived the War of Independence, their preoccupation with the immense task of taking possession of the stretch of the continent from the Atlantic to the Pacific, their acceptance of the slavery as the issue of their formative constitutional period, but not least of all their isolation and freedom from military threat and rivalry. It is not native to the American to feel that he may further his own interests by controlling and governing others.

*   *   *

On the other hand, the democracies of Europe have accustomed themselves to struggle for freedom at home while their governments have ruled with autocratic power other peoples beyond the seas or even at their very doors. It involves no contradiction in habits for the German social democrat to make terms with their government which give the people enlarged power at home while it gives the governing feudal and commercial group dominions stretching from Hamburg to Bagdad and beyond. Our historic development has given our democracy no such adaptability. It has left us with the uncompromising habit of accepting home rule abroad because we demand it at home.

If war as the arbiter of national disputes opens the door to imperialism, and who will deny it who has passed in review the projects which have appeared on both sides for the reconstruction of the map of the world, America will be found instinctively ranging herself with those who seek to make the outcome of this war the forced abdication of military power as the adjudicator between nations. If this is the issue, America will fight with the force of all her history, all her traditions and her whole genius.

READING 4E

DEMOCRACY'S ISSUES IN THE WORLD WAR[16]

Looking back over the three years of the war, realizing that we ourselves are entering into the valley of its shadow of death,[17] accepting the spiritual bankruptcy of war which has been the logical outcome of its efficiency, seeing all its pomp and trappings hopelessly mired in the trenches and the deliberate modern barbarities that demand retaliatory barbarities, we recognize that war can no more be accepted as part of the mechanism of modern society than filth, diseases and blights and famines which have stalked as "Gods agents" through human history.

But the last three years have accomplished this, they have transformed what began as a vast imperial and commercial raid on the world by Germany and Austria into a contest between democracy and autocracy, and the entrance of Russian and American democracy into the fight have underscored the transformation. It remains to be seen how far the democratic forces of the Western world can realize this change and with what intelligence they can direct its fortunes.

In Russia we can see as yet only huge popular upheavals and depressions, with heroic figures struggling to master its disorganization and give effective direction to its titanic forces. In the western countries of Europe the socialistic parties that have so largely directed the action of the masses have begun to assert themselves again, seeking on the one hand, for greater democratic control at home and, on the other, with more uncertainty to revive their internationalism.

*   *   *

We can only wait, with patience and profound sympathy, the outcome of the Russian revolution. It is not as yet articulate. The socialistic international we can better understand and more clearly envisage. We must not conceive it in terms of American socialism, for socialism has never been the articulate voice of democracy or even labor in America.

Socialism abroad has been the outcome of popular struggle against governments which have been in the hands of privileged classes. It has logically pitted against the privileged classes the laboring masses. It has undertaken to give them a class consciousness and a class program with which to fight the dominant classes. It has been democracy's fighting formation when opposed to a modern feudalism. But it has been a fighting formation, and has opposed the program of socialistic state to the feudal order it conceived itself to be fighting. Not unnaturally it sought to endow the classes in control of its own state program with the same powers which it would wrest from the privileged classes.

Just because it has been a battle formation of the laboring classes it has never represented the democratic attitude of a whole community and its internationalism has stood only for the solidarity of the laborers in the different countries in their opposition to the privileged groups. It has never stood for the common spirit of a society made up of different nations. It has been unable to enter into vital relation with the national self-consciousness which is of such overwhelming importance in the present struggle.

In a word, socialism, in its international attitude, is unable to express the individual spirit of one community entering into relation with another in a society of peoples.

*   *   *

When the declarations of war came socialism's internationalism was shown to have no roots in the larger society of the world. And even now, when the socialistic groups come forward with formulae for peace which are free from the tenets of their doctrines, they are suspect at home to the governments they oppose on principle and abroad because they have supported their own governments in their war aims.

The real assumption of democracy inside the society of a nation and with the society of different nations is that there is always to be discovered a common social interest in which can be found the solution of social strifes. Democratic institutions recognize this assumption in giving political power to all groups and individuals, confident that out of the political struggle of the conflicting aims and interests of individuals and groups the common interest must eventually arise to command the allegiance of all.

Democratic advance, therefore, has always been in the direction of breaking down the social barriers and vested privileges which have kept men from finding the common denominators of conflicting interests which have been at war with each other, because they have been incommensurable.

*   *   *

The same democratic assumption in the relation of nations insists that there are no irreconcilable conflicts between peoples if only there is adequate opportunity for bringing these conflicting interests in deliberative contact with each other, backed by a public opinion that enforces a thrashing out of the questions, before resort is had to force.

It is the laboring masses of all communities that are more interested in the assertion of this democratic assumption than the vested interests. In war they suffer most and profit least. They have more at stake, for they are the beneficiaries of every democratic advance, and no advance can be of such importance as that which dispossesses autocracy of its last hold on militarism.

Thus there has arisen a great opportunity for democracy in America, and especially for labor, which must be most jealous of its security, an opportunity to give to the war, so far as we are concerned in it, the paramount issue of the elimination of war by the democratic principle. This implies the rights of nationalities, government by the consent of the governed, the opportunity for the full discussion of international disputes under conditions which open the discussion to the public opinion of the world before war may be declared, and such a league of nations as will enforce this appeal to the democratic principle.

*   *   *

With Russia still inarticulate, with the European nations compromised by their earlier formulations of terms of peace and the uncertain note of the socialistic parties, America is in a peculiar degree called upon to interpret the import of the struggle between democracy and autocracy.

The principles have been presented by President Wilson. It remains for the American people and their most democratic groups to make these principles consciously their own as the issues of the war.

Notes

1. The great human rights document, the *Magna Carta*, signed on 10 June 1215 in England limited the powers of the king toward his subjects.
2. Addams was denied an honorary degree at the University of Chicago in perhaps 1906 and again in 1916. Mead and Small had championed her acceptance in 1916, again revealing their alliance with Addams even during war-time (Deegan 1988, 175-77).
3. See Addams' (in Addams, Balch and Hamilton, 1915) critique of war slogans as emotional and irrational symbolic language.
4. *Chicago Herald* (26 July): 4, cols. 4-5.
5. *Chicago Herald* (27 July 1918): 4, cols. 4-5.
6. A famous munitions manufacturer.
7. There were two battles of the Marne in WWI. The first occurred in August 1915 when Germany tried to take Paris but failed. French losses totaled 250,000 with approximately the same number of German loses (the latter numbers were never confirmed). The second battle occurred between 15 July and 16 September 1918. It was the first major Allied offensive victory and turned the war in favor of the Allied forces. Mead is writing just as this battle recorded its first successes.
8. Dr. Suedekum and Phillipp Scheidemann organized a labor movement in German to have a more participatory form of government.
9. The social democracy of 1914 supported German imperialism and war. Socialists who took this position broke with the Second International which stated that workers across nations were united in one cause for labor.
10. *Chicago Herald* (2 August): 4, cols. 4-5.
11. Mead is paraphrasing Edmund Burke in his "Speech on Conciliation With America."
12. Mead is not addressing the form of pacifism supported by Addams and Balch.
13. Addams did not use this argument and at this point in time Mead would have considered her pacifist stance traitorous.
14. (Chicago) *Herald*, 2 August 1917, box 9, folder 34, the Mead Papers, Regenstein Library, Special Collections Research Center (Hereafter referred to as "Mead papers.")
15. Friedrich Nietschze's (1901/1924) ideas, especially the "will to power," influenced German militarists in WWI and WWII.
16. *Chicago Herald* (4 August): 4, cols. 4-5.
17. This phrase,"the shadow of death," comes from Psalm Twenty-Three, *King James Bible*.

5

Academic Publications during War-Time: Academic Citizenship

> *"America finally entered this world war because*
> *its issue became that of democracy, democracy*
> *defined as the right of peoples to self-government,*
> *the right of a people to determine the foreign policy*
> *of its government, the right of the small nations to*
> *existence because the are nations, and the right of*
> *the whole Western world to be free from the threat*
> *of imperialistic militarism." (See reading 5B).*

Mead published four significant articles during WWI where he employed his formal language as a sociologist and generated working hypotheses on the relations between the citizen, the nation, and war. These include his analysis of the conscientious objector; Veblen's book on socialism and peace, *The Nature of Peace and the Terms of Its Perpetuation*; the welfare state as a product of social reconstruction in response to national upheaval; and the psychology of punitive justice. His criticism of the conscientious objector as engaged in illegitimate civil disobedience reveals his conservative nativism (Bennett 2004). His continued arguments against American, conflict-based socialism, discussed in chapter 4, appeared in his critique of Veblen's pragmatism. His definite support for a form of Fabian socialism, also shared with Addams and Fabian sociologists in Great Britain (Deegan 1988; Shalin 1987, 1988), is his model of how to reconstruct American society to fulfill its democratic ideals. Finally, his rejection of punitive justice is vital to understand his dashed hopes for democracy and a just peace after the punitive Versailles Treaty was signed.

Mead on "The Conscientious Objector" (1918)

Mead originally submitted his pamphlet on the "Conscientious Objector) to the Chicago City Club (CCC) for publication, but it was rejected (see G. H. Mead to Irene Mead, 22 October 1917, p. 2, Mead papers, box 1, folder 14). Instead, the National Security League, a conservative group, ultimately accepted and sponsored it. This alliance reflects the basic similarity between Mead's politics on this issue and that of an organization on the political right.

Henry David Thoreau (1849/1993) is justly famous for his concept of "civil disobedience" wherein he argues that each individual has the responsibility to follow his or her understanding of moral action, especially when a group supports an unjust law. This transcendentalist notion, civil disobedience, is one path to interpret American ideals, but it challenges Mead's understanding of these same values. Thoreau's concept could have been compatible intellectually with Mead's analysis of the role of conscientious objectors during WWI. Mead, however, did not accept a secular reason to reject war, and his hawkish perspective defined such an objection as illegal and cowardly. He did not support the secular, political, or economic reasoning that would lead an American citizen to reject participation in an unfair war. He particularly opposed such behavior if socialism was the reason for resisting American's capitalist, national ideology. As noted in chapter four, Mead stated that Americans did not need Marxist socialism because they did not struggle against an aristocracy and the democratic state reflected the will of the people. Dewey did not accept civil disobedience, either, but he did not ground his objection in Mead's understanding of economic democracy.

Thus Mead stressed the need to obey the law in a democratic society. He began with this statement in support of American participation in the war:

> its issue became that of democracy, democracy defined as the right of peoples to self-government, the right of a people to determine the foreign policy of its government, the right of the small nations to existence because they are nations, and the right of the whole Western world to be free from the threat of imperialistic militarism. We are fighting for the larger world society which democratic attitudes and principles make possible. . . a fight for the inviolability of peoples, for the right of a people to determine itself and its life in self-respecting intercourse with other nations (Mead 1918, see reading 5A here).

In Mead's view, these moral stances needed to be adopted by a citizen in a just state. Although his pamphlet, "The Conscientious Objector" (see reading 5A) was a progressive analysis for a patriot during WWI, when few people supported any conscientious objection, it was not a radical one. If an objector's resistance emerged from an organized religious belief, which is the case with the Quakers in general and Addams in particular, then Mead supported this behavior. Once again, he strongly supported Addams' pacifism, a position that Dewey did not share.

Mead offered one other exception to his demand for citizen obedience: he recognized the need for civil disobedience during the Civil War. Like Addams and Dewey, Mead was a neo-abolitionist whose home and family vehemently rejected slavery. He applauded the people who fought slavery through the Underground Railroad and disobeyed unjust laws that reinforced slavery (Deegan

2002a). Dewey did not compare this form of civil disobedience to pacifists during WWI, however.

Mead considered the case of a person who felt this moral repugnance for war. When this moral objection was based on an individual's and not a group's arguments, then to fight in WWI would be unacceptable for that individual. Such a person would have to acknowledge their violation of the state's legitimate right to command obedience and be morally obligated to accept incarceration and punishment as a just response. Thus Mead acknowledged the possibility of civil disobedience, but the state could not determine who was justifiably opposed to combat versus those who merely shirked their duty:

> Whenever and wherever an act runs so counter to man's moral nature that he cannot carry it out and still keep house with himself, his refusal in the face of any and all authority commands our instant respect. If such men could be certified to the exemption board beyond a doubt, any thinking, self-respecting community would demand their exemption. If they cannot be so isolated that their real spiritual lineaments can be clearly discerned they will still refuse to serve and will accept this penalty which a community which could not identify them has laid upon them, because it could not distinguish them (Mead 1918, see reading 5A here).

Mead argued here for free speech and dissent, but not for freedom of action when it was against the law. On the one hand, minority views could be heard and used to persuade people to change their laws. On the other hand, behavior could be demanded by the group, however, and the state's rights superseded the rights of the individual. Again Mead's position is more progressive than Dewey's when the latter limited Bourne's (Bourne 1917, 1964) right to criticize him and his arguments. Mead allowed for the moral refusal to fight by servicemen, which Dewey did not, but both men supported incarceration of such dissenters during the war.

Political and economic views that run counter to the majority's widely accepted views during war-time have gained more legitimacy since 1918, particularly after many Americans expressed their deep moral struggle over the Vietnam War. This stance has never been popular, nonetheless, and Addams' (1922, 1930; Deegan 1988) persecution for her condemnation of WWI — the religious minority's rights defended by Mead — remains a typical price paid by conscientious objectors in the United States.

Mead on the "Camouflage of the Conscientious Objector"

In late December, 1917 Mead (1917g) published a very important national article in the *New York Times* (see reading 5B). It complemented many points that he had raised in his pamphlet, but the article immediately reached a much larger audience.

Again, Mead finds the secular or ethical conscientious objector subject to the state's laws concerning military service. Although he argues that a prison sentence can only be imposed once for the same crime, unlike the position of the English government during WWI which re-incarcerated conscientious objectors who had served their sentence, the English objective could be met by delivering a lengthy sentence for the disobedience.

Mead fears that any objection other than a religious one can hide cowardly, greedy, or malicious disobedience. Accepting social or ethical objections could lead to a "camouflage" for the morally unfit. It encourages the unworthy to hide behind the exemption of an ethical argument.

Mead blindly assumed here that human nature emerged from man's biological nature to be aggressive and women's biological nature to be passive which exempted the latter from military service. He supported, therefore, the Doctrine of the Separate Spheres for men and women in war-time. He even argued that the subject of the state must obey the call of those in control of the state. Contrary to this article and his *Chicago Herald* articles (see readings 4A to 4E), Mead supported education and rational thought for each individual, and not state control. Mead's position logically would have opposed Americans fighting the English in the American Revolution, because the English represented the state. According to this argument, Mead opposed the War for Independence, a stance he not did not hold to be true here or in other writings. Thus his war fever made him considerably less logical in his philosophical arguments in order to justify his defense of WWI.

Mead on Veblen's
The Nature of Peace and the Terms of Its Perpetuation

On 21 March 1918 Mead ruefully wrote his daughter-in-law Irene Mead that he was late in submitting a review of Veblen's book *The Nature of Peace and the Terms of Its Perpetuation* (1917). In this letter he unequivocally states that he liked reading the book very much:

> It is exciting and exhilarating to get into a book of Veblen's again. With so much one can cry ["]yea and amen. ["] I think the only ground for dissent and it is a fundamental one, is that for him patriotism is only a characteristic of man that is entirely irrational not only in the losses and costs involved in its exercise, but also in its psychology, It never seems to occur to him to connect patriotism with the process by which [the] personality of the individual has been gained in the consciousness of the group and to see in this but the further growth of the same consciousness in the larger society. This personality has had an unquestioned function in social behavior. The more highly organized personality of a larger society will not lack — does not lack [—] its function. Patriotism as Veblen sketches it is[,] of course[,] only that phase of the growth which appears at the points of inhibition, and checked development.

Reading only the review, however, a very different impression of Mead's response is created.

Thus Mead spends a considerable portion of his review (see reading 5C) pointing to the narrowness of Veblen's position and suggests that if Veblen had had access to the Fabian socialist's program, Veblen's position would have been different. Since the Fabians had outlined many of their assumptions about the economy and the state by 1917, Veblen did have access to these ideas and Mead's argument is difficult to accept. Mead's enthusiasm for the book noted in his letter to Irene is also absent, and a long review of the more correct ideas, according to Mead and his war-time theory, is presented.

An even greater problem with Mead's review is that he does not mention that Veblen's book was inspired by Immanuel Kant's essay on the need for a "perpetual peace." This eighteenth century argument inspired Veblen's title and helped organize the book. In fact, Veblen specifically opposed many of the ideas that inspired Mead and William James. Thus Veblen perceived the heady power of fighting against an enemy and being a strong citizen of a nation, as did Mead and James, but Veblen came to the conclusion that this attachment through war and violence was unacceptable and a barrier to world peace.

Mead on *Social Work, Standards of Living and the War* (1918)

Mead chaired the "Division Committee for 1917-1918 on Social Problems of the War and Reconstruction" for the National Conference of Social Work. He led a large committee of nineteen members, including Breckinridge, and they were responsible for numerous papers that were presented at the national meeting in 1918. Mead wrote a plenary paper on "Social Work, Standards of Living and the War" that was presented at a general session for the whole convention (see reading 5D). Here he defends a massive growth of the American social welfare state based on Fabian socialism and similar programs established in England.

Addams again shared the platform with Mead on this occasion and was invited to speak by Mead's committee. Addams discussed "World Food and World Politics" (Addams 1918, pp. 650-56). By addressing world poverty and hunger exacerbated by war, Addams tried to find some common ground with the nativists then vilifying her for her pacifism. For Mead to share the rostrum with her was a courageous sign of support as well as intellectual recognition, similar to his work with Addams at the CCC in 1917 discussed above.

Katharine Bement Davis, a Chicago-trained sociologist (Deegan 2002b) was also on the agenda with a paper on "How the Public May Help" (pp. 673-74). Florence Kelley and E. C. Hayes, also Chicago sociologists, presented a panel on the topic of war and industry ("Future Prospect of Leading War-time Efforts and Movements" p. 675). All of these articles were published in the annual *Proceedings of the National Conference of Social Workers*.

Mead's analysis of the intersection between Fabian socialist programs, social work, standards of living, and war-time social programs reveals his commitment to the emerging welfare state in the United States as a form of social reconstruction. Dimitri Shalin is one of the few scholars to examine this article, but he misunderstood the type of socialism that Mead supports. That is, Mead consistently criticized Marxist, conflict-based socialism while he systematically allied himself with the development of a broad welfare state based on Fabian socialism. Shalin, however, indicates that Mead stopped supporting socialism, but Mead never denied Fabian socialism nor policies supporting it in any of his future writings. Mead did reduce the number of his writings on policy issues and social reform after the war (Deegan 1999, 2001) indicating a change in emphasis, but not a rejection of his politics and position on the welfare state. Shalin (1988) also views Mead's position as representative of progressive thought, but many progressives, especially men, were far more conservative that Mead (Sklar 1995; Skocpol 1992). Many male progressives represented capitalist interests that limited the development of the American welfare state, and Mead's position is significantly closer to that of the feminist pragmatists, Fabian sociologists, and what some scholars call the "maternalist welfare state" (e.g., Skocpol 1992), or "the social justice welfare state" (Goodwin 1991), or more accurately here, the "feminist pragmatist state" (Deegan 2005).

Mead also transcends the gender division that Katherine Sklar (1995) calls the "female political culture" or Robin Muncy (1997) calls the "female dominion." Mead was closer to these "female" political perspectives than Dewey was during the war. This is a continuity in Mead's thought that embraces the three chronological eras on self, war, and society examined here.

Mead on *"The Psychology of Punitive Justice"* (1918)

Mead opposed punishment as a response to crime. He was committed to integrating a criminal into the community after the group had delivered a just and fair verdict for the injury inflicted upon the group by the criminal behavior. The "psychology of punitive justice" inflicted harm not only on those disciplined, but also on the friends and relatives of the law-breaker. The community needed to help the violator return to a productive place within the everyday life of the group (See reading 5E). Mead identified four flaws within this punitive justice system: the blatant failure to identify the importance of social conditions, the failure to ameliorate the causes of crime, the stigma attached to criminals, and the capitalist ideology which underlies the system.

According to Mead, our fundamental instincts create an organized form of social conduct (the expected conduct of the individual in the group). One of our fundamental instincts, however, is the hostile attitude. When the hostile attitude emerges through a breakdown of the organization of the social act, crimes of passion emerge. The public responds punitively to attain two ideals: retribution and prevention. These ideals are characterized by the following statement: "It is just that a criminal should suffer in proportion to the evil that he has done. On the other hand it is just that the criminal should suffer so much and in such a manner that his penalty will serve to deter him and others from committing the like offense in the future" (1918, 582).

Punitive justice, like utilitarian principles, is maintained by the idea that justice is served by impartial enforcement of the common will to protect the individual interest in the common good. Recognition of this protection of the common will brings a personal "responsibility to obey and support the law in its enforcement" (Mead 1918, 584). This is not to say that flaws do not exist in laws and their administration. Respect for the law, however, is based on the values that the law conserves, not the actual laws and their administration. Respect for the law, based on the protection of the interests of the common good, means that when crime occurs, a personal enemy becomes a public enemy, and punitive justice becomes the weapon of defense and attack.

Mead never dreamed that the war would end with punitive punishment instead of signaling the end of all wars. If Mead's non-punitive view had governed the Treaty of Versailles, which determined the terms for peace and war based on punitive punishment, then the disaster generated by punitive psychology could have been prevented. This horrible mistake by several "victorious" nations dashed Mead's dream of a just, new, international, democratic society created by the war.

Mead made an important contribution to criminology in this essay, and it connects his ideas across the stages of the war, too. Thus he was active in the Juvenile Court, along with Addams, and he understood the importance of reconstructing the self to successfully return the law-breaker to the community (Deegan 1988; Neeley and Deegan 2005). He did not connect his knowledge of hostility within the criminal and within the state, despite his use of a model discussing impulses, mind, and aggression in both cases.

Conclusion

Mead's war-time articles reveal his continuing justification of WWI as a battle for democracy. He supported religious conscientious objectors, but not ethical or secular objectors who could "camouflage" the unworthy and the unfit. He anticipated a just response to former enemies after the war ended, declining class differences, and increasing progress for the feminist pragmatist welfare state.

His formal publications during war-time were less vehemently anti-German in his attacks on the aristocracy, military, and "Kultur" than his newspaper articles in the *Chicago Herald*. In 1917 and 1918 Mead supported Wilson, and his son's and daughter-in-law's gendered participation at the warfront. The international society is temporarily in abeyance for Mead, because democracy and American ideals are threatened. The psychology of patriots and patriotism are part of the mind, self, and society of citizens. Democratic laborers help create the community and American laborers' participation is part of a just society. Laws are not merely negative and blindly obeyed. To Mead, they are part of the fiber of citizenship.

THE CONSCIENTIOUS OBJECTOR[1]

America finally entered this world war, because its issue became that of democracy, democracy defined as the right of peoples to self-government, the right of a people to determine the foreign policy of its government, the right of the small nations to existence because they are nations, and the right of the whole Western world to be free from the threat of imperialistic militarism. We are fighting for the larger world society which democratic attitudes and principles make possible. In such a fight for the inviolability of peoples, for the right of a people to determine itself and its life in self-respecting intercourse with other nations, in this contest for a higher individualism among nations, are we transgressing the rights of the individual at home? In a war for democracy what should be our attitude toward the conscientious objector and how should we proceed with reference to his refusal to fight at the call of his country?

The conscientious objector has no recognition in the legislation which is mobilizing our new army, except as a member of a religious sect whose tenets forbid fighting. Membership in a political or other social organization with such tenets conveys no immunity from military service, nor does the fact that a man himself entertains conscientious objections to military service grant the individual freedom from service in the army. If the conscientious objectors number is called and he is not a *bona fide* member of such a religious organization, he will be certified to the army and there, if he refuses to serve in accordance with the orders given him by the officers of the army, he becomes subject to military discipline, and will undergo such penalties as any private suffers who refuses to obey orders. These penalties are or may be severe, for obedience to orders is the foundation of all army organization and the first condition of all military achievement. The position of the conscientious objector is also prejudiced by another circumstance. When he has suffered the penalty which a court martial has laid upon him, he returns automatically to the service, and if he remains a conscientious objector, he will again refuse to obey the military orders which direct him to do what runs contrary to his judgment of right conduct, and again he will find himself subject to court martial and again serving another sentence for what is in fact only the same offence, though in point of martial law it is a new offence. Thus a conscientious objector in the army cannot escape from the round of sentences which succeed each other automatically. He can never satisfy the law under which he finds himself placed. A consistent and logical application of the statute and the customary military criminal procedure will keep a conscientious objector under penalty for the rest of his life.

Continuous Offence

It is this feature of the situation of the conscientious objector which has called out perhaps the most serious reflections in England upon this manner of dealing with his offence. In civil procedure, a man may be punished but once for the same offence. While the continuance of the attitude of the conscientious objector, on the part of the drafted man who finds himself unwillingly in the army, involves a continuance of offenses each of which subjects him to penalty, the real offence is not in the separate refusal of the conscientious objector, but in the attitude from which these refusals arise. A single uniform punishment should be inflicted for the offence. When this sentence has been served, the individual should be again returned to society as any other offender who has committed an offence and suffered the penalty prescribed by law. It is to be hoped and expected that this particular injustice in the treatment of the conscientious objector which characterizes the English procedure will be avoided here, if the war lasts so long that this automatic repetition of the technical offence arises under the operation of army discipline. This is however only a subsidiary matter, one of procedure. It may lead to serious injustice. This can be readily avoided by the recognition of the real as distinguished from the technical position of the offender. The more fundamental matter is that of punishment for acting in accordance with the dictates of one's own moral judgment. The recognition of conscientious objection to fighting appears definitely in the exemption given to those whose religious tenets forbid army service. This exemption not only recognizes the objection but admits that it constitutes a valid ground for not accepting the draft. Why then should not the exemption extend to all those who have such conscientious objection, but who for other reasons do not belong to these non-resistant religious sects? Our government has sedulously avoided all ecclesiastical association. It recognizes religious bodies only in so far as it proclaims its complete toleration. Why then should the government extend this freedom from military service to those belonging to a particular sect, refusing it to others? The answer is found in the supposition that the government is ready to recognize the legitimacy of the claim of the conscientious objector, but is at a loss when it seeks to determine the genuineness of the objection. Actual membership in a church which forbids bearing arms is at least *prima facie* evidence of the reality of the scruple, and the government has accepted it as such.

The long and honorable history of the Quakers [e g., Jane Addams] in this matter lends weight to the evidence which the individual member of the denomination presents in regard to his scruples against fighting. If there existed any acid test by which it could be determined that the assertion of conscientious objections by others was in fact correct, we must assume that the government would exempt them also from its draft. No such test exists.

Dishonest Plea

A hundred reasons may make a man unwilling to fight, ranging all the way from physical timidity or business losses to disbelief in the justification for this war or, for that matter, for any but a defensive war, not to mention the profound influence of racial sympathies. A man moved by any of these reasons could cover them up under the dishonest plea of a conscientious objection if this claim were accepted by the exemption board whenever presented. The excuse would be the more readily offered because it is easy to construe one's objection to fighting a particular war, with a specific enemy, at the risk of one's own life and the loss of one's own business, into a conscientious objection to fighting at all. The group that bulks the largest among those that could use the plea of conscientious objection is the socialist party — that is that portion of the party which is orthodox, if there is still any orthodoxy in socialism — for the orthodox doctrine, according to the socialist economic interpretation of society and its history, condemns every war as a capitalists' war, except the last battle in which the proletariat is to dispossess the bourgeoisie in the control of the state. A convinced Marxian socialist [Marx and Engels 1848/1932], who devoutly believed that in this, as in any other war except the ultimate revolution, he would be fighting inevitably in the service of an economic system which was exploiting the mass of the community in the interest of an inconsiderable fraction, and that, whether he fought on one side or the other, such a devout socialist might well claim to the complete satisfaction of his own conscience that he was a conscientious objector. But this is not the conscientious objection that the government contemplates in its exemption version. The conscientious objection, which the present law allows, has nothing to do with the causes of the war nor its beneficiaries; it concerns the very act of fighting. As theft, treachery, perjury or any other heinous crime could not be laid as a duty upon an honorable man even by an act of Congress, so an act of Congress ought not to compel that man to fight who conscientiously objects to fighting as inherently wrong. Perhaps the most pertinent comparison is that to be made with those who refused to obey the runaway slave laws, and in defiance of Congress and the interpretation of the Supreme Court helped runaway slaves on the way to Canada via the Underground Railway. Whenever and wherever an act runs so counter to man's moral nature that he cannot carry it out and still keep house with himself, his refusal in the face of any and all authority commands our instant respect. If such men could be certified to the exemption board beyond a doubt, any thinking, self-respecting community would demand their exemption. If they cannot be so isolated that their real spiritual lineaments can be clearly discerned they will still refuse to serve and will accept this penalty which a community which could not identify them has laid upon them, because it could not distinguish them. It must be recognized on the other hand that there are not many conscientious objectors in the sense in which they have been defined.

The Non-Resistant[2]

Most men do not regard fighting as immoral in itself. Even most of those who regard warfare as an evil which must be removed and therefore immoral are willing to fight to bring this about. The conscientious objector, if he is logical, is a non-resistant,[3] and most human nature is not non-resistant. One may realize to the full the fatuity of war, its hideous wastefulness, its debasing influence; one may conceivably believe that any peace is better than any war and still not be a conscientious objector. For the man who resents war because of its uselessness and its wastefulness of the values which we esteem most in the community is still weighing values against each other, and may reluctantly accept a war that the community wills as he accepts a corrupt and pernicious government, while he allies himself with the forces that will make for better conditions. The community may legitimately conscript such a citizen in its wars. It is the man to whom fighting for any cause, good, bad or indifferent, is uniformly evil, to whom any act of fighting would be a sacrifice of his personality, who is the conscientious objector. And there are not many of them. The Quakers have always been a small sect, and a considerable proportion of the Quakers have been willing to fight in certain wars, such as those of self-defence. [4] If we simply consider the fundamental impulses out of which human nature is made up, and the large part which the hostile impulse takes in this material, one will realize that there cannot be many in whom so dominant a human trait can be absent or sufficiently suppressed or sublimated to make the exercise of force under any conditions abhorrent.

What will be the attitude of the real conscientious objector who, standing outside the church which could guarantee his scruple, still maintains his conscience against the prescription of the government? Inevitably he must consider the ordinance, which seeks to compel him to do what he regards as wrong, as entirely unjust. He will however also recognize that such changes as his doctrine calls for in human nature must be slow in their development and that his quarrel is not so much with the government whose laws he refuses to obey as with the society of which the government is but an expression. If he can give any impartial study to his propaganda, he must realize that, while within the not too distant future wars are likely to be relegated to the outworn devices whose upkeep and cost are too hideously expensive to be longer endured, the revolution in human nature which would be called for in rendering all forms of fighting under all conditions evil is not likely to be secured in the future that we can foresee. The conscientious objector must realize that, so long as there is no acid test for sincerity of his attitude, his is a doctrine that renders martyrdom almost inevitable, when his country is involved in a war that seriously threatens its existence or whatever values the country insists on fighting for.

Specific Objectors

So far we have been considering the conscientious objector contemplated by the exemption provision of the draft law. A more serious question is the justification for enlisting by force citizens who oppose the war, perhaps regard it as utterly wrong, who are thus compelled to surrender everything up to life itself for an undertaking which may run entirely counter to their profoundest inclinations and most unquestioned judgments. These may be men who are quite willing to fight for causes they consider worthy of the sacrifice. Can they be legitimately called upon for the supreme sacrifice for a cause which in their minds is utterly unworthy? Where does the right of a state to conscript its citizens find its limit? There seems to be no limit to the sacrifices which the state may call upon its citizens to make, if the community decisively demands them in the interest of the community. Even the limits set upon the action of the government by the constitution may be set aside by a procedure which the constitution itself lays down. Ethically there seems to be no limit except that which is found in the conscience of the individual, and as we have seen where this cannot be evidenced in a conclusive manner the individual may still be legitimately subjected to penalties for failing to obey the direction of the state. We recognize this quite definitely in the laying of taxes. However unworthy the uses to which the state may put the money it raises by taxation, the individual may not refuse to pay them unless again he is willing to undergo the penalty which accompanies the compulsory distraint of his goods. [5] The individual's remedy in a democratic community lies in his ability to arouse a public sentiment which condemns and leads to the repeal of the law. Here indeed the individual may in answer to his own conscience suffer the penalty rather than transgress his own conscience, and he may find in the publicity which this brings with it assistance in arousing the public sentiment he is seeking to create. Instances of such conduct have been frequent in the history of modern communities, but they do not indicate that the state is proceeding in an unethical manner in laying the taxes which the community authorizes.

If there is a type of conduct which a citizen may not under any circumstances undertake without transgressing his own conscience, it is unjust that the state should compel him to suffer a penalty because he will not act contrary to his conscience at the command of the law. None the less the state, in its inability to determine whether the man is really presenting his own convictions or merely simulating them, is still justified in laying a penalty to prevent the evil which would arise from illegitimate use of conscientious objection as an excuse to avoid public duties and burdens.

Where however the action prescribed by the law is not itself at variance with a man's conscience — as for example the payment of taxes — then the fact that the law prescribes the use of the tax funds for purposes which the man disapproves does not absolve him from the obligation of paying the tax levied upon him. His remedy must lie in changing the governing body or its policies or its manner of administration. Otherwise a democratic government would be clearly impossible.

Rights of Minority

The man then who admits that under some conditions fighting is moral and that conditions may arise under which the community may call upon him to fight, cannot claim that his objection to the issues of the actual war can be made an excuse for his not registering and responding to the draft. The logic of such conduct would free every man in a defeated party from the duty of obeying the laws which were enacted by the party whose policies he disapproves, when they may have won a victory at the polls.

Here, as in other cases of governmental compulsion that run counter to individual judgment, the remedy lies in the freedom to influence public opinion so as to change what the judgment of the individual condemns. The minority's right is the right of propaganda, not the right of refusal to obey the ordinances which have the authority of the state behind them. Such propaganda was undertaken and vigorously pushed during the Boer War by Sir Henry Campbell-Bannerman and the present English premier, Mr. Lloyd George, and in the end met with such success that the peace which was made after that war was quite opposite in spirit from that in which the war was undertaken and fought. A similar propaganda was embodied in the *Bigelow Papers* (1848) by James Russell Lowell,[6] during the Mexican War in this country.

It is important that we should realize that what constitutes the freedom in a democracy is not absence of restraint upon action through laws and ordinances, but the presence of the ideas and interests of all groups and even individuals in making the laws and ordinances. It is not conscription of bodies that threatens democracy but the conscription of ideas. Acceptance by the people from a power above itself of the policies and objectives of the state stamps the peoples as subject, whether the policies come from an autocrat or an aristocratic group of landholders, or imperialistic financiers and entrepreneurs, or from a political boss. Obedience to a law has never constituted a man a slave, while his ideas and those of the other citizens go to make and remake the laws; nor does the acceptance of policies and regulations by the community make them free if their ideas have not gone into the making of the policies and the regulation of life that follows from them, nor yet is a community free because within wide limits there is no regulation of life, provided the final ordering of the conduct of the community is determined by others than the community itself. The right of the minority is the right to be heard. Given this right and any regulation by the community may be enforced without invading the rights of the individual under the limitations to which reference has already been made. It should be added that as the right of the minority does not include disobedience to laws of which they disapprove so it does not include the right to undertake organized effort to keep others from obeying the laws. Not only is the man who is out of sympathy with his country's position in this war still subject to conscription, he is also bound to take no steps to induce others to disobey the conscription act. His right is to work for the change of the law not against its enforcement.

Right to Discussion

Furthermore war brings about exceptional conditions. For a war may involve the very existence of the country itself. Questions of policy which are debatable and must be debated under a democracy, if they involve the war itself and its successful conduct, cannot be debated while it is going on. Such discussion may very well involve a serious weakening of the country in its fight and even lead to its defeat, and the loss of the very institutions of democracy itself. No government in war-time can suffer a movement at home against the armies of the country and their conduct, any more than it will give way willingly before the enemy in the field.

It is perhaps impossible to lay down any fixed rules of practice to cover governmental conduct in this field. If the struggle is one in which the very existence of the nation is seriously imperiled, the action of a minority in opposing the war becomes a veritable attack upon the nation itself, while such a struggle as that between England and the Boers in South Africa may be one that involves governmental policies rather than the integrity of the nation, nor would any intelligent man regard the Bigelow Papers[7] as a monument of disloyalty. But while it is probably impossible to lay down any procedure with reference to minorities in war-time that would not be subject to numerous exceptions, it is possible to indicate the principle that should underlie any procedure. That principle is that of clear definition in each case of the field that is open to discussion and that which is withdrawn from discussion in the public interest, and in case of procedure by the government through its departments against an individual there should be an appeal to a court or commission whose public sense and impartiality would command the respect of the whole community. No man should be in doubt as to what he may do and say without transgressing the government's exceptional provisions, nor should he feel that his final judge is to be an administrative officer who is likely to be narrowly interested in the exercise of his departmental authority. Secondly, it would be obviously a most serious detriment to the country if suppression of supposedly unpatriotic speech and publication should suppress that criticism which is essential to efficient public action in a democracy. Efficiency is never attained even in the techniques of exact science by the following merely of rigid rules, but by a continual checking up of results. In a community governed by the expression of public sentiment, the necessity of the continual checking up by a criticism that is free but not hostile has been so often evidenced by the results both of its presence and its absence that it requires no demonstration.

Conservation of Ideas

And finally, intelligence in war-time should reach the point of recognizing the value of that stimulation to individual thought and interest which the war brings with it and not be willing to suppress the individual response because it is different — even from current formulae. The conservation of ideas is as essential as a conservation of foodstuffs. It behooves a government even in setting aside the customary rights and privileges of citizens in a democratic country to show solicitude for the rights of minorities, for the protection of which the very war is being fought. Such solicitude is demanded not only by the sense of honor of those chosen to govern the whole people and not a majority alone, but it is demanded by the good sense of the statesmen, who must know that it is most serious to run counter to profound political habits and attitudes of the community, especially those upon which men depend when they assert the right that belongs to them as free members of a democratic community.

READING 5B

CAMOUFLAGE OF THE CONSCIENTIOUS OBJECTOR[8]

Those Who Think They Are and Are Not — Those Who Say They Are and Know That They Are Not — Only Religious Tenets Recognized By Law

America finally entered this world war because its issue became that of democracy, democracy defined as the right of peoples to self-government, the right of a people to determine the foreign policy of its government, the right of the small nations to existence because they are nations, and the right of the whole Western world to be free from the threat of imperialistic militarism. We are fighting for the larger world society which democratic attitudes and principals make possible. In such a fight for the inviolability of peoples, for the right of a people to determine itself and its life in self-respecting intercourse with other nations, in this contest for a higher individualism among nations, are we transgressing the rights of the individual at home? In a war for democracy what should be our attitude toward the conscientious objector and how should we proceed with reference to his refusal to fight at the call of his country?

The conscientious objector has no recognition in the legislation which is mobilizing our new army, except as a member of a religious sect whose tenets forbid fighting. Membership in a political or other social organization was such tenets conveys no immunity from military service, nor does the fact that a man himself entertains conscientious objections to military service grant the individual freedom from service in the army. If the conscientious objector's number is called and he is not a *bona-fide* member of such a religious organization, he will be certified to the army then and there, if he refuses to serve in accordance with the orders given him by the officers of the army, he becomes subject to military discipline, and will undergo such penalties as any private suffers who refuses to obey orders. These penalties are or may be severe, for obedience to orders is the foundation of all army organization and the first condition of all military achievement. The position of the conscientious objector is also prejudiced by another circumstance. When he has suffered the penalty which a court-martial has laid upon him, he returns automatically to the service, and if he remains a conscientious objector, he will again refuse to obey the military orders which direct him to do what runs counter to his judgment of right conduct, and again he will find himself subject to court-martial, and again serving another sentence for what is in fact only the same offense, though in point of martial law it is a new offense.

It is this feature of the situation of a conscientious objector which has called out perhaps the most serious reflections in England upon this manner of dealing with his offense. In civil procedure, a man may be punished but once for the same offense. While the continuance of the attitude of a conscientious objector, on the part of the drafted man who finds himself unwillingly in the army, involves a continuance of offensives each of which subjects him to penalty, the real offense is not in the separate refusals of a conscientious objector, but in the attitude from which these refusals arise. A single uniform punishment should be inflicted for the offense.

The more fundamental matter is that the punishment for acting in accordance with the dictates of one's own moral judgment. The recognition of conscientious objection to fighting appears definitely given in the exemption given to those whose religious tenets forbid army service. This exemption not only recognizes the objection but admits that it constitutes a valid grounds for not accepting the draft. Why then, should not the exception extend to all those who have such conscientious objection, but who for other reasons do not belong to these non-resistant religious sects? Our Government has sedulously avoided all ecclesiastical association. It recognizes religious bodies only insofar as it proclaims its complete toleration. Why, then, should the Government extend its freedom from military service to those belonging to a particular sect, refusing it to others? The answer is found in the supposition that the Government is ready to recognize the legitimacy of the claim of a conscientious objector, but is at a loss when it seeks to determine the genuineness of the objection. Actual membership in a church which forbids bearing arms is at least *prima facie* evidence of the reality of the scruple, and the Government has accepted it as such.

A hundred reasons may make a man unwilling to fight, ranging all the way for a physical timidity or business losses to disbelief in the justification and for this war, or, for that matter, for any but a defensive war, not to mention the profound influence of racial sympathies. A man moved by any these reasons could cover them up under the dishonest plea of a conscientious objection, if this claim were accepted by the exemption board whenever presented. The excuse would be the more readily offered because it is easy to construe one's objection to fighting a particular war, with a specific enemy, at the risk of one's own life and the loss of one's own business into a conscientious objection to fighting at all. The group that bulks the largest among those that could use the pleas of conscientious objection is the Socialist Party — that is, that portion of the party which is orthodox, if there still be any orthodoxy in socialism — for the orthodox doctrine, according to the Socialist economic interpretation of society and its history, condemns every war as a capitalists' war, except the last battle in which the proletariat is to dispossess the bourgeoisie in the control of the State. But this is not the conscientious objection that the Government contemplates in its exemption provision. The conscientious objection which the present law allows has nothing to do with the causes of the war nor its beneficiaries; it concerns the very act of fighting.

Whenever and wherever an act runs so counter to a man's moral nature that he cannot carry it out and still keep house with himself, his refusal in the face of any and all authority commands our instant respect. If such men could be certified to the exemption board beyond a doubt, any thinking, self-respecting community would demand their exemption. If they cannot be so isolated that their real spiritual lineaments can be clearly discerned, they will still refuse to serve and accept the penalty which a community which could not identify them has laid upon them. It must be recognized on the other hand that there are not many conscious objectors in the sense in which they have been defined.

What will be the attitude of the real conscientious objector who, standing outside the church which could guarantee his scruple, still maintains his conscience against the prescription of the Government? Inevitably he must consider the ordinance which seeks to compel him to do what he regards as wrong as entirely unjust. He will, however, also recognize that such changes as his doctrine calls for in human nature must be slow and their development and his quarrel is not so much with the Government whose laws he refuses to obey as with the society of which the Government is but an expression. If he can give any impartial study to his propaganda, he must realize that, while within the not too distant future wars are likely to be relegated to the outworn devices whose upkeep and costs are too hideously expensive to be longer endured, the revolution in human nature which would be called for in rendering all forms of fighting under all conditions evil is not likely in the future that we can foresee.

So far we have been considering the conscience objector contemplated by the exemption provision of the draft law. A more serious question is the justification for enlisting by force citizens who oppose the war, perhaps regard it as utterly wrong, who are thus compelled to surrender everything up to life itself for an undertaking which may run entirely counter to their profoundest inclinations and most unquestioned judgments. These may be men who were quite willing to fight for causes they consider worthy of the sacrifice. Can they be legitimately called upon for the supreme sacrifice for a cause which in their minds is utterly unworthy? Where does the right of a State to conscript its citizens find its limit?

If there is a type of conduct which a citizen may not under any circumstances undertake without transgressing his own conscience, it is unjust that the State should compel him to suffer a penalty because he will not act contrary to his conscience at the command of the law. Nonetheless the State, in its inability to determine whether the man is really presenting his own convictions or really simulating them, is still justified in laying a penalty to prevent the evil which would arise from illegitimate use of conscientious objection as an excuse to avoid public duties and burdens.

Where, however, the action prescribed by the law is not in itself at variance with a man's conscience — as, for example, the payment of taxes — then the fact that the law prescribes the use of the tax funds for purposes which the man disapproves does not absolve him from the obligation of paying the tax levied upon him. His remedy must lie in changing the governing body or its policies or its manner of administration, in the freedom to influence public opinion so as to change what the judgment of the individual condemns. The minority's right is the right of propaganda, not the right of refusal to obey the ordinances which have the authority of the State behind them.

It is important that we should realize that what constitutes the freedom in a democracy is not absence of restraint upon action through laws and ordinances, but the presence of the ideas and interests of all groups, and even individuals, in making the laws and ordinances. It is not conscription of bodies that threatens democracy, but the conscription of ideas. Acceptance by the people from a power above itself of the policies and objectives of the State stamps the people as subject whether the policies come from an autocrat or an aristocratic group of landholders, or imperialistic financiers and entrepreneurs, or from a political boss.

The right of the minority is the right to be heard. Given this right, and any regulation by the community may be enforced without invading the rights of the individual under the limitations to which reference has been already made. It should be added that, as the right to the minority does not include disobedience of laws of which they disapprove, so it does not include the right to undertake organized effort to keep others from obeying the laws. Not only is the man who is out of sympathy with his country's position in this war still subject to conscription; he is also bound to take no steps to induce others to disobey the conscription act.

Furthermore, war brings about exceptional conditions. For a war may involve the very existence of the country itself. Questions of policy which are debatable and must be debated under a democracy, if they involve the war itself and its successful conduct, cannot be debated while it is going on. Such discussion may very well involve a serious weakening of the country in its fight, and even lead to its defeat and the loss of the very institutions of democracy itself.

It is perhaps impossible to lay down any fixed rules of practice to cover Governmental conduct in this field. If the struggle is one in which the very existence of the nation is seriously imperiled, the action of a minority in opposing the war becomes a veritable attack upon the nation itself. But while it is probably impossible to lay down any procedure with reference to minorities in war-time that would not be subject to numerous exceptions, it is possible to indicate the principle that should underlie any procedure. That principle is that of clear definition in each case of the field that is open to discussion and that which is withdrawn from discussion in the public interest, and in case of procedure by the Government through its departments against an individual there should be an appeal to a court or commission whose public sense and impartiality would command the respect of the whole community. No man should be in doubt as to what he may do and say without transgressing the Government's exceptional provisions, nor should he feel that his final judge is to be an administrative officer who is likely to be narrowly interested in the exercise of his departmental authority. Secondly, it would be obviously a most serious detriment to the country if suppression of supposedly unpatriotic speech and publication should suppress that criticism which is essential to efficient public action in democracy.

And, finally, intelligence in war-time should reach the point of recognizing the value of that stimulation to individual thought and interest which the war brings with it and not be willing to suppress the individual response because it is different — even from current formulae. The conservation of ideas is as essential as conservation of foodstuffs. It behooves a Government, even in setting aside the customary rights and privileges of citizens in a democratic country, to show solicitude for the rights of minorities, for the protection of which the very war is being fought.

READING 5C

REVIEW OF *THE NATURE OF PEACE AND THE TERMS OF ITS PERPETUATION*, BY THORSTEIN VEBLEN[9]

The Nature of Peace and the Terms of Its Perpetuation By THORSTEIN VEBLEN. New York: Macmillan, 1917. 8vo, PP xiii + 367. $2.00.

Mr. Veblen has applied the conception which he entertains of the present economic order of society to the problem of securing a permanent peace. Mr. Veblen's conception of existing society his readers have found in *The Theory of the Leisure Class* [1899] and *The Theory of Business Enterprise* [1904]. In brief, it contemplates a society in which the usufruct of the creative industry of the community passes into the hands of the small fraction of those who own and control the community's wealth and the opportunities for labor. From this is subtracted what goes to the upkeep of the masses, including some expenditures which are not necessary for upkeep, but represent needs which have arisen through imitation of the well-to-do and wealthy. These expenditures, however, tend to be kept within narrow bounds in proportion as the business organization of the community is effective and clear-headed. The expenditures of those who possess or control the wealth of the community beyond what is involved in upkeep and investment fall under the Veblenian category of "pecuniary waste and personal futility," a category of expenditure which is indefinitely extensible.

Such a society moves inevitably toward the sharpest opposition of interests, on the one hand those of the masses made up of the common people, i.e., the operatives, together with the farmers who entertain the illusion that they are in control of the agricultural industry of the country, and on the other those of the wealthy who control the usufruct of the industry of the community, together with the well-to-do, who, as agents of those in possession, find their advantage to go with that of their masters. This clash of interests is favored by certain characteristics of this modern industrial period, especially the breakdown of the earlier feudal loyalties of the man for his master due to the attention shifting from persons, in their social relations, to things, i.e., the mechanisms of industry. Machinery in breaking up the crafts industry with its emphasis upon persons has also tended to destroy the social structure of mediaeval Europe with its habitual unthinking sub-ordination of the lower groups to the ruling or economically "kept" class. The preservation of a certain amount of competition still gives the employee a measure of independence, and inventions at times bring within his reach a higher standard of living. Such an industrial life furnishes the economic background of the war.

Politically the distinction of first importance is that between the dynastic states and those with so-called liberal institutions. The important instances of the former class are imperial Germany and imperial Japan. While the general attitude of the liberal states with more democratic institutions is "to live and let live," the inevitable push of the dynastic state is toward domination and more domination. It can exist only in the continual exercise of this impulse. It must therefore depend upon military organization within the state and upon conquest and the threat of conquest in its relations with other states. Two social attitudes render the dynastic state possible, that of feudal loyalty for the dynastic ruler and that of patriotism. The preservation of this first trait, that of feudal loyalty, in the German and Japanese people is due to their being politically less developed or, as Veblen states it, less mature. In course of time the operation of machine industry in the community will presumably deprive the people of these communities also of this capacity for dynastic loyalty, but for the present the perilous circumstance for Europe and America is that such dynasties have, in Veblen's opinion, complete control of their peoples, despite their industrial efficiency, and must act militantly, i.e., must be true to their nature. The other trait, that of patriotism, is common to both types of states, the dynastic and the more democratic communities.

In passing it is well to correct the impression that actual political control, according to Veblen, belongs to the masses in democratic communities; on the contrary, it rests inevitably with the small fraction who control the wealth of the community. The difference in the two types of communities lies in the disappearance, through neglect, of the trait of dynastic loyalty. It is also well to note that, according to Veblen, in the liberal or "night-watchman" state the material interests of the possessing class on the one hand and of the common man on the other are so diverse that no patriotic enterprise can be of common interest to both. In fact no patriotic enterprise can possibly be of benefit to the community at large in a material sense.

> In its economic, biologic, and cultural incidence patriotism seems to be an untoward trait of human nature; which of course has nothing to say as to its moral excellence, its aesthetic value, or its indispensability to a worthy life.... Its moral and aesthetic value signify for the purposes of this argument nothing more than that the patriotic animus meets the unqualified approval of men because they are, all and severally, infected with it (p. 47). [10]
>
> The emulative spirit that comes under the head of patriotism commonly if not invariably seeks its differential advantage by injury of the rival rather than by increase of the homebred well-being (p. 33).
>
> Apart from prestige values these things (the so-called moral commend a war to the community, such as "National Honor," "A Place in the Sun," "The Freedom of the Seas," "The Open Door," and the like) are worth fighting for only as prospective means of fighting (p. 37).
>
> So that the chief material use of the patriotic bent in modern populations appears to be its use to a limited class of persons engaged in foreign trade, or in business that comes in competition with foreign industry. It serves their private gain by lending effectual countenance to such restraint of international trade as would not be tolerated within the national domain. In so doing it has the secondary and more sinister effect of dividing nations on lines of rivalry and setting up irreconcilable claims and ambitions, of no material value but of far-reaching effect in the way of provocation to further international estrangement and eventual breach of the peace (pp. 75 and 76).
>
> The aggregate cost to the community of such an enterprise in retardation (*i.e.,* patriotic enterprises in military or trade wars) is always more than the gains it brings to those who may benefit by it (p. 54).
>
> Into this cultural and technological system of the modern world the patriotic spirit fits like dust in the eyes and sand in the bearings.... The patriotic spirit is at cross-purposes with modern life, but in any test of the case it is found that the claims of life yield before those of patriotism; and any voice that dissents from this is a voice crying in the wilderness (pp. 40 and 41).

Finally we have Veblen's definition of patriotism as "a sense of partisan solidarity in respect of prestige," and "a sense of undivided joint interest in a collective body of prestige."[11] The prestige here referred to is the feeling of national superiority arising out of national invidious comparisons, though dependent on an organization of impulses which are physically inherited. Patriotism is then an attitude of mind which is socially inherited, and according to the author is very uniformly present in all the populations of Europe and among the Japanese, though absent from the Chinese. It is the only important common social trait of the common man in the community and the member of the wealthy class, so that when appealed to it unifies the community for the time being.

It does need as long an argument as Veblen gives to the undertaking to prove from these premises that a permanent peace is possible only with the elimination of the dynastic states on the one hand and on the other of those issues which call out the "emulative spirit that comes under the head of patriotism" [p. 33].

These issues are found in the national support of the claims of the citizen abroad, in the favoring of national industry by protective tariffs and trade wars, and in the imperial control of weaker communities by the stronger in the supposed interest of home industry and commerce, or in the interest of national prestige. In the interstices of the authors too-elaborate argument one finds a number of alternatives imbedded that prove to be of considerable interest. Assuming that the dynastic states cannot be eliminated, we must contemplate the other alternatives, that of submission and that of some agreement with the preservation of the balance of power.

In the consideration of the alternative of the acceptance of submission on the part of the democratic countries to the imperial establishment of Germany, Veblen dwells upon two phases of the social situation. The first of these is that so far as the material interests of the common man are concerned he would suffer no loss in such submission. The present order of private ownership with the concentration of financial control in the hands of the few takes away from the common man the means and the incentive to a life in which he is able personally to control the manner and ends of his living. On the one hand he finds himself in a vast system in which efficiency means the reduction of his wage to the level of maintenance of himself and those dependent on him, with the few crumbs that drop to him from the inventors and managers table increasing incidentally his comfort and the standard of his living. On the other hand he is psychologically bound, according to Veblen, in his expenditures beyond the limits of the demand for food, shelter, and covering his and his wife's and children's nakedness to imitate the pecuniary waste and personal futility which characterizes the spending of the possessing and well-to-do classes. In the so-called democratic countries he does not even get the benefit of a wide community view of the physique and morale of the operative, for under the system of private control of the country's wealth and competition between capitalists the employer feels no responsibility for the upkeep of his man power. When this is worn out it renews itself. If his machinery wears out he must replace it at his own expense. If his workers are worn out they are replaced at the expense of those who come to take the positions of the workers who have been scrapped. Veblen draws out at some length and with his accustomed power of innuendo the advantages which would accrue to the common man from the German imperial control of the social order. All the advantages which he lists would arise from the imperial (Veblen always capitalizes "Imperial") control of private industry, in this way approaching the overthrow of the present system of the business man's control over the industries of the country.

Probably no more effective way of presenting the disabilities of the operative in the modern machine industry could be found than in emphasizing the material advantages which would accrue to him in case he accepted complete political subjection to a foreign imperialistic power.

Evidently if the common man of the modern nations that are prospectively to be brought under the tutelage of the Imperial government could be brought to the frame of mind that is habitual with his Chinese counterpart, there should be a fair hope that pacific counsels would prevail and that Christendom would so come in for a regime of peace by submission under this Imperial tutelage. But there are always those preconceptions of self-will and insubordination to be counted with among these nations, and there is the ancient habit of contentious national solidarity in defense of the nation's prestige, more urgent among these peoples than any sentiment of solidarity with mankind at large, or any ulterior gain in civilization that might come of continued discipline in the virtues of patience and diligence under distasteful circumstances. The occidental conception of manhood is in some considerable measure drawn in negative terms. So much so that whenever a question of the manly virtues comes under controversy it presently appears that at least the indispensable minimum, and indeed the ordinary marginal modicum, of what is requisite to a worthy life is habitually formulated in terms of what is not.... The indispensable demands of modern manhood take the form of refusal to obey extraneous authority on compulsion; of exemption from coercive direction and subservience; of insubordination, in short. But it is always understood as a matter of course that this insubordination is a refusal to submit to irresponsible or autocratic rule. Stated from the positive side it would be the freedom from restraint by, or obedience to, any authority not constituted by express advice and consent of the governed.... The common man, in these modern communities, shows a brittle temper when any overt move is made against this heritage of civil liberty. He may not be well advised in respect to what liberties he will defend and what he will submit to; but the fact is to be counted with in any projected peace that there is always this refractory residue of terms not open to negotiation or compromise. Now it so happens that these residual principles of civil liberty have come to blend and coalesce with a stubborn preconception of national integrity and national prestige. So that in the work-day apprehension of the common man not given to analytic excursions any infraction of the national integrity or any abatement of the national prestige has come to figure as an insufferable infringement on his personal liberty and on those principles of humanity that makes up the categorical articles of the secular creed of Christendom. The fact may be patent on reflection that the common man's substantial interest in the national integrity is slight and elusive, and that in sober common sense the national prestige has something less than a neutral value to him; but this state of the substantially pertinent facts is not greatly to the essence of the case, since his preconceptions in these premises do not run to that effect, and since they are of too hard-and-fast a texture to suffer any serious abatement within such a space of time as can come in question here and now (pp. 182-185).

Veblen nowhere recognizes in the society within a nation, nor in the relations of nations to each other, any comprehensive principle of social growth.

In a few words, the common man gets no advantage out of the structure of society which he fights to protect. He fights to protect it because through historical causes he has come to resent direction in which he has no voice; and although it is true that he is not able to control his own industrial condition through the operation of liberal institutions, still he has identified his independence with these institutions and the institutions with the national prestige. Veblen regards these identifications as largely accidental, but recognizes them, not only as everywhere present in the so-called democratic communities, but as so grounded in fixed habits that there is no likelihood of their changing in the near future. Therefore the workingman will not adopt the Chinaman's attitude and will not accept the domination of a German autocracy though it would be on the whole to his material advantage.

On the other hand the German will remain in his attitude of feudal loyalty for the same reason, i.e., the force of secular habits. Here Veblen sees a necessary change in the end. The machine ordering of life, the dependence on things instead of persons which characterizes our technological industry and the life that is shaped by dominant industry, will in the end make a feudal loyalty to the Prussian dynasty impossible, but it will be a long process in which old custom will slowly die from disuse. Veblen sees no revolution on the horizon in Germany. Neither through submission to the imperial establishment of Germany nor through the liberalizing of the institution of Germany is a permanent peace to be realized, at least within the lifetime of the oncoming generation.

There remains the alternative of the conquest of the military government of Germany and its elimination from a decisive position in the Western world. What prospects of permanent peace would this bring with it? Nothing in the fundamental attitudes of the peoples of the democratic countries offers a serious obstacle to such a permanent peace. There will still be dangers from the sense of the national prestige, but there is nothing inconceivable in working out a system by which difficulties of this sort could be met. There is nothing in the institutions of the Western *entente* powers which fundamentally opposes the idea of peace as does the will to domination which is the very nature of the German autocracy and, one should add, of the Japanese autocracy. War is a necessity for a monarchy which rests upon a military basis. No such logical contrary to peace exists in the structure of the communities which are fighting the Central Powers. What is necessary to reach such an understanding that war could be avoided is the abandonment of the causes of war. These are the domination of colonies and spheres of influence for avowedly commercial reasons; the national support of concessions and investments made by citizens of one country in the enterprises of another, protective tariffs and trade wars, and finally the absence of neutralization of citizenship.

Although this last elimination of a cause of war is referred to quite frequently by the author, it is most unsatisfactorily treated. His illustration is found in the large numbers of foreign citizens who live quite contentedly in the United States without becoming naturalized. He does not discuss their loss of the privileges of political life in America nor the detriment to our community of the presence of large numbers who are intimately affected by the political conditions which they cannot help to control. Nor does he discuss the manner in which without change of citizenship people could become a part of the governing body of the community within which they happen to reside. Presumably Veblen contemplates a situation in which national consciousness would largely if not entirely disappear, and with it any citizenship which would have to be protected when the individual found himself in foreign parts. This seems a fair assumption because the author finds nothing in a national consciousness which has any other function than that of providing possible causes for hostilities between different communities.

Not only does the removal of these occasions for war involve no fundamental conflict with the structure of liberal states of the Western world, but Veblen could sense a real movement in the direction of these changes in international life when his book was published in February of last year. Since then the demand for such measures for the safeguarding of peace has become much more articulate. They are logical expressions of the animus of the liberal state to live and let live. The author, however, sees another danger to peace which successful accomplishment of all these measures would not remove. A peace in our modern industrial state would quicken the industrial process under its present financial control. It would hasten the process by which the community is being divided into the nine-tenths who are without possession and the social control which possession gives and the tenth which includes those in possession and control and those who are their immediate managerial, legal, engineering, and scientific satellites. The material interests of these two groups in the community are so opposed that a condition favorable to their sharp differentiation must tend to precipitate a struggle between them, a struggle whose issue would be the continued control of the process of industry in the interest of private financial gain. The appearance of this revolution or the serious threat of it would complicate the peace of the world, for no more effective damper upon revolution could be found than the awakening of patriotic fervor by an attack upon another country, and the danger of the spread of revolutionary spirit from one country to others might well lead those countries which viewed with alarm a revolution elsewhere to come to the assistance of the propertied classes with their military power. Thus even a peace which had been won by the elimination of the dynastic power of Germany would carry in its own bosom the germs of social disorder and the threat of later international strife.

The rigidity of the Veblenian categories is occasionally relieved by an apparent recognition of other forces which are there and at work, though they have no logical place in the economic world. Thus the author recognizes a sense of a "community" which has been independent of dynastic loyalty and has been an inheritance in France possibly from Roman times. The English attained a national sense through their earlier revolution in which the dynasty lost its hold on the loyalty of the people; and yet the attitude of these peoples, commonly called democratic, is referred to by Veblen as a habit of "insubordination." He recognizes that the spirit of these people with so-called liberal institutions is "to live and let live," though the reason for this more social attitude is found only in the absence of an imperial establishment. In a word, there is no indication of positive social forces in society which in the midst of imperialistic, political, and economic movements tend toward democratic control. It is of course true that Veblen is writing, not an exposition of the social order, but an account of the prospects for a permanent peace, and yet the reasons he gives for his conclusions could not be adequate if they left out of account profound social forces that work with or against those which he has depicted. The authors account is of the hostile self-assertion of nations over against each other and of economic groups within these nations.

After all, these conflicts are taking place within societies. The economic struggle between the possession-employing class and the workers of the nation is at the worst within a community in which there are common interests, and common interests beside common national hatreds. The vivid international economic, artistic, scientific, socialistic, religious, and humanitarian movements that affected all classes in all the countries of the Western world before the war are sufficient evidence that there existed an international society within which this catastrophic struggle has arisen. One need not be a Hegelian and maintain that all movements are contradictories arising out of a social situation and leading to a synthesis that harmonizes them to recognize that society exists because it has a principle of life within it, and that the present struggle may very well make possible a higher organization within it, as the conflicts of groups and individual interests have in the past made for a more highly organized community. Veblen isolates the forces of national and class self-assertion in dynastic and capitalistic control and insists that they inevitably work out in social exploitation alone. Yet in the history of human society self-assertion in groups and individuals has led through rivalries, competitions, and finally co-operations to new types of individuals. The present-day legal and political citizens are individuals who have slowly evolved with the institutions which have grown out of group-struggles and a feudal society whose entire occupation was internecine warfare. During the period of this feudal chaos there was indeed an international consciousness which found its expression in the Holy Catholic church and the Holy Roman Empire, for there have always been forms of social conduct which have held people together, as well as the fights in which groups and individuals have sought to destroy and exploit each other. It is true that self-assertion either in the group or in the individual has been universally hostile in its early forms, for a social order in which one can assert himself or his group while he asserts and respects the rights of others comes later and is a development out of the earlier hostile attitude. What Veblen calls patriotism is the attitude of members of a hostile group. A "sense of solidarity in prestige" is the sense of group-superiority which one always possesses or seeks to possess in a fight. If by definition patriotism is to be restricted to the hostile consciousness, all that Veblen says of it is true. But if it is to include the attitude of members of the community toward other communities in their co-operations and arbitrations and satisfactions of mutual claims, or even in their rivalries and competitions which are conducted in other ways than fighting, a "sense of solidarity in prestige" is not an adequate definition. As the attitude of hostility develops into that of national individuality with the growth of international organization, patriotism in the Veblenian sense will be an early stage in the development of such a community sense as can function in an international society.

The passage of feudal loyalty into loyalty to a national monarch was due to mediation by this latter loyalty of a consciousness of a larger society. It was not simply the transfer of a blind attitude of subordination from one master to another. Nor was the formation of the German Empire the result of a blind transfer of loyalties. It was the achievement of the German national conscious-ness that made this loyalty to the Hohenzollerns[12] possible. This positive content of national consciousness Veblen's doctrine of patriotism ignores. It is a consciousness that comes with the feel of the greater values that belong to more complete community life. In all fields of social endeavor it is the sense of value for the community that is the basis of the final estimate, and the more complete this community sense can be the truer will be our estimates. To resolve this social consciousness into its negative expression in fighting is to lose, not only its positive import, but also the recognition of its passage from the negative form into that which can animate a society of nations. It is entirely true that a dynastic state must stand on a militaristic foundation and under any condition must be a continual threat of war. But the dynastic state may dig its own grave by advancing social organization, as indeed the German bureaucracy was doing till it took refuge in the present war. The opportunity of the German government after the formation of the empire, lay in the fact that its militaristic state was independent alike of the capitalistic employer and the masses of the laborers. This superiority over the industrial and financial group enabled the German government to inaugurate a program of social legislation which na-tions with liberal institutions have but tardily undertaken. In the countries with liberal institutions the financial and industrial magnates have so dominated their governments that this German legislation, though undertaken in the interests of the workingman, has been but slowly copied. Two powerful influences in the support of the German dynastic government are then the achievement of the German nation and of a continuous program of progressive social legislation. Veblen's account considers nothing but the age-long habit of loyalty to dynastic masters in German land. Though habits so ingrained change of themselves but slowly, a government that is dependent for its popular support upon its recent social achievements may well fall when such accomplishments fail. Veblen's formula is too simple and abstract.

Veblen's book was written before the publication of the program of the Eng-lish Labor party [see reading 5E here] and the author was unable to comment on it. It is a program that assumes that the wealth of the community can and may be commandeered for the common good. All governments among the belligerents are acting today upon that principle. Unquestionably such a program would not have been formulated by the English Labor party at this time but for the war, but it is after all an outcome of the democratic movement in our modern industrial democracies. It is not a movement to abolish private property. It aims to proceed slowly and experimentally. It has been dependent on the development of many forces besides the growing power of organized labor. Education, sanitary science, the prevention and elimination of disease, improved housing, and other social undertakings have contributed to the formation of the present conception of what should be the standard of life, and this is responsible for the recognition that the wealth of the community can be and should be spent by the community for those community values which can be obtained in no other way. Now this movement which gives the content to the program by the English Labor party gets no recognition from Veblen, who sees only the tendency of wealth to gravitate into the hands of the few, and their tendency to spend it for purposes of conspicuous waste or, to use his other formula, "pecuniary waste and personal futility." Veblen's formulas are too simple and abstract to do justice either to social movements or to the psychology of the individual.

READING 5D

THE PSYCHOLOGY OF PUNITIVE JUSTICE[13]

The study of instincts on the one side and of the motor character of human conduct upon the other has given us a different picture of human nature from that which a dogmatic doctrine of the soul and an intellectualistic psychology presented to an earlier generation. [14]

The instincts even in the lower animal forms have lost their rigidity [Mead 2001]. They are found to be subject to modification by experience, and the nature of the animal is found to be not a bundle of instincts but an organization within which these congenital habits function[15] to bring about complex acts — acts which are in many cases the result of instincts which have modified each other. [16] Thus new activities arise which are not the simple expression of bare instincts. A striking illustration of this is found in play, especially among young animal forms, in which the hostile instinct is modified and held in check by the others that dominate the social life of the animals [Mead 1999]. Again the care which the parent form gives to the infant animal admits of hostile features which, however, do not attain the full expression of attack and destruction usually involved in the instinct from which they arise. Nor is this merging and interaction of such divergent instinctive acts a process of alternate dominance of now one and now another instinct.

Play and parental care may be and generally are of a piece, in which the inhibition of one tendency by the others has entered into the structure of the animals' nature and seemingly even of its congenital nervous organization. [17] Another illustration of such a merging of divergent instincts is found in the elaborate wooing of the female among the birds [2001].

Back of all this type of organization of instinctive conduct lies the social life within which there must be co-operation of the different individuals, and therefore a continual adjustment of the responses to the changing attitudes of the animals that participate in the corporate acts. It is this body of organized instinctive reactions to one another which makes up the social nature of these forms, and it is from a social nature of this kind exhibited in the conduct of lower forms that our human nature is evolved. An elaborate analysis of this is still in the making, but certain great features in it stand out with sufficient clearness to warrant comment.

We find two opposing groups of instincts, those which we have named hostile and those which may be termed friendly, the latter being largely combinations of the parental and sexual instincts. The import of a herding instinct lying back of them all is still very uncertain if not dubious. [18] What we do find is that individuals adjust themselves to each other in common social processes, but come into conflict with each other frequently in the process, that the expression of this individual hostility within the whole social act is primarily that of the destructive hostile type modified and molded by the organized social reaction, that where this modification and control breaks down, as, e.g. , in the rivalry of males in the herd or pack, the hostile instinct may assert itself in its native ruthlessness. [19]

If we turn to the human nature that has developed out of the social nature of lower animals, we find in addition to the organization of social conduct that I have indicated a vast elaboration of the process of adjustment of individuals to each other. This elaboration of gesture, to use Wundt's [Mead 1934; Deegan 1999] generalized term, reaches its most developed expression in language. Now language was first the attitude, glance of the eye, movement of the body and its parts indicating the oncoming social act to which the other individuals must adjust their conduct. It becomes language in the narrower sense when it is a common speech of whatever form; that is when through his gesture the individual addresses himself as well as the others who are involved in the act. His speech is their speech. He can address himself in their gestures and thus present to himself the whole social situation[20] within which he is involved, so that not only is conduct social but consciousness becomes social as well.

It is out of this conduct and this consciousness that human society grows. What gives it its human character is that the individual through language addresses himself in the role of the others in the group and thus becomes aware of them in his own conduct. But while this phase of evolution is perhaps the most critical in the development of man, it is after all only an elaboration of the social conduct of lower forms. Self-conscious conduct is only an exponent which raises the possible complications of group activity to a higher degree. It does not change the character of the social nature that is elaborated and complicated, nor does it change the principles of its organization. Human nature still remains an organization of instincts which have mutually affected each other.

Out of such fundamental instincts as those of sex, parenthood, and hostility has arisen an organized type of social conduct, the conduct of the individual within the group. The attack upon the other individuals of the group has been modified and softened so that the individual asserts himself as over against the others in play, in courting, in care of the young, in certain common attitudes of attack and defense, without the attempted destruction of the individuals attacked. If we use the common terminology we shall account for these modifications by the process of trial and error within the evolution out of which has arisen the social form. Out of the hostile instinct has arisen conduct modified by the social instincts that has served to delimit the conduct springing from sex, parenthood, and mutual defense and attack. It has been the function of the hostile instinct to provide the reaction by which the individual asserts himself within a social process, thus modifying that process while the hostile conduct is itself modified *pro tanto* [only to that extent]. The result is the appearance of new individuals, certain types of sex mates, playmates, parent and child forms, mates in fight and mates in defense. While this assertion of the individual within the social process delimits and checks the social act at various points it leads to a modified social response with a new field of operation which did not exist for the unmodified instincts. The source of these higher complexes of social conduct appears suddenly when through a breakdown of the organization of the social act there is enacted a crime of passion, the direct outcome of self-assertion within sex, family, or other group responses. Unmodified self-assertion under these conditions means the destruction of the individual attacked.

When now, through the exponent of self-consciousness, the complexities of social conduct are raised to the nth power, when the individual addresses himself as well as the others, by his gestures when in the role of another he can respond to his own stimulus, all the range of possible activities is brought within the field of social conduct. He finds himself within groups of varied sorts. The size of the group to which he can belong is limited only by his ability to co-operate with its members. Now the common control over the food process lifts these instincts out of the level of the mechanical response to biologically determined stimuli and brings them within the sweep of self-conscious direction inside of the larger group activity. And these varied groupings multiply the occasions of individual oppositions. Here again the instinct of hostility becomes the method of self-assertion, but while the oppositions are self-conscious the process of readjustment and the molding of the hostile attitudes by the larger social process remains in principle the same, though the long road of trial and error may be at times abandoned for the short cuts which the symbolism of language provides.

On the other hand the consciousness of self through consciousness of others is responsible for a more profound sense of hostility — that of the members of the groups to those opposed to it, or even to those merely outside it. And this hostility has the backing of the whole inner organization of the group. It provides the most favorable condition for the sense of group solidarity because in the common attack upon the common enemy the individual differences are obliterated. But in the development of these group hostilities we find the same self-assertion with the attempted elimination of the enemy giving way before the larger social whole within which the conflicting groups find themselves. The hostile self-assertion passes over into functional activities in the new type of conduct as it has taken place in play even among lower animal forms. The individual becomes aware of himself, not through the conquest of the other, but through the distinction of function. [21] It is not so much that the actual hostile reactions are themselves transformed as that the individual who is conscious of himself as over against the enemy finds other opportunities for conduct which remove the immediate stimuli for destroying the enemy. Thus the conqueror who realized himself in his power of life or death over the captive found in the industrial value of the slave a new attitude which removed the sense of hostility and opened the door to that economic development which finally placed the two — upon the same ground of common citizenship.

It is in so far as the opposition reveals a larger underlying relationship within which the hostile individuals arouse non-hostile reactions that the hostile reactions themselves become modified into a type of self-assertion which is balanced against the self-assertion of those who had been enemies, until finally these oppositions become the compensating activities of different individuals in a new social conduct. In other words the hostile instinct has the function of the *assertion* of the social self when this self comes into existence in the evolution of human behavior. The man who has achieved an economic, a legal, or any type of social triumph does not feel the impulse to physically annihilate his opponent, and ultimately the mere sense of the security of his social position may rob the stimulus to attack of all of its power.

The moral of this is, and one is certainly justified in emphasizing it at this time of a profound democratic movement in the midst of a world-war, that advance takes place in bringing to consciousness the larger social whole within which hostile attitudes pass over into self-assertions that are functional instead of destructive.

The following pages discuss the hostile attitude as it appears especially in punitive justice.

In the criminal court it is the purpose of the proceeding to prove that the defendant did or did not commit a certain act, that in case the defendant did commit the act this act falls under such and such a category of crime or misdemeanor as defined by the statute, and that, as a consequence, he is subject to such and such punishment. It is the assumption of this procedure that conviction and punishment are the accomplishment of justice and also that it is for the good of society, that is, that it is both just and expedient, though it is not assumed that in any particular case the meting out to [the] criminal of the legal recompense of his crime will accomplish an immediate social good which will outweigh the immediate social evil that may result to him, his family, and society itself from conviction and imprisonment. [John] Galsworthy's (1910) play *Justice* turns upon the wide discrepancy between legal justice and social good in a particular case. On the other side lies the belief that without this legal justice with all its miscarriages and disintegrating results society itself would be impossible. In the back of the public mind lie both these standards of criminal justice, that of retribution and that of prevention. It is just that a criminal should suffer in proportion to the evil that he has done. On the other hand it is just that the criminal should suffer so much and in such a manner that his penalty will serve to deter him and others from committing the like offense in the future. There has been a manifest shift in the emphasis upon these two standards. During the Middle Ages, when courts of justice were the antechambers to chambers of torture, the emphasis lay upon the nice proportioning of the suffering to the offense. In the grand epic manner Dante [1895] projected this torture chamber, as the accomplishment of justice, against the sphere of the heavens, and produced those magnificent distortions and magnifications of human primitive vengeance that the mediaeval heart and imagination accepted as divine.

There existed, however, even then no commensurability between retributory sufferings and the evil for which the criminal was held responsible. In the last analysis he suffered until satisfaction had been given to the outraged sentiments of the injured person, or of his kith and kin, or of the community, or of an angry God. To satisfy the latter an eternity might be too short, while a merciful death ultimately carried away from the most exacting community the victim who was paying for his sin in the coin of his own agony. Commensurability does not exist between sin and suffering but does exist roughly between the sin and the amount and kind of suffering that will satisfy those who feel themselves aggrieved and yet it has become the judgment of our common moral consciousness that satisfaction in the suffering of the criminal has no legitimate place in assessing his punishment. Even in its sublimated form, as a part of righteous indignation,[22] we recognize its legitimacy only in resenting and condemning injury, not in rendering justice for the evil done. It was therefore natural that in measuring the punishment the emphasis should shift from retribution to prevention, for there is a rough quantitative relation between the severity of the penalty and the fear which it inspires. This shift to the standard of expediency in determining the severity of the penalty does not mean that retribution is no longer the justification for punishment either in the popular mind or in legal theory, for however expedient it may be to visit crimes with condign punishments in the interest of the welfare of society, the justification for inflicting the suffering at all is found in the assumption that the criminal owes retributive suffering to the community; a debt which the community may collect in the form and amount which is most expedient to itself.

This curious combination of the concepts of retributive suffering which is the justification for punishment but may not be the standard for the amount and degree of the punishment, and of a social expediency which may not be the justification for the punishment itself but is the standard of the amount and kind of punishment inflicted, is evidently not the whole story. If retribution were the only justification for punishment it is hard to believe that punishment would not itself have disappeared when society came to recognize that a possible theory of punishment could not be worked out or maintained on the basis of retribution; especially when we recognize that a system of punishments assessed with reference to their deterrent powers not only works very inadequately in repressing crime but also preserves a criminal class. This other part of the story, which neither retribution nor social expediency tells, reveals itself in the assumed solemnity of criminal court procedure, in the majesty of the law, in the supposedly impartial and impersonal character of justice. These characters are not involved in the concept of retribution nor in that of deterrence. Lynch law is the very essence of retribution and is inspired with the grim assurance that such summary justice must strike terror into the heart of the prospective criminal, and lynch law lacks solemnity, and majesty, and is anything but impersonal or impartial. These characters inhere, not in the primitive impulses out of which punitive justice has arisen nor in the cautious prudence with which society devises protection for its goods, but in the judicial institution which theoretically acts on rule and not upon impulse and whose justice is to be done though the heavens fall. [23]

What, then, are these values evidenced in and maintained by the laws of punitive justice? The most patent value is the theoretically impartial enforcement of the common will. It is a procedure which undertakes to recognize and protect the individual in the interest of the common good and by the common will. In his acceptance of the law and dependence upon it the individual is at one with the community, while this very attitude carries with it the recognition of his responsibility to obey and support the law in its enforcement. So conceived the common law is an affirmation of citizenship. It is, however, a grave mistake to assume that the law itself and men's attitudes toward it can exist *in abstracto*. It is a grave mistake, for too often the respect for law as law is what we demand of members of the community, while we are able to regard with comparative indifference defects both in the concrete laws and in their administration. It is not only a mistake, it is also a fundamental error, for all emotional attitudes — and even respect for law and a sense of responsibility are emotional attitudes — arise in response to concrete impulses. We do not respect law in the abstract but the values which the laws of the community conserve. We have no sense of responsibility as such but an emotional recognition of duties which our position in the community entails.

Nor are these impulses and emotional reactions less concrete because they are so organized into complex habits that some slight but appropriate stimulus sets a whole complex of impulses into operation. A man who defends an apparently unimportant right on principle is defending the whole body of analogous rights which a vast complex of social habits tends to preserve. His emotional attitude, which is seemingly out of proportion to the immediate issue, answers to all of those social goods toward which the different impulses in the organized body of habits are directed. Nor may we assume that because our emotions answer to concrete impulses they are therefore necessarily egoistic or self-regarding. No small portion of the impulses which make up the human individual are immediately concerned with the good of others. The escape from selfishness is not by the Kantian (see Mead on Kant and war, reading 6A here) road of an emotional response to the abstract universal, but by the recognition of the genuinely social character of human nature.

An important instance of this illusory respect for abstract law appears in our attitude of dependence upon the law and its enforcement for the defense of our goods and those of others with whom we identify our interests.

A threatened attack upon these values places us in an attitude of defense, and as this defense is largely entrusted to the operation of the laws of the land we gain a respect for the laws which is in proportion to the goods which they defend. There is, however, another attitude more easily aroused under these conditions which is, I think, largely responsible for our respect for law as law. I refer to the attitude of hostility to the lawbreaker as an enemy to the society to which it belongs. In this attitude we are defending the social structure against an enemy with all the animus which the threat to our own interests calls out. It is not the detailed operation of the law in defining the invasion of rights and their proper preservation that is the center of our interest but the capture and punishment of the personal enemy, who is also the public enemy. The law is the bulwark of our interests, and the hostile procedure against the enemy arouses a feeling of attachment due to the means put at our disposal for satisfying the hostile impulse. The law has become the weapon for overwhelming the thief of our purses, our good names, or even of our lives. We feel toward it as we feel toward the police officer who rescues us from a murderous assault. The respect for the law is the obverse side of our hatred for the criminal aggressor. Furthermore the court procedure, after the man accused of the crime is put under arrest and has been brought to trial, emphasizes this emotional attitude. The state's attorney seeks a conviction. The aggrieved person and the community find in this officer of the government their champion. A legal battle takes the place of the former physical struggle which lead up to the arrest. The emotions called out are the emotions of battle. The impartiality of the court who sits as the adjudicator is the impartiality of the umpire between the contending parties. The assumption that contending parties will each do his utmost to win, places upon each, even upon the states attorney, the obligation to get a verdict for his own side rather than to bring about a result which will be for the best interests of all concerned. The doctrine that the strict enforcement of the law in this fashion is for the best interest of all concerned has no bearing upon the point which I am trying to emphasize. This point is that the emotional attitude of the injured individual and of the other party to the proceedings — the community — towards the law is that engendered by the hostile enterprise in which the law has become the ponderous weapon of defense and attack. [24]

There is another emotional content involved in this attitude of respect for law as law, which is perhaps of like importance with the other. I refer to that accompanying stigma[25] placed upon the criminal. The revulsions against criminality reveal themselves in a sense of solidarity with the group, a sense of being a citizen which on the one hand excludes those who have transgressed the laws of the group and on the other inhibits tendencies to criminal acts in the citizen himself. It is this emotional reaction against conduct which excludes from society that gives to the moral taboos of the group such impressiveness. The majesty of the law is that of the angel with the fiery sword at the gate who can cut one off from the world to which he belongs. The majesty of the law is the dominance of the group over the individual, and the paraphernalia of criminal law serves not only to exile the rebellious individual from the group, but also to awaken in law-abiding members of society the inhibitions which make rebellion impossible to them. The formulation of these inhibitions is the basis of criminal law. The emotional content that accompanies them is a large part of the respect for law as law. In both these elements of our respect for law as law, in the respect for the common instrument of defense from and attack upon the enemy of ourselves and of society, and in the respect for that body of formulated custom which at once identifies us with the whole community and excludes those who break its commandments, we recognize concrete impulses — those of attack upon the enemy of ourselves and at the same time of the community, and those of inhibition and restraint through which we feel the common will, in the identity of prohibition and of exclusion. They are concrete impulses which at once identify us with the predominant whole and at the same time place us on the level of every other member of the group, and thus set up that theoretical impartiality and evenhandedness of punitive justice which calls out in no small degree our sense of loyalty and respect. And it is out of the universality that belongs to the sense of common action springing out of these impulses that the institutions of law and of regulative and repressive justice arise. While these impulses are concrete in respect of their immediate object, *i.e.*, the criminal, the values which this hostile attitude toward the criminal protects either in society or in ourselves are negatively and abstractly conceived. Instinctively we estimate the worth of the goods protected by the procedure against the criminal and in terms of this hostile procedure. These goods are not simply the physical articles but include the more precious values of self-respect, in not allowing one's self to be overridden, in downing the enemy of the group, in affirming the maxims of the group and its institutions against invasions. Now in all of this we have our backs toward that which we protect and our faces toward the actual or potential enemy. These goods are regarded as valuable because we are willing to fight and even die for them in certain exigencies, but their value is neither affirmed nor considered in the legal proceeding. The values thus obtained are not their values in use but sacrifice values. To many a man his country has become infinitely valuable because he finds himself willing to fight and die for it when the common impulse of attack upon the common enemy has been aroused, and yet he may have been, in his daily life, a traitor to the social values he is dying to protect because there was no emotional situation within which these values appeared in his consciousness. It is difficult to bring into commensurable relationship to each other a man's willingness to cheat his country out of its legitimate taxes and his willingness to fight and die for the same country. The reactions spring from different sets of impulses and lead to evaluations which seem to have nothing in common with each other. The type of valuation of social goods that arises out of the hostile attitude toward the criminal is negative, because it does not present the positive social function of the goods that the hostile procedure protects. From the standpoint of protection one thing behind the wall has the same import as anything else that lies behind the same defense. The respect for law as law thus is found to be a respect for a social organization of defense against the enemy of the group and a legal and judicial procedure that are oriented with reference to the criminal. The attempt to utilize these social attitudes and procedures to remove the causes of crime, to assess the kind and amount of punishment which the criminal should suffer in the interest of society, or to reinstate the criminal as a law-abiding citizen has failed utterly. For while the institutions which inspire our respect are concrete institutions with a definite function, they are responsible for a quite abstract and inadequate evaluation of society and its goods. These legal and political institutions organized with reference to the enemy or at least the outsider give a statement of social goods which is based upon defense and not upon function. The aim of the criminal proceeding is to determine whether the accused is innocent, i.e., still belongs to the group or whether he is guilty, i.e. , is put under the ban which criminal punishment carries with it. The technical statement of this is found in the loss of the privileges of a citizen, in sentences of any severity, but the more serious ban is found in the fixed attitude of hostility on the part of the community toward a jailbird. One effect of this is to define the goods and privileges of the members of the community as theirs in virtue of their being law-abiding, and their responsibilities as exhausted by the statutes which determine the nature of criminal conduct. This effect is not due alone to the logical tendency to maintain the same definition of the institution of property over against the conduct of the thief and that of the law-abiding citizen. It is due in far greater degree to the feeling that we all stand together in the protection of property. In the positive definition of property, that is in terms of its social uses and functions, we are met by wide diversity of opinion, especially where the theoretically wide freedom of control over private property, asserted over against the thief, is restrained in the interest of problematic public goods. Out of this attitude toward the goods which the criminal law protects arises that fundamental difficulty in social reform which is due, not to mere difference in opinion nor to conscious selfishness, but to the fact that what we term opinions are profound social attitudes which, once assumed, fuse all conflicting tendencies over against the enemy of the people.

The respect for law as law in its positive use in defense of social goods becomes unwittingly a respect for the conceptions of these goods which the attitude of defense has fashioned. Property becomes sacred not because of its social uses but because all the community is as one in its defense, and this conception of property, taken over into the social struggle to make property serve its functions in the community, becomes the bulwark of these in possession, *beati possidentes* [the happy who are possessors]. [26]

Beside property other institutions have arisen, that of the person with its rights, that of the family with its rights, and that of the government with its rights. Wherever rights exist, invasion of those rights may be punished, and a definition of these institutions is formulated in protecting the right against trespass. The definition is again the voice of the community as a whole proclaiming and penalizing the one whose conduct has placed him under the ban. There is the same unfortunate circumstance that the law speaking against the criminal gives the sanction of the sovereign authority of the community to the negative definition of the right. It is defined in terms of its contemplated invasion. The individual who is defending his own rights against the trespasser is led to state even his family and more general social interests in abstract individualistic terms. Abstract individualism and a negative conception of liberty in terms of the freedom from restraints become the working ideas in the community. They have the prestige of battle cries in the fight for freedom against privilege. They are still the countersigns of the descendants of those who cast off the bonds of political and social restraint in their defense and assertion of the rights their forefathers won. Wherever criminal justice, the modern elaborate development of the taboo, the ban, and their consequences in a primitive society, organizes and formulates public sentiment in defense of social goods and institutions against actual or prospective enemies, there we find that the definition of the enemies, in other words the criminals, carries with it the definition of the goods and institutions. It is the revenge of the criminal upon the society which crushes him. The concentration of public sentiment upon the criminal which mobilizes the institution of justice, paralyzes the undertaking to conceive our common goods in terms of their uses. The majesty of the law is that of the sword drawn against a common enemy. The evenhandedness of justice is that of universal conscription against a common enemy, and that of the abstract definition of rights which places the ban upon anyone who falls outside of its rigid terms.

Thus we see society almost helpless in the grip of the hostile attitude it has taken toward those who break its laws and contravene its institutions. Hostility toward the lawbreaker inevitably brings with it the attitudes of retribution, repression, and exclusion. These provide no principles for the eradication of crime, for returning the delinquent to normal social relations, nor for stating the transgressed rights and institutions in terms of their positive social functions.

On the other side of the ledger stands the fact that the attitude of hostility toward the lawbreaker has the unique advantage of uniting all members of the community in the emotional solidarity of aggression. While the most admirable of humanitarian efforts are sure to run counter to the individual interests of very many in the community, or fail to touch the interest and imagination of the multitude and to leave the community divided or indifferent, the cry of thief or murder is attuned to profound complexes, lying below the surface of competing individual effort, and citizens who have separated by divergent interests stand together against the common enemy. Furthermore, the attitude reveals common, universal values which underlie like a bedrock the divergent structures of individual ends that are mutually closed and hostile to each other. Seemingly without the criminal the cohesiveness of society would disappear and the universal goods of the community would crumble into mutually repellent individual particles. The criminal does not seriously endanger the structure of society by his destructive activities, and on the other hand he is responsible for a sense of solidarity, aroused among those whose attention would be otherwise centered upon interests quite divergent from those of each other. Thus courts of criminal justice may be essential to the preservation of society even when we take account of the impotence of the criminal over against society, and the clumsy failure of criminal law in the repression and suppression of crime. I am willing to admit that this statement is distorted, not however in its analysis of the efficacy of the procedure against the criminal, but in its failure to recognize the growing consciousness of the many common interests which is slowly changing our institutional conception of society, and its consequent exaggerated estimate upon the import of the criminal. But it is important that we should realize what the implications of this attitude of hostility are within our society. We should especially recognize the inevitable limitations which the attitude carries with it. Social organization which arises out of hostility at once emphasizes the character which is the basis of the opposition and tends to suppress all other characters in the members of the group. The cry of "stop thief" unites us all as property owners against the robber. We all stand shoulder to shoulder as Americans against a possible invader. Just in proportion as we organize by hostility do we suppress individuality. In a political campaign that is fought on party lines the members of the party surrender themselves to the party. They become simply members of the party whose conscious aim is to defeat the rival organization. For this purpose the party member becomes merely a republican or a democrat. The party symbol expresses everything. Where simple social aggression or defense with the purpose of eliminating or encysting an enemy is the purpose of the community, organization through the common attitude of hostility is normal and effective. But as long as the social organization is dominated by the attitude of hostility the individuals or groups who are the objectives of this organization will remain enemies. It is quite impossible psychologically to hate the sin and love the sinner. We are very much given to cheating ourselves in this regard. We assume that we can detect, pursue, indict, prosecute, and punish the criminal and still retain toward him the attitude of reinstating him in the community as soon as he indicates a change in social attitude himself, that we can at the same time watch for the definite transgression of the statute to catch and overwhelm the offender, and comprehend the situation out of which the offense grows. But the two attitudes, that of control of crime by the hostile procedure of the law and that of control through comprehension of social and psychological conditions, cannot be combined. To understand is to forgive and the social procedure seems to deny the very responsibility which the law affirms, and on the other hand the pursuit by criminal justice inevitably awakens the hostile attitude in the offender and renders the attitude of mutual comprehension practically impossible. The social worker in the court is the sentimentalist, and the legalist in the social settlement in spite of his learned doctrine is the ignoramus.

While then the attitude of hostility, either against the transgressor of the laws or against the external enemy, gives to the group a sense of solidarity which most readily arouses like a burning flame and which consumes the differences of individual interests, the price paid for this solidarity of feeling is great and at times disastrous. [27] Though human attitudes are far older than any human institutions and seem to retain identities of structure that make us at home in the heart of every man whose story has come down to us from the written and unwritten past, yet these attitudes take on new forms as they gather new social contents. The hostilities which flamed up between man and man, between family and family, and fixed the forms of old societies have changed as men came to realize the common whole within which these deadly struggles were fought out. Through rivalries, competitions, and co-operations men achieved the conception of a social state in which they asserted themselves while they at the same time affirmed the status of the others, on the basis not only of common rights and privileges but also on the basis of differences of interest and function, in an organization of more varied individuals. In the modern economic world a man is able to assert himself much more effectively against others through his acknowledgment of common property rights underlying their whole economic activity; while he demands acknowledgment for his individual competitive effort by recognizing and utilizing the varied activities and economic functions of others in the whole business complex.

This evolution reaches a still richer content when the self-assertion appears in the consciousness of social contribution that obtains the esteem of the others whose activities it complements and renders possible. In the world of scientific research rivalries do not preclude the warm recognition of the service which the work of one scientist renders to the whole co-operative undertaking of the *monde savante* [learned world]. It is evident that such a social organization is not obtainable at will, but is dependent upon the slow growth of very varied and intricate social mechanisms. While no clearly definable set of conditions can be presented as responsible for this growth, it will I think be admitted that a very necessary condition, perhaps the most important one, is that of overcoming the temporal and spatial separations of men so that they are brought into closer interrelation with each other. Means of intercommunications have been the great civilizing agents. The multiple social stimulation of an indefinite number of varied contacts of a vast number of individuals with each other is the fertile field out of which spring social organizations, for these make possible the larger social life that can absorb the hostilities of different groups. When this condition has been supplied there seems to be an inherent tendency in social groups to advance from the hostile attitudes of individuals and groups toward each other through rivalries, competitions, and co-operations toward a functional self-assertion which recognizes and utilizes other selves and groups of selves in the activities in which social human nature expresses itself. And yet the attitude of hostility of a community toward those who have transgressed its laws or customs, *i.e.*., its criminals, and toward the outer enemies has remained as a great solidifying power. The passionate appreciation of our religious, political, property, and family institutions has arisen in the attack upon those who individually or collectively have assailed or violated them, and hostility toward the actual or prospective enemies of our country has been the never-failing source of patriotism.

If then we undertake to deal with the causes of crime in a fundamental way, and as dispassionately as we are dealing with the causes of disease, and if we wish to substitute negotiation and international adjudication for war in settling disputes between nations, it is of some importance to consider what sort of emotional solidarity we can secure to replace that which the traditional procedures have supplied. It is in the Juvenile Court that we meet the undertaking to reach and understand the causes of social and individual breakdown, to mend if possible the defective situation and reinstate the individual at fault. This is not attended with any weakening of the sense of the values that are at stake, but a great part of the paraphernalia of hostile procedure is absent. The judge sits down with the child who has been committed to the court, with members of the family, parole officers, and others who may help to make the situation comprehensible and indicates what steps can be taken to bring matters to a normal condition. We find the beginnings of scientific technique in this study in the presence of the psychologist and medical officer who can report upon the mental and physical condition of the child, of the social workers who can report upon the situation of the families and neighborhood involved. Then there are other institutions beside the jails to which the children can be sent for prolonged observation and change of immediate environment. In centering interest upon reinstatement the sense of forward-looking moral responsibility is not only not weakened but is strengthened, for the court undertakes to determine what the child must do and be to take up normal social relations again. Where the responsibility rests upon others this can be brought out in much greater detail and with greater effect since it is not defined under abstract legal categories and the aim in determining responsibility is not to place punishment but to obtain future results. Out of this arises a much fuller presentation of the facts that are essential for dealing with the problem than can possibly appear in a criminal court procedure that aims to establish simply responsibility for a legally defined offense with the purpose of inflicting punishment. Of far greater importance is the appearance of the values of family relations, of schools, of training of all sorts, of opportunities to work, and of all the other factors that go to make up that which is worthwhile in the life of a child or an adult. Before the Juvenile Court it is possible to present all of these and all of them can enter the consideration of what action is to be taken. These are the things that are worthwhile. They are the ends that should determine conduct. It is impossible to discover their real import unless they can all be brought into relationship with each other.

It is impossible to deal with the problem of what the attitude and conduct of the community should be toward the individual who has broken its laws, or what his responsibility is in terms of future action, unless all the facts and all the values with reference to which the facts must be interpreted are there and can be impartially considered, just as it is impossible to deal scientifically with any problem without recognizing all the facts and all the values involved. The attitude of hostility which places the criminal under the ban, and thus takes him out of society, and prescribes a hostile procedure by which he is secured, tried, and punished can take into account only those features of his conduct which constitute infraction of the law, and can state the relation of the criminal and society only in the terms of trial for fixing guilt and of punishment. All else is irrelevant. The adult criminal court is not undertaking to readjust a broken-down social situation, but to determine by the application of fixed rules whether the man is a member of society in good and regular standing or is an outcast. In accordance with these fixed rules what does not come under the legal definition not only does not naturally appear but it is actually excluded. Thus there exists a field of facts bearing upon the social problems that come into our courts and governmental administrative bureaus, facts which cannot be brought into direct use in solving these problems. It is with this material that the social scientist and the voluntary social worker and his organizations are occupied. In the juvenile court we have a striking instance of this material forcing its way into the institution of the court itself and compelling such a change in method that the material can be actually used. Recent changes of attitude toward the family permit facts bearing upon the care of children which earlier lay outside the purview of the court to enter into its consideration.

Other illustrations could be cited of this change in the structure and function of institutions by the pressure of data which the earlier form of the institution had excluded. One may cite the earlier theory of charity that it was a virtue of those in fortunate circumstances which is exercised toward the poor whom we have always with us, in its contrast with the conception of organized charity whose aim is not the exercise of an individual virtue but such a change in the condition of the individual case and of the community within which the cases arise that a poverty which requires charity may disappear. The author of a mediaeval treatise on charity considering the lepers as a field for good works contemplated the possibility of their disappearance with the ejaculation "which may God forbid!" The Juvenile Court is but one instance of an institution in which the consideration of facts which had been regarded as irrelevant or exceptional has carried with it a radical change in the institution. But it is of particular interest because the court is the objective form of the attitude of hostility on the part of the community toward the one who transgresses its laws and customs, and it is of further interest because it throws into relief the two types of emotional attitudes which answer to two types of social organization. Over against the emotional solidarity of the group opposing the enemy we find the interests which spring up around the effort to meet and solve a social problem. These interests are at first in opposition to each other. The interest in the individual delinquent opposes the interest in property and the social order dependent upon it. The interest in the change of the conditions which foster the delinquent is opposed to that identified with our positions in society as now ordered, and the resentment at added responsibilities which had not been formerly recognized or accepted. [28]

But the genuine effort to deal with the actual problem brings with it tentative reconstructions which awaken new interests and emotional values. Such are the interests in better housing conditions, in different and more adequate schooling, in playgrounds and small parks, in controlling child labor and in vocational guidance, in improved sanitation and hygiene, and in community and social centers. In the place of the emotional solidarity which makes us all one against the criminal there appears the cumulation of varied interests unconnected in the past which not only bring new meaning to the delinquent but which also bring the sense of growth, development, and achievement. This reconstructive attitude offers the cumulative interest which comes with interlocking diversified values. The discovery that tuberculosis, alcoholism, unemployment, school retardation, adolescent delinquency, among other social evils, reach their highest percentages in the same areas not only awakens the interest we have in combatting each of these evils, but creates a definite object, that of human misery, which focuses endeavor and builds up a concrete object of human welfare which is a complex of values. Such an organization of effort gives rise to an individual or self with a new content of character, a self that is effective since the impulses which lead to conduct are organized with reference to a clearly defined object.

It is of interest to compare this self with that which responds to the community call for defense of itself or its institutions. The dominant emotional coloring of the latter is found in the standing together of all the group against the common enemy. The consciousness which one has of others is stripped of the instinctive oppositions which in varying forms are aroused in us by the mere presence of others. These may be merely the slight rivalries and differences of opinion and of social attitude and position, or just the reserves which we all preserve over against those about us. In the common cause these can disappear. Their disappearance means a removal of resistance and friction and adds exhilaration and enthusiasm to the expression of one of the most powerful of human impulses. The result is a certain enlargement of the self in which one seems to be at one with everyone else in the group. It is not a self-consciousness in the way of contrasting one's self with others. One loses himself in the whole group in some sense and may attain the attitude in which he undergoes suffering and death for the common cause. In fact just as war removes the inhibitions from the attitude of hostility so it quickens and commends the attitude of self-assertion of a self which is fused with all the others in the community. The ban upon self-assertion which the consciousness of others in the group to which one belongs carries with it disappears when the assertion is directed against an object of common hostility or dislike. Even in times of peace we feel as a rule little if any disapproval of arrogance toward those of another nationality, and national self-conceit and the denigration of the achievements of other peoples may become virtues. The same tendency exists in varying degree among those who unite against the criminal or against the party foe. Attitudes of difference and opposition between members of the community or group are in abeyance and there is given the greater freedom for self-assertion against the enemy. Through these experiences come the powerful emotions which serve to evaluate for the time being what the whole community stands for in comparison with the interests of the individual who is opposed to the group. These experiences, however, serve only to set off against each other what the group stands for and the meager birthright of the individual who cuts himself off from the group.

What we all fight for, what we all protect, what we all affirm against the detractor, confers upon each in some measure the heritage of all, while to be outside the community is to be an Esau without heritage and with every man's hand against him. Self-assertion against the common enemy, suppressing as it does the oppositions of individuals within the group and thus identifying them all in a common effort, is after all the self-assertion of the fight in which the opposing selves strive each to eliminate the other, and in so doing are setting up their own survival and the destruction of the others as the end. I know that many ideals have been the ends of war, at least in the minds of many of the fighters; that in so far the fighting was not to destroy the fighters but some pernicious institution, such as slavery, that many have fought bloody wars for liberty and freedom. No champions however, of such causes have ever failed to identify the causes in the struggle with themselves. The battle is for the survival of the right party and the death of the wrong. Over against the enemy we reach the ultimate form of self-assertion, whether it is the patriotic national self, or the party, or the schismatic self, or the institutional self, or simply the self of the hand to hand *melee*. It is the self whose existence calls for the destruction, or defeat, or subjection, or reduction of the enemy. It is a self that finds expression in vivid, concentrated activity and under appropriate conditions of the most violent type. The instinct of hostility which provides the structure for this self when fully aroused and put in competition with the other powerful human complexes of conduct, those of sex, of hunger, and of parenthood and of possession has proved itself as more dominant than they. It also carries with it the stimulus for readier and, for the time being, more complete socialization than any other instinctive organization. There is no ground upon which men get together so readily as that of a common enemy, while a common object of the instinct of sex, of possession, or of hunger leads to instant opposition, and even the common object of the parental instinct may be the spring of jealousy. The socializing agency of common hostility is marked, as I have above indicated, by its own defects. In so far as it is the dominant instinct it does not organize the other instincts for its object. It suppresses or holds the others in abeyance. While hostility itself may be a constituent part of the execution of any instinct, for they all involve oppositions, there is no other instinctive act of the human self which is a constituent part of the immediate instinctive process of fighting, while struggle with a possible opponent plays its part in the carrying out of every other instinctive activity. As a result those who fight together against common enemies instinctively tend to ignore the other social activities within which oppositions between the individuals engaged normally arise.

It is this temporary relief from the social frictions which attend upon all other co-operative activities which is largely responsible for the emotional upheavals of patriotism, of mob consciousness, and the extremes of party warfare, as well as for the gusto of malicious gossiping and scandal-mongering. Furthermore, in the exercise of this instinct success implies the triumph of the self over the enemy. The achievement of the process is the defeat of certain persons and the victory of others. The end takes the form of that sense of self-enlargement and assurance which comes with superiority of the self over others. The attention is directed toward the relative position of the self toward others. The values involved are those that only can be expressed in terms of interests and relations of the self in its differences from others. From the standpoint of one set of antagonists their victory is that of efficient civilization while the other regards their victory as that of liberal ideas. All the way from the Tamerlanes[29] who create a desert and call it peace to the idealistic warriors who fight and die for ideas, victory means the survival of one set of personalities and the elimination of others, and the ideas and ideals that become issues in the contest must perforce be personified if they are to appear in the struggles that arise out of the hostile instinct. War, whether it is physical, economic, or political, contemplates the elimination of the physical, economic, or political opponent. It is possible to confine the operation of this instinct within certain specific limitations and fields. In the prize fights as in the olden tourneys the annihilation of the enemy is ceremonially halted at a fixed stage in the struggle. In a football game the defeated team leaves the field to the champion. Successful competition in its sharpest form eliminates its competitor. The victor at the polls drives the opponent from the field of political administration. If the struggle can be *a outrance* [to the uttermost] within any field and [a person] contemplates the removal of the enemy from that field, the instinct of hostility has this power of uniting and fusing the contesting groups, but since victory is the aim of the fight and it is the victory of one party over the other, the issues of battle must be conceived in terms of the victor and the vanquished.

Other types of social organization growing out of the other instincts, such as possession, hunger, or parenthood, imply ends which are not as such identified with selves in their oppositions to other selves, though the objects toward which these instinctive activities are directed may be occasion for the exercise of the hostile instinct. The social organizations which arise about these objects are in good part due to the inhibitions placed upon the hostile impulse, inhibitions which are exercised by the other groups of impulses which the same situations call out. The possession by one individual in a family or clan group of a desirable object is an occasion for an attack on the part of other members of the group, but his characters as a member of the group are stimuli to family and clan responses which check the attack. It may be mere repression with smoldering antagonisms, or there may be such a social reorganization that the hostility can be given a function under social control, as in the party, political, and economic contests, in which certain party, political, and economic selves are driven from the field leaving others that carry out the social activity. Here the contest being restricted the most serious evils of the warfare are removed, while the contest has at least the value of the rough selection. The contest is regarded in some degree from the standpoint of the social function, not simply from that of the elimination of an enemy. As the field of constructive social activity widens the operation of the hostile impulse in its instinctive form decreases. This does not, however, mean that the reactions that go to make up the impulse or instinct have ceased to function. It does mean that the impulse ceases to be an undertaking to get rid of the offending object by injury and destruction, that is, an undertaking directed against another social being with capacities for suffering and death — physical, economical or political — like his own. It becomes in its organization with other impulses an undertaking to deal with a situation by removing obstacles. We still speak of him as fighting against his difficulties. The force of the original impulse is not lost but its objective is no longer the elimination of a person, but such a reconstruction that the profounder social activities may find their continued and fuller expression. The energy that expressed itself in burning witches as the causes of plagues expends itself at present in medical research and sanitary regulations and may still be called a fight with disease. In all these changes the interest shifts from the enemy to the reconstruction of social conditions. The self-assertion of the soldier and conqueror becomes that of the competitor in industry or business or politics, of the reformer, the administrator, of the physician or other social functionary. The test of success of this self lies in the change and construction of the social conditions which make the self possible, not in the conquest and elimination of other selves. His emotions are not those of mass consciousness dependent upon suppressed individualities, but arise out of the cumulative interests of varied undertakings converging upon a common problem of social reconstruction. This individual and his social organization are more difficult of accomplishment and subject to vastly greater friction than those which spring out of war. Their emotional content may not be so vivid, but they are the only remedy for war, and they meet the challenge which the continued existence of war in human society has thrown down to human intelligence.

READING 5E

SOCIAL WORK, STANDARDS OF LIVING AND THE WAR[30]

Domestic Policy and International Adjustment

The program of the English Labor Party is one of the most important of the war documents. It has lifted the war, by its definition of the social issues that the war has made conceivable and possible, into a struggle for a new order of things. This new order of things when accepted makes of the war an entirely different struggle. It stands in this manner upon the level with the greatest of President Wilson's papers. The League to Enforce Peace, the right of self-determination of nations, the demand for full security of the small nations, all of these are part of the *magna carta*[31] [great charter] of an international society. But they approach the form of this international society from the outside, and by their structure they do not consider the inner nature of communities which may belong to such a society. The demand that diplomacy shall be open, that it shall be under the control of the people, is, to be sure, a step toward a reconstruction of inner order; but these measures also look toward the outer relations of nations with each other.

The program of the English Labor Party, on the other hand, is that of a country which approaches the problem of international life from the inside. In a cruder form the Russian revolution undertook also to reconstruct Russia from within from the standpoint of a society of peoples who can regulate their international affairs without armed conflict. They too have assumed that wars arise from an inner order of the states, and that a change in that order is the essential step in eliminating warfare. That they failed was due in part to their inadequate conception of the economic and political structure of the modern community, and in part to the failure of the Allied communities to realize the strategic advantage of the Russian attitude. There remains this in common between the English Labor Party's program and the Russian Revolution, that they assume that changed inner conditions, within the countries involved in this world war, would make war itself impossible.

The emphasis in both undertakings has been laid upon change in the economic conditions of the laboring classes. In the program of the Bolsheviki this change was to be accomplished with the sweep of a single revolutionary movement. The capitalistic society was to be at once set aside, and a new order substituted. Unfortunately the plans for this new order of things were hopelessly impracticable, and had been taken over not from constructively thought-out social programs, but from gospels of the revolution. Its tenets were those which aroused to battle those who were not on all fours with the forces which were at work in our industrial society, not in touch with the methods which in our pragmatic age must be adopted in changing social conditions.

In both these respects the program of the English Labor Party stands in sharp contrast with those of the Russian revolution. The changes that this program advocates are in the direction of those that have been steadily at work, and have been vastly stimulated by the efforts to attain supreme efficiency in the life-and-death struggles of the nations. The demand for a standard of living in determining wages, for the government direction of the wealth produced by the community toward the welfare of the community, the definition of the living conditions which should obtain throughout the nation and especially among its members who are economically the weakest, of the socially necessary education, and of the opportunities for political control for the groups which have been for various reasons politically handicapped, and finally of the foreign policy which such a renovated society must demand — these tenets are but further developments of movements which antedate the war, and which the war has heavily underscored. Nor have the English Labor Party presented their program as one which can be at once attained, nor indeed have they ventured to sketch in detail the actual changes which must take place. They confidently indicate the directions which are already plotted in recent social history, and they recognize that the method of advance here as in the domain of physical and biological sciences must be experimental.

Progress, Aristocracy, and Legislation

Now the application of the experimental methods to the solution of social problems has hitherto been subject to a capital difficulty — the absence of recognized social values by which to test projects of reforms. Who was to assure us that any scheme of social betterment was not fraught with losses which would outweigh what advantages it promised, even if they could be attained? The order of society as it exists carries with it certain values which have been secured. We have art and science, the culture which is the distilled essence of our past, and a system of training which fits at least certain classes to attain these values. The projects of social reform seem, to endanger these achievements. We are still living under the psychology of a religious philosophy which accepts a world in which the absolute values are the possession of the few. Ideals, moral elevation, beauty of character, as well as the wealth, culture and the constructions of art and science, are regretfully recognized as the possessions of the minority and a small minority of the community, *Beati possidentes* [the happy who are possessors]. [32] Projects of fundamental reform threaten these absolute values, for on the one hand they fasten the attention upon the interests of the mass of the community, and upon interests which appear material and mechanical, and, on the other hand, they have to do with changes which can be brought about by legislation and can be enforced by the police power of the community. These absolute values of religious experience, of art and creative science can none of them be attained in this fashion. Intelligent ordering of society may favor their appearance in those who are endowed for such achievement. They cannot be legislated into existence. To test our social and spiritual vigor by the results which can be assured by legislative enactment promises to level all values to those which can be attained by change in the external conditions in the community. Such programs are denounced as leveling, bound to arrest the free expression of the creative minds, and eliminate the great personalities together with the cultured few who can sit beside their nectar in their golden houses girdled with the gleaming world, those favored few who keep the beauty and distinction of the past alive by enjoying them.

Perhaps we are not perceptibly nearer a solution of the problems of the absolute values of goodness, beauty and truth, if these values are absolute, but we are nearer a statement of the things that are so worthwhile that they can form a usable test of programs for social reconstruction, and whatever the social import of religion and science and art may be, we recognize that these things that are worthwhile cannot endanger this import. We are confident of this, for science has become the method of social progress, and social progress itself has become a religion; and the most dominant form of modern art, the novel, has been the medium of the imagery, the concrete pictures, by which the minds of men of all groups and classes have passed into each other. If there is such a thing as a culture that exists by itself, careless of mankind, it must soon atrophy and die.

Social Work Emboldened by the War

It is these things that are so unquestionably worthwhile that they are the tests of social undertakings and hypotheses, that the social worker stands for and has stood for. We may generalize them as the standards of living. They connote health, and education, and opportunity to realize enough of the social world in which we live to interpret our lives, and the opportunity to exercise the part in social control which our occupations and capacities demand. I have no intention of analyzing these standards of living either in their earlier or in their present war statements. I desire only to emphasize their growing authority and the change which this authority added to the program of the social worker brings to the social worker himself. Since the days in which we accepted the doctrine that the poor, being always with us, constituted the field for good works, the laying up of treasure in heaven, and the means of perfecting the character of the charitable — especially since the Western world accepted the doctrine of the Manchester school that the economic process carried with it not only its own control but the direction of the life of the community — there has been a slow accretion of community assistance to the handicapped, to those in misery, the submerged members of the community, which has uniformly begun with private charity, that in its turn has become more and more organized, passing with varying success into the legislative enactment.

It is this series of changes with which the social workers have been identified. They have never spoken with authority. They have carried with them the burden of responsibility for unhealthful social conditions which the community has been unwilling to acknowledge, and has accepted only in meager fashion and always with protest. And this reluctance of the community to acknowledge their responsibility for the conditions which the social workers have undertaken to present has had its effect upon the social workers. In great measure they have had to assume the attitude which would bring them such measure of success as they gain. They could not come as the prophet who spoke the words which they had received from the mouth of the Lord; nor in their effort to assist those immediately overborne by conditions within and without them, could they base their appeals upon judgments of public policy, or condemnation of social injustice. These could be made the platforms of a political party, that of the radical groups of various types. To present them as grounds for help to those in distress, would have closed both the minds and the pocketbooks from which assistance had to be sought. The social workers have had in great measure to come with the compliance of the beggar, the beggar in the cause of humanity. The social workers have been in great degree committed to the presentation of cases, and cases which they dared not generalize, and the method of approach has in great measure molded those who have used it.

In the meantime organization has given the prestige which comes with numbers and system, and without authority they have become impressive. The passage of uplift measures into legislation has brought the weight which attaches to what can be enforced by the court. Still more important has been the recognition of scientific method, the traffic in tables of statistics, which inevitably generalize the case, and slowly force upon the community in impersonal fashion the moral of the misery which a charitable response comfortably covers up. But the passage of remedial individual assistance into remedial legislation has been occasional, and had not been sensed by the community as a fundamental shift in the method of social control. Mr. [Theodore] Roosevelt did indeed realize that there was a reality implied in social work that offered a new observation point from which to get the range upon the enemy, and incorporated a program of social work into the platform of the Progressive party (see Addams 1930, 10-48). However, Mr. Roosevelt inevitably remains the dominant issue in any campaign in which he is involved, and it was impossible for him or the community, to feel the actual import of the material which he had incorporated in the tenets of the Progressive party.

It is against this background that the war has come with its revolution in methods and standpoints of procedure. In securing efficiency the government has committed itself to a living wage, to a program of adequate housing for its employees in the shipping yards, to the principle of collective bargaining. The Federal Suffrage Amendment, with the endorsement of the President, has been started on its road toward adoption. The federal amendment abolishing the sale of alcoholic liquors is before the country, and prohibition has been accepted as essential to the efficiency of our soldiers. There has never been a record in control of venereal diseases dependent not only on the control of the men, but upon the co-operation of the surrounding community such as that obtained in the cantonments of our armies in this country.

The war has brought a sense of dependence of public effort upon individual economy, not simply in financial savings but in the avoidance of waste, such as we have not seen before. In the conduct of the government there has been a recognition of the right and expediency of the governments making as large a use of the income of the country as the needs of the country, in our exigency, require. If a continued prosecution of the war demands finally the conscription of capital to meet the country's necessity there is an attitude both in the country at large, and in the government which will undertake it. The present war has gone further in advancing the social program which social workers have recognized as essential to reaching and attaining the welfare of the community, than any of us have dreamed could be reached in several generations. For not only have such positive measures as I have listed above been actually undertaken, but the acceptance of these measures as the conditions of efficiency in the entire community organization and conduct of the war, has at last clothed these programs and those that are their champions with an authority which they have not before possessed. If any undertaking as huge and momentous as this war is on foot such a program is essential to its success, and any nation in the struggle that neglects it is handicapping itself as definitely as if it omitted part of the program of munitions and big guns.

Continued Progress or Reaction after the War?

Will it be possible for governments falling into the hands of reactionaries to maintain that in times of peace such a program is not only unnecessary but would be actually destructive of the institutions and the social goods which they conserve? Such claims will indeed be made, together with such disparagement as is possible of the value of these radical measures during the war. They will be admitted as valuable for the organization of popular support — especially the support of the laboring classes, whose devotion had to be secured at any cost. It would not be difficult to forecast a *post bellum* [postwar] treatise of [W. H.] Mallock (1920) in demonstrating both the lack of economy and the lack of justice in the social program even during the war. However, these reactionary attempts to discredit the social organizations and tactics with which the war is being fought will not produce any other effect than to solidify those who are in advance and in principle opposed to them. It will be their political power in high and low places which we will have to fight, not their ideas.

The social programs in operation in England and in France and those we are putting into operation in America have been effective, not because they are technical military measures, to be discarded with the dying down of the battle; they have been effective because they have increased industrial efficiency, because they have revealed the sources of wealth taxable for common social purposes, and methods of taxation which do not dry up the springs of wealth; because they have indicated not only the manner in which children should be trained for social efficiency but the conceptions of common good in whose interest men recognize that such methods must be used. Most important of all, they indicate the conditions under which the interest of all the people can be secured for common ends; and their success in war-time has demonstrated that they can be inaugurated and that they do produce the results which they have promised. In other words, they have become the touchstone of all political undertakings which claim to enlist the interest of the whole community.

Class legislation always advances as a program for the common good, and however acute and destructive may be the criticism by which the social scientist overwhelms it, the average man caught in the wheels of a society organized largely in the immediate interest of the few, sees no escape from those measures which secure him his livelihood as a part of the whole mechanism. The situation will be changed after the war, when men can apply to these undertakings the test of meeting the conditions which the war has shown alone could carry the whole country with it; and conditions immediately after the war will favor the application of this test, for the problems which the world will face, while not hanging for their solution upon military success, will be so international in their character, will demand such united action on the part of the whole community, will so definitely face the issue of removing the causes and occasions of war, that governments will need the same unanimity in the communities back of them for their solution.

It has, of course, been the history of wars in the past, with the possible exception of the Boer War, that the general weariness and reaction after the high tension which fighting carries with it, have left democratic issues, that call for large vision and sustained interest on the part of all, to the mercy of those whose immediate profit lies in exploiting the situation, and this private interest is most naturally found in so handling the vast debts which war leaves behind that the financial group may make their profit out of them. The stakes will be higher after this colossal struggle than they have ever been in the past, and there will be astute minds engaged in reaping their post bellum harvest. Still we can reasonably hope that the other issues of getting the world again on its feet—proper caring for the wounded and disabled, demobilizing forces such as have never before stood under arms, organizing the supply of materials for which all nations will be crying, refashioning the international fabric, will be so dominant that community interest will perforce remain vivid and possibly united.

Projection of War Programs into the Future

However, optimism in this regard is unwise. It will be true then as before that it will be the unexpected that happens, and we may be bitterly disillusioned in the immediate outcome of the peace. But even disheartening results will not take away this achievement of war. Whether our communities arise sooner or later to their social tasks, they will have the touchstone of the social programs of the war — of labor conditions, of child welfare and education, of housing and sanitation, of control of venereal diseases, of proper political representation of all groups in the community, of common democratic statement of the issues at stake, — to apply to campaigns and platforms. I do not mean that such programs will be the actual issues involved, though they will certainly be part of aims which will be sought in the political struggle. This program will be the test of the common interest and the community good to which every political campaign must lay claim. An intelligent, effective community response is dependent upon such a social program; and measures and men whose interest finds them in opposition to such measures will be forced to admit they do not seek the aroused, intelligent response of the whole country. The agencies of this war have forced even reactionary governments to discover how the community as a whole can get into a public undertaking with sustained interest; and the method, being based on human social psychology and the economic and political structures of our communities, has the same validity in times of peace as in times of war.

But apart from the recognition of the new authority of the social program, there are practical considerations that deserve attention. The success of the program after the war is in large measure dependent upon the manner of conducting it during the war. A vast store of social statistics such as America has never gathered before with reference to her population, is gathering in the Provost General's office. It contains other information beside that bearing on military features. Men are catalogued with reference to occupations and capacities. Vital statistics with reference to their families are accumulated. The effort to determine how many can be spared for the fighting force without dangerously depleting the working force at home, gives a picture of fanning and industrial conditions which are new. The direction of laborers to occupations where they will be most effective starts us on a project of labor distribution which the government has never faced in the past. Beginning of vocational training for adults and development and intensification of vocational training for children are already under consideration. It is of the highest importance that those who realize the necessity of knowledge for the direction of social effort should come into touch with these efforts and further the methods which will pass naturally into the operations of peace. The veil which has been lifted from the contraction and spread of venereal diseases in communities which have never before faced the situation must not be allowed to fall again. The housing programs undertaken for industrial communities suddenly called into existence must be so carried out that they will be permanent, and remain as evidences of the duties of our communities for the housing of their workmen.

The problem of properly training the physiques of our children and older citizens must especially be faced, that the illogical conclusion be not drawn that only by arousing the fears and enmities upon which depend the program of a nation in arms can we obtain a physically fit generation. The opportunities for insurance of those in the war zone must be studied and feasible plans for universal governmental insurance must be worked out. It is of peculiar importance that the interest in education should be intelligently utilized to give us not only efficiency, but the attitude of social responsibility that will extend beyond the exigencies of this conflict. The willingness to recognize the individual child or man or woman as a precious asset to the community, whose conservation must be secured even by changing formerly fixed social conditions, must be emphasized and generalized in such forms that they will reach into times of peace. Through the actions of the state councils of defense and their subsidiary committees throughout the state, the information in regard to the favorable conditions of conducting the war should come to all our citizens and through interest in what they can do, that sustained interest which is necessary to the conduct of the war be kept in being. From such neighborhood centers an intelligent interest in conditions which will face us after the war will radiate into the problems of industry and democratic control. The spread of knowledge of our crops, the actual measures in selection of seed and method of cultivation which are known to the experts but still hidden from most of our farmers should be carried out in such fashion that the machinery will continue in operation when peace is declared. The whole problem of farm labor must be studied under favorable conditions not only for the good of the whole community, but for the special advantage of the rural community. The lists of possible fields of intensive work all looking toward social reconstruction now and after peace is declared could proceed for many pages. They present the only opportunity for legitimate profiteering which the war offers. The social worker in his organization should speak with the authority after the war with which so many of them are speaking now.

Finally, should there not arise out of this organization and the trained men and women gathered here, a central body which will make it its business to come into touch with all the war-time social activities, to fix the location of the social material which is coming into being, to indicate possible lines of development as well as exploitation, to serve not only as a clearing house, but as a means of stimulating and directing other groups of individuals in fashioning out of our present activities the social balance which the community can draw from the conflict? It would lead, perhaps, not to such a program as that of the English Labor Party, but to a statement of what the conditions are which will be necessary for an intelligent response of the whole country to the national and international problems we must face in the immediate future.

Notes

1. *The Conscientious Objector*, National Security League, Patriotism through Education Series, pamphlet No 33. (New York, 1918).
2. Mead refers here to the non-resistant movement led by the abolitionist William Lloyd Garrison (1904/1924) who opposed both slavery and the Civil War.
3. For the concept of "non-resistant" see the writings of Garrison, Tolstoy (Villard 1924), and Addams (e.g., 1910, 1928).
4. This was the position of Jane Addams' (1910) father, John Addams, on the Civil War.
5. Some Americans today refuse to pay taxes because of the large portion that goes to militarization. This is the position of the tax resistance movement, many of who are religious pacifists.
6. The correct title is *Meliboeus-Hipponax: The Bigelow Papers* (Lowell 1848).
7. See ftn. 3, p. 150.
8. The by-line read: "By Dr. George Herbert Mead. Head of the Department of Philosophy in the University of Chicago." *New York Times* (23 December 1917): 56, cols. 1-4.
9. *Journal of Political Economy* 26 (July 1918): 752-63.
10. Mead sometimes quotes passages and sometimes paraphrased them. I left his words as he wrote them.
11. Veblen (1917: 31) defined patriotism as "a sense of partisan solidarity in respect of prestige," and "a sense of undivided joint interest in a collective body of prestige."
12. The Hohenzollerns were a German dynasty governing Brandenburg, Prussia, and Germany during WWI. Their followers supported an aggressive nationalism.
13. "The Psychology of Punitive Justice," *American Journal of Sociology* 23 (March 1918): 577-602.
14. Mead studied comparative psychology under Wilhelm Wundt who was part of this earlier generation. See Mead (1999, 2001).
15. Mead is combining the development of "habits" with "functions" that organize the self, institutions, and even nation-states.
16. See Mead (2001) for a discussion of instincts and comparative psychology.
17. Mead (2001) discusses the animal instincts in his earliest writings and then develops them for humans. See also Mead (1934, 1999).
18. Mead does not accept the Freudian concept of the "herd instinct" here.
19. Freud's theory of "the primal horde" argued that each male has this tendency within the id.

20. "Social situation" is a concept usually attributed to W. I. Thomas, but Mead used it in the early 1890s when Thomas was his student. This suggests that Thomas learned it from Mead, and the former elaborated on it.

21. Mead's "functional psychology" from the 1890s appears to be continued here. See Deegan (1999).

22. Freud uses "sublimation" to refer to the occasion when the mind directs object-libido energies toward objects that have nothing to do with sexual satisfaction. See *On Narcissism* (1991).

23. See discussion of lynching by Addams (1901) and Ida B. Wells-Barnett (1901).

24. [Mead provided the following annotation]: I am referring here to criminal law and its enforcement, not only because respect for the law and the majesty of the law have reference almost entirely to criminal justice, but also because a very large part, perhaps the largest part, of civil law proceedings are undertaken and carried out with the intent of defining and readjusting social situations without the hostile attitudes which characterize the criminal procedure. The parties to the civil proceedings belong to the same group and continue to belong to this group, whatever decision is rendered. No stigma attaches to the one who loses. Our emotional attitude toward this body of law is that of interest, of condemnation and approval as it fails or succeeds in its social function. It is not an institution that must be respected even in its disastrous failures. On the contrary it must be changed. It is hedged about in our feelings by no majesty. It is efficient or inefficient and as such awakens satisfaction or dissatisfaction and an interest in its reform which is in proportion to the social values concerned.

25. Mead anticipates Erving Goffman's (1963) discussion of *Stigma* here.

26. This is a phrase taken from Euripides (480 B.C.-406 B.C.) referring to happy or blessed people who possess things, and I assume Mead is using the phrase to refer to the happiness of people before the war began, a happiness that cannot be restored during the war.

27. This argument is similar to one that results in Mead supporting war, instead of seeing the price of solidarity as being too high.

28. Mead rarely discusses competing interests so this is an important discussion.

29. "Tamerlane" is Edgar Allen Poe's first published poem which he privately printed in 1827.

30. *Proceedings of the National Conference of Social Work* at the 45th Annual Session held in Kansas City, Missouri (1918): 637-644. Mead served as 1917-1918 Chairman of the Division of Social Problems of War and Reconstruction and organized the papers presented for this section. Breckinridge, Charles F. Neill, and Harriet E. Vittum were associated with Chicago social settlements at some point and served on the committee under his guidance. Mead included papers by Addams, Katherine B. Davis, Florence Kelley and other Hull-House allies in this project.

31. See ftn. 1, p. 95.

32. See ftn. 26 above.

33. "The Manchester school" refers to a British political and economic approach to free trade, radical libertarianism, and government withdrawal from the economy. It supports free enterprise capitalism along with many liberal values.

Part 4

Mead's Unpublished Writings after America Entered World War I: Teaching His Formal Ideas on War and Peace

6

Unpublished Lectures during War-Time: The Intellectual Background

> *"I am taking up the burden of the war course next*
> *quarter, lecturing on the intellectual background*
> *to the war, a working over of the Movements of*
> *Thought in the Nineteenth Century [Mead 1938].*
> *It will have from sixty to seventy five in it, and will*
> *require a lot of work on my part, that is if I get any*
> *work out of the students. I will undertake to present*
> *the ideas behind and involved in the nineteenth*
> *century state, industry, science, art, and religion*
> *and something of the form these ideas took in phi-*
> *losophy though I will eschew technical philosophy."*
> *(G. H. Mead to Henry Mead, p. 1, 15 March 1918,*
> *box 1, folder 9, Mead papers)*

In the spring of 1918 Mead offered a course on the "Intellectual Background to the War" (see Lewis and Smith 1980, 279).[1] A number of unpublished, hand-written, and heavily edited manuscripts on war are in the Mead papers at the University of Chicago and are the basis of this next lengthy section of the book. I assume theses essays were part of his course preparation, if not the substance of the lectures themselves. He worked through his position on a number of issues related to the United States and their role in WWI in this large body of previously unpublished work. This set of unpublished papers is a rich source of Mead's macro-analysis of the relations between self, war, and society: he focused on the relations between nation states who are either America's friends or enemies. He used American democracy, ideals, values, and laborers as standards for behavior and justification for state violence. He also analyzed the individual, citizenship, and the state, as well as the relation between the individual and citizens of other states. Finally, he considered the ethics of war and peace.

Despite his expectation of a large enrollment of sixty to seventy-five students (see the opening citation to this chapter) Mead had only five students. He had written lengthy lectures, nonetheless, as this volume attests. If he had had a larger class, he might have created different lectures. These fortunate students were the only ones to benefit from Mead's extended macro-sociology on self, war, and society. Clearly he intended these lectures to be epistemologically linked to his course on the Movements of Thought in the Nineteenth Century, but the ties to his advanced social psychology course are evident, too (Mead 1932, 1936).

Unpublished Lectures during War-Time-Germany as the Enemy and Nationalism Gone Awry

As noted in chapter 1, Mead loved Germany — its culture and people — as a graduate student living there in 1888-1889. He shared this attachment with his best friend Henry Castle and the latter's first wife, M. Frieda Steckner, their German landlady's daughter whom he married in 1889. Helen Castle, Henry's sister and Mead's future bride, also received graduate training in Germany and shared their attachment to Germany. Many of their friends, especially at the University of Chicago (Deegan 1999, 2001), studied and enjoyed German life, too. They developed a deep and passionate bond to Germany and embraced the intellectual life of its philosophers, psychologists, literature, and cuisine. Prior to World War I, Germany was part of Mead's "international self" and perspective (Deegan 1992). He loved both the United States and Germany. He specialized in the study of Immanuel Kant (see reading 6A here), Wilhelm Wundt, and Wilhelm Dilthey (For Wundt and Dilthey, see Mead 1999, 2001). He offered separate coursework on Kant and studied both social reform and psychology from their joint perspective.

Mead's perception of and relation to Germany dramatically turned from love to hate during war-time. This sea-change is evident in most of the readings in this section of the book. It reflects a dualistic stance where the United States is good and Germany is bad. Such a dramatic turn emerged from the power of his previously positive feelings. Mead was not rational but passionate in his patriotism during war-time.

Immanuel Kant on Peace and Democracy

In reading 6A, Mead focuses on the errors he finds specifically in Kant, which are echoed in the philosophy of German idealism, which co-existed with an aristocracy and oppression of the worker and masses. Authority is tempered in France, England, and the United States, argued Mead, but the rigidity of the military and class structure in Germany created an insupportable control by the ruling classes. Although German poetry, music, and other forms of culture are innovative and creative, political life is not. Mead also criticizes Kant as lacking specific laws, too abstract to be workable, and not empirical. Thus Kant's categorical imperatives are not universal in application.

Dewey shared Mead's view of Kant, albeit Dewey developed it earlier. Thus in 1915 Dewey argued that Kant, and not Hegel or Nietzsche, sharpened the dangerous traits of Germans. Dewey (1915) developed this point in *German Philosophy and Politics* in great detail. Dewey argued that Germanic dualism distorted the work of Kant and again was reflected in German *Kultur*. Steven C. Rockefeller (1991, 301) summarizes Dewey's position as similar to Mead's.

Mead argued that German intellectuals, artists, poets, philosophers, and scientists live in a world that is open to possibility and ideas. German politicians, aristocrats, military, and economy were much more rigid, controlling, and punishing. This split is seen in Kant's categorical imperatives which assume that each person is part of an ideal moral universe that determines right and wrong. This idealistic assumption ignores the *realpolitik* of German *Kultur* based in a political and national apparatus of aggression, power, and control. This dichotomous situation is the foundation of the destructive German nation-state. Mead did not seriously examine Kant's pacifism (Veblen 1917) and avoided a direct confrontation with this vitally relevant part of Kant's position.

Mead's differences with the German romantic movement is important to understand, because Meadian scholars often describe this group of idealists as integral to Mead's theory. In this reading, however, Mead documented that he saw himself as not only distinct from but also in disagreement with it. This was an intellectual and practical separation he tried to maintain throughout his work after WWI. Mead argued that German romantics did not fight evil but merely avoided confronting its effects. This failure to respond to real problems left a vacuum of intellectual analysis and criticism that the aristocrats and military were happy to fill. Scientists, philosophers, literary figures, and artists were left with little choice during war-time between either supporting the state or becoming revolutionaries. These romantics were the foundation for international-mindedness, but they did not have the power or authority to materially influence the aristocracy or military.

Mead raised an important argument that is the opposite of that offered by many critical theorists, especially Theodor Adorno et al. (1950), who saw the German people and culture as authoritarian. The latter's aggressiveness and need for control supported a belligerent nation. Mead argued, instead, that Germans were too passive and trusting. They recognized that control and authority resided in the aristocracy and military and everyday people needed to obey the orders of the hierarchy above them. Thus the idealism reflected in Kant was embraced in everyday life leaving a gap in politics filled by the state without a voice for the citizenry.

Mead on the Government of the State and War

Mead held that the American government — reflected in the Constitution, the Bill of Rights, the Declaration of Independence, and the American Revolution which ended aristocracy in the nation — was crucial to establishing a progressive society. He therefore found the liberal institutions of England and France as more flawed than in the United States. He also preferred the separation of church and state found in America, and its greater emphasis on education. Pragmatic action on behalf of other communities that wanted to demand rights and freedoms found in America would be the best basis for a world society and the consciousness it generated. For Mead, WWI was a crucial mechanism to create such a world with a new, widespread form of democracy and social justice (see reading 6B).

Mead's view of democracy and social reconstruction, even during war-time, had elements of internationalism, anti-militarism, and world peace epitomized in new international organizations such as the League of Nations. In a lengthy passage he summarizes all these structural assumptions that preceded and followed the war:

> Democratic governments arise out of the interaction of all groups and classes in the country. Through such governments the individuality of the whole community may express itself.
>
> If, then, democracies are not militaristic and instinctively favor the development of institutions whose function it is to solve international difficulties without war, the defeat of autocracy in this war means that the world hopes that democratic nations can bring about a more perfect society of nations, in which each will retain its own individuality and make this the basis of its dealings with other nations. To state the implication in another form, democracies instinctively favor a League to Enforce Peace and the development of the Hague tribunals, but they favor as instinctively the principle of nationality in the settlement of the problems out of which the war has arisen.

Mead argued that war brings out the best and the worst in people, institutions, and the nation. During war, people equate the government with the state (see "The Government of the State and War," reading 6B here). Social integration and large-scale change can occur more rapidly than in the more stable times of peace.

Mead on Germany versus International Life

"Germany Versus International Life" (see reading 6C here) posits Germany as a nation state concerned primarily with itself and its domination of other states. It opposes "internationalism." Mead argues again that labor is "essentially international," although he opposes the imposition of one class vision on the proletariat from different nations. "A society of nations" must be called on to generate and define a program of social reconstruction. This group could chart new ideas and hypotheses: "It is impossible to give a nation definition of the golden rule," because specific steps are needed to meet new situations.

Mead discussed many "social reconstructions" to improve society, but his strongest "working hypothesis" for institutional change was the Juvenile Court (an innovation where Addams played a major role, see Addams et al. 1927).

His perspective links his ideas of progressive education with justice defined in terms of the child's own interests (Mead 1999, 2001). This is a joint interest with Addams, and in turn, with Dewey (Deegan 1999, 2001).

Mead also adopted the LTEP as a model for social reconstruction. He accepted an "enforced peace" after the war. Addams accurately perceived that this concept is contradictory: an enforced peace is not peace but a form of coercion. Mead was anticipating the "end" of the war was not an end to force by liberal nation states against the governments and states comprising the Central Powers. Mead's belief in the LTEP is reiterated in some of the following readings and in others he wrote during the war. As flawed as the LTEP was, however, it was not as disastrous a plan as the Versailles Treaty which "ended" the war by stripping the Central Powers of financial control in the future and breaking the spirit of the "conquered" people.

Conclusion

Mead's unpublished lectures were presented probably in the spring of 1918 in his war-time course on "The Intellectual Background to the War." During this class Germany was an enemy nation. He portrayed German idealism as a costly separate culture which flourished in literature, philosophy, and the arts while the governing of the state was left in the hands of the aristocrats and military, a brutal class that ignored the rights of the laborer. War became a force for throwing out these ruling classes and the reason why communism and socialism attracted workers in Europe but not the United States. European theorists as a group explained unjust societies which made their arguments invalid in the more democratic and egalitarian society in America.

The German enemy would be eliminated when democracy ended the blind might of the aristocrats and military. He saw congruence between communism and democracy because they shared the goals of worker's rights. The flaws of a capitalist democracy were invisible to him. Although his language is slightly more temperate here than in his newspaper articles, Mead uncritically supports violence between national states, believing that America was being attacked. He, therefore, adopted the "self-defense" argument he had criticized in his earlier writings.

READING 6A

IMMANUEL KANT ON PEACE AND DEMOCRACY[2]

Immanuel Kant is the Koenigsburg philosopher to whom the present King of Prussia ascribes in good part the achievements which Germany[,] under the guidance of God and the Hohenzollerns[,][3] have made in the past century, and those which he expects Germany to make in this war and thereafter. The representative of the House of Hohenzollerns who sat on the throne of Prussia when Kant was lecturing in Koenigsburg regarded the philosopher of transcendentalism with suspicion and frankly snubbed him for his views of the possibility of perpetual peace. Immanuel Kant could see no hope of peace among nations except under a democratic regime. His brochure on the subject is an early edition of President Wilson's doctrine that only in a world that is safe for democracy can differences of nations be settled without the appeal to arms: that only in a world of republics could right stand higher than might. In a very real sense Kant's philosophy is an expression of that independence of the reason of the individual which found its outstanding evidence in the drama of the French Revolution. Kant affirmed, that it is the nature of the mind that gives laws to nature, that we find in the heavens above in the earth beneath and in the moral order of the universe only the law which we bring in the structure of our own understandings and our own reasons and our own wills. A more thoroughgoing rejection of external authority over the mind and will of man than that involved in Kant's doctrine could not be found even in the execution of monarchs, the disestablishment of the Church and the establishment of the religion of reason, and government by the common will of the common people. It was the final and summary burying of the principle of authority. Kant put his lance at rest against the principle as it appeared in philosophic dogma, but philosophic dogma is but the abstract statement of the dogma of the church and of the state. If philosophical dogma could no longer abide the examination of the critical doctrine it was beyond question impossible for arbitrary authority on the ecclesiastical and secular thrones to abide the day of reckoning. I do [not] imply that the advent of critical philosophy crowns and mitres automatically fell, but only that the presence of criticism as a philosophical creed securely entrenched meant that no institution could [any] longer [continue to] justify itself in society through its own authority. Dynastic and ecclesiastical thrones might still rest upon the foundation of custom and for the time being draw support form extraneous sources, and yet the advent of the critical philosophy, its acceptance and the sweep of its influence was the most definite interment of the principle of arbitrary authority which had dominated the world during the medieval age, and remained in many forms in the feudal order of things ecclesiastical and governmental and in the stratification of society. It was not in German philosophy that this passing of the authoritative was marked.

In England the change had taken place more gradually, in the preceding revolutions which had set aside the monarch, Charles the First, who undertook to stand squarely upon his divine right to rule, and thus relieve his authority from any responsibility to the community he governed, and in the later revolution in which the Stuarts were removed from the throne and new monarchs, William and Mary[,] were placed there upon the authority of the parliament which represented if not the people of England at least the organized community of the country. The break with Rome under the Tudors had in an analogous fashion shifted the principle of authority from the Papacy to England herself. England was quite satisfied with the results of these revolutions. They desired no abstract theory of what they had done. As long as the precedent was there, that at bottom the ultimate authority in the community was its representative assembly, they were pleased to utilize institutions which in their spirit and in the actual operations were still in no slight measure feudal.

In France the issue had become more sharply drawn. What Charles had attempted with disastrous results to himself and his dynasty, the Bourbons had succeeded in accomplishing in France. Authority was ultimate and arbitrary in the monarch who announced himself as the state. The feudal order was not a mere survival but a part of the order of things. The attack upon the order of things demanded another theory which could take the place of that which was in vogue, and Rousseau[4] supplied it, supplied the theory that human nature unspoiled by the arbitrary conventions of the age was itself good, that the evils which the state was supposed to suppress were the product of itself, that sovereignty must reside in the body of the citizens, and that its expression must be by the general will of the people. Here was no English compromise. The two doctrines could not occupy the field together. The French Revolution was the decisive defeat of the principle of authority within the domain of government, and even the reaction after the fall of Napoleon could not reinstate it.

In Germany the process of the amalgamation of the smaller feudal states which had taken place in France, in England, and in Spain was never completed during the middle ages. This process of nationalization had gone on through the growth of the power of the monarch and the weakening of the feudal lords and their principalities. In Germany during the earlier part of the middle ages the great prize was the iron crown of the Holy Roman Empire. To secure it and hold it meant the presence of the Emperor in Italy with powerful armies, and these could be secured only [by] bribing the feudal lords of Germany with privileges and added lands, or else by crushing them under the royal hand. The Emperor could not do the latter and fight the battles of the Empire beyond the Alps. The natural development of the German nation was balked by the struggle of the Holy Roman Empire. Finally this became but an empty title[;] and Germany remained a land made up of principalities[,] little and big[,] but not a nation. In the wars of Europe the other countries had been welded together as men of one land, speaking one tongue, and bound by a single national tradition. In Germany and Italy this was never the case. German principalities were on opposite sides in every conflict. Their language and their culture were radical but they did not connote a single state. The principle of organization was dynastic not national. Loyalty to a dynasty could not pass into the sense of national solidarity.

In England and France it was this national solidarity, this feeling of belonging to the national whole which made possible those revolutions by which the nation was placed above the monarch which could become a political principle. It took up into itself the literature, the history, and the cult of its heroes. In Germany too there grew up a German literature, German Universities, German Philosophy, German Science, German Art, and German Artisanship. But they constituted a land of the spirit not the political habitat of a people. A medieval feudalism shackled the political life of the German people. They were subdivided in innumerable principalities, and their literature, art, science, philosophy, and handicraft could not give them the sense of national solidarity in which they could undertake the task of achieving self-government. Spiritual life in Germany has been always politically ineffective. It has either existed outside of the political life, and the social consciousness in which this is found, and then its representation has been the abstract, impractical German professor and learned man, or it has accepted the subservience which the dynastic overlord requires. The *pronunciamento* signed by the most distinguished German men of learning at the beginning of the war was in strict historical keeping.

It is necessary to keep this in mind when we consider the sweep of Kant's doctrine. It is true that he finds in the nature of the mind of the individual the laws of nature, the condition of a moral order of the world, the presuppositions which carry with them the idea of an intelligent God, an immortality and the freedom of the will. Man's reason gives laws to nature. The imperative demand of systematizing his experience requires him to conceive of a God whom he cannot conceive without falling into contradictions. It is the impossibility of harmonizing the demands of the human desires for pleasure with the demand of the reason that man act only with reference to law that compels Kant to conceive of an infinite life after death, within which these irreconcilables may be reconciled. If we ask what these laws of nature are which are given by the reason, we find that they are principally the law of causality — the law that each event is necessarily connected with that which precedes it — and that of substance and attribute, that qualities must inhere in a substance. But we do not learn what events are connected in causal order, nor what are the substances in which the multitudinous qualities of our sensuous experience inhere. The human mind gives us only the abstract forms of the laws of nature, not the law which Newton discovered. The human mind demands that our conduct should be rational[;] that is[,] that we should formulate the maxims of our conduct in universal laws which could bind the conduct of all men under the same conditions, but it does not tell us what we should do in a specific occasion though Kant futilely undertook to show that it did. Kant's categorical imperative demands obedience to law on the part of the moral being. It does not state what the law is to which we should be obedient. Kant's whole doctrine belonged to abstract human beings that lived outside of the political communities, outside the happenings of empirical science. There was nothing in this doctrine which a dynastic ruler needed to fear. Kant's moral law was empty and the state could give it its content, and yet the authority of the dynastic state had to be found elsewhere than in the divine appointed monarch who was placed on his throne to fulfil God's purpose through his church. This was the principle of authority in the medieval state. Kant's critical philosophy made this no longer possible. The *raison d'être* [meaning for existence] of the dynastic monarch had to be found in other and more mundane ends.

It was Napoleon who provided the first of these ends: that of organizing the people of the German states so that they could throw the invader out of their lands. After this had been accomplished the task of giving a national state to the German peoples remained the great task which the dynastic state had to accomplish. Its other great task was that of the efficient inner organization of the people for the economic and social reconstruction that followed the Napoleonic wars. Now these great tasks were undertaken by the statesmen and bureaucracies of the states. They were not undertaken by the people. There was a feeble attempt made in 1848 to establish a national German state on a popular basis, but it failed. The period of the *Befreiungskrieg* during which Germany gathered herself together to drive the armies of Napoleon from German soil, was the period of [the] Romantic Movement. Here too arise great characteristic philosophies, those of [Johann Gottlieb] Fichte, [Friedrich Wilhelm Joseph] Schelling and [Georg Wilhelm Friedrich] Hegel. [5] During this period rise the great geniuses of Schiller and Goethe. Fichte was a fiery moral teacher as well as idealistic philosopher. He expresses [this more] than any other[:] that rousing of the national consciousness which the defense of the Fatherland demanded. His philosophy demanded that the individual should realize in his moral effort that he was part of the Absolute Self which comprised the whole of reality. Schelling who followed him called for the same realization of the identity of the self with the Absolute Self but with him the emphasis lay in the creative power of the artist. Hegel [1807/1977] finally finds in thought the identity of the self with the Absolute Self. In all these systems the aim is that of bringing the abstract individual of Kant into the concrete world both physical and social. It is to be accomplished through the identification of the inner life of the individual, moral, aesthetic, and reflective with the principle of reality of the universe through its inner life. The Absolute Self is the inner life of the universe, and our selves are but parts of this Absolute Self. It is a definite attempt to overcome the abstractness of the Kantian individual, to put content into his laws, his moral imperatives, and his antinomies by finding one's self in the universe and the universe in one's self.

In the vast and subtle structures of the idealistic systems of philosophy I wish to point out only one thing, and that is that the individual's undertaking is to realize himself in all and all in himself, but [it is] not himself [that can] change the order of the universe[—] no[r] indeed [that] of his own country and nation. The same may be said of the culture of Goethe. Its aim was to be at home in any place in the world. It was a being at home in the world by appreciating it, and its technique called for such a development of the inner life that it would reflect all that it experienced. The oppositions and contradictions of the world are annulled in their recognition by the larger and fuller self. The Romantic Idealist is a recalcitrant against conventional order and ideas, insofar as these fetter his own nature. He demanded that he be allowed to be himself and so a part of the world soul, the Absolute Self, the Oversoul. He did not demand the freedom to get into the evil and error of the world and fight and correct it. His task was to reach an elevation of moral, attitude, of aesthetic appreciation, of reflective comprehension, which would enable [him] to be a conscious part of the process of development that was going on. If he were only allowed to be himself in purpose, in feeling and thought he will agree to find himself in the order of things which gives him this opportunity of being identified with it. It is this romantic attitude in which the world of early nineteenth century revelled in the medieval world. They attained thrills of self-realization in taking the roles of knights errant, of thirteenth century saints, of aesthetic adoration in Gothic cathedrals, it is this attitude that as readily found itself in Hegel's loyalty to the dynastic state of Prussia[:] Loyalty to the absolute even in its expression in a state ruled by Hohenzollern kings and their efficient bureaucracy. Hegel has but given the most profound, the most grandiose, the most subtle expression to the attitude of loyal self-realization of the German subject in identifying himself with the state personalized in his sovereign lord.

The stimulus which this romantic attitude offered to the monarchs, but more especially to the ministers who did their thinking for them, one must read [Heinrich] von Treitschke. [6] The latter gives vivid expression to the demand of the nation to be powerfully led and efficiently governed. In Wilhelm the Second the German people have created a god in their own image, which probably only a Heine could adequately stigmatize. But forget for the moment the personalizing of this government in its monarch, what Hegel deprecatingly called dotting the-i-of state, and in no country in the Western world will you find the task of government so vividly and conscientiously conceived and so thoroughly executed as in Germany. If the romantic demand on the part of the German people to be masterfully and efficiently governed acted as a powerful stimulus on the governing group, their reaction was proportionately impressive. It is not necessary to particularize as to the effectiveness of this governing machine. The Germans themselves have been sufficiently explicit about the marvels of the machine, and from their own point of view they have not greatly exaggerated the comparative superiority of their governing mechanism over that of the other nations of Europe and America.

There are but two comments that are to be made upon it even if we accept the German estimate of the merits of the machine. One of these is that only in one sense can the Germans be said to be responsible for this government. That sense is that they have passionately and even bitterly sought for national unity while on the other hand in their highly reflective and informed docility have almost as passionately called for the trained and competent direction from above. Out the depths of their many principalities the German people, with a national feeling already awakened in the uplands of ideas, of art, and science, called for a national state, and out of multifarious and at times even learned tractability acquired at the hands of feudal masters and Lutheran pastors[,] they looked for a government capable of directing them in the doing of all the things in which their diversified docility sought expression. The other comment is that a government which arises in response to such popular demands and attitudes is bound to be a government whose first attribute is that of force. For the German people sought for a government that would tell them not simply how to do what they wanted to do, but what they should do, a government that would determine their ends for them as well as prescribe the appropriate means. When [one] seeks expert assistance in doing what one has before him, which is his own project; the authority exercised by the expert is not that whose attribute is force, but that of intelligence. The expert directs because he has the technique of the operation, but the other determines whether the prescribed manner accomplishes what he wished. The final authority lies with the man who seeks the expert for his guidance. But the individual who comes to another and places himself so completely in his hands that he asks him to determine what he shall do as well as the manner in which he shall do it, can himself take no effective part in the direction. The direction which prescribes the purpose of conduct must always be one of compulsion.

The Imperial government of Germany characteristically keeps in the hands of the council of the monarchs the *Bundesrath* — that council within which the Prussian king is the dominant power, — the initiative in all legislation. The imperial government of Germany tells its subject what they are to undertake. After this it is willing to consult with them in the Reichstag upon the means. The articulate representatives of Germany have all recognized this and placed as the first attribute of the state that of irresistible force. Germany is militaristic not because the people are by nature pugnacious or filled with the joy of battle. It is militaristic because the feudal type of government which Germany has adopted must rest upon force even in its reaction to its own subjects, not because it is superimposed upon a people who are hostile to it, the opposite of this is true, but because the German people has had and has wished to have no say [nor] share in determining what they will undertake.

The logic that lies back of the German military system is evident throughout the organization of German society, in its schools, the ordering of its business establishments, its family life, even in the relation of the rank and file of the Social Democratic party to its directorate. In all these expressions of authority is found this same assumption of the policy and purpose of the social activity, and where authority goes with this function it inevitably implies the appeal to force as of its very nature. It is further characteristic of such an attitude on the part of the Germans that their own historians and commentators affirm that they lack political ability. Certainly members of the German governing class have not shown lack of such ability, nor have Germans who have gone to other countries and become a part of those communities. It is the German attitude of looking to those above for direction in the policies which they are to undertake that naturally deprives them of the interest in thinking out and presenting for public consideration, and backing with their whole personal force the policies which the community is to adopt, and it is this lack of individual share in the initiative in government which inevitably carries with it the assumption that a government must be the expression of the force which is called up to dictate to a community what are to be its purposes and undertakings. It is on such a foundation that a militaristic state arises and it is such a social attitude that calls forth militarism in other situations. For example foreign policies have been to a very considerable extent determined by the government rather than by the people even in democratic governments. And diplomacy through which foreign policy is carried on has in the past always looked to a backing of force. Wherever a measure is to be enforced which does [not] or cannot be made to appeal to the intelligence of the community force is the inevitable implication, while recognition of the value of the measure and comprehension of its technique at once change the character of its enforcement. The enlistment of the interest of the public in the purpose of the undertaking at once makes the enforcement of the regulation something in which all are a part.

Let me recapitulate. With the end of the eighteenth century the principle of arbitrary authority that was embodied in the Church and State of the medieval world had so far lapsed that it could no long be appealed to maintain the institutions of society. Kant's doctrine which found in man's own nature the form of nature's laws and those of the moral universe and the implications from which had to be derived the conceptions of God, immortality, and the freedom of the will, was a fitting epitaph of that medieval principle of authority. But Kant's doctrine was still but formal in its character. It found in man's nature the forms of natural laws, but not in the immediate experiences of men. It found in his reason the categorical imperative that called for law-abiding conduct, but it did not find there what conduct was moral. The romantic philosophies which followed hard upon Kant's critical doctrine, undertook to supply this content which Kant's formal statements so completely lacked. They sought this in the inner life of the individual — in the self — and the identification of this self with the Absolute Self. But while these systems sought to find the content of the world in man, this content could be gained only in appreciation. The romantic philosophies could not present man as an active agent in the construction of his world either social or physical. The Hegelian doctrine found itself a welcome court philosophy in Berlin since it found in the state the highest expression of spirit on earth, and saw in the subject of the state a dependent being who could attain a full social consciousness only insofar as he realized himself in the state.

Two great impulses were present in the German people, one toward national organization and the other toward efficient organized government. The people of Germany were unable, largely through their own historic background, to determine the manner in which they should reach this national existence, nor yet what the directions and aims of government should be. It remained for the

Prussian state through the exercise of force to weld together the different German principalities in a single national whole, and to form a superstate which undertook to determine what should be the aims and purposes of the nation itself. Such a state could by definition only rest upon force. Militarism became the necessary form of its life. As none of the spiritual expressions of German life undertook to present the aims of German national life except as these were indicated by the government, its scientists, its philosophers, its literary men and other artists became spokesmen and officials of the government whenever the policies of the nation were involved, or they left Germany, or were regarded as rebels who were admitted to varying degrees of toleration. The intellectual background of the growth of Germany during the past century has been filled with vivid intellectual life, and has presented some of the great achievements of the human spirit in all time. What has been noted as singular in their character is that they did not enter into the task of helping the people as a people to fashion their own national state, or determine its policies, and in taking this subservient attitude toward the state, and of state policies, they have inevitably left the state upon the foundation of force, a force to which ideas are under the conditions necessarily subordinate.

The nations with liberal institutions found their philosophy in the English empirical thinkers. Hobbes[7] is contemplating human nature, especially the impulses that find their expression in self assertion and those that appear in the desire for possession[. He] despaired of any state which did not stand upon the absolute power of the monarch, but Locke, a generation later writing the justification of the Whig revolution which drove out James the Third could see in human nature not only impulses leading to self assertion but social instincts which bound men together and made the framework to society the natural expression of human nature. Rousseau in France presented, only in more passionate fashion, this same faith, and drew from it equalitarian conclusions. The conception of the intellectual individual which had come to clear consciousness in the Age of the Enlightenment was carried by the mass upheaval of the revolution to the ranks of the common people. The rights of man were the center about which was organized an individual who could assert himself and yet enter into a society and build up the fabric of the state. In defense of their common rights they could get together and tear down the structure of the authoritative state. But could they stand together in their jealous consciousness of their individual rights and find the method of governing in the voices of the majority? Was a state of the abstract individual possible with nothing, but the rights for which the French proletariat fought so fiercely?

An examination of the statement of the rights of man given in the Constitutions of the revolution shows but negative definitions. Liberty is defined in terms of taking away liberty and other rights still to be defined, equality in terms of the absence of legal distinctions, security in terms of its source, property in terms of the absence of interference with its use. But to the minds of the men of the revolution these definitions had definite contents, because they were undertaking to determine the conditions under which certain powers which it did not even occur to them to define, might be exercised. The positive rights are those of self government through direct vote or through representatives, and those of property. It is about these that the individual of the nineteenth century was built up.

Other rights and powers are corollaries of these, or extension of the conceptions that belong to them, into other fields. Thus the right to property involves that of exchange, and out of this grows up the vastly important category of contract, which has been so widely applied in all the fields of modern life. The right of self government, carries with it that freedom of expression and opportunity of combination [that] has shown itself wherever authority has been exercised under other institutions, such as the church, the family, the school and the direction of labor in industry. It is indeed the triumph of this century that society has been reconstituted upon such elements in human nature. For the right of self government finds its mechanism of expression in the hostile self assertion in which the individual repels others of the group to which he belongs. Property springs out of the impulse to have and to hold which isolates the possessor of his booty unless he is overpowered by a stronger competitor for the prize. Such impulses are not promising materials out of which to build up a social structure, and it is the achievement of the countries of liberal institutions that they have been able to make these stones rejected by the earlier builders the head stones of the edifice. It could be done only in a society of rational beings who recognized that a reasonable being could only make claims for himself which he recognized as claims on the part of others under like conditions. It is the principle of which Kant conceived that he could build up a whole moral universe. A rational being may see that his claim for self determination must accept the same in others if they are to accept it when he makes his demand. One may only make possible the right to his own property when he respects the property of others. And yet these remain empty forms[,] the meaning and value of which must come from other sources. For what is to be the aim of government? To maintain the right of self government? What is the function of property? Merely to have and to hold?

Now it is to the relation between these two, between the form and the content of the institutions of an individualistic society that we must [understand] for the interpretation of the states with liberal institutions and their history leading to this war. It was not about the impulse of self assertion, nor about that of property even that medieval society was organized, nor did these form the principles out of which primitive society sprang. Back of medieval society lay the conception of New Jerusalem. The ecclesiastical structure was that which gave form and meaning even to the secular governments. Family — or the clan — was the principle of primitive society, and in the medieval world it continued to be one of the most powerful of the cohesive factors. Education, art, festivals and recreations were [governed by] church and state affairs in one way or another. The demand for self government was regarded as heretical and anarchical. Property was constantly subordinated to church and dynastic purposes. Its rights were by no means sacred and the right to the increment upon wealth, to interest, to usury or interest was frankly denied by the church. The doctrinaires of the French Revolution undertook to translate as much as possible of this positive content of medieval society into the language and method of their movement. But a religion of reason died a-borning and other attempts at reconstruction went the same way. The real structure of society after the upheavals of the revolution and the reaction remained to a surprising degree the same. The outstanding illustration of this is found in the so-called Victorian period (1837-1901) in England, where the feudal order remained in social strata and social prestige, where the right to possession of land carried with it all sorts of social values and earlier the real membership in the governing class, where religion in the middle class consciousness played so dominant a part in the direction of life and the ordering of it, where the highest prizes bought with accumulated wealth were social stations, the right to wear orders and enter an outworn aristocracy. The content and meaning of life is at least expressed in its culture of the century [which] has been in the past. Nothing could be beautiful nor spiritually significant, nor indeed decent[,] which had not received the refinement of the past. These communities had accepted liberal institutions but the wine in the new container was the old wine of a world that had been outgrown.

Not that the concerned advocates of the new order did not face the issue. They undertook to formulate the end and purpose for which [life] should be lived by men in a democratic state. The battle cry of this valiant group [of] keen liberals in England was [Jeremy] Bentham's dictum — The greatest Good of the greatest Number. This good was to be measured in terms of the experience of [the] individual, his pleasures and relief from pain. Sum up all the pleasures of all the members of society, allowing one man to count for one and only one and subtract all the pains and privations and you have the end for which society exists and which it is the business of government to realize to the limit of its capacity. This was the most thoroughgoing of the attempted translations of old social values and ends into modern terms, but the attempt was made all the way around. Religion was a matter of the conscience of the individual; the family was a contract between individuals; taste and artistic creation the affair of the individual artist and those who appreciated him; even the common festivals and the recreations about which so much of earlier social life had gathered, became the picnics, the excursions, the dances whose democracy was only expressed in their commercialization.

It is impossible to make a sum of pleasures and subtract the sufferings of humanity. Men live and die for things that cannot by any possible dictionary be translated into terms of satisfaction. What made the translation seemingly possible was the economic movement, the introduction of the factory system, and the more or less unconscious statement of pleasures and pains in terms of wages and the essentials of existence which these could buy. The factory was the most potent influence in breaking up the remaining feudal order of society. It took vast numbers of workers from the land and carried them to the great centers of manufacture. It created a proletariat, a mass of wage-workers who had no other position in the community except that which the economic situation gave them. Inasmuch as the operation of the iron laws of industry and trade reduced the wage to very limit of the essentials of existence[.] Money in the form of wages came to represent pretty well the sum of pleasures[,] and the absence of it the sum of pains which the mass of laborers could experience. It might be heresy to identify money with the higher, intellectual, aesthetic and social pleasures, but for men and women living on a starvation wage money can well be the *summum bonum*. Especially insofar as reform and philanthropic efforts is centered in removing misery does the increase of the means of subsistence through increased wage become the goal of the socially minded statesman. And on the other side[,] money became the means for obtaining a host of other goods which under earlier conditions could not be bought. It could give education, travel, association with choice sp[iri]ts, social position. We are so in the habit of decrying the charge that our aims are materialistic, when we make money the end of all effort, and assert that money can buy anything, that we overlook the truth that lies behind the statements. That truth is that insofar as money in an economic age has opened the doors to social positions and callings and means of training and appreciation, it has been the great democratizing force. In a world that could piously say that the poor we have always with us, it was a needed response that the poor we have with us only so long as the laborers wage is held at the lowest possible figure. It is of immense importance to translate human misery into economic terms for then the possibility of removing it is at hand. It is of immense importance to provide golden keys to the doors opening into learning, and science, and art, and nature, for these are keys that are theoretically within the reach of all in an economic society. It was the economic era that gave a meaning and content to the democratic movement. To translate the goods of society into the medium of exchange, a medium of exchange which was in some quantity in everybody's hands was a means of presenting a conceivable democratic society, for there was not only a society of individuals with natural rights, of self government and property, but also a universal medium in everybody's hands through which all the *desiderata* of human society could be come at. It was this economic situation that mediated between the individual with the abstract rights and no social content, and the older medieval order of things still preserved in the structure of society and its goods and values.

The countries with the liberal institutions had a frame of political society which reduced as far as possible all political and other social functions to natural rights and their corollaries. While these natural rights gave the form of the individual they did not give the content. This was in large measure taken over from the older world. The real mediating link between this form and content was that economic medium, which was so rapidly undermining the order of things. Out of this arose socialism as a great spiritual movement, which a[waken]ed the democratic implications of the economic doctrine. This movement of the laboring men accepted the economic structure of things, and drew the conclusion that those who had economic control had the access to the good of society. From these premises there was only one conclusion to be drawn, and that was that the control should be in the hands of the greatest number, that their good might be obtained.

Socialism is the logical outgrowth both of the economic theory of the industry of the beginning of the nineteenth century but also of the democratic school of the Benthamites. It is not for me to discuss the practicability of socialistic schemes, for our purposes the important thing to realize is that socialism presented at least for some decades the goal that society must contemplate[,] whether it will or not, a democratic society in which the means of social expressions and satisfactions are placed at the disposal of the members of the whole community. That socialism had to arise to state the aim which the countries with the liberal institutions should have faced, is one convincing piece of evidence that democracy was in these countries an unrealized form of society. It placed the individuals on a theoretical level, but it left the former stratifications largely unchanged, and did not place the values of life in society at their disposal. Socialism at least understood to accomplish this in accordance with current economic doctrine. It is a strange and almost disconcerting fact that these countries have had to wait for the tragedy of this war to awake to what it is possible to do for the better ordering of life in the community. All the governments in the communities are recognizing the need to better wages, better education, better sanitation, better care of personal health, better housing, better recreations, more control of the laborer over the conditions of labor, larger sharing on his part in the profits, and this not by way of concession to a restless proletariat, but as making for higher efficiency when the community is in need of the greatest possible returns in the shortest possible time. While a good part of the program of socialism is being put into practice, the striking difference lies in the fact that it [is] being undertaken not by the proletariat but by the whole community under the eager guidance of captains of industry, commanding generals, research scientists and conservative statesmen. A real democracy in which the theoretical political power is not simply in the hands of a voting majority, but in which the community life expresses the interests of all[:] that is the goal which has never been so sharply put before us as in the efforts of these countries with liberal institutions to become sufficiently efficient to win the war.

Socialism though it sprang out of the democratic states, and found its gospel in the political philosophy of the Manchester School,[8] to reach its goal had to attack both the natural rights on which are based our democratic states. The socialistic state was one which was not to be bounded by the natural rights of the individual, either to self government or to the complete control over his property. It was natural that its most completely logical statement should appear in Germany and not in England nor in France.

When Karl Marx issued his *Communist Manifesto* in the [eighteen] fifties[9] there was hardly any expression of the nationalism which has played such an increasing part in the life of modern Europe[. Nationalism] has put the socialistic *internationale*[10] in its grave, and united laborers of every country with the other groups in a unified national whole. Of course nationalism is not a new phenomenon. But its recent expression has characters which are new. During this last half century it has played an increasingly important part in the politics of all countries in which are found peoples of different races. The oppositions of these races has not been simple racial antipathy. What has turned it into nationalism has been the demand for full determination of their social life. The first item in the program has always been the demand for a recognition of the language of the group. There has appeared a new interest in the history and literature that belongs to the group. Schools, church affiliation and a right of association with others of the same race are parts of the demand culminating[,] where this is possible[,] in the demand for full independence of political control. Beginning with the Balkans this movement has swept over Europe carrying its quarrels into Austria, Hungary, Germany, Italy, England and Russia. Everywhere nationalism has stood for a closer and more intimate life in the group than that which has existed before, for a deepening of the social consciousness, and for the right to self control which goes with vivid group consciousness. It has been a divisive factor insofar [as] peoples have come to consciousness of themselves in their opposition to others, and especially insofar as they have undertaken to break the yoke which has subjected them to other peoples and to dynasties foreign to themselves. But there is no movement which has so quickened the conscious life of the society of the Western world as this growth of nationalism. It has brought together peoples [who] have found that in their differences they had common interests. It has awakened sympathetic response in those who are of different tongue and race. Every increase in the consciousness of the selfhood of a community has meant an increase in the awareness of other groups and has laid the foundation for the community of interest and endeavor which has had its greatest expression in the formation of the League of Nations which is opposed to the Central Powers of Europe.

In a real sense nationalism has done in part what neither liberal institutions nor socialism has accomplished. It has brought together the whole community in a common interest, and made the whole community realize that they were one. Liberal institutions left the community which was united only in the possession of abstract common right divided in the conflicting interests of classes. There was no occasion outside of hostility to another people which brought all together in emotional unity. Socialism runs right across national boundaries [.I]t gives class consciousness but neglects the organization of society within which the laborers are at home. National development has changed the character of socialism in all the countries. Nationalism has been the most potent force in forcing the problem of internationalism upon the world, in compelling men to ask the question how can nations that are vividly conscious of themselves live law abiding relations with others. The League to Enforce Peace is the direct growth of the nationalistic movement. All the smaller nations look to it as the natural society within which each can exist in peaceful relations with each other. Self determination of nations is as genuinely a part of the cause of the Allies as making the world safe for democracy. Every movement which organizes the inner life of a people and brings it to more definite realization of itself as a whole[,] with a common interest belonging to all its groups and parts[,] draws it into the league which is fighting the present Germany and its ally empire of the Hapsburgs.

Thus we see the background of this war. I am not referring to the occasions out of which it arose, nor to the interests that at first sought to profit by its possible results, but to that more profound problem which existed in Western society and which with every year of the war has come to more definite expression. We call it the issue of democracy. A democratic order of society is one in which individuals who respect each other's rights in asserting their own, who demand right of self determination in recognizing that others must determine their own lives, who claim to control their own in affirming the possessions of others. Beside this there has arisen with ever clearer vision in men's mind the end which such a society must have—that so ordering the social life that the interests of all shall be regarded and conserved, and what the war has emphasized more than any teaching of philanthropists or theorists is that the one cannot be carried out without the other. Efficiency in the common activity is dependent on the recognition of the interest of the individual and *vice versa*. But more important still it has become evident that this cannot be accomplished in one nation without the recognition of the same undertaking in others, that the attempt to exploit other peoples inevitably carries with it the subordination of the interest of weaker groups at home to those who alone can profit by the exploitation.

The German military class organized under its dynasty and working with its imperialistic industrial and financial group have come to stand out as the power which cannot find its ends in the healthfully organized life of its own people in natural social intercourse with other peoples. When a people cannot determine its own life, those who can must be a necessary danger to others. It can maintain itself at home only by the principle of force, and it can find expression for that force only by the actual or threatened conflict attack upon those without. Its purposes must be at variance with those of the great mass of its own people and to pursue them it must emphasize its own power and render continually more efficient its own military arms. It can live only by war.

On the other hand just insofar as countries with liberal institutions can face and solve the real problem of democracy[,] just insofar [as] they render more natural and peaceful their intercourse with others, not by giving up their national consciousness but by quickening it in the realization and solution of the common problems of the whole country.

The problem, the fundamental problem that has come into view in the war[,] may not reach its solution but it is clearer than it has ever been[,] and the result of the final victory of the nations that are fighting for a society of nations can but bring it nearer solution.

READING 6B

THE GOVERNMENT OF THE STATE AND WAR[11]

The two sides of our emotional life upon which emphasis has been laid — the hate and the devotion — which are both called out by war indicates the two aspects of the state which appear in the paradox — that the state on the one hand represents the highest values, while on the other it makes not only possible[,] but almost legitimate[,] all the vices in the calendar. In the contests of states with each other men pass beyond every standard which they held in peace. The only mission which is never forgotten is defeat, any contract which organizes victory is justified by its success.

This point of view has its own logic — that it is only through the state that all the values of society may exist. With the attack upon the state we pass beyond the canons of conduct within the state. Over against the state's enemy there is no law but law's destruction.

The assumption underlying this is that the state as the organized institutions of the community can be identified with society — an assumption that is false. Attention has already been drawn to the chasm existing between the society of Europe and the government of Europe. On the other hand the states are not simple survivals, not simple vestiges of the older order of things which should drop away of themselves. This is the Doctrine of philosophical anarchy. Unfortunately for this Doctrine, the institutions of society have not been decreasing either in number or in importance. Modern government involves more rather than less mechanism.

It is[,] of course[,] true that it undertakes vastly more than government has ever undertaken in the past, and it is possible that could an actual comparison be made between the undertaking of the government a hundred years ago and today, it might be found that present day governments make propositions that use institutional mechanisms less than did those of our grandfathers, but this quantitative test would be beside the mark. The real questions is not the amount, even the relative amount[,] of institutional mechanism formed. It is found rather in the relation of the state institution to the social organization.

In the first place, the institution simply facilitates and extends social relations, which have the ground for existence in this social nature of men. It does not create relations nor has it any value apart from these relations which it mediates. It is further true that the control which is exercised by and through the institution becomes more effective as it becomes less institutional. In other words, the most effective government is through public opinion. Social control[,] insofar as it is institutional[, involves prisons,] and fails to carry with it that recognition of the identity of interests which must be the foundation of proper social control.

Social integration implies the continual transfer of control from governmental institutions to the quickened and enlarged consciousness of the community. What appeared first as governmental prescription becomes awareness of the new meaning of our interaction with others. Compulsory industrial insurance grows into a sense of the fuller responsibility of the industry to its employees and the community. [12] The manufacturer comes to feel that it is an essential part of the economies of his enterprise, and looks back to the practice of fighting claims in court as not only barbarous but unintelligent. The normal citizen is not controlled by the police. To acquire and own private property carries him beyond the possibility of picking pockets.

The increase of industrial, commercial, and biological supervision by the government does not contradict this. It is normal that the new relations in a society which is growing and developing should be at first largely external to the individuals, and it is normal that the healthfulness and integrity of these relations should be evidenced by their gradually becoming part of the individuals themselves. The number and extent of governmental prescriptions are simply coefficients of the new developments in the organization of the group, provided that there is no arrest in the passage from the less adequate to the more adequate form of social control, from the institution to public opinion.

So far then is the institutionized state from being logically the highest phase of social development, that it stands for social organization that has not yet been fully realized. To fix and perpetuate this external authority of the state over the individual, and present it as the most adequate expression of the relation between the two is to substitute [an] arrested stage for a process of continuous growth. There are two phases of the authority of the community over its constituent individuals. In one case [on the one hand] the individual through his participation in the larger life of the community becomes a part of the governing whole. The institutional control[,] on the other hand, represents relations which are not so completed that they can come to full consciousness of their social meaning. The institution serves as an external representative of the whole community which does not yet appear directly and fully in the consciousness of the individual.

Now, to my mind, it is important, at this moment, when states have appealed to the *ultima ratio* [last argument, last resort] of states, we recognize that the organized institutions of a community which we call the state, are merely mechanisms that arise to trace out the field for further socialization. They tend to lapse as men come into more and more direct connections with each other. There is no prospect of their disappearance in any future [to] which we can look forward, but we perceive that men are recognizing more and more that the institution is merely a means never to be installed as an end, a means to be constantly judged by its tendency to foster direct social control in the place of the external institutional control, a means that is to be at any time refashioned to meet changing social situations.

The flagrant crime of the Western world and we are involved in it through war [but not] as deeply as Europe, thanks solely to our geographical position, has been that, while in very many respects the true nature of the institution has been recognized in the inner life of nations, we have refused to recognize it in the international life of Christendom.

This I take it to be [is the] fundamental definition of militarism — that the state has the right to exist and to maintain itself against any judgement from within or without, not because of its functions in the community of nations but because it is the reality and meaning of the society it represents.

If the state is the end and not the means [,] militarism is logical and moral. If the state is the means and not the end[,] international legislation must take the place of war and [in] that diplomacy the weight of whose arguments is found in the relative powers of destruction of the states which it represents.

READING 6C

GERMANY VERSUS INTERNATIONAL LIFE[13]

The most serious injury which can be dealt to the cause of Germany is to identify it with the doctrine that might is the determining principle of international society. For the nation or alliance of nations that asserts and maintains this doctrine makes itself the champion of war and the apologist for its horrors. The man in the trenches and those returning from the trenches refuse to accept war as the legitimate means of conducting the common affairs of peoples and their states. War has been generally accepted as the necessity of self defense. The German nation, flushed with victory and confident of future achievement accepted for a time war as a means of becoming the masters of Europe and the world. But this acceptance of war depended upon the success of the war plans of the militarist party and government in Germany. That plan has not been carried to fulfillment. It is not now generally allowed that this plan can succeed. A swift mighty war carried to undisputed victory leaving the fruits of victory in the hands of the victors, such a war was planned by Germany's military governing class, and when it was in its seemingly irresistible march the German people including even the Social Democrat adopted its program and accepted its doctrine of international life. In the place of this almost universal acceptance there is in Germany today bitter strife. The *Vaterland* party espousing the militarist's program is unable to hold its meetings in many German cities because peace by conciliation has become the watchword of the larger number. In Austria the unwillingness to accept the principle of might is still greater and is inspired by motives drawn from inner political life and struggle. In the gradual emergence of the issues of international right as the determining principle of the common life of peoples[,] the nations involved in this struggle are becoming aware more and more clearly of two things. The first of these is that no defeat of the military power of Germany can be so complete or so final as an undertaking by which right should be substituted for might in the conduct of international affairs. The second of these is that it is a solution that cannot be put through without very serious changes in the political attitudes, points of view, and even inner organization of the Allied as well as of the Central Powers.

Let us consider first the latter fact, to wit that Germany cannot be made the sole champion of the doctrine that might makes right in international affairs unless the opponents of Germany are themselves willing to surrender the appeal to might in support of their own international contentions. The formulation of the League to Enforce Peace has put the implications of the abandonment of war as the arbiter of nations' conflicts in fairly evident outline. Justiciable issues will go to various sorts of international courts while issues which the contending nations are unwilling to regard as justiciable are to be referred to boards of arbitration. It is true that this plan — and it is only one plan, though the best considered one yet before the world — still contemplates the decision of the issues on the field of battle in case no solution [is] reached by the board of arbitration which the contending states are both minded to accept. However unless a year is allowed to elapse during this period of attempted arbitration and while the findings of the court of arbitration are presented not only to the peoples at issue with each other but also to the world at large, the whole league will join in support of the nation attacked. It is confidently assumed that no issue can reach the trenches which must wait a year under judicial consideration and the discussion of the world. If it was a question of considerable doubt before this war, there is now I imagine little doubt in the mind of anybody that a year's discussion would force a solution. The masses of the people in any community would insist that a sufficiently reasonable proposition be made so that the agony of war be avoided. The meaning of a scientifically organized entirely competent nation at war has been made too evident to leave in question the willingness of a modern people to approach in a reasonable spirit an opposing nation seeking adjustment of an outstanding dispute. We know that it was under conditions fairly comparable to these that private vengeance gave way to public prosecution and punishment. The expense to the community of the private right of vengeance became intolerable. The escape from the situation did not lie in perfecting the means of vengeance but in the substitution of a public right for a private might, backing up the public right by the might of all — a might however which it is difficult to organize and render effective. This is of course more true as the exercise of force becomes more mechanical, more elaborate, and involving highly organized bodies of men as well as highly elaborated machinery.

More effective than the actual fear of the exercise of the might of all in the enforcement of public right, has been what we term the force of public opinion. The dependence of men upon the community to which they belong is so complete that no man or group of men can long resist the judgment of the members of the community when it is directed upon him or them. It must be further recognized that the term private vengeance is a misnomer. The avenger of blood was but the next of kin; he was the representative of the clan, and the evil which became intolerable was not the murder of the individual by the individual, but the clan feuds and wars, which decimated the larger community that was coming to consciousness of itself as a community. The real bridge by which the community passed from the old vengeance to the new law was that of the larger social consciousness which acknowledged the larger social whole. In passing, it should be emphasized that the passage from the membership in the clan to that in the larger community was not attended by any loss of individuality. Nor will the passage of the citizen of the national state to that of the larger community bring with it any loss of individuality. Nor will it diminish the sense of national citizenship anymore than national citizenship has diminished the meaning of family relationship. In general so much has been proved by the development of society; that where the larger social group has served a definite social function, it has always given greater meaning and content to the smaller groups within it. It is possible today to give a more concrete meaning to a family, a school, a legislature, a court, or a church than could be given to a clan, the initiation of youth, a folks' moot, the gathering of magicians and elders on an *Areopagus*, or a sacrificial meal.

It is however becoming evident that even such an epochal reconstruction as that involved in a League to Enforce Peace is not the limit of the innovations which the passage from might to right in the government of the relation of peoples and their states to each other. The further change that is indicated by the attitudes of the populations of Europe[,] and in some degree those of America[,] is expressed vaguely by the recognition that this has become a war of Democracy. At first this statement meant simply that England and France were the dominant members of the alliance against the central autocratic powers, and that in England and France were to be found institutions which are considered democratic, [or] at least are governments in which the way is open for popular control. It was a fight between people under liberal institutions and those under government from above. With revolution in Russia this situation has changed fundamentally. I refer to the profound popular attitudes and movements of feeling and thought. More and more definitely in France and England as well as in Russia since this revolution, there has come to expression the sentiment that in all these countries — in the countries under liberal institutions as well as in those subject to autocratic power — imperialism, based on militarism and predatory finance, must be met by the entrance of the laboring people into control in the colonial politics and those of foreign industry and trade, which have been the field of imperialism, whether the institutions have been liberal or autocratic.

No clearer expression of this could be given than in the pronouncement of the laborers of England in their recent congress. The sum and substance of those pronouncements have been that the democracy of England is to find its issues formulated by the Labor Party. As a Labor Party they have come to realize that the self determination of populations in distant colonial possessions is tied up with their own liberties, with the control over economic conditions which they have learned they must exercise at home.

The League to Enforce Peace formulated at first by conservative gentleman such as Messrs [Elihu] Root and [William Howard] Taft[14] has been found to be a necessary institution in a democracy that determines to be done with se-cret diplomacy and the international finance which depends on governmental influence in obtaining contracts and concessions, in insuring investments and collecting debts. The Internationale has gone, but the demand of self conscious labor parties is for a world society within which war with all its uncompen-sated evils for the masses of the community can be replaced by other means of facing international disputes. From the standpoint of Germany's militaristic and financial groups[,] a League to Enforce Peace would enforce a peace in a world in which the prestige of English empire will remain unbroken, in which an unpopular Germany will drive an unprofitable commerce. Free to employ might[,] Germany is confident she can hew her way to a place in the sun vastly more impressive, profitable, and satisfying to her irritable sense of her own supreme importance than she can possibl[y] hope to attain in a world in which might is subjected to an international right. If a League to Enforce Peace is to be the League of Germany's enemies in the contest of might, a league whose province it is to keep the *status quo ante*, shaped now as the field of Germany's defeat, it is a League into which Germany can enter only as a beaten power who must make the best of the lot of the conquered. So regarded it is a political devise of the *Entente* in their effort to closely organize themselves and preserve the union by which they hope to vanquish the common enemy and hold him in a harmless condition in the future. As such[,] it has little if any value in weakening the Central Powers.

It must be the expression of a really different order of society, if it is to have any influence on the present society of Germany and Austria. Let me emphasize again that it is of the utmost importance that we study the conditions under which the political offensive against Germany and Austria can be made most effective. If the League to Enforce Peace is viewed as it has just been presented[,] it has no power over the German community. It will not stand to them for another order of the world in which the barbarity of war is to be abandoned in favor of more efficient, less expensive, and more worth[-while] methods of reaching international agreements[,] but as an intimate political, economic, and spiritual alliance of the enemies of the German empire and her allies, to bring about their defeat in the struggle for world supremacy and more especially to close all the doors against her in the economic and political competitions after the war.

It is a question whether the League to Enforce Peace and its corollaries belong to the old order or to a new order of the world. The old order was one in which war had its recognized place, not only for purposes of self defense, but as a source of empire and economic power. From the standpoint of the old order war was a ticklish undertaking. It was of the utmost importance that the nation should always appear as defending only its existence and just rights in its entrance into the war. When however the nation was once in the struggle broad lands, imperial argosies, fields of unhampered influence leading to the most valuable concessions and the exclusive control over the richest opportunities of exploitation became the legitimate prizes of the contest. Right must be somewhat scrupulously considered in the entrance into the fight, but thereafter force was the arbiter and might the umpire. Such was the old order. There had grown up within it a body of international law, a body of rules of procedure in peace and war which was gradually restricting the field of force. It was limiting the horizon of the battlefield. This body of constricting custom, standard, and legislation Germany has hacked through without hesitation. She has been determined that before the new order comes, which this growth of international law and precedents typifies, she will have garnered all that resolute might might harvest. This she considered England has done in the past. She insists that England is simply profiting by the new body of international custom and regulation to secure her title to what she has won by the sword and render that title indefensible. In this mixture of might and right which characterizes the old order, the German nationalist sees a right which safeguards what might has seized. It is perfectly possible for the German nationalist to present the League to Enforce Peace as but a further ingenious piece of policy for insuring present[-]day titles, a sort of super-Torrens[15] system in international affairs. I am not arguing the justice of the German attitude of mind, and his passionate will to power[16] in the world. I am simply emphasizing the fact that policies which undertake to put things back where they were with the same order of things and with the same *beati possidentes*,[17] do not constitute parts of an effective political offensive against the Central Powers. If the *entente* powers are confident that they can crush Germany and her allies on the battlefield, the German people have nothing to urge against the harshest dictum of victory. Those that by preference draw the sword may not resent its weight in the balance when the final settlement is made. But this willingness to leave the decision to the sword is not found among the Allies. President Wilson has with his earliest war papers commenced a political offensive against Germany. He has insisted that America with no foreign policy to defend except that of the Monroe Doctrine, the non-interference of imperialistic powers in this hemisphere, and that with no interest in a single foot of soil that now owes another allegiance, with a fixed determination to be done with all predatory commerce America represents a new attitude, one that deliberately refuses to recognize might as the source of right in the affairs of nations.

And the America for which Mr. Wilson spoke had not only a pure heart but clean hands. But America spoke for herself and not for Europe, and America was not nearly so articulate as her spokesman President Wilson. It has been the Russian revolution and the Bolsheviki offer of peace on the basis [of] no indemnity, no annexation, and the right of all peoples to self determination that has given the world a sudden realization of a possible new order of things in which the issue of democracy takes on another meaning beside that of a fight between nations with parliamentary governments and those whose governing ministers and bureaucrats derive their authority from monarchs and not from representative assemblies, or directly from the electorate. I do not at all mean that we who felt this new meaning have accepted the particular doctrine of Lenine and Trotsky, that they have even recognized the coming of some form of socialistic state.

What they have recognized in the attitude of the Russian people is a new national consciousness which is as international as it is national. It is attitude of a people that are able and desire to be conscious of themselves not through opposition to nor in competition with other peoples but in the friendly wish that other peoples may have the same freedom of government and the same right to determine their own allegiance which the people of Russia have maintained against their Czar and the autocracy of which he is the incarnation. It is a generous attitude which may not endure longer than endured the same generous wish for liberty abroad as well as at home, which inspired the hearts of the French populace in the earlier years of the French Revolution. It has behind it the naive mind of the Russian peasant whose life is the simplest of that of any population in the Western world.

While industrialism flourishes in a few centers in Russia in the vast mass of its peoples it has not yet become the dominant manner of life and thought. But both the life and thought of Western Europe is industrial. Its sophisticated consciousness has sprung out of the intricacies of its products and the miseries of its factory system. It is out of the wrongs which the factory system has inflicted upon the laborer that has arisen the more adequate recognition of the duty of the community to the individual. Our modern social conscience has sprung from industrialism. While this industrialism is reflected in the socialism of Lenine and Trotsky it is not the order of mind and feeling that animates the Russian peasant. And yet though the present phase of the Russian mind cannot be expected to be lasting, this spontaneous national consciousness which is at the same time international has produced a profound impression throughout the Western world. The socialism which the present leaders of Russia affect is not in sympathy with the type of constructive socialism[s] which are to be found in other European communities, yet there is a profound response to the demand that the governing ideas in the society of the Western world must be those of financial growth, or as it is expressed in the jargon of the socialistic revolutionary, those of the bourgeoisie. What is compelling in the Russian Revolution, what calls to the laboring classes in other countries as deep calls to deep, is the demand for social reconstruction in the interest of the laborers, the masses of the community. That it is a nationalism which is international. It would however be a most serious error to assume that it obliterates or minimizes national consciousness. While it is hostile to the national aims which are divisive, which array peoples against peoples hostile to the imperialism which feeds the sense of national and racial prestige by supremacy over subject nations, to the predatory finance which exploits weaker groups by the exercise of force or by the threat of force, and the militarism upon which both of these are built. It is hostile to them because they inevitably run counter to the undertakings of social reform which are becoming more and more insistent and which make more and more demands upon the national conscience and the common interest. It was Germany's great undertaking to preserve and quicken the consciousness which springs out of war with other nations in commerce and arms, while a supergovernment that fostered and rested upon militarism at the same time effected such social reforms as its imperial aims admitted. It has been a titanic experiment which has failed. The attempt to use the discipline of a nation trained to arms and the authority of an imperial military government to solve problem of social and economic reconstruction has failed. It has failed if for no other reason because it invites war, and war has proved too vast a price to pay for the sense of national prestige and the social amelioration which an imperialistic state can include in its program. It is, however, important to recognize just what it has been in the German state which enabled it to set the pace in labor insurance and in other features of the modern social program. It has certainty not been greater sympathy or social intelligence on the part of the German employers of labor and captains of industry. Nor has the general German public been more interested in the problems of social reform than other communities.

What history makes quite evident is that Bismarck[18] with extraordinary foresight recognized the ominous growth of a democratic labor proletariat, and, on the other hand, the strategic position of the monarchical state above and independent of both labor and capital. The German government could dictate to both. It was possible for the German state to force upon the industry of the community measures which it has required thirty years and more of industrial struggle to compel English industry to undertake. The German government had a base independent of industrial institutions. This base was military organization of German society. It left in the minds of the citizens a sense of a state with irresistible force subject neither to the immediate demands of the populace, nor to those of the financial magnate who in the modern industrial society has elsewhere secured the *pas* over all others. It is this independence both of direct popular control and of domination by the captains of industry which has cultivated in the German mind the belief that they have a form of government superior to the parliamentary types found elsewhere in the Western world.

But it has failed because the very independence which militarism has given to its government has left the military clique to steer the state into a conflict that has arrayed the whole world against Germany. It is not in a life and death struggle for the domination of the world that the German proletariat will gain the improved economic and social conditions for which they have been fighting. The cause of the masses cannot be hitched to the star of a military imperialism. While military government ruled by a war-lord could claim to be using its force of arms to keep the world's peace, and at the same time to be giving the German proletariat better conditions than could be found in the countries that boasted of their liberal institutions, the German socialist could be superior to the laborites, and socialists of other communities as were the German scientists, and financiers and commercial magnates, and Junkers to those of other lands. But as soon as militarism provokes the war of the world it becomes evident that only imperialism and the classes and commerce that live on the preparation for war, and a predatory commerce can ultimately flourish in the militaristic state. They are intensely national and hostile to internationalism. The other expressions of national life are not hostile to internationalism. In particular the cause of labor is felt to be essentially international. It is in a society of nations that the standards and values which are involved in the program of social reconstruction receive their clearest definition, and every forward movement toward the realization of this program, emphasizes the larger whole within which all lesser communities lie. It is impossible to give a nation definition of the golden rule, nor to the democratic battle cry of the greatest good of the greatest number, nor to the rights of the individual to political and economic freedom.

Notes

1. This class is not found in the course catalogs at the University of Chicago.
2. Box 2, folder 27, Mead Addenda
3. The aristocratic family who ruled the Austria-Hungarian Empire.
4. See ftn. 20, p. 72.
5. These German philosophers are part of the movement called German idealism. They argued the basis of culture was produced in the creative power of the mind, and they challenged the priority of rationalism and empiricism. The latter two assumptions were important in the Enlightenment and in Chicago pragmatism.
6. See ftn. 30, p. 72.
7. See ftn. 18, p. 72.
8. The Manchester School refers to a British political and economic approach to free trade, radical libertarianism, and governmental withdrawal from the economy. It supports free enterprise capitalism along with many liberal values. See, "The

Manchester School," http://cepa. newschool. edu/het/schools/manchester. htm. Captured 13 June 2006.

9.   Mead is referring to the work by Karl Marx and Friedrich Engels, *Manifesto of the Communist Party,* published in 1848.

10.   This is the world-wide movement of workers to gain control over their labor.

11.   This document is found in box 3, folder 26, Mead Addenda. It is partially handwritten and partially typed and heavily edited. When I am unsure of the legibility of the writing, I indicate this with a question mark. If I add an edited letter or punctuation I put it in brackets.

12.   Mead supported such federal measures and indicates here that they can institute changes in public opinion.

13.   Box 2, folder 32, Mead Addenda.

14.   Elihu Root (1845-1937) was a lawyer, U. S. Senator, and 1912 recipient of the Nobel Peace Prize. He was President of the Carnegie Endowment for International Peace from 1910-1925. William Howard Taft (1857-1930) was the 27th President of the United States and specialized in international arbitration.

15.   "Torrens" is a system of land registration and transfer. Mead served as a surveyor briefly after his graduation from Oberlin in 1883 and would have known about such land measurements and titles (Deegan 1998, xxxiv).

16.   Nietzsche's phrase the "will to power" was a key concept in his over-all philosophy. It refers to the human drive to dominate others. This idea was important in Germany's national aggression in both WWI and WWII. This phrase became the title of a famous, posthumous book of that title. See Nietzsche 1901/1924.

17.   See ftn. 22, p. 151.

18.   Otto von Bismarck (1815-1898) was a Prussian aristocrat who led two wars against first Austria and then France to help build the German state. In 1871 he became Chancellor of the German Empire. He was asked to resin from this office in 1890.

7

Unpublished Lectures during War-Time: Labor and War

*"In the first place the laboring men and women of
the country have the same interest in the victory of
our military forces which belongs to every citizen.
Notwithstanding the conflicting interests and attitudes of different groups in the community all who
are conscious members of the community will be
exalted by the victory of the nation or humiliated
by its defeat. There is a fundamental patriotism that
arises simply because all are fighting the common
enemy. Conflicting interests disappear for the time
being and we all have the exhilaration of feeling as
one in united hostility" (see reading 7B here).*

Mead's weakest areas of analysis are the institutional processes where dif-
ferential power creates massive inequality and social injustice between two
groups. Anything he writes on labor is, therefore, of great interest. In this
brief chapter Mead continues many of the themes he addressed in chapter five
and his popular articles on laborers and the war. Although he was committed
to labor unions during an era when such a stance was radical, he believed a
democratic society would respond to the demands of labor, and the strategies
and mechanisms to enable this response were part of the continuing social
reconstruction of America.

Again Mead addresses the need for class conflict in order to overthrow
aristocracy and, in the case of Germany, the military elite. American workers,
in contrast to German workers, could organize the community to listen to their
voice, so they did not conflict with capitalists and owners of the means of production. Mead wrote about socialism as early as 1899(a), and he was sympathetic
with the goals of social justice. He did not see a universal worker, however,
and American laborers could turn to the vote, arbitration, labor protests, and
citizens such as himself to help obtain a more just society.

Mead on Socialism and the War

In "Socialism and the War" (see reading 7A here) Mead criticizes Marxist socialism. He does not adopt the model of class conflict, historical materialism, or dialectical change proposed by Marx and Engel. He does support the Fabian socialism of England and the welfare state it created there. Many contemporary scholars seem confused by these two types of socialism and Mead's intellectual relation to them.

Mead, however, is highly consistent in his Fabian analysis and he did not abandon it after the war, as Dimitri Shalin (1988) argues he did. As Mead wrote in his prewar writings (see especially reading 3B) and in the previous chapter's readings, liberal rights were fundamental to his worldview. He maintained this commitment to liberal values his entire career. He also believed in social and economic justice for all, and he supported minimal state subsides in housing, medicine, income, and employment. Liberal institutions needed to be active, strong, and responsive to the needs of the citizen and community (see reading 7B here). He was an ardent advocate of public education and linked becoming a citizen to the right of every child, from kindergarten through high school, to a superb, comprehensive, non-capitalist education (Mead 1999, 2001).

Mead was a co-operative theorist and believed all members of the community were needed in a just society. Thus he opposed the Marxist approach defining justice as achieved through revolution. Marx argued that liberal rights were weak and hegemonic: they served the interests of the powerful while providing lip-service to ideas of social equality and rights. He rejected labor unions for the same reasons. These were intolerable assumptions to Mead. Clearly Mead and Marx differed on their understanding of the role of language and speech, too. The material world created social realities, including ideas and words. For Mead the world was both material and ideational. Ideas and words helped create the self and the other: they made the social world possible.

Mead on the Specific Interests of Labor in the War

Mead asked "What are the Specific Interests of Labor in the War?" (reading 7B) and answered that democratic rights could solve the problems of workers in an aristocracy. This essay follows the arguments Mead raised in his newspaper articles in the Chicago Herald in the summer of 1917 (see readings 4A to E and chapter 6 here). Mead argued that American labor's specific interests did not result in divided classes: "There is a fundamental patriotism that arises simply because all are fighting the common enemy." All Americans were united and exhilarated by their commonality. He notes: "In the first place the laboring men and women of the country have the same interest in the victory of our military forces which belongs to every citizen." Although Mead observed that German socialists were opposed to the war, American laborers were not socialists because their voices could be heard in a democracy.

Mead on the Failure of Liberal Institutions in England and America

"The Failure of Liberal Institutions in England and America" (see reading 7C) resulted, of course, from not enough participation by the citizens in political control. This was the same flaw in the German government, but Americans had mechanisms and rights to prevent this failure. The public, and particularly labor, could popularly control the government, but they often failed to exert this control. As a result, power elites exercised too much control. The latter group emerged from privileges derived from money, education, and family connections. They represented the interests of the few over the many and Mead condemned this imbalance of power. Like he averred in the previous reading, the workers have interests, too, and needed to exercise their legitimate rights to govern politics. Again Mead is a democratic theorist, failures in democracy could be remedied by more participation by all citizens in the social construction of the state.

Conclusion

Mead's theory of democracy and politics, liberal rights and the voice of the governed explained the failures of both the German and American states. The Germans, however, had an explicitly unfair state which left no voice for the everyday person, especially the workers, in government and state control. Marxists were wrong when they argued for an international proletariat. Each ethnic group and nation had separate interests that needed representation in each nation.

The Americans developed a state apparatus where everyone could be heard, but for many reasons the privileged few garnered power and influence. This was a failure of liberal institutions in the way they operated, not in the way they were designed. Like Addams (1902), problems in a democracy called for more democracy in order to resolve them.

Reading 7A

Socialism and the War[1]

I recognize that there are many socialist doctrines, and still more social attitudes among those who class themselves as socialists. I will not undertake to present these; either the doctrines or the attitudes in their details. Probably I would not be able to do them justice as doctrines and still less would I be able to do justice to the individuals, especially at a time when there is such a searching of hearts and men find the values have so shifted in their thought and in that region of subconscious reaction which generally lies out of the reach of reflection.

I shall address myself to one attitude in socialist literature and expression, that I have met, in reports of campaign speeches in the election for judges in this city and in the election of the mayor in New York and in the pronouncements of the soviets in Russia as well as in conversations I have held with socialist acquaintances.

This finds its most frequent expression in the statement that in this war as in the wars of the past the economic causes are as dominant as they are in the everyday life and organization of society. It follows from this for many of the socialists that the conclusion of the war will find society still under the same domination of the capitalist group. The enormity of the field of struggle, the unprecedented number of combatants, the almost inconceivable mobilization of the property, the industry, the commerce, the science, the education, and of all the inner life of men, women, and children does not for these socialists change the dominant causation in this Armageddon, and for this reason it does not change their attitude in refusing to accept the economic order, or to feel that they are under obligation to fight its battles. In fact from this standpoint the more things differ, the more they are the same thing. The economic order appears to these thinkers in its titanic struggle to be pulling down its own structure upon its own head. Why should those who have condemned it in times of political peace and have preached in season and out of season the fundamental injustice and inhumanity of the system involve themselves [in] the tragic realization of this injustice and this inhumanity, when the very logic of events display them in such gigantic and horrible conclusiveness. Must those who have not profited by this economic order of things, who make up as they conceive the self-conscious-members of the proletariat who have always suffered under it, who have regarded it as a disease of the commonwealth, must they abandon their own clear vision and identify themselves with these social convulsions and voluntarily take on their own shoulders the consequences of conditions they have never been willing to accept?

Some such attitude of mind in varying degrees of definiteness I have met in the expressions of socialists on the platform and in conversation. It has not been the attitude of men who would let others fight their battles for them. I have personally met neither fear of the dangers and sufferings of the trenches nor sympathy with the cause of the enemy. These may exist. If they do under the cloak of a socialist doctrine they deserve neither intellectual consideration nor respect.[2]

In passing allow me to refer to the case of the conscientious objector. The law exempts such, if they belong to religious sects whose tenets forbid fighting. Whatever may be said for or against this criterion of the genuineness of the conscientious objector, its implication is that only the man to whom fighting under any situation is wrong may be exempted from military service. Only the man who is a non-resistant on moral grounds is a conscientious objector in the eyes of this law. The implication is that the state may not compel a man to do what in itself is wrong in his own eyes. This does not[,] of course[,] mean that if the cause is wrong in the eyes of the citizen he is absolved from fighting, or paying taxes, or carrying out the other ordinances of the government. Under such an interpretation any government[,] and especially a democratic government[,] would be impossible. Under this interpretation every change in governmental parties would free those of the defeated party from the obligation to obey the laws enacted by those whose policy it disapproves.

The drafted socialist who considers the war a capitalists' war, and one therefore in which he has no concern, is under the same obligation to obey the draft law as he is to pay the war taxes in time of peace. The remedy of the man in a democracy, whose party is out, is to use the ballot to place in power those whose views are in accord with his own.

The matter of more profound interest, however, is the detachment of the socialist, his otherworldliness. It is his refusal to take the responsibility with the rest of us for the direction of the evolution that is going on about him. One may agree with the socialist, as does Mr. [Frederic C.] Howe (1917) in the last number of the *Atlantic* [*Monthly*], that since Palmerston sent a British cruiser to Greece to look after English investments in the early Victorian period,[3] the set of events that has led to this catastrophe has been dominated by financial diplomacy, an evil expression of capitalism. If the outcome of the war were to be the mere determination of that national group which is to control the field of foreign investments and exploitations, there would be no place in it for any democratically minded people. There are financial groups in all the nations, on both sides, that hope to make the victory or the settlement in the war the open door for governmentally insured investments, and contracts, and concessions. They are powerful groups, but they can control the policy of the government only in case the country as a whole fails to realize its opportunities, or realizing them chooses to abdicate in favor of the powers of international finance. For there are issues in the war which are not financial and they have been the interest which have grown in importance and clearness of definition with the progress of the three years' fighting.

The first of these is that identified with the invasion and conquest of Belgium by the German armies on the advance to Paris that never reached its goal. It is the issue of the small nation. This has been emphasized by the fact that Germany has never been willing to admit that her outrage upon Belgium called for reparation. The widespread and generally accepted demand among the industrialists, and their financiers supported by resolutions passed by assemblies of university professors and of pastors and higher church officials for the retention of the coal and iron districts of France as well as Belgium has thrown into clearer relief the acceptance by the intellectual and moral circles in Germany of the right of the stronger nation to dominate the weaker. This issue involves the entire doctrine of the community of nations. It involves the internationalism which has been dear to the heart of socialism. A triumphant Germany with Belgium and northern France subjugated, with Servia in bonds would inevitably place the whole world insofar as it was not willing to accept German overlordship in determined military preparation to preserve national identity and to be ready for the next struggle.

It is true that Belgium is not the first outrage in history that other nations[,] and among them both England and France but preeminently England[,] have sinned against the weaker nation in the past. But past history is that out of which the present world has risen. The socialists with their history of the three stages are well aware of this. The present issue is that which the nations make in their present conduct. Germany has so definitely affirmed the justification of force exercised by the stronger upon the weaker nation, she has so fashioned in the sweep of her plan the career of an empire resting upon force and recognizing no rights against her superior power, her project and her attitude have been so completely unveiled by her conduct and the expression of her own chosen mouthpieces that she, in the consciousness of her might and her conception of her opportunity, has made the issue of the right of the mighty nation to dominate the weaker and to sweep away what society there was of nations and refashion it, as one of our eminent professors of international law stated, to meet the demands of the German state and the German *Kultur*, Germany has made this issue her own. And those who have fought her have inevitably fought upon this issue, for the issue has entered deep into the consciousness of people. This issue of the right to existence of the small nation has appeared in this war as it has never appeared before.

It has required the martyrdom of Belgium and the consistent logic of war's frightfulness as Germany has made war her occupation, to make Germany the confessed present day champion of the doctrine that in international life might is the only right. She could not come victorious out of this struggle without the affirmation of this doctrine in the intercourse and common life of nations. Whatever may have been the attitudes of governments and influential groups in finance and industry and politics the issue was made by Germany herself. It was as democratic people refusing to accept what was the confessed aims of Germany after she had once entered upon the war that the rest of Europe found itself in opposition to her armies and her imperialistic program. The mere contemplation of the result which would inevitably succeed to German triumph, made the cause of the Allies[,] the struggle against subjection to a government dominated by a militaristic class[,] in alliance with imperialistic industry, commerce and finance.

In the realization of this issue the czardom fell in Russia and with it the imperialistic program in Russia. The formulations of Allied policy have been steadily shaping themselves in the sense of this democratic issue. In Germany itself the Social Democrats have their formula of a peace with every nation back in the boundaries which they held before the war. Unfortunately this German democracy has been unable [to] oust its own government nor has Germany's government ever been willing to commit itself not to get any advantage in territory and power which its arms could secure. As Mr. Asquith[4] has often pointed out[,] the German government has never been willing to refer to Belgium's condition after the war or to disown the ambitious program of the commercial and Junker groups that call for its retention. Germany insists on having every inch of soil she has occupied with her armies as trading goods at the peace conference, even if not as permanent possessions. This issue which is the flower and fruit of Germany's occupation and intended retention of peaceful Belgium, is the first great issue of the war, which dwarfs and pushes into a dusty background any questions as to the events of the beginning of the war. It is the issue which Germany has made and must abide by.

The other issue which is closely allied with this is that of war itself. More clearly than ever before the peoples of all Europe and now of America [are] facing the question whether arms regimented by science and backed by the entire economic and social life of the communities of the Western world are to be retained as the means of settling disputes between competing peoples. Never have such vast numbers in all these countries engaged in the fighting itself. Never has the fighting been of more determined character. Never have the entire communities so resolutely accepted the terrible undertaking, and never have those who have borne the struggle in all its horror been so articulate or so aware of what the fundamental causes are for which they are fighting, so that never has the world been so clearly able to realize the infinitely exaggerated price which is being paid for whatever political or economic or nationalistic advantages might be gained from victory. In a world in which all the great nations would be ready for war, no war could by any conceivable standard be worthwhile. And the one question which remains is this; is it a necessity forced upon us by the inability of modern communities to come to agreement upon their disputes? Is it a psychological necessity? Is human nature, when found in world communities that must and do have close and continually close relations with each other, unable to take the steps toward resolving conflicting national interests which[,] within every community[,] have been taken in solving the conflicting interests of individual citizens? That these steps can be taken, if the communities of the world through their governments, seriously attempt it[,] there can now be no serious doubt, since these steps have been discussed and tentatively sketched and in principle approved by the commanding statesmen in all the Allied countries. There has even come some dubious approval of them from the Central Powers. The development of commissions to deal with justiciable disputes, of arbitration boards to deal with those that fall outside these boundaries, of a League to Enforce Peace until all methods [are exhausted before a] continuously sitting international legislative body to consider the legislation of international law, such a development of our international machinery, it is generally believed will obviate war as the arbiter of the disputes of people.

To secure such measures there is needed but the will on the part of the peoples of the different countries. But that this will may find its expression in governmental action it is necessary that the people through their representative assemblies should be able to determine the policies of their governments, and until the Central Powers are ready insofar to democratize their governments that this will of the people is sure of fulfillment by their governments there can be no assurance that such steps will be taken. Indeed it is difficult to conceive that the German government at least would be willing to take such steps toward international settlement of disputes, for this government rests upon not only a monarchical foundation but still more profoundly upon the military order of the state.

Until the German people insofar realize their inevitable defeat in a continued struggle that they will force their will upon their own government or until the people of Germany adopt this program and fashion the governmental machinery for its enforcement, this great possible achievement of the war cannot be anticipated.

These are the two great issues that have arisen in the war, the issue of a community of states within which the weaker states can be secure, the issue of an international right that stands higher and is more potent than national might, and the issue already implied in this of a development of international institutions for settling the disputes between nations, [conceded, so that] the further integration of the society of nations till war becomes unnecessary, as it [war] has become, when determinately pursued, an unmitigated catastrophe. The victory of Germany spells the inevitable defeat on both these issues. [In] the logic of events both of these issues have become those of the Allied nations. If the Allies gain the decision in the war and are determined to achieve these ends, they will lie entirely within their power.

I do not deny that there are, even in the event of the victory of the Allied nations, other issues, which are of secondary importance when compared with these, which will arise to immensely complicate a democratic settlement of the war. Such problems are those involved in the future of Poland[,] the subject Slavic races in Austria-Hungary, the Balkan States, the German colonies, Alsace and Loraine, and the Trentino and other Italian portions of Austria. Their settlement in one way or another threatens to continue the war after the war. They are all possible grounds for future wars. This very fact is an indication of the reason for their secondary importance as compared with the democratic issues of the war. If a society of nations is recognized in which right is dominant instead of might, and if institutions of investigation, conciliation, arbitration, and legislation are allowed to arise to give articulate international expression to this right, just these issues referred to above, those of boundaries, of small nationalities access to raw materials and competing spheres of political and commercial influence, just these issues outline the field within which these international institutions will operate. It is of greatest importance therefore that the war should result in the opening of ways for dealing intelligently with just such casus belli [causes of war], for the opportunity then exists for reaching a solution without planting the seeds for later wars. It is possible, I think, to indicate the chances of success of such an attempt. For it has been demonstrated that in a world prepared for war, or in a world in which it is possible to hold a prepared nation long enough to bring into the field the opposing forces, there is and can be no objective that it is worthwhile starting a world war to obtain. I mean worthwhile to those who have to actually fight and suffer and endure, and these are the great mass of the community. We all know that there are always those who in our communities who want various sorts of roast pig and are willing to profit by a world conflagration to get it, but the people who live in the houses do not consider that these sorts of roast pig are worth the fuel that is necessary to roast it.

In ot[her words, the peoples of] the world are sufficiently alive to the fact that wars do not pay and especially do not pay those who have actually the fighting to do, they [now] insist on the settlements being made in a different fashion and at less expense. These mechanisms if intelligently and determinedly tried must succeed if the people of the world demand that they succeed. The only reason for their not succeeding would be found in the unwillingness of the governments of the communities of the world to allow them to succeed.

This then outlines the spiritual front in the war. It arises sharply out of the smoke of battle in the fierce "never again" that comes back from the trenches, the cry that has revealed the presence of a profounder reason for dying than any that had as yet appeared. Those that shout this back to us ask for no respite from death but that they shall not have died in vain. In the first place the war cannot be won on this front if the Central Powers win on the other fronts. Even the return to the status quo ante [the earlier social order] with the same monarchical institutions, the same military caste with its imperialistic commercial and industrial allies in control of the fortunes of Germany, and hence of her impotent ally Austria Hungary, would by definition and automatically shut and bolt the door in the face of this democratic peace. A democratic peace can be made if it can be guaranteed by the people of Germany, otherwise it is futile to consider it. Mr. Wilson has traced the outline of this spiritual front with the clearest approach to authority and finality. In [the] second place victory on this front demands a democratic sentiment at home that recognizes its world, its cosmical opportunity. Let us not labor under illusions and harbor vain hopes. It is only those who feel in their bodies and souls the price which whey are paying for this war who will enforce upon their governments the drawing up of a democratic peace, but they can do it. Nothing that the masses of the people demand can be refused by any government, even a government of the Central Powers if they will make their demand insistent. It has the authority, this democratic peace, of all the [world, especially the [Alli]ed powers, but the final authority[,] and the only authority that will be final[,] is that of public sentiment at home. For there are too many interests bound up with the profits, spiritual and material, of nationalistic victories, of a victory of revenge, and of a commercial victory, interests that are wont to be dominant in governments and which know who to formulate and enact to the advantage that looms up largest to them. The democratic peace will not be signed by the trained diplomat. The politician with his eye on the election issues to be wrung from the war, nor by the industrial and financial magnates. If it is signed it will be signed by those who feel with and speak for all of us in a common determination of "never again."

Now in the face of this situation, this demand for an intelligent public sentiment that will utilize this opportunity whose vast saecular importance is proportionate to the horror of the Valley of the Shadow of Death[5] out of which it arises, the socialist rises to remark that this is a capitalists' war. It is a lame and impotent conclusion, and to my mind it is a fatuous remark, for the war will belong to those who can find their issues there. Of course capital will seek profit out of the war. It seeks profit wherever it can find it. This is the necessity of its own existence, as no one preaches more insistently in season and out of season than the socialist. If out of the settlement of the war there can be made opportunities for higher rates of interests or fields for exclusive exploitation, the Marxian socialist at least is not the one among us to throw the first stone. Or let us turn to the parables. The capitalist sees in the war an opportunity to put his five talents out to the usurer and to get five other talents, while the socialist wraps his talent in a napkin rolling his eyes in pious disapproval of the profits which capital brings back from its quest.[6] Now there is an issue in the war for all of us—all of us is what the socialist calls the proletariat - which far outweighs the wealth of Ormus or of Ind[ia:]

Or where the East with richest hand

Pours on her kings barbaric pearl and gold[7]

and that issue is the conscious beginning of the world society whose tissues and organization can in their growth make war unnecessary as national law has taken the weapon out of the hand of the private citizen in the name of a principle of right. It is the internationalism which the socialist like the ancient prophets have hailed from the distance but which they refuse to recognize when it appears within us. If this is a capitalists' war it is because the people and their spokesmen refuse to enter into possession of it. And yet they have fought it and are fighting it, and no one can cast a shadow of doubt upon their title. They have bought it with their agony and blood. If the democratic peace is not signed it will be simply because they have allowed the decision on the spiritual front to go by default, though they conquer in France and Belgium, in Italy and the Balkans, in Palestine and Mesopotamia.

There are but two things necessary for this victory, a military decision against the powers of autocracy, and a clear consciousness that it is in the hands of the democracies of the world to set up and foster other methods of finding out a right in the contests of nations than that of fighting. It is this spiritual front that is in danger, in greater danger than the eastern or the southern fronts, for if this popular attitude toward the real issue of the war were once recognized all the world over, the people of the Central Powers would respond to it as deep answers to deep.

It is on this front that the socialist leaders should be found by profession. They proclaim themselves the spokesmen of the proletariat, of the people. If we may believe them they are the thinkers for the working classes, and here in America and over in Russia they are living proof of their calling by calling this a capitalist's war, and by preaching popular abdication of the spiritual direction of the war they are doing what they can to make it a war that the capitalist may exploit.

It may be that the socialist has so preached class consciousness and sought to arouse it by separating [the workers and owners where the [interes]ts of all come together they are un[willing] to see the identity of interest.

It is the irony of the situation that the socialists who have seen the society of nations approaching from afar, who have preached an economic otherworldliness, who alone have made of internationalism a cult, should take what steps they can to frustrate its arrival.

Of course I refer only [to] those socialists who have taken this attitude. There is a significant group among the American socialists who have seen otherwise and seen farther. In the Allied countries also the socialists and the working classes have had a far clearer vision of this spiritual front, and what are the issues that [are] bound up with it. It is in my view because American socialism has actually functioned far less as the mind of the workers than it has abroad that it is more bound by the academic tradition and less responsive to the actualities of the situation within which it is playing, I think, so poor a role.

I have called this a pragmatic criticism, because pragmatism finds all its values in the midst of the problem, and does not hesitate to recognize them because they appear in suspected garb. Especially does the pragmatist deny that the solution of our problems can be found in any vision given in the mount of prearranged order of society. He finds certain of the socialists still in the thrall of abstraction and the bonds of metaphysics, but let me say in conclusion that what has been said has been said with a profound realization of the past and future import of its economic gospel, even if it has been a gospel only according to Marx.

It is because I see the world stage cleared for the prophets of democracy and the socialists afraid to answer to the cue because the stage hands are not all unionized, that I am disappointed.[8]

READING 7B

WHAT ARE THE SPECIFIC INTERESTS OF LABOR IN THE WAR?[9]

In the first place the laboring men and women of the country have the same interest in the victory of our military forces which belongs to every citizen. Notwithstanding the conflicting interests and attitudes of different groups in the community all who are conscious members of the community will be exalted by the victory of the nation or humiliated by its defeat. There is a fundamental patriotism that arises simply because all are fighting the common enemy. Conflicting interests disappear for the time being and we all have the exhilaration of feeling as one in united hostility. This primitive response however ignores the actual cause for which we are fighting that should give reason to the primitive impulses that find their expression in the sentiment "My country right or wrong."[10]

The causes for which America fights in joining the Allies in their conflict with Germany has in one respect been unanimously formulated. The cause is with common consent that of democracy against autocracy. It has been the overturn of the Czardom in Russia that has given this formula its peculiar force. It has been subscribed to by all the Allies. It is not the only issue but it has become the dominant issue. By its definition many of the other issues have been taken up into that democracy. Insofar as democracy can be identified with government by the consent of the governed; insofar as nationalism is reduced to the right of separate races to govern themselves; insofar as the Allies demand that they shall treat with a German government that is responsible to the people of Germany instead of a monarch who rules in his own right through a bureaucracy independent of a representative assembly; insofar as the restitution of Belgium and Serbia, the future of Poland and of the Balkan states, and even of Alsace and Lorraine can be made corollaries of the principle of democracy; and finally insofar as the settlement of future international disputes through arbitration and adjudication, under the enforcement of a League to Enforce Peace, can be regarded as application of the democratic principle to the society of nations, insofar democracy has become the great issue for which the Allies are fighting. But it would be too vast a claim to reduce all of the issues involved in the war to that of democracy. There are going to be problems of organization of the state of Austria-Hungary, in the relations of the Balkan states to Europe and to each other, in the disposition of Polish territories and those of Alsace and Lorraine, and of subject races of Turkey, not to mention the conquered German colonies, and the conditions under which the countries of the world will be willing to do business with each other after the war which cannot be solved by the a priori application of an abstract principle of democracy. In any case predatory interests[—] political, narrowly national and financial,[—] represented by men who know exactly what they want will have powerful influence in the final settlement. The slogan of "war for democracy" will be used intelligently, and also with a sentimental vagueness that may be more dangerous than a frank support of autocracy, honestly, and with the intent to cover up designs that do not wish to be recognized.[11]

And yet there is a genuine democratic issue involved in this struggle, and it would be as stupid to fail to realize this, as it would be to be deceived by the dishonest use of the slogan.

The war was begun by the frankly imperialistic Central Powers for imperialistic ends. The immediate opposition they called out was that of the nations whose imperialistic interests were affected. Germany and Austria sought to get control of the Balkans and the way to the near East by the th[reat of] war. Russia's imperialistic interests in the Balkans called out Russia's support of Serbia and the following steps were the logical consequences of the premises. France supported her ally Russia. The opportunity was thus offered Germany of crushing the enemy at the door. Belgium could be seized as the shortest cut to Paris and essential to Germany's instantaneous victory and would leave Germany in possession of [the Belgium coast of Flanders] and Antwerp, the pistol at England's head. It has been France's heroic fight for her own territory and indeed for her own existence, and the response of the English people to the outrage upon Belgium that began the reshaping of the character of the struggle from an imperialistic war, in which the destinies of the peoples of the world were to be fixed by the exercise of efficient brute force and frightfulness, into a struggle in which the rights of peoples to govern themselves and determine their own foreign policies are seen to be pitted against the power of autocratic governments to control the lives of their own peoples as well as others in the interest of a militaristic and commercial imperialism. This changing character of the war has been heavily underscored by the overthrow of Russian autocracy and the entrance of America into the war.

This is the issue that is emerging. It is acclaimed by the Allies, especially in dealing with the new Russia and in opening the door to the entrance of the United States upon their side. It is, however, needless to say that in the counties of the Allies there are reactionary, militaristic, and financial forces which are quite out of sympathy with the growth of democratic power. It remains to be seen whether the democratic formulae are to be the genuine expressions of the issues of the war, or simply empty phrases that express no more than the original differences between the more liberal political institutions of England and France and those of Germany and Austria. That earlier difference did not obviate the war. Even the democracies of England and France had left the immediate control of foreign affairs to their foreign offices, and found themselves plunged into the world war as the result of steps for which the peoples themselves were not responsible. European labor parties have left their centralized governments largely untrammeled in their foreign doings, concentrating upon their efforts to win greater political power at home. That democracy, which is becoming the issue of the war, it is assumed will control foreign policies, will be non-militaristic in its attitude, and respectful of the rights of nationalities. The implication of the issue of democracy versus autocracy is that while democracy has not in the past undertaken the responsibilities of international life it cannot assume those responsibilities without changing that life profoundly, especially in the elimination of war. A League to Enforce Peace is regarded as the natural outcome of democratic influence upon international affairs.

It is very evident that back of these assumptions lies the belief that the mass of the people in all of the countries at war are hostile to war itself, and there can be no doubt that this is the attitude of the mass of the people in the United States, while the masses of the populations of the European warring communities show willingness and determination to fight only as they regard themselves as fighting in self-defense or against war itself. It is of course true that human nature in autocratic communities is like that to be found in democratic states, and if modern serious warfare could be the result of the mere ebullition of popular anger and racial antipathies, democracies might be more in danger of militancy than autocratic states. But modern warfare cannot be successfully waged without long preparation and long sustained drilling of the entire community to the undertaking. Intelligent warfare, if such is conceivable today, peremptorily demands the direction of an autocratic state. As, on the other hand, democracies cannot afford to conduct their foreign affairs with actual warfare or the threat of it, [democratic] intelligence demands the substitution of other means of asserting and defending their interests in international competitions than the challenge to national extinction. It is this issue that is taking shape, such an ending of the war that the threat of war need no longer be the ominous background of all dealings between nations; that democracy's most serious handicap, militarism may lose its categorical imperative; the imperative based on the assumption that [militarism] alone can insure national existence and give national self consciousness; that the real basis for the society of nations is the government by the people within the different nations.

We must however recognize that the import of democracy for the society of nations is not identical with the "international" of European socialism. This rests upon the common cause which socialism has assumed all laboring groups have against the capitalistic classes. In the first place this has completely broken down when put to the test of the war. In the second place socialist parties have been always organized and inspired by class conflicts. There are democratic governments. There are no socialistic governments. A world society arising out of the "international" of socialism would be a single society, if it could exist at all. National organization and consciousness would disappear. There would be nothing in the common interests of the different proletariats over against the capitalistic groups to differentiate one national community from another. Democratic governments arise out of the interaction of all groups and classes in the country. Through such governments the individuality of the whole community may express itself.

If, then, democracies are not militaristic and instinctively favor the development of institutions whose function it is to solve international difficulties without war, the defeat of autocracy in this war means that the world hopes that democratic nations can bring about a more perfect society of nations, in which each will retain its own individuality and make this the basis of its dealings with other's nations. To state the implication in another form, democracies instinctively favor a League to Enforce Peace and the development of the Hague tribunals, but they favor as instinctively the principle of nationality in the settlement of the problems out of which the war has arisen.

It is, however, true that the labor groups in all the nations at war have occupied a peculiar position such as they have never taken in any other war. In every nation it has been recognized that only as labor as a separate group has identified itself with the conduct of the war could the necessary solidarity of the nation for the war's successful prosecution be attained. It has also been felt that the laboring masses in taking this attitude have made a conscious sacrifice for the country which is greater than that of other classes. For in the actual fighting they bear the brunt of the loss and that without the prestige and heightened self consciousness of the officers and commanding staff. They also have in the past been the greatest sufferers from the depressions and losses that follow upon war, and they get no proportionate share of the profits which profiteering in war-times brings with it, while the autocratic tendencies which militarism always favors are regarded by labor as dangerous to its organizations and their achievements in increased wages and better labor conditions. These greater sacrifices of the masses of the community in previous wars have not had the character of a self conscious class attitude. The enlisted or drafted man has come as an individual to the colors. That the great majority of those in the ranks belonged to the labor group was not in evidence. It has remained for this war to recognize in some degree this situation. The recognition has been the result of labor's organization in times of peace. But back of this has lain the consciousness that recognition of labor has given the government a representation of the most important class in the community for the conduct of the war, and made possible an efficiency of industrial organization which has proved a [condition] sine qua non of efficient twentieth century fighting.

I have no wish to exaggerate the weight and importance of organized labor in the community. I know that organized labor is but a small fraction of all the labor in the community. I know that labor has had in general to depend upon the socialists for its leaders, outside of specific union contests. In most of the European countries the socialist parties have been the recognized spokesmen for labor. In England the national trades union body which speaks for labor is not a socialist party though the socialists among them are close to a majority. In the United States the [American] Federation of Labor of which Mr. [Samuel] Gompers is the head is a unionist body with but a small and uninfluential minority of socialists. But, in every country that organized body which could speak for labor has been accepted by the government as the spokesman for labor in the community at large. This more or less official representative of labor has had the recognized function of acting for labor in matters affecting laboring conditions during the war, the settlement of labor disputes, the suspension of union rules and like questions. It has had another function, in the European countries, that of discussing the attitude which the workers of the nation should take toward the war. The resolutions adopted at their congresses have been a certain barometer of the feeling of the great mass of the community, and the governments in these countries have made representatives of the labor parties members of their ministries. In this country the action of the administrative body of the American Federation of Labor, the presence of its president Samuel Gompers on the advisory committee at Washington, the appointment of [Alfred] Barnes on the Central Industrial Committee[12], and the presence of representatives of organized labor on the state and city war councils have been the analogous steps. But they have not identified the labor organizations and those whom they represent with the government in its war undertaking to any such extent, as the action of the foreign labor bodies has identified the laboring masses with the action of their governments.

This is due in part to the fact that labor has had up to the present no regular political representation either in Congress or in the Assemblies of the different states. This attitude of keeping out of the party politics of the country has been the definite policy of our labor bodies, and[,] as has been above indicated[,] the socialists have not played either in the councils of the labor organizations or in politics any decisive part in the program of labor activities. It is not therefore natural for the representatives of organized labor in the country at present to undertake to play a considerable part in the governmental activities of the war. It would have been contrary to their traditions, and it would have placed upon the labor leaders and those whom they led a responsibility such as they had not assumed before. Their organization has not been fitted to taking or carrying such responsibility. While therefore the action of administrative bodies in labor circles has greatly reduced the difficulties which would otherwise have arisen in the industrial situation caused by our entering the war, and while the patriotic attitude of labor leaders has greatly steadied the country in these days, labor has not been in a position to influence the policies of the government, nor to present the position of labor in Congress.

The other circumstance which has held the representatives of organized labor back from taking more decisive steps in identifying labor with the government and its polices has been, undoubtedly, the large number of foreign born in the ranks of labor, a very large group of whom are if not sympathetic with the Central Powers at least [are] not interested in the United States entering war against them on the side of the Allies. This situation makes it difficult for the labor party to take a responsible direction of the sentiment and opinion which they stand for in the country. An unquestioned sentiment and opinion is either not there or it is inarticulate, and the labor organization with its traditions clustered so closely about the narrow and immediate interests of the labor unions, has neither the attitude nor the mechanism for making sentiment [or] opinion among the masses of the community; those masses, nevertheless[,] which labor leaders and officials in responsible positions at Washington and elsewhere are supposed to represent. These leaders and officials seem hardly to welcome the responsibility which has been thrust upon them. However, one must recognize that an attempt to seize this opportunity and formulate and give vigorous expression to the sentiment of the large portion of the community, for whom they are called upon to speak and act, would be fraught with danger to their positions and perhaps to the interests they legitimately feel that they have in their keeping. And yet the position which representatives of labor take on the boards and councils which are assisting in organizing the country for war is one which carries with it both opportunity and responsibility. The larger part of the membership in these boards and councils is necessarily from among the business managers of the great industries, for the purpose of these councils is in great measure the organization of industry and commerce, as it faces the country's supreme needs in the Great War. Labor is represented because labor is so essential a part of the process of industry and commerce that it must be recognized in any undertaking to which these boards and councils put their hands. The problems which these labor representatives are dealing with and with which they will have to deal in the future are not simply those of the most effective organization of the machinery of industry and commerce. The problems are bound up with the most serious questions in a democratic community. The situation in our industrial democracy is such that the business manager and the workmen are parties in opposition. The history of industry in England during the war period has shown in great detail that the issues between the employers and the employed in the country's industry have not been kept in abeyance and, taking human nature as it is, are not likely to be. The stronger position of business as compared with that of labor appears under the autocratic form of war government as it does in times of peace, and many of the real issues of democracy at home, the democracy which we are fighting for abroad, assert themselves and have to be met.

When these issues arise the responsibility of the labor representatives becomes very great. It will be none the less because into these labor troubles will be injected the disaffection of great bodies of laborers with foreign sympathies. The labor representatives of labor will stand alone, probably without the support which they can command under normal conditions from the community at large. It will be easy to represent the laborer as unpatriotic in this [demand], merely because [this demand] interferes with the industry so essential for the conduct of the war, and to this will be added the suspicion that disaffection lies behind the contest over wages and labor conditions. These boards do not have in their membership the representatives of intellectual and liberal minded group[s] that mediate between autocratic business and militant labor. If then these labor representatives, finding themselves in an actual conflict and overruled, undertake to insist on what they consider labor's legitimate interests, they may be able to do this only by stopping the wheels of industry. They may have to make serious trouble to be heard.

Not only will their responsibility be great. Their opportunity will be equally great. In all the European countries[,] the three years of the war have given the labor group a recognized position in the conduct of the country. It is to no purpose to speculate as to the form that this added power will take after the war. There is however no question that the added power is there. In these countries there are labor parties in politics and they will be able to make use of the position of added power which the war has given them. The war offers the American labor organizations the opportunity for such a consolidation and orientation with reference to politics that they can commence to carry their issues over from the field of industrial struggle into politics where under our liberal institutions they belong.

The term ["]industrial democracy["] is a misnomer. Liberal institutions have placed so-called political issues within democratic control. In a certain sense the revolution which overthrew dynastic governments at the end of the eighteenth and beginning of the nineteenth centuries has been incorporated into modern representative governments. Under liberal governments the people are at liberty [at] any time by political means and by regular procedure to change the form of government and mold their institutions to meet the wishes of the community. Government by the will of the people means that orderly revolution is a part of the institution of the government. Problems and conflicts provoked by governmental methods, national or local, are all in politics and may be settled directly or indirectly by the will of the people through representative institutions. This is true only in a very limited degree of industrial struggles. On the contrary it has remained true that both the management of business and organized labor have seemingly preferred to fight out their battles in a kind of border warfare, on the edges of the field of democratic institutions. Both parties get into politics to keep the other from using the legislatures, the courts, the sheriffs, and the police on one side or the other of their [perspectives] in their lock-outs and strikes.

From the business man's point of view governmental regulation of business in a democratic community will destroy efficient management and loot business itself in a shortsighted effort to improve the condition of the laborer. From the standpoint of organized labor governmental regulation will fall under the control of the financial interests and deprive the laborers of the only weapon in which they have confidence — the strike. Thus in modern industry and commerce we have the autocracy of business management, checked by a somewhat restricted revolution, in other words by the strike and the lock-out. The natural results are extreme developments, on the one hand organized business undertaking to crush out all organization of labor, on the other [hand] the I.W.W. s[13] or syndicalists maintaining continued guerrilla warfare against the business within which they are employed. There is evidently no solution of this situation except by the steady increase of democratic governmental control in industry which is already being undertaken in a hesitating manner.

In a democracy the essential and unavoidable issues that arise between groups and individuals must become political questions. The unwillingness on the part of the European and American communities with popular governments to frankly accept this challenge of the industrial order has placed them in the embarrassing position of having to grudgingly [and] halfheartedly undertake the program of labor legislation which autocratic Germany initiated. Germany's militaristic government standing above both business management and organized, [and] class-conscious labor could accept and put into operation just such portions of the program of labor as it chose. And the democratic countries of the Western world have been forced to confess that an autocracy has dealt more intelligently than they with the issues which touch most closely the masses of the people. However these democratic communities have traveled many leagues since the beginning of the war. They have demonstrated capacity for governmental control and efficient management in countries with popular governments and the possibility of dealing with extraordinary problems in what has been regarded as an exceptional procedure. Institutions after the war will become, as never before, tools for dealing with social problems, gradually ceasing to be fixed structures which serve as protections for entrenched interests, whether those of capital or labor.

[It is] not likely that these changes will take place suddenly. Probably there will be no revolution in [our] social order, but the passage of industrial problems into the field of politics is going to be rapid as compared with the tardy progress in our so-called industrial democracies in the past, and labor cannot afford to [have] the direction given nor the pace set by business management alone. If organization and leadership among the workers of the nation is to be intelligent and effective it must be ready to get effectively into politics.

It is this situation with its probable development that emphasizes and interprets the interests of labor in the war and its outcome.

The immediate and central interest of labor in the war is that which is becoming more articulate all the world over, that this war shall be [the] last war. Either through the democratization of the only two powerful autocracies still left, or through general disarmament and a League to Enforce Peace, together with the development of the Hague international tribunals and arbitration treaties, militaristic foreign policies with the preparation and drilling of the nations for their support shall disappear.

There can [be] no other issues that is of so much importance to labor as that of the disappearance of militarism, for the interest of labor is in the awakening determination of society that all of its citizens shall have the economic means for normal physical and social life, in bringing social control to bear upon problems of municipal and rural life[;] in a word[,] in the working out of the social problem. As I have already indicated more of the program of social reform has been carried out in autocratic Germany than in countries with popular governments. Nor is this entirely without parallel in other countries. There has arisen in England a new Toryism which has distinguished itself from that of the reactionary conservatives by accepting the social problem, while it has asserted that only a state directed by a dominating upper class could solve it. In the gospel of efficiency in America there is the same suggestion that only intelligent direction from trained intellects above is necessary to the solution of social problems. In certain circles of socialists the same aristocratic dogma has appeared in the doctrine of the government by experts.

It has remained for this war to lift the fundamental fallacy in these doctrines and attitudes into the unquestionable light of day. The fallacy is the old one that out of mere interest in good government an autocratic power above can govern in the interest of all. On the contrary the power, the prestige, and wealth of the upper caste will inevitably subordinate to themselves the good of the whole community. The masses of Germany as well as those of the other European communities have paid and are paying with their blood for the social program of labor insurance[:] industrial, educational, and municipal reform which autocracy through its bureaucratic government has carried out in Germany. Now that we realize that no efficiency in governing even in the field of labor and social reform can justify a government standing on a militaristic foundation[,] the last intelligible ground for preserving war as the means of settling international differences disappears.

But if other means of solving international problems are perfected and the state can no longer insist that preparedness to fight for its own preservation is the first duty of the community, the social reforms and reconstructions which are of paramount importance to labor will beyond doubt become the dominant issues. Those groups and interests in the community, which are either hostile to such a program or are fearful of democracy's ability to deal with it, will be unwilling to accept the conclusion that the community must not be eternally ready to fight, that means of international adjudication and Leagues to Enforce Peace can relegate the military function of the government and the will to power to a place subordinate to the legislative undertaking to adjust the structure of society so as to meet the immediate needs of the community. Those interests which are entrenched will seek to preserve the status quo and push to the front military preparation as of supreme importance to the community. Through various types of propaganda they will endeavor to keep the country in the attitude of anticipating and fearing war, and especially they will insist that changes which tend to deprive business management of its autocratic power over labor and those which recognize the social necessity of better wages, labor, housing, educational, and recreational conditions of the works and their families will tend to destroy the authority of government and break down the morale of the rank and file of those who are to be the fighters of the nation. They will magnify causes of difference with other peoples and governments and forms of foreign policy which are contentious and seek to increase the military activity of the government in every manner so as to secure the means of maintaining the fixed order against programs of reform which they consider revolutionary.

Labor is then supremely interested in bringing the war to an end which through a League to Enforce Peace, through the development of adjudication of international differences, — through the recognition of the right of the governed to determine their own government, the principle of nationality, through the control of foreign policy by the representatives of the people — the principle of the parliamentary responsibility of those powers that determine peace and war, will render war unnecessary and ultimately impossible. They are interested as all the world is interested in ridding the world of the scourge of war, but they are very especially interested in reducing to their lowest terms militaristic tendencies which will be in competition with the programs of social betterment through governmental control in industry. There is no group in the community to which the disappearance of war as a recognized method of settling international disputes can be of so much importance as to labor. It is this interest which must add still more determination to their support of the war against the Central Powers. For every month of the war has served to bring more and more clearly to light the inevitably military foundations of their present governments. If it ever has been in doubt that a government not responsible to its people can exist only by the organization and magnification of the irresponsible force upon which it stands, that doubt is set at rest by this conflict. What is equally evident is that such a mobilizing of the military force of the nation at the command of its monarch is possible only if the nation regards itself as in constant danger of attack by its neighbors. To abolish war as a necessary condition of national safety is by the same stroke to abolish autocracy. War is essential to the existence of autocracy. It is unnecessary in a democratic world. As autocracy can live only by wars and the threat of war, there can be no peace even for non-militaristic nations until governments that are not responsible to the people have given way to popular governments.

The second issue which labor has in the war is the freedom to work out in a democratic manner, that is by political methods, the problems which our industrial life has forced upon us. The Western world will never have the freedom of institutions, nor the freedom of mind, necessary to deal fearlessly and intelligently with the conditions that produce human misery, and ignorance, and disease, and crime while our attention is held by the fear of hostile neighbors and that preparation for fighting which abstracts from immediate social conditions in concentration upon the external enemy. Perhaps the most important change of attitude that our modern attack upon social problem demands is that involved in looking upon government not primarily as the expression of the force of the community[,] but as the expression of its organized intelligence in meeting and overcoming the difficulties and solving the problem which common life brings with it. The power of the community is the servant of its intelligence and not its master.

It is this change of attitude which the present ruling caste in Germany can never accept. It will be willing to be in many respect an intelligent ruler of the people, as was its prototype Frederick the Great,[14] but only for the purposes of its own determination, and with the guarantee of the force of the community centered in its monarch and his government; a guarantee which can only be obtained in the martialling of the nation against possible as well as actual enemies. Eventually there can be no peace between autocracy and democracy. Labor should be willing to fight this war to the finish. But if labor demands the extreme sacrifice in fighting this war for democracy, it should demand it only upon the condition that the peace is to be one which rests upon no imperialistic aims or presuppositions. The power of autocracy must be broken either by the democratization of Germany or thoroughgoing disarmament with a League to Enforce Peace. Whatever changes are to be made in the map of Europe must be made upon the principle of nationality, that is government with the consent of the governed.

These are issues which are of critical importance and of immense importance to the workers of America, but that they should take them up as their issues is an undertaking that is dependent upon their very definitely realizing them as labor issues, which they should fight for not only as American citizens but as a group that have grave political stakes in our modern democracy. It would mean a change of attitude of labor toward the war.

At present labor is loyal so far as it has given organized expression to its sentiments. Its great undertaking however is to hold in check, as far as possible, strikes and other labor disturbances which would interfere with the effective conduct of the war. Beyond this most considerable undertaking the administration of the [American] Federation of Labor only calls upon its members to be loyal citizens. It has not undertaken to present the issues of the war as having a peculiar importance to the workers of the nation. As an organization its attitude toward these issues is then negative. Its present organization could not probably take any other attitude without quite contradicting its own traditions. While an active movement in labor circles to espouse the issues of democracy in the war, because of their peculiar import to labor itself, could arise within the same group as that of the [American] Federation of Labor[,] it would have to have a different inspiration and a different leadership. If such a movement were effective and widespread it could not find its organization nor its leadership among the socialists, because they are a minority and a hostile minority in the labor group and because the minority of the socialist leader[s] have chosen to see in the war only a capitalists' undertaking not an opportunity for democracy. Furthermore the interest behind such a labor movement should be in the American democracy which does not contemplate a society dominated by a single class, as do socialist programs especially in America.

It is very doubtful whether such a movement is possible. But there is no doubt of the immense value it would be to the country now and after the war and of the critical importance it would have for the labor itself. The momentum it would get in fighting vigorously for the war and its proper conclusion would carry it over after the war into a labor party that could bring industrial issues into politics. The situation presents a great opportunity.

READING 7C

THE FAILURE OF LIBERAL INSTITUTIONS IN ENGLAND AND AMERICA[15]

In the face of the problem of our modern industrial society, it is but just to recognize that the liberal institutions of England and America failed quite definitely to fulfill the function which they had exercised when the problem of political control emerged. Political control passed from the hands of privileged classes through representative institutions in the direction of which popular vote could register the actual political attitudes and wills of a majority of individuals in the community. However inadequate the practice of this popular control might be in comparison with the perfection of its theory; however great the preponderance of the upper-class minorities with their prestige of traditional ideals of and governmental offices with their old time authorities never completely divorced from the classes to which in England[,] at least through education and family tradition[,] they have still naturally fallen, however easy it has been for astute politicians to keep the control of popular institutions themselves in the hands of the industrial and commercial interests that have employed them[—], still the political machinery remains capable of popular control[.]

When ideas have formulated themselves in the mind of the people and have become articulate[,] these liberal institutions have at once made the people sovereign. The final achievement of the English revolutions of the seventeenth and eighteenth centuries was to embody the mechanism of these revolutions in the structure of government. The government in power must at the behest of people step down and give place to such a government as can obtain the suffrages of a majority of the electors. As long as the traditions of the use of this electoral machinery remains intact in the habits of the people[,] critical social problems will receive their immediate solutions at the ballot box and not at the barricade.

A problem of like social dimensions has arisen in industry. Control of the economic returns to the laborer in industry and of the conditions under which he works remains still without institutional recourse to the people [and remains] in the hands of the owners and their managers of the industry. When the vast majority of those engaged in industry have refused to accept the direction of the managers and owners of the industries their recourse has been to revolution[.] Not the revolution which has undertaken a complete political reconstruction, but the forcible resistance to the authorities in the business and even attack upon them in the exercise of their managerial powers.

Notes

1.   Box 2, folder 20, Mead Addenda.

2. See chapter 5 and readings 5A and 5B here.
3. Henry Temple, 3rd Viscount Palmerston (1784-1865) was Prime Minister of England twice during the mid-nineteenth century. In 1850 he argued that a British subject should be defended by the British government anywhere in the world.
4. Herbert Henry Asquith (1852-1928) was England's Prime Minister who brought his country into the fighting after Germany invaded Belgium. His disastrous leadership during the war led to his resignation in 1916.
5. This phrase, "the Shadow of Death" comes from Psalm Twenty-three, King James Bible.
6. "The Parable of the Talents" is found in St. Matthew 25, 14-30. *Holy Bible*. King James Version, 2000.
7. John Milton (1608-1674), in *Paradise Lost, Book II*, line 1.
8. Traces of a lightly penciled phrase remain but are now illegible.
9. Box 2, folder 9, Mead Addendum.
10. "My country right or wrong" is a phrase used by several writers and has entered the general stock of knowledge instead of being recognized as belonging to one author.
11. Addams (1915/2003, 83-91) sharply criticized the mindlessness of war slogans and their use to stop criticism and reflection by everyday citizens.
12. Alfred Barnes was a Fabian socialist in England who wrote a few, now-obscure, pamphlets.
13. The International Workers of the World, or Wobblies, are radical trade unionists. They were founded in 1905 and follow a Marxist model of a world-wide proletariat.
14. Frederick II of Prussia, known as Frederick the Great, was part of the Hohenzollern dynasty. He ruled Prussia from 1740 to 1786 and became the King of Prussia in 1772. He led a series of wars against German states, Austria, and parts of Poland. He modernized the military and civil affairs. A gifted linguist, he enjoyed architecture, music, and other arts.
15. Box 2, file 28, Mead Papers.

8

Unpublished Lectures during War-Time: Citizenship, the Self, Peace, and War

> *"It is not necessary to review the gradual increase and spread of the functions of government, its inevitable interference with the inhumanities of the factory system, its unwilling shouldering of the cost and direction of the education of the children of the community, its less grudging assumption of the task of encouraging and housing and displaying of the national art, its spasmodic undertaking under popular pressure of some degree of control over corporate business and transportation, its slow recognition of the necessity of public control of health conditions and recreation. It has been the spirit in which these innovations have been made that is of especial importance. They have been made always as concessions, without frank recognition of their propriety" (see reading 8D here).*

The connection of the individual to the state was a vital issue to Mead. War required numerous sacrifices and only a strong bond between the self and the state made such sacrifices logical, necessary, and voluntary by the individual. James and Mead both celebrated the war virtues generating such emotions and loyalties, but they also acknowledged that creating and maintaining such social objects were fraught with problems. Predictably, Mead turned to democracy as integral to the formation of the co-operative unity between the self and the nation in America.

Mead on Citizenship

Mead raised the central question: "How Can a Sense of Citizenship Be Secured? (see reading 8A here) because he argued that citizenship is below awareness in times of peace. Individual differences are stressed in peacetime, but war-time emphasized commonality, and not differences. Citizenship became a primary identification during these extraordinary situations, and the self changed its relationship to the state accordingly. He, thereby, defined citizenship as the central mechanism connecting the self and the state:

> Being a citizen lies back of all living in the community, but it stands for the group of habitual processes which are so fundamental and universal and continuously in operation that in times of peace one may be unaware of them. It is the unconscious foundation for all the negations of each other's ends and ideas which produces the diversities of individuals in the social whole.

Citizenship is part of everyday life and does not call out conscious reflection during peace. During war, it becomes conscious and creates a society composed of selves who willingly sacrifice everything to re-establish a peaceful society.

Mead explicitly discussed the varying relation between the self and institutions as a function of war. The feeling of being part of a nation-state — or the organization of what he later called "the generalized other" (Mead 1934) — took on new arrangements:

> The actual social whole to which the individual belongs and which is responsible for his self consciousness varies enormously. In a professional army it may be the army itself. For the religious recluse the community that gives him his awareness of himself may be spiritual figures that inhabit the mind. One's country may be the republic of letters. It may be one's family or an uncertain group in the underworld.

A "fighting citizen" depended on an attitude that accepted state violence.

Mead on the Definite Attitude of Fighting during War-time

Once America made the declaration of war, a "Completely Definite Attitude of a Fighting Power at War" emerged. This new attitude involved war budgets, a new role for the President, the draft, a military build-up including forming an army of over a million soldiers to send into combat in Europe, new experts on war, and new alliances with other nation states. Mead mentions the formation of numerous committees, many headed by civilians like himself, who aided in the war effort at home through lectures, money, enthusiasm, and the promotion of unquestioning loyalty to the war effort. These behaviors led to the emergence of a "completely definite attitude" toward the sacrifices demanded by the state (See reading 8B). Mead describes this situation, one that applies to himself, as follows:

> There is abroad the sense of a people's getting ready, the evidences of multiple activities and responses which reinforce each other and under favoring conditions should lead to effective and powerful organization. Do we see a "nation, rousing herself like a strong man after sleep, and shaking her invincible locks"?[1] There is the favorable evidence of wide-spread interest.

The new attitude of war-time obviously contradicted Addams' "newer ideals of peace" that resisted the emergence of the new belligerent relation between the self and people of other nations.

Mead on the Moral Psychology of War

The just state demanded moral conduct during national conflicts, which Mead discussed in "Psychology and the Moral Conduct of War" (see reading 8C). Fighting a war required more than "definite attitudes," it needed new behaviors. Although violence might be required of a soldier, it was specific, limited, and done with a spirit of justice.

Mead on the Rising Tide of Nationalism

Nations and identification with them were changing around the world. This global movement mitigated against an international labor movement, as Mead repeatedly argued. "The Rising Tide of Nationalism" (see reading 8D) called out new attitudes, communities, institutions, and relations between the self and a specific state. International institutions of law and control over conflict were needed to respond to this new world order. War was a violent attempt to dominate and control these new social structures and behaviors. Preventing inter-state violence needed to be a duty of a co-operative global understanding. Increasing nationalism made the defense of new states necessary and recognition of the right for peoples to develop their own nations was also necessary.

Many points raised in this essay compare with those discussed in his Movements of Thought in the Nineteenth Century (1936). This posthumous book emerged from a course of this title which he taught many times over a period of years. This essay on nationalism is an important addition to this aspect of his social thought. Mead developed an international "multi-cultural" argument, here, an understanding of the need for "multi-national" recognition supported by new legal, political institutions. The World Court, the League of Nations, and new attitudes opposed to militarism (discussed in the next reading) were specific steps to protecting new nations from aggressive older ones with more power.

Mead's Defense of War and Its Association with a Changing Attitude toward Militarism

"The Changing Attitude Toward Militarism" (reading 8E) is a handwritten essay with some unclear handwriting in spots. This hastily written and unpolished essay is worth salvaging, nonetheless, because Mead wrote about new ideas, sometimes in quite surprising ways, in this essay (I indicate my best guess about a word or phrase with brackets).

Always opposed to the build-up of armaments, he hoped that his attitude would become more popular after the war. He predicted that "The changes will come piecemeal, in the gradual determination of the arbitration treaties, and the power of Hague tribunals." The state, Mead wrote, was identified with the sum of the values of society that men believe to be true. States, like individuals, emerged from each other and interacted. The state can experience a revolution but order will be restored because the state was a "resistant institution." A new self would emerge from this new attitude shared by the post-war citizen.

Conclusion

Citizenship was called out in war-time to create a unifying relationship between the individuals and the wider society. The self and the generalized other changed. Mead continued his uncritical view of American politics, policies, and class relations in these essays and justified the world-wide violence. He suspended but did not abandon his prewar international pacifism.

He saw new institutions emerging as a result of WWI: more democratic states, especially the weakening of the military and aristocracy in the nations of the Central Powers; a new global attitude of acceptance of new nation-states and their rights to govern; the end of the definite attitudes of obedience needed for a nation at war; and the spread of new ideals and moral conducts called out by the new citizens and new world order. All of his reasons for supporting the global conflict depended on a just peace, the spread of democracy, and world-wide co-operation. He did not foresee the vindictive Treaty of Versailles, the rejection of Wilson's Fourteen Points and the League of Nations by the U.S. Congress, and the ultimate revelation of America's belligerence toward the Central Powers before Americans declared war.

During WWI Mead had a "completely definite attitude" toward the fighting. After the war, his war-time ideas and attitudes were shattered, but generally he neither analyzed nor corrected them.

READING 8A

HOW CAN A SENSE OF CITENSHIP BE SECURED?[2]

In time of war the spiritual experience of the most profound importance is the emotional realization of the supreme value of citizenship in the nation to which one belongs. The psychology of this experience is not hard [to] discover. Unification of all parties in the community brings with it the suppression of all the differences which call for the continual social readjustments that make up the life of the community. The every-day[,] tangible and superficial ends of existence are for the time being forgotten, and the consciousness of everyone finds but one problem, the mutually exclusive alternative either the continued life of the society that is responsible for his own existence, or the particular sacrifice which he is asked to make. The fact that the enemy directs his attack against the life of the community throws up into consciousness the fundamental processes of being a citizen while the unification of all individuals abstracts from all those specific ends which differentiates one individual from another. Being a citizen lies back of all living in the community, but it stands for the group of habitual processes which are so fundamental and universal and continuously in operation that in times of peace one may be unaware of them. It is the unconscious foundation for all the negations of each other's ends and ideas which produces the diversities of individuals in the social whole.

In times of peace[—] just because each is occupied in expressing himself and being himself in contradiction from others[—] he cannot [make his citizenship conscious] unless he undertakes to reconstruct society[. It may] very well be that which he [has] in common with everyone else, [being] a citizen of the community and nothing more. Nor does his consciousness of his rights and privileges as a citizen when he appeals to them in support of his cause against that of others, in the courts of law or in the primaries or the election of candidates of his party, emphasize the worth of citizenship except by implication. The immediate value he has in mind is of his cause or measure of interest which he maintains [that] expresses this citizenship while the opposing cause or measure or interest would express it not at all or but inadequately in comparison with his own. Thus the conflict of values is between relative and competing forms of citizenship and does not bring to consciousness the value of citizenship itself. It seems to require a situation in which there arises simply the alternatives of the continued existence of the community, or the life and comfort of the individual with the community wiped out. When the English shopkeeper objects to the officer who would enroll [enlist] him [in the military], that his shop with its business would go to pieces if he left it, the reply is, what is the good of the shop if the Germans conquer? The unendurableness of living under such conditions overbalances the individual loss, probable suffering and even death. With the great majority of people there is little hesitancy in responding to this alternative[,] if the two alternatives can be made to appear the only ones and mutually exclusive. Human nature protects itself against this disjunctive judgment by refusing to accept it. The citizen refuses to believe either that the society is in reality in serious danger, or that his preference of his own comfort and life would destroy the community so far as he is concerned, i.e. would deprive him of citizenship and the social self that is dependent upon this fellowship.

When the disjunction has been successfully constructed[,] the value to the individual of his relationship to the community is brought finally into consciousness in competition with any other values that may arise in competition. It is so brought into consciousness by the threat of its annihilation. Either he may continue to live while the community in which alone he desires to live is destroyed or he may continue to live and the community also may survive but he is physically or spiritually cast out of it. In either case the emotional value of his citizenship does come to consciousness. When the disjunction has been once successfully constructed there is no doubt as to the outcome of the evaluation.

It is a contradiction in terms to assume that a social being can will to destroy the ground upon which alone he can rest his existence. It is true that physical impulses which are not under the control of the social self may make of the soldier at the moment of peril a so-called coward who winces before the physical ordeal, but the number of such cowards is but an insignificant percentage of those who make up the community. Panics and defeats are generally social and not physical phenomena. The lack of the specific training which welds the units of the army together, the absence of the clearly cut alternatives in the minds of the people, the lack of confidence in the leadership of nations and armies, such are the causes of the breakdown of morale and these are social causes. The most favorable situation for the construction of the alternative is found in a war of defense, and it is the function of statesmanship in any community which is approaching the probability of war, to impress upon the people that they are face to face with enemies who are seeking to destroy the nation.

The actual social whole to which the individual belongs and which is responsible for his self consciousness varies enormously. In a professional army it may be the army itself. For the religious recluse the community that gives him his awareness of himself may be spiritual figures that inhabit the mind. One's country may be the republic of letters. It may be one's family or an uncertain group in the underworld. If the logic of the social situation can only be used there is some community of which every social being is ready to die, if only the alternative can be so shaped that he realizes it; that that is in danger without which continued life is psychologically impossible for him.

While such an experience brings to emotional realization the import of the group to which we belong, it is accomplished at inevitable loss. The loss is due to the submerging of values in which the individual asserts himself over against the other members of the society. Striking illustrations of this tendency of the mobilizing of the minds of the community for war can be found in the extreme anxiety of organized labor in England and of the Home Rulers in Ireland because of the peremptory shelving of the causes for which they had been [fighting]. Hours of labor that are recognized as destructive to the health of the laborer are accepted. Children are taken out of school so early and allowed to work so long that the effect must be to stunt their growth. Women undertake tasks which legislation and court decrees had forbidden in times of peace. Social propaganda suddenly lapses. To the logic of this tendency we cannot take exception. An interest that can demand the sacrifice of the best blood of the country on the field of battle can surely demand sacrifices of the mobilized arm of industry at home that is as essential to the defense of the country as is the devotion of soldiers on the battle field. The more serious injury appears in the attitude of mind which persists in the community after the war. In a period of great emotional stress these values have been sacrificed for the supreme social value. They stand as relatively unimportant. They have been discarded as spiritual impedimenta, thrown away to save the fundamentals. It may take the life of [a] generation to bring people to the recognition of the fact that the fundamentals are after all only valuable as the foundation for the other values which for the time being have been forgotten in the life and death struggle to save the foundations. It is the sacrifice of the cargo to save the ship, and yet the end and purpose of ships is to carry cargos. It required twenty five years to distract the political attention of America from the fact that the union had been saved by the Republican Party and direct it to the social interests for which alone the union can exist. And during that period this absorption of political sentiment in an issue that was already passed [emancipation of slaves], left corruption free to flourish in all corners of [the] republic.

The welding of a united Germany through blood and iron made militarism such a symbol of unity that Germany has been unable to think nationally, except in terms of a Kriegsherr [war gentleman or warlord,] a Schwertadel [aristocracy] and a world armed against her. She conceives of her application of trained intelligence to social problems which has been made possible in no small part through the detachment of her militaristic government, as a *Kultur* [culture] which can conceivably be spread through the world by force of arms. It has remained for Germany to conceive of that most international of all things — civilization as a national achievement and possession, to be propagated by the sword. Thus in the evaluation of citizenship in time of war we are called upon to sacrifice for it just that which to a large degree gives it its value. And this is not simply the paradox of giving up one's life for what can be only enjoyed through life. In the period of preparation for war as well as after war[,] we are forced constantly to give a supreme value to military interests and operation because in theory they protect the fundamentals of the state. The conclusion which military classes and interests and those dependent upon them seek to draw from this is that, these fundamentals being counted as more valuable than all the rest, the same supreme value must be accorded to them when they come into conflict with the constructive activities of the community.

It is this situation which presents a challenge to [the] psychological doctrine of social values. Is it possible to bring to consciousness the value of one's relationship to the whole community in these constructive activities of daily life, which presuppose it, while they seem to ignore it[?]; or is it only the by sacrificing them all for community that we can reach an emotional sense of the worth of the society to which we belong[?] Must we lose our lives to save them?

Psychologically the condition for the solution of the problem is the production of a situation that will bring the community in its relation to ourselves into the field of awareness and interest, in some other fashion than through the danger of losing it. The theoretical statement of the solution of the problem is not difficult. If we conceive that one course of action conserves the social structure while another threatens it, that one program means life and that more abundantly while another restricts and finally quenches the life of society, in these competing hypotheses for the solution of social problems the value of the life to be saved and enlarged should appear over against the program which promises to sacrifice it. In a word it seems possible that one should appreciate the value of fundamental social relations in their fullest realization especially when contrasted with a scheme of conduct which will fail of this realization. And yet this is exactly what is lacking in our response to reform measures and movements. The candidates who claims that his program will save the country is met with a shrug of the shoulders or a contemptuous smile. The reformer's vision of a reorganized society is the surest indication to the public mind that the reformer is an unpractical dreamer. I am not referring to the lack of proportion between a plan of action and the accomplishment which the program-maker promises, nor to the visionary character of social utopias, but to the suspicion we feel at once of an undertaking which is supported by an emotional appeal to the results which it is to obtain. The orator or reformer who presents a picture of happiness in any other terms than those of the alleviation of immediate misery is classed as a sentimentalist, and even the picture of misery, may fall into the same category. In the pulpit it is legitimate to state in emotional terms the ends of human conduct apart from any statement of the definite means by which these may be obtained — except in a New Jerusalem — while the social scientist must formulate his ends largely in terms of fixed institutions and their stereotyped formulations of the ends of social life.

Universal education, equal justice, order, popular government must [be established] and [fulfill] the rest of the ideals of liberalism. And the exceptions prove the rule. Our experimental schools have in some degree made it possible to state the ends of education in the immediate emotional interests of the child. The Junior George Republics[3] and the Juvenile Courts[4] deliberately undertake to state in terms of affective experience the results of governmental procedure and judicial control. This is confessedly easier in the problems of childhood than in those of the adult. But the initiative and referendum are bungling methods of asking the individual voter to present to himself how he enjoys the prospect of this measure or that. The domestic relations courts and the pathological clinics and parole systems in the adult courts are extensions of the method of the Juvenile Court of looking at its problems in terms of immediate human situations which means that we are willing to regard our emotional responses to the social problem and to the measure suggested for their solution as permissible in the scientific procedure.

This seems at least to be the most striking difference between the older institutional procedure and that of the Juvenile Court. In the former the actual human situation with its evaluations must be forced into the formalized evaluations of the institution. What is right or wrong, what good or bad is determined by the standards and rules already determined. Conflict between such judgments and the attitude of the individual gives rise to the pathos of the Greek tragedy, the resignation of the religious devotee in the presence of suffering which he regards as the chastisement of a divine hand, the sense of an abstract majesty of law, or the revolt of the religious or political revisionist, and anarchist. These emotional states may serve thus for the statement of another individual problem, but not for the statement of the problem with which the institution deals. The statement of this problem is fixed in advance by the norms of the institution. The norms of the institution are not flexible[,] provisional means of bringing out the social problem as it appears in the individual's experience. Nor can the result of the operation of the judicial procedure be tested by the actual effect which it will have in the individual's experience. Quite the opposite attitude belongs to the Juvenile Court[.] Sympathetic interrogation reconstructs as far as possible the actual situation, its motives, its values, its purposes. It becomes a tacit assumption of the procedure in this court that the statement of the court will be on all fours with the estimates and standards of the child, and the test that is most insistently applied to the final decision is that it will bring about the most satisfactory result in the immediate relations of the child to [the] community that surrounds him.

In the habitual social life of the community where the fundamental relations are not called in question, they are, as was remarked earlier, practically below the level of consciousness, and where they are thrown up into consciousness by conflict between the interests of the individual and the formulated interests of the whole group the situation is not favorable for the emotional appreciation on the part of the individual of his citizenship in the community. Only insofar as in the attitude of contrition he accepts the estimate of the community upon his conduct will he [be] possessed by an emotional sense of the import of the state. Here again the result is attained by the sacrifice of the individual. He does not realize himself in the whole, but he realizes the whole in the negation of the self. It is possible but in the last degree unusual for the individual taking this attitude to undertake the reconstruction of his character upon the model of the institutional standards. The usual result is the revolt of the individual against the judgment of the institution and the community that is in his mind identified with it. The products of our prisons are defective and maimed personalities. The other situation, that typified by the Juvenile Court, is favorable to just this emotional realization of the fundamental relation of the individual and the community. For here there is mutual adjustment. That which the child feels to be valuable to himself is recognized and stated to him in terms of the community and the community's rights and attitudes are presented to him in terms of his values, while there is the ever present test of the continuance of social relations to determine whether the statement of the problem and of its solution is a working and workable statement.

There is nothing novel in this statement of the moral judgment. It is the experience of every parent who has gone beyond the conception of building up his child's character by breaking his will, and compelling him to obey for the bare obedience's sake. The Juvenile Court has simply carried over this experience of the parent into the relation of the state to the child. I am however confident that we have not fully realized the full implications of the change. Consider for example our discussion of property with the child and compare it with the attitude which the community takes toward its disinherited members in their resentment at their disinheritance. In our argument with our children we are quite free to go back of the institution of property and to present it as a method of giving them the control they demand over their goods and chattels, and thus protecting others in the control of their own. A sensible father does not start with rights. He starts with the social situation of which the child is a part and within which the child insists on being and remaining a part and works out his instruction in terms of the child's own interests, while he keeps before him the child's own conscious dependence upon the family and the neighborhood. I would not of course imply that society can meet its I.W.W. s [International Workers of the World[5]] in this simple fashion. Certainly it cannot until it has found a way of convincing them that they are at home in the community in the same fashion as that in which the member of the family feels himself at home under the family tree. And yet the manner of procedure with the child is the logical procedure. It is the scientific manner of stating the problem and testing its solution. It is willing to define its object in terms of an ongoing social process, and is ready therefore to bring any right or social sacrament into discussion and to a possible reconstruction. That such a problem may be formulated — such e.g. as the social justification of property — it is necessary that one should state the values that come to him by immemorial rights in form of functions they perform. If he has property or wishes to have and keep property he will find himself estimating his citizenship in terms of such possession. If he has no possessions in goods and chattels but feels the justice of getting the social opportunities and the personal development which possessions give[,] he must conceive of his citizenship in the community as productive of the opportunities and personal development which the goods buy. In either case he will be in the attitude of realizing his relation to the community and of the community to himself in terms of the immediate values of personal problems.

This is not at present the situation which we face in approaching the problems of social science. Property and marriage are institutions which cannot be brought into the statement of a personal problem of conduct in the same fashion that one brings in the values of studies which are possible parts of one's curriculum in a university course or alternative uses of money already in one's possession, when the justice of the possession is not itself disputed. In fact it is the very nature of the fixed institution that they are to [be] accepted as the preconditions of the solution of personal problems of those who are members of the society to [which] the institutions belong. As, however, these institutions are themselves the expressions of the fundamental organization of the community, all the social values guaranteed by them are lifted out of the realm of scientific assessment and reconstruction. It is of course true that by the indirect methods of legislation and referendum we may change these institutions and amend our

Bills of Rights and our Constitutions. But the fundamental institutions are not as a rule changed by direct conscious undertaking.

After men have chafed under old forms and by subterfuge have escaped this or that implication of the institution, thus undermining it and slowly building up new attitudes and forms of conduct[,] our legislation or decisions of court[,] register changes which have already taken place. While thus our institutions can change and evolve we are robbed of the conscious import of the process of change, and in especial we are not able to bring to consciousness the fundamental social values which are wrapped up in these institutions, except when these institutions and their values are attacked by the enemy from without. If we could attack the institution by way of continual reconstruction we would have as real an opportunity of feeling its import as we have of the value of meeting a friend when we reconstruct our program giving up this[,] that[,] or the other privilege to compass this opportunity. We get hardly more immediate meaning out of the constant process of the evolution of social institutions than we do out of the processes of dialectical changes which take place unconsciously in our mouths to be registered by coming [to] Grimms[6] as great laws of speech. We have indeed all the wear and tear of the problems of misery, of divorce, of abuse of childhood, et al., but the particular case of misery may not be used as the direct evaluation for the property scheme which we have now and as a datum in an immediate change to be wrought out to solve this problem. We have the misery and the faith that out of it in the slow process of the ages is arising a better form of the state which will have eliminated this suffering and injustice, but we can neither get rid of the misery nor take conscious part in the reconstruction. We can neither have our cake nor eat it. It is not my thesis that we might change all this and at once attack the social problems in the same completeness of method as that with which we can attack those of disease or the velocity and mass of an electron, what I do maintain is that until we can do this we cannot got an emotional realization of the value of citizenship, except when our institutions and their values are in danger of destruction *vi et armis* [by force and arms];[7] for we are stopped from any direct evaluation of them in the process of social reconstruction.

When men accepted the order of society as final and its structure as divinely arranged, in their resignation and acceptance of the order of the world they registered the metaphysical value set by them through the sacrifices they made to them. But when we assume that changes are taking place which will tend to eliminate the losses we decry, and recognize that it is only because men in society have not yet got the control over the process of change as we are getting in control over that of physiology we admit that we cannot consciously live the life of reconstruction that is both that of the individual and of the community. It is no longer possible to draw water from these wells of salvation.

When we can apply scientific method completely to social problems we will [be] able to consciously live the life which we are at present to a large part only existing, or viewing with the Epimethean eye of the historian.[8]

THE COMPLETELY DEFINITE ATTITUDE OF A FIGHTING POWER AT WAR[9]

Out of a situation of great confusion, judgment, and uncertainty of issues, America has passed into the completely definite attitude of a fighting power at war with Germany and her allies[; i.e., the Central Powers] and Allied with England, France, Russia and Italy against them.

Out of this situation has arisen certain definite activities. Congress has done what is immediately demanded by this passage from neutrality to hostility, not only have they passed measures appropriating huge war budgets, but we have largely upon the judgment of the President at once accepted conscription and set on foot the preparation for the formation and drilling of an army of a million men to be sent into the battlefields of Europe as soon as their preparation justifies this in the opinion not only of our own military experts but in that of our Allies across the sea. We have undertaken to profit as well as we could from the mistakes made [by] our present Allies in their first steps in preparation. Numerous committees have been formed to bring into common action and common mind all groups and classes of men, women, and children. It is not unnatural that those who dominate these groups at present should be the men of action not only in military life but in that of business, commerce and especially production. For it has been borne in upon us that the winning of the war is quite as much a matter of production and transportation as it is of military readiness and competency, and then the first step dictated imperatively by the situation which [is] not of our making was the mobilizing of our wealth in the form which would most aid England and France. The first aid has been that of the banker and the captain of industry. He has naturally headed our Committee of Defense and filled with his affairs and his demands upon us the horizon of our attention. But other phases of the war-time activity have been largely in evidence. The anxiety as to our crops and their sufficiency to meet the common needs of our Allies and ourselves have aroused an interest in soil production such as the country has never seen before. There is not only the intelligence of [an] agriculturalist with the backing of science and the wide and detailed knowledge of foreign conditions and methods, the exigencies and the superfluities of the world, but a willingness and even an eagerness to use the interpretation of experience and the scientific training of the expert. Economy is taking on an interest which that hard virtue does not arouse in normal times. There is abroad the sense of a people's getting ready, the evidences of multiple activities and responses which reinforce each other and under favoring conditions should lead to effective and powerful organization. Do we see a "nation, rousing herself like a strong man after sleep, and shaking her invincible locks"?[10] There is the favorable evidence of wide-spread interest. It is fortunate that the beginning of the war stimulates us at many points and to many responses, that men, women and children in varying ways can respond to the summons. However the steps which we have thus far taken are but the first into the valley of the shadow of death[11] into which we are entering and within which so many other peoples are engaged in the death struggle. Can we maintain the peace we have set ourselves? Can the nation assume and keep the athletic form which we picture us adopting?

The answer to those questions cannot be made with assurance at the present moment, for the people are not articulate. The press on the whole is loyal but every body and organ that is articulate must in war-time be loyal or suspect. There are certain groups who on account of their natural sympathies with Germany in this European struggle have been against the war. There [are] socialists whose creed calls for an antimilitaristic attitude and program and who attack the war professedly because of this creed. There are convinced antimilitarists who are still fighting the war. It is impossible to judge how widely such sentiment is spread abroad. It crops up here and there. But it dare not be much in evidence. There is a widespread confidence that such anti-war sentiment will be negligible if the country as a whole is convinced and determined in prosecuting the war. There is no group or groups in the county who will undertake to set themselves up against the conscious will of the community. Such centers of disaffection then can be of importance only if the people are themselves uncertain of the issues at stake or are uncertain of themselves, and we come back with the greater insistence to the question whether those issues are in people's minds. What would be the answer if put to the mass of people[—]if from each one could extract an answer to the demand, why is America in this conflict?

[The] President must bear the great responsibility, not only for the actual precipitation of the nation into the conflict, but for the movement of minds that has made the relatively rapid swing into the current possible. The people have followed Wilson. They have been willing to take his judgement that there was no alternative that America could consider. They have been willing to take his judgement not because they have felt that the break with Germany was the logical conclusion from Wilson's own premises, or that the President and his Secretary have pursued consistent paths in their diplomacy. Perhaps because the way has been tortuous and because the conduct has not always been consistent[,] men have realized that the administration at Washington have found themselves in the face of conditions that were too terrible and too grim to be logical, and have felt the more that every legitimate step was being taken to keep [us] out of the Armageddon. When President Wilson accepted the necessity there were but few who felt that the conclusion could be avoided. Men knew that the step had been taken not only in view of the invasions of the nation's rights but also in view of the consequences which this step carries with it. The decision was fully matured. The country has been willing to believe that it was inevitable.

The sense of inevitableness has been deepened by the appeal which Mr. Wilson has made to the country's democratic ideals and principles. The encroachments which Germany has made upon the rights of the United States have been presented in their full colors as outrageous not only upon our rights but upon those of humanity, but we have been given to feel that what has been of more importance has been the frame of mind, the type of government, that was responsible for the outrages. They had to be understood by means of the ideas and principles of conduct which dictated the ruthless sub-marine campaign.

This frame of ruling mind, this type of government we call an autocracy. But the United States of America is not necessarily at war with every autocracy. For a long period of time we had no ambassador at Petrograd because the Russian autocracy refused to recognize the American citizenship of Jews who left Russia to become American citizens. There was no danger of our falling out of this attitude of refusal[—] to condone the affront Russia put upon us in her ruthless treatment of the Jews even after they had become citizens of our country[—] into that hostility.[12] The Russian autocracy was certainly abhorrent, not only to our thought but also to our deepest political instincts, but this attitude of mind and national nature did not demand war, did not suggest war.

READING 8C

PSYCHOLOGY AND THE MORAL CONDUCT OF WAR[13]

There are certain inheritances of an intellectualistic psychology which have more than an academic interest. They affect the actual conduct of war affairs and, in the form of outworn opinion, they hamper us in the moment of action. Instances of this are to be found both in our schools and in our churches. We have so long assumed that ideas are the meaning of words rather than plans of action, that we can with difficulty adjust our school to the dependence of ideas upon conduct and the interest that springs from practice. The traditional view of salvation has so expressed the judgement that moral conduct is only possible as the result of right beliefs that the church finds itself without any standards of morality in discovering what [should be] the search for right beliefs in the face of new problems. An outstanding instance of the embarrassing effects of the psychology of ideas is to be found in our own attitude toward the democratic ideals which we assume to be [at] stake in the fight with Germany.

It has been with some embarrassment that we have seen the formulae of the equality of rights to national existence, and of government only with the consent of the governed, which we have heard on [the] Fourth of July, or from the rhetorical Southern orators, appear as the actual issues of the struggle in which the entire world is involved. Can ideas which have lost all their meaning in our actual political life become political possessions so precious that we are prepared to sell our lives for them? We have been fighting for freedom from the dominance of the boss in municipal, state and national politics [Addams 1898], for control over public utilities, for improved sanitary conditions in our slums, for better housing, for more education for the workman, for the whole social program which [we] are now somewhat ashamed to say has been better carried out in Germany than in any one of the communities among the Allies. We have been telling each other that liberty, equality, consent of the governed, are negative conceptions, while the forward movement in social reconstruction demands a positive program. It is startling to suddenly find that what we considered the rhodementade of the period of the Revolution, the declamations over our freedom, contrasted with Europe shackled by its tyrants[,] arises from the past, which we thought was as dead, and clothed in President Wilson's eloquence, call upon America to make the world free for democracy. It is too simple a reply to this embarrassment to point out that while freedom from autocracy at home cannot give use freedom from the domination of the political machine, nor from an outworn economic order, nor liberties purchased by earlier struggles must still be defended against a new imperialism which threatens us as truly as did the autocracy of George the Third. But it is not the danger to our own liberties which has brought us into the war. Our isolation is indeed gone, but not merely because the Atlantic has become an ineffectual barrier, but much more because we have become so real a part of the Western world that we find we find we cannot divorce ourselves from its tragic struggle. The country at large is not moved by fear that Germany will conquer the United States and subject us to a regimen of the Poles in Posen. The consequences for the Monroe Doctrine of German domination in the world present themselves more definitely to the imagination, and perhaps people at large realize that German victory will mean the abandonment of America's claim to exclude European imperialism from this hemisphere. But the Monroe Doctrine has been in process of change during these later years. It is not welcome in its earlier pronouncements to the states of South America. What its future forms will be is not clear, nor is it clear just what the issue would be, if the Monroe Doctrine became the stake of our war with Germany. The issue in the souls of the American people is not a narrowly American issue. On the contrary it is the issue of the whole Western world rising against the project of such a military domination as that planned by the general staff of the armies of the Central Powers. We have found ourselves so essentially a part of this world that we are involved in a struggle which this German threat has made inevitable and all but universal. The issue in the War of Independence was the right of the American Colonies to self government. The issue of the present war is the right of individual nations in a highly organized international society to live with each other free from the threat of conquest by force.

Can these older ideas of the American community which have not been thrown into relief for over a century, except insofar as they have been used for an unmeaning and somewhat pompous comparison of America with Europe, be now appealed to successfully by the war into which we have entered and given their proper emotional content? Can we realize that a war to make the world safe for democracy is essentially an American war, and thus make the outcome of the war a definite one with which we passionately identify ourselves?

It is the answer to this question which is confused by an intellectualistic psychology, for we assume that ideas and ideals are simply conceptions to which we do or do not give consent, and that our action follows upon acceptance or failure to approve the ideas. If then an idea has shown that it has exhausted its emotional content, is worn out in fact, we can anticipate no forceful conduct to follow from its enunciation. If our liberal institutions which this war calls upon us to protect against the aggression of a German autocracy, seems to us to fail to give the control of community life into the hands of the people as a whole, if on the contrary they seem to leave the control in a great degree in the hands of political machines and interests which make use of the machines; the ideas of which these institutions are the expressions will call all but a languid response even if they are threatened by a foreign hostile power. We may fight to defend ourselves against a hostile power, [but] the nation will hardly mobilize itself to defend ideas which have become to us hardly more than sounding brass and tinkling cymbals.

If, however, our forefathers did not fight for an abstract liberty, an ideal of freedom, but rather formulated the Declaration of Independence as the justi-fication to themselves and the world at large of their determination to control themselves and their own affairs as a separate nation, if the idea grew out of the conduct and not the conduct out of the idea, then political habits and at-titudes answering to those which gave rise to the Declaration of Independence, may today give rise to new formulations if these attitudes and impulses oppose themselves to the aggression of the Central powers. The possibility of such new formulations will be found in the international attitude of the country. What is involved in the present struggle is not democracy of home but the relation of democratic attitudes of the different Western peoples to the International life of the Western world.

There is in American democracy a generalization that is not merely national but harks back to the formulations of the French Revolutionary period, and the attitude is one has been preserved, largely, it is fair to assume, because our isolation has kept us out of the imperialistic regime which has dominated the self conscious life of the European nations. Our own manifest destiny was so evidently the occupation of the continent, we were so completely absorbed with the application of our democratic doctrine to the problem of slavery, that we have never reached the frame of national mind that accepts what [Rudyard] Kipling calls euphemistically the white man's burden, the governing of others against their wills.[14] When the question has been definitely presented to the American community, as it has in the outcome of the Spanish [-American] war, we gave Cuba her independence and after undertaking to exercise an imperialistic power in the Philippines we have found that we could not come to terms with our own political habits without promising the Philippines their independence within the near future. In this respect our democracy has been at variance with the democracies of European countries. These democracies have been occupied with the freeing of the masses of the communities from the disabilities of old feudalisms and fighting those battles of economic freedom for the laborer which arose earlier in Europe than in America. The demand for freedom at home has not carried with it any antagonism to colonial and imperialistic policies abroad, especially insofar as these empires had been supposed to favor industrial conditions at home.

This American attitude however has been negative. Our very separation from the rest of the world has kept us from a positive application of our democratic attitude to the rights of other states, caught in the wheels and interests of European diplomacy. Our sympathies have always been with the small oppressed nationality whether it was found in Ireland, or in Posen or in Armenia, but we have never recognized any mission to espouse either by arms or diplomacy the causes which aroused our sympathies. If than we are to put a positive content into the political attitude which is expressed in the dogma that there is no legitimate government without the consent of the governed[,] it must come out of our reaction to the new situation. Our response will determine our ideas.

That reaction has been defined in a measure by President Wilson. It is primarily a fight against German imperialism, an imperialism which has undertaken to dictate to the rest of the world an order pleasing to its own idea of German power and mastery, while it has asserted military advantage as sufficient justification for treading down lesser nations and casting aside international agreements, laws and usage when they would have stood in the way of German aggression. That Germany has but given ruthless completeness to military practices which in varying degrees have characterized all other wars, becomes of great importance in attempting to estimate what America's attitude will come to be in this struggle. For we are not fighting Germany simply because of the Lusitania, nor Belgium nor the attempted crushing of France, but because of the ruthless logic of her use of military force to determine what is to be the form and manner of the life of nations. It is impossible to live with a nation whose conduct follows such a logic. If this becomes the definite objective of America in the war, there will arise an ideal of organized international life based upon the attitude of the people themselves. Already this has been presented in the reply which President Wilson has sent to the Pope's appeal for peace negotiations. This reply finds in a control of our own foreign affairs by the German people the one secure basis for immediate and future peace. Assuming our own non-imperialistic attitude we assume also that there are no questions that will arise between peoples themselves which they will not prefer to settle by arbitration or adjudication to a settlement by war. The implications of democracy are not that a majority of the people are more powerful than any minority, class or monarchical group and should therefore govern by right of superior might. The implication of democracy is that there is always a basis of common interest in the community upon which differences can be better settled then through the exercise of force, if only the conflicting interests can be brought into the field of an enlightened

public opinion of the whole society. The failure or success of democratic institutions depends upon their success in bringing these issues into the field of an
enlightened public sentiment. A militaristic order of the state, on the other hand,
denies a common field of interest which can be the ground for the deliberative
settlement of international differences. Military readiness and effectiveness seeks
the chance for sudden and unexpected attack and seeks to minimize if not to
destroy the democratic attitude of appeal to instructed public opinion. It is for
this reason that democratic and militaristic states, such as that of Germany are
inevitably opposed to each other. It is for this reason that democratic societies
insofar as they are democratic cannot be imperialistic.

Insofar then as America recognizes in the militaristic government of Germany its real enemy, America will inevitably give new content to its democratic
ideas and ideals, which in their earlier expression answered only the assertion
by the colonies of their right to independence. Out of her attack upon the state
whose form rests upon the theory that force is the legitimate and logical arbiter of international differences, will arise the conception of common interest
between peoples which can serve as the medium for the adjudication of their
disputes. America will have gained a new idea of the implications of her democracy on German imperialism as the actual objective in the war[.] In the
minds of the people will be the source of the ideas by which Americans will
interpret to themselves and others the struggle they are entering and will carry
to its conclusion.

READING 8D

THE RISING TIDE OF NATIONALISM[15]

Since the middle of the nineteenth century there has been a rising tide of
nationalism throughout the world. It has run across the policies of most of the
nations. Out of it has arisen the seething cauldron of the Balkan peninsula, the
deadly struggle that has grown to formidable proportions in the empire of the
Habsburgs, and given birth to the war in which the whole world is now engaged.
It has compelled a diametrical change in the policy of the English empire toward
its colonies and possessions, and has produced upon this crowded stage the
culmination of the age-long Irish problem. In America it has appeared in the
form of the negro [sic] question, and the exclusion of the Chinese and Japanese
[Deegan 2002b]. With the force of an unseen irresistible current it has swept
the internationale of Marxian socialism into the realm of myths. It appears
glorified in the devotion of the French to France. In Belgium it reaches the
majesty of complete tragedy, while in Hungary and Posen it takes on the form
of hideous oppression. We feel it in the unified sentiment with which America
has come into the war.

For nationalism, race consciousness, patriotism, mob consciousness are
psychologically all one. Whether it appears in a lynching, or in the last devo-

tion in a trench, or [in] the bowels of the torpedoed transport, or [in] the fiery furnace of a falling aeroplane, or in the arrogance of a *Kultur* that sets itself beyond right and wrong, in all cases it is the expression of the relation of the individual to the group to which he belongs, of the social possession that takes him out of himself. From the time that men passed into the clan down to the present it has represented that mechanism of human nature which has proliferated into all forms of society. Out of it has sprung all the spiritual treasures of the race and most of the inhumanities of man to man. But it is too intimate[,] too subconscious to admit of ready analysis. We applaud and objurgate, we do not study, nor control it. We recognize the gesture and the passion in the enemy who is swept on by the same current by which we are borne against him. We fail to identify the force nor do we determinately seek for the technique by which it may be brought under our direction, and yet men's escape from the domination of the [other has al]ways been by way of the realization of some larger social relation with that by which have bound. In fact it has been the specific function of religion — the universal religions — to provide the sense of this larger whole which could transcend restricted social groups, and open the door for the larger spiritual life which clan and national cults could not offer. Plato's [ca. 360 B. C. /2003] city beyond the heavens, and [St] Paul's city not built with hands[,] eternal in the heavens, the saints and sages "in solemn troops and sweet societies"[16] that entertain the soul that is not at home in this world and whose citizenship is in heaven, the soul that loses itself in God, and even the soul that escapes individuality in the Nirvana of Indian philosophy, all affirm another social habitat as the condition of escape from that which actually confines and constricts the individual. The major premise of every syllogism in social reconstruction is the actual existence of a social order which includes the particular reform in question there[,] as a specific instance. It is not however essential that this other social order should be in the heavens nor in Atlantis, nor the Sun nor in Mars, nor, to express it in other words, is it necessary that the social reformer should believe firmly in the existence of a Utopia in actual existence somewhere in the heavens or on the earth. If he does he is an idealist.

[The empiricist proceeds on other assumptions and presents his projects on a stage set with much more modest properties. He cannot escape from the necessity of the major premise, but he finds it not in a vision given in the mount, but in certain universal characters in human society as it exists in our experience, from which, the empiricist affirms, there follow conclusions in reformation of the institutions under which we are living. The empiricist has found two such universal characters which find their expression[:] one in Democracy and the other in Property. The principle of democracy is that there are common ends in which men are individually interested, and that these individual interests in community ends may be made the basis of government. Different schools have very different ways of accounting for the individual's acquiring an interest in a community end, but they all affirm that it finally appears, and that with its appearance comes the possibility of democratic institutions, and they are confident that this situation is present in all human societies in which civilization exists, though the democratic conclusions may not have been drawn from the premises. It may be necessary to inaugurate revolutions to oust privileged classes and monarchs from power, but the material for the erection of democratic institutions is present, and requires only the freedom of the individual from restraint, and sufficient education to recognize the community ends which are also his own, to reach their fruition.

Such community ends are frequently defined as natural rights, and refer to the individual impulses, such as those which find their expression in the family, in property, and in the acquirement of knowledge, in the free utterance of opinion not to mention the negative rights — that is the freedom from interference on the part of others in the exercise of one's positive rights. There have been wide variations in the statement of these so-called rights, but what has been common to all statements of them is this interest of the individual in their exercise, and the like interest of the community in the individual's possessing them and exercising them. All recognize that in the common individual and community interest lies the possibility of popular government. The result of such uncertainty as to just what the rights and the functions of the individual are is that he remains a very abstract person.

The Declaration of Independence says that he should be free and un-burdened by a privileged class above him, that his rights are to life, liberty and the pursuit of happiness, certainly a vague definition of the political individual. Has he a right to an education for example, even if he is not able to meet the expense of an education out of his own pocket? What are the mutual rights of the members of a family, beyond this that they may all pursue happiness? Do his rights include those of healthful surroundings and adequate return from his labor to meet normal standards of living? Has he a right to the opportunity to labor at all? We are unquestionably nearer an answer to these questions than were those who wrote the Declaration of Independence and the Constitution but even in countries with so-called liberal institutions there is as yet no clear answer, and yet they all have to do with interests which are both those of the individual and of the community, and in which what is to [be] the genuine interest of the community must [be] to that of the individual and vice versa.

The second conception in which, the interest of individual and the community coincide is found in property. Property is a universal. You cannot claim it yourself without recognizing it in the possessions of your neighbor. To safeguard his property is to protect your own. Your most insistent emphasis upon your own property rights is the affirmation of those of all the community. The rights of the individual to and over his property include that of exchange and the contract which is a part of the process, especially when it is extended in time and space. Property is of course one of the fundamental rights which go to make up the political individual. Under conditions of detail production that is consumed within the political community, and an exchange of goods that is found also mainly at home, going abroad only at great risk and in search of high profits and then as a part of the foreign political policy of the country, a part of the colonial system, or the extension of empire; under these conditions property is merely a category of the rights of man that goes to make up the political individual, the individual whose interests are sufficiently identical with those of the community to enable him to enter into the government of the country.

While such political individuals were sufficiently abstract and universal to make the idea of a larger society than that of any single nation comprehensible, the interest in the political individual centered in his relationship to the government within the national communities. Democracy was quite confined to revolutionary and reform movements inside the nations, and did not become the basis for international speculation or agitation to any considerable degree. But in the development of the factory system, with its wholesale production of the commodities of everyday life, and the economic theories of [David] Hume and Adam Smith[17] that grew out of it, an international economic life arose, which was not the field of abstract speculation but of intense concrete economic activity The economic man in distinction from the political man did not find his habitat within the political community. The favorite spot for settling him by the speculative economists was a desert island where with only a few other economic individuals, he commenced his production and exchanges under the simplest conditions. It was the boast of these economists that these simple conditions were those to which the most complex and complicated of economic processes could be reduced. They had nothing to do with political boundaries, except as the governments of different countries introduced pernicious barriers, protective and exclusion tariffs, to interfere with the action of the inherent laws of production and distribution. It was out of this economic process with its conceptions of the economic man and the international economic regime, that modern industry and finance and the internationale of socialism arose. Back of all interference with the economic process lay the conception of the free production under the most favorable economic conditions, the free distribution where the best markets could be secured, and a vivid reform movement for free trade in the interest of cheaper food, was pushed on the one hand and the revolutionary movement for the control of industry by the masses of the laborers in their own interest on the other. Neither of these movements was national. The passionate free trader believed that it would inaugurate an era of peace, by removing all economic causes for warfare. The socialist had no other interest in the political organization of his country except to get control of it for the purpose of taking over a capitalistic industry, converting it into an industry conducted in the interests of the vast number of producers.

The conception of political man opened the door to the reform movements in the direction of popular control over government. The conception of the economic man opened the door to revolutionary movements which sought to overthrow present governments, or to reduce governmental activities to the minimum of police supervision, of a process that would run of itself.

It is interesting to note how slow, haphazard, and inconsiderable has been the democratic evolution since the period of the French Revolution. With the exception of tardy enlargement of the electorate up to the present[,] half of the community has been shut out on inconsequent sex lines, and the introduction of popular education, which has not been adapted to its purpose of acquainting the rising generation with their physical and social opportunities and has therefore been largely ineffective, with these exceptions it is not too much to say that political democracy has been sterile and ineffectual. Thus while the vote has been placed in more and more hands, and the schools have been opened to more and more children[,] the political control in the community has remained with much the same classes in whose hands it reposed at the beginning of the century. The common interest of the individual and the community have not been greatly widened. They still rest largely with the so-called natural rights. The common interests gathering about the family, really popular education, the great fields of recreation and aesthetic enjoyment, and the varied human contacts which these involve, have been most meagerly occupied. This is illustrated both in the city and in the country. In the city where men and children are massed together and subject to the spell of the crowd, none of this concentration of emotional life has been put into intelligent cooperation in constructive activity, or in recreation, while city politics have retained the type of corruption that was invested and perfected in 1850. In the country where the most interesting of occupation is still largely unspecialized and there remains a field for artisanship, where there is the opportunity to apply scientific training with immediate results[,] the methods of production have remained more stationary than in any other form of creating wealth. There are a host of human interests, which have too little or no influence at all, that should enter into the organization of social forces that bring about social control, in other words into the government of the community. We express this absence of important social interests from the governing institutions of the community by the distinction drawn between social control through these institutions and that exercised by public opinion. Into public opinion enters all that has any place in the consciousness of the community, while political control is exercised only through the interests which go to make up the political individual.

It would be wrong to fail to recognize the considerable additions to the content of the political individual, that have come by way of preservation of the health of the community[;] through control of disease, regulation of housing, of working conditions in the interest of health, especially those of women and children[;] through universal public education, and the grants for higher technical and even so-called cultural training. All of these indicate that the individual which the community recognizes has added both rights and duties to his nature which had no place in that of the eighteenth century individual. On the other hand it would be equally wrong to assume that these rights and duties stand for clearly defined principles which can be logically applied. The earlier conception of property was such a principle, and its applications have made the most logical part of governmental administration. This remains the most consistent part of government administration today, notwithstanding the invasions upon former rigid conceptions of property which are found in more recent legislation and court interpretations. No one could say that the modern individual has such a right to good health, and the conditions essential to its preservation, as that which he possesses to his property. No one could clearly outline the amount of enlightenment to which a citizen of a modern community may lay claim. These innovations have come by way of police regulations in the interest of public welfare. Ignorance, disease, and unsanitary conditions are suppressed as public nuisances[;] municipal invasion into the fields of the aesthetic and of recreation are uncertain[;] and without even as much logical organization as those[,] into the fields of education and health. The difference between these two fields, that of definite rights belonging to the political individual, and that of privileges coming to him through the exercise of public police power in the interest of the general welfare, appears in the different conceptions of liberty that the two imply. The liberty that grows out of rights inhering in the nature of individual such as that of self-defense, or property, is one which is not restrained by the definition of the right, and this definition carries with it the conditions under which the power may be exercised, but does not thereby restrict the right.

Thus the right of property is defined [in] terms of the full control which one may exercise over one's own. This definition does not restrict its use, it indicates the field of its use. The definition of a right presents the territory within which it may be exercised without restraint. Restrictions which legislation and court interpretation have introduced are regarded as defining that which is property rather than restraining a right. Thus an ordinance may prohibit building which is not safeguarded against danger of fire upon land owned in a certain district. The prohibition deprives the owner of a certain possession in that land. His possession is in it as a site for certain types of structures, but not in it as a site for others. When a right has been defined the door has been opened for its exercise. The advantages which accrue to the children of citizens through attendance upon public schools, on the other hand, reach them if the public has acted in creating the schools. They come as privileges rather than as rights, and the definition of these privileges leaves the individual dependent upon public action for his profit by them. Thus our social policy implies individuals who control their property, while it may determine in what that property may consist. It desiderates enlightened citizens and opens schools for the education of each advancing generation. He is free to do what he will with his own, he may take advantage, indeed may be required to take advantage, of the opportunities of educating his children, but the right to educate his children does not spring from his own parental interest in the children, but from permissive or compelling legislation. While the distinction here indicated cannot be made hard and fast, and the privilege tends to under exercise and long tenure to become a right, it yet does mark an important difference in the nature of our liberties. Those that are conceived of as springing from natural rights which form the basis for the individualism of the nineteenth century, while the liberties which accrue to the individual from the privileges extended by society, when conceived of as rights as well as privileges, lay the foundations for the socialistic doctrines which are characteristic of the latter part of the same century.

The whole of social doctrine has gathered about this distinction. The determination to keep the structure of the community within the lines indicated by the political individual has left the privileges that accrue from social control and reconstruction without any vital relation to natural rights. The dominant reason for this is to be found in the economic situation, which has placed in the hands of those in controlling possession of the wealth of the community a ruling influence in the country. In the vivid industrial life of the last century and this, the right of control of one's property has put in the keeping of those who control the country's wealth the increasingly complex and rich social activities which are dependent on the expenditure of the country's income. Slowly the governmental control of this wealth when its influence reaches important social undertakings such as education, public health, transportation and the like, has assumed a new function which an earlier economic doctrine refused to admit. The conflict lies between the conception of these undertakings and that of the independent individual. The social control invades what had been considered as his rights. On the other hand the undertakings to give the individual the training and opportunity for physical well-being, the larger social experience, with access to the finer sorts of values, have inevitably led to a new conception of what the individual should be, but the individual, who should be has no authority over against the well-entrenched political individual, who is in possession. This is the contention of the socialists. As has been already indicated[,] socialist doctrine stands upon the translation of the privileges extended to the individual by society, in the interests of the community as a whole, into rights. The refusal to recognize these as rights to which all members of the community may lay claim, is laid at the door of the economic exploitation which private property in the hands of the older individual has made possible. The socialistic remedy for this evil is abrogation of property in the means of production of wealth. Thus they would extend the character of privilege from the fields such as those of education, health, enjoyment of art, and recreation to that of all property in capital.

All rights then would come from the state to the individual, and an absolute state would be erected over the individuals from which all their rights would come as privileges. This socialistic doctrine is no less a logical result of the abstract individual, than the political theory and practice which has allowed community control to pass so largely into the hands of the possessing class.

The individual is abstract because only the impulse of having and holding, the impulse out of which property arises in the community, and that of hostile self assertion which, under social conditions such as have arisen in modern democracies, becomes that of self government are recognized as preconditions of our social order. With individuals who can assert themselves in the demand for government of their own making, and who are free to control what is their own in the group[,] a modern society may be built. With other powers and prerogatives they are endowed by the state. This situation has a double effect. On the one side community action leading to the change in the conception and definition of property is regarded as attacking the foundations of society, while on the other hand activities springing from impulses that give rise to the family, education and science, art and recreation are conceived of as dependent upon the action of the state. There is of course no fundamental reason in human nature for this distinction. The rights of self government and that of property are no less dependent upon social organization for their actual form and validity, than are those that spring from the impulses of sex, parental and filial responses, and those of social adjustments and intercommunication. There is at bottom as good a right to express oneself through constructive workmanship[18] as through property, and on the other hand there is an ever increasing recognition that the conditions under which property control is to be exercised must be under community supervision. The two foci about which the modern community revolves are the individual and the state. In the conception of the Manchester School,[19] the state could [be] reduced to a minimum, and the individual with his two fundamental attitudes of demand for self government and for property, could be left with nothing but the barest modicum of police control.

The opposite pole is that which finds in government control the principle of social organization, and erects the state entirely above any individual expression. The bureaucratic German state is the corresponding instance in contrast with the individualistic English society. It is indeed the achievement of human society that it has been able to socialize these resistant individualist impulses, that of hostile self-assertion, and that of property: that attitude which resists with physical force [any] direction from another and that which excludes others from the use of what is within one's possession. In the opinion of [Thomas] Hobbes[20] these two impulses, especially the latter, can lead to nothing but the war of all against all. In his view complete surrender of all so-called rights to an absolute sovereign was the only solution of the problem of forming a society out [of] recalcitrant human nature. Modern democracy actually in existence means that men can reach the position of respecting the rights of others when demanding the right of self-government for themselves, as they can demand protection for their own property in the respect which they pay to the ownership of others. For it was not about these human impulses that primitive societies arose. Clan organization appealed to the family as its cohesive principle. Cooperative interest in hunting, in magic control of nature and disease, in the primitive art of decoration and the dance, in the initiation of children into the tribe, in the care of flocks and herds, and finally in the common fight against the enemies of the tribe, these were the socializing influences in early human organization. Modern democratic society has deliberately undertaken to eliminate the family, religion, art, and recreation, and the community training of children from its method of government. Primarily the state is supposed to be constituted out of freemen, who in asserting their independence of outer control, agree to respect the independence of others and to join in the obedience only to the common will in undertakings which affect the community as a whole. The most definite common interest, beyond that of defense against the aggression of powers that are still organized on the tribal principles, that is feudal, religious, and dynastic principles, has been that of property. The democratic state was primarily instituted for the defense of the freedom and the property of [all citizens.]

Other interests were regarded as far as possible as individual affairs. Religion was the matter of one's conscience. The training of one's children lay within the regulation of the father. So far as possible the family was considered the property of the head of the family. The earnings and other property of the wife or minor children belonged to the head of the family. Festivals[,] theater[,] dance and works of art, education and science had no governmental significance. They belonged in the private lives of the citizens. However conduct on the part of the citizen which affected the comfort, health, and safety of the citizens could be their corporate action be abated or regulated, but sacred precedents, bills of rights, and written constitutions jealously protected the individual against invasion of his rights, and the rigorous theorist of the school wished these police regulations to be reduced to the lowest terms. It was the "nightwatchman state."[21]

It is not necessary to review the gradual increase and spread of the functions of government, its inevitable interference with the inhumanities of the factory system, its unwilling shouldering of the cost and direction of the education of the children of the community, its less grudging assumption of the task of encouraging and housing and displaying of the national art, its spasmodic undertaking under popular pressure of some degree of control over corporate business and transportation, its slow recognition of the necessity of public control of health conditions and recreation. It has been the spirit in which these innovations have been made that is of especial importance. They have been made always as concessions, without frank recognition of their propriety. They have represented compromises in which the possessing classes and the governments that they inspired never admitted the public obligation to do what they grudgingly undertook. It was the expense that was always presented [as] an unanswerable argument. Each concession was regarded as a step down a fatal incline into a gulf which was bottomless. The distribution of the country's income in accordance with the existing economic order was the presupposition of all consideration of community responsibility for other than political and economic expressions of human nature. If diversions of funds to the government for such so-called humanitarian and philanthropic purposes could take place without disturbing the healthful normal operation of business, further taxation for these purposes could [be] allowed, but always with an eye to the danger of the precedent established. The whole procedure emphasized the divorce between the abstract political and economic man from the rest of human interest, impulse, and endeavor. And yet the actual structure of society depends as necessarily upon the other sides of human nature as upon these, and in the end it cannot be possible to so grudgingly recognize other than political and economic activities in the operation of social control, that operation which we call government, with the consent of the governed.

Under simpler conditions of earlier American life the divorce was not definitely felt because education was but a slight affair. Science had not presented the avoidable evils which public control can obviate. National values had not taken on the forms of self-conscious art, and economic processes did not need the supervision which became so crying a demand of later times. But the effect of development of the industrial nineteenth century has been to bring about a complex social organization in which men have become much more interdependent that was formerly the case.

Starting with the institution of property we find a constantly widening group involved in its acquirement and in its expenditure. The outstanding evidence of this may be found in the fast organization of business, the centralizing of financing of industrial undertakings, the growth of investment in corporations with its divorce of ownership and control. On the other hand stands the organization of labor. The coming together of men in new social relations because of their dependence upon the factory system that employs them in great numbers and without reference to their status; the social issues that are raised in the contests between organized labor and organized capital, and the multitudinous contacts in the crowded city existence which centers about the great factory industries all involve a new social order in which the present institutions of property fails to express the values and fulfil the functions which the institution implies. Its great political function is to give the individual independence, so that he may order his life to meet the obligations which his relat[ions with others impose] upon him, and obtain the larger social experiences which are essential [to] his full being. Such a man is prepared to take up his political duties and exercise his political privileges. Without these he is not a freeman, but dependent upon others for what is essential to his normal social expression. Furthermore property involves control over the means and tools which he makes use of in the productive activity by which he justifies his existence in the community. Inadequate return for labor, which results from unjust distribution of the profits of industry deprives a large percentage of the population in our industrial communities of this economic independence which is the foundation of a country of freemen. Factory methods, insufficient training, and the absence of the voice of labor in determining the conditions of work, deprive the laborer of the control over what is apt to be his sole property, his capacity to work and his skill. On the other hand the disproportionate returns which goes to the owners of the capital invested in the industry, and to those who control the sources from which capital flows into industry has not only the results to which reference has just been made, but encourages forms of expenditure which set up prestige values as the social function of property. These social aims become dominant not only in the attitudes of those who have considerable surplus to expend, but they tend to set the fashion subconsciously in the expenditures and the social aims these imply on the part of the whole community.

READING 8E

THE CHANGING ATTITUDE TOWARD MILITARISM[22]

This change of attitude, as had already been indicated, will probably take place because of a conscious determination to pass beyond a militarist order of society. If it does take place it will be the result of impending [?] changes which sign for this without intention. The countries of the Western world may be willing to reduce their armaments, and the people may demand control of foreign policy.

The general growth of democracy may crowd out these upper classes, the [generals] them[selves] who supply the natural materials for officers of a supernational army, one that is a sacred mystification, the specialization of the state and at the same time may make the subjugation of the people to the drill sergeant no longer possible. The changes will come piecemeal, in the gradual determination of the arbitration treaties, and the power of Hague tribunals. This manner of change may be so quickened by the terrible experiences of this war that actually such a catastrophe will become in consequence no longer possible and [for each] person that the ethical problem will not be faced[, there is] a whole [range of?] ethical values and the mechanisms [that] are dependent upon subconscious organizations of habits.

Because the state is the mechanism by which the community undertakes its deliberate corporate action, it gets the value of the society itself. Upon social organization depend all our values and those who are still functionaries certainly do not hesitate to demonize any attack upon the mechanisms of the state as one directed against society[;] and, in the case of hostilities between state[s,] men assume that war with all its machinery of destructions is leveled at all the values which society and the men whom society makes possible continu[es] until some mechanism of the society within which states exist [appears?].

Whereas men [seldom exist] in society with each other without fighting, men will inevitably assume that the destruction which war threatens is directed against the society whose instrument the state is, and without which the society cannot be articulate or consciously active, and it will become possible for men to realize the possibility of such intention of the states in the crucial interests of the larger whole when such interaction has managed to take place and has in taking place left a mechanism by means of which further reorganization may take place in the future.

The state is identified with all the values of society in men's minds — they are not aware that states imply the existence of each other as much as do individuals — that states as such are but instruments of the communities — that the problem is to work out a mechanism for interaction of the common states over against each other [to] have the same sort of value and function as that which belong to institutions within the state. These are recognized as dependent upon their formation in the community and the community has provided a mechanism by means of which these may change in their interaction and under the stress of conflict — revolution has been embodied with[in] the organization of the institutions. The institutions have not in this last [situation] then reality or meaning — an uncertain landless war must be embodied in international organization — a process which will neither destroy nor weaken actual states. Until situations have attained this possibility of materially affecting each other[:] they are evidences of incomplete socialization and do not accomplish this full function. The state [is] a resistant institution.

Notes

1. The phrase a "nation, rousing herself like a strong man after sleep, and shaking her invincible locks" is found in *Areopagita,* Part III, by John Milton.
2. Box 2, folder 3, Mead Addenda.
3. Junior George Republic was an American industrial institution in Freeville, New York where children stayed several years and engaged in self-government. Similar institutions were founded throughout the United States in the late nineteenth century.
4. Addams was a prime mover in the first Juvenile Court, an organization which Mead enthusiastically supported. See Deegan (1999, lxiv).
5. This labor union wanted more freedom for workers, not merely more money or job benefits like most American organizations. Popularly called "the Wobblies," they were more radical than the more typical union, such as the garment workers unions, that Mead supported (Deegan 1988). See also ftn. 118 above.
6. The Grimm brothers, Jacob and Wilhelm, were philologists, as was Mead's mentor Wilhelm Wundt. The brothers' fairy tales are famous worldwide.
7. This is a phrase from Cicero (106 B. C.-43 B. C.), a Roman author and politician.
8. Epimetheus was the brother of Prometheus in Greek mythology. Epimetheus was blessed with hindsight while Prometheus was blessed with foresight.
9. Box 2, folder 19, Mead Addenda papers.
10. See endnote 21 above.
11. See ftn. 17, p. 95.
12. Mead was committed deeply to preventing Rudovitz, a Russian immigrant, from being deported to Russia for what that government considered political crimes. See Deegan (1988, 117-18).

13. Box 3, folder 22, Mead Addenda.
14. Rudyard Kipling (1865-1936) was a popular British author and poet. His poem, "The White Man's Burden" (1899) describes the colonial attitude towards the people and countries they exploit. The poem has been seen by many as an egregious attitude by Kipling who was born in India and of English descent. Some interpreters, however, believe Kipling was mocking such an attitude.
15. Box 3, folder 2, Mead Addenda.
16. These phrases are from Milton's (1909-1914) "Lycidas" published in 1637.
17. See ftn. 9, p. 184.
18. See discussion of "instinct of workmanship" in Veblen (1914).
19. See ftn. 8, p. 184.
20. See ftn. 18, p. 72.
21. See ftn. 9, p. 150.
22. Handwritten, box 3, folder 1, Mead Addenda

Part 5

The Chicago City Club and Mead's Writings during and Immediately Post-World War I

9

War, Mead's Leadership of the Chicago City Club, and Public Citizenship

> *"This evening we went as usual to the City Club*
> *for War issues, and discussed the British Labor*
> *Party's Program. It is the only program that makes*
> *an industry and commerce of exploitation impos-*
> *sible, and would therefore make such a war as*
> *the present impossible, this being justified by the*
> *conquest of markets. But our labor people have not*
> *got far enough along to accept and stand for this*
> *admirable document." (Mead to his son Henry on 3*
> *March 1918, Mead papers, box 1, folder 9)*

Chicago was a hotbed of reform from 1892 until WWI. To a considerable degree the people studied here were central to this tumult and the repeated challenges to the status quo. They agitated for social legislation, collected information on social problems, exercised their bureaucratic skills, delivered speeches and lectures, and systematically combined their talents through numerous organizations. Similar activities occurred throughout the country at the same time, but Chicago provided much of the initiative and leadership for what historians have dubbed "urban progressivism." Stephen Diner (1980, 5), in his outstanding analysis of these Chicago reformers, noted that of the 169 leading men, 113 were members of the City Club of Chicago (CCC). Founded in 1905, this male only group discussed and debated civic issues. Through an extensive committee structure, they virtually covered every area of urban problems. These committees formed the basis for concerted action on any given issue. Oriented to the collection of facts on a given problem, each committee led a municipal drive to achieve its goals. They were frequently powerful and successful advocates. Addams was often a guest lecturer,[1] but it was the men who controlled and organized the group.

The CCC provided Mead with a major outlet for his public leadership. He was a member of the CCC from its founding in 1907 until the 1920s. In 1917 he was one of several influential city leaders who called for more information before making recommendation for increased taxes for city planning changes ("'Show Us,' Say Civic Bodies To Suppliant City" 1917). Most importantly before the war, he served on the education committee for years, developing several statistical studies that are crucial to understanding his scholarship, reform commitments, and ties to sociology. He was elected president of the organization for two terms, from 1918 until 1920, and frequently served on the board of directors. Charles R. Henderson, the Chicago sociologist, served on the employment committee, Charles Zeublin, another Chicago sociologist, was on its municipal parks committee, and W. I. Thomas was a member for two years.[2] Thus this group formed a subunit of collegial contacts within the world of Chicago pragmatism, organizing the men around specific municipal interests and united in one organization for urban planning and reform.

The Education Committee of the Chicago City Club

Mead worked from 1910 until 1916 on the Chicago City Club's Education Committee. This group was a significant force in Chicago's school system, and Mead was its chair. Their vocational training report in 1912 was based on voluminous statistical data collected from several cities. In it, the committee members documented the high rate of dropouts among youth between the ages of fourteen and sixteen (Mead, Wreidt, and Bogan 1912). This study was similar to the educational and housing surveys sponsored by the University of Chicago Settlement where Mead served as the treasurer. The vocational training report of the City Club was one of a number of studies urging more progressive education, the raising of mandatory school age from fourteen to sixteen, and the establishment of vocational programs in public schools (Deegan 1988, 1999).

This committee also worked to revise the services of the Chicago Public Library. A series of changes were then instituted and managed under the auspices of the City Club's Library Committee with George Vincent, another Chicago sociologist (Deegan 1988, 92-98), as a supervisory member. One of the first steps was hiring a professional librarian to head the service, instead of making a political appointment. The wider circulation of books and the more efficient use and location of facilities throughout the city were other policies that were implemented and modeled after programs suggested first by John Ruskin and adopted in Chicago at Hull-House (Deegan and Wahl 2003). Mead's work in these areas was based on a scholarly model similar to that used by other Chicago sociologists, including Henderson, Abbott, and Breckinridge, and involved statistical analysis and documentation, empirical methods that many contemporary symbolic interactionists eschew (e.g., Manis and Meltzer 1979; Fine 1995).

Mead's Wartime and Postwar Presidency of the CCC, 1918-1920

As the brutal war continued in Europe, the CCC members became increasingly militant, sponsored more war debates, and encouraged "citizenship" involvement. Beginning in 1917 and continuing into 1919 the CCC sponsored speakers almost every week who discussed the war, the Russian Revolution, the dwindling food supply in Europe, the need for an emerging homeland for Israel (Kallen 1918), "community gardens" to grow food in Chicago (Rogers 1918), children's horrible fate during war, and the impact of the war on India, Lithuania, Asia, and especially England (see table 9.1). Mead symbolized these positions through his election to a virtually unprecedented two terms of office as the club president, from 1918 to 1920. He was a vigorous and involved officer during and immediately after the war. In the letter to his son which opens this chapter, Mead writes of the centrality of the CCC and its discussions of the war.

Table 9.1
Typical CCC Speakers and Topics During 1918.

Dernby, Karl. G. 1918. "The Finnish Revolution." City Club Bulletin 11 (24 June): 207-208.

Frey, John B. 1918. "A Menace to Morale." City Club Bulletin 11 (15 July): 219-20.

Hamilton, Alice. 1918. "Munitions Workers Risk Death." City Club Bulletin 11 (18 February): 63-64.

Harper, Samuel N. 1918. "Munitions Workers Risk Death." City Club Bulletin 11 (15 April): 131-32.

Johnson, James Weldon. 1918. "Negro Soldier Praised." City Club Bulletin 11 (6 May): 160.

Kallen, Horace. 1918. "The Jewish People and the War." City Club Bulletin 11 (15 April): 135-36.

Lowden, Frank P. 1918 "Should We Amend Our Constitution in Wartime?" City Club Bulletin 11 (24 June): 211.

Lucas, W. P. 1918. "Children of the War Zone." City Club Bulletin 11 (17 June): 201-202.

Ratcliffe, S. K. 1918. "A Picture of British Politics." City Club Bulletin 11 (18 March): 93.

The men of the city club joined forces with the Women's City Club (WCC), a gender-parallel organization (Goffman 1977) where the women of Hull-House and the wives of the men of the CCC worked together. Growing food and protecting children were important joint efforts. The research arm of the CSCP, headed by Breckinridge and E. Abbott, conducted a joint survey on housing with the CCC members who acted on a request for information from the government ("Housing War Workers in Chicago 1918). A remarkable series of war memoirs were presented and published by the CCC during and after WWI. The speakers included Fabian socialists, American politicians, intellectuals writing on the war, and everyday citizens struggling with the new issues, especially the members of the CCC.

The CCC also collected money to buy their own ambulance that was driven in Europe by a club member, Rembert C. Anderson. In June 1918 Anderson (1918, 198) wrote the club members that "Our Ambulance in France" was serving in a quiet sector where the new American soldiers "generally stand out and watch shells break." He observed that the men did not run for cover because the war remained a novelty for them.

One of the wartime links between Mead and Addams was their mutual friendship with George Hooker. Mead worked closely with Hooker who served as the Civic Secretary of the CCC. Mead (1919b, 101) wrote that Hooker at an unspecified location "has worked continuously and at high pressure on one of the Exemption Boards throughout the whole period of the war. It is unnecessary to add that Hooker contributed generously of his time and effort outside of the hours ordinarily given to Club duties" (see reading 9C here). Hooker also used Hull-House for his wartime activities, despite the overwhelming opposition of Addams and many other residents to the war. This has led some scholars, notably Harriet Alonso (1995), to mistakenly interpret Addams as vacillating in her commitment to peace (Deegan 1996b). But Hooker had been a Hull-House resident for decades, and Addams believed the social settlement was a home where she did not force her beliefs and policies upon the residents. Thus Hooker served as a recruiting agent for the military at Hull-House. This is a fine example of Addams' complete acceptance of non-violence and her belief in the settlement as the home of the residents where she was "Head" but never "Director." All these Hull-House friends balanced their deeply felt conflicting feelings so that their friendships could continue. Mead tried to maintain this balance, too, but he had the advantage of living and working outside of Hull-House in his separate world of work and home.

Immediately after the war, Wilson's commitment to the League of Nation and his "fourteen points" for a better world society fell apart. McDowell (1919) spoke at the CCC against the politics barring the signing of America's support for the League. Mead shared McDowell's position and immediately acted on her recommendations for action. Mead, of course, thought these were the raison d'être for the war while Senator Medill McCormick, who was part of the wealthy family of McCormick reaper fame and the Chicago Tribune, did not. As a formidable senator from Illinois, McCormick led the opposition to the League of Nations. Through local and even national newspapers, Mead and McCormick publicly debated America's entry into the League of Nations (see further discussion later in this chapter).

In the summer of 1919, Chicago experienced a horrendous race riot and Mead supported the appointment of a commission to study the event and its causes. Addams (1922) later testified before this group and was integral to the commission's formation and investigations.

But this was only one pressing problem facing her: The "Red Summer" of 1919 hit the women of Hull-House very hard as the government targeted them as unpatriotic communists. The CCC swept into the fray and sided with the feminist pragmatists, another sign of the men's return to their previous positions on war and peace. Thus the CCC sponsored a symposium analyzing "Americanization" and the anti-immigrant laws limiting entry into the United States. Although various speakers offered different ideas and represented a range of politics, the weight of the arguments was closer to those advocated by Addams and the pre-war positions of Mead than to those who restricted immigration and favored nativism.

Mead's stature in the CCC led to his offering his opinion on political issues. Thus on 2 November 1918, he released two statements on the need for a new law to provide more public transportation ("Reports Show Tide Rising for Car Ordinance" 1918; "How Chicago Will Profit" 1918). He also protested against the appointment of some public school administrators earlier that year ("Hanson Holds Up Shoop's Last Two Appointees." 1918). Finally, one of Mead's most important municipal services in conjunction with his presidency of the CCC was his role as a public citizen advisor.

Mead as President of the CCC and a Public Citizen Advisor, 1918-1920

The mayor of Chicago organized a "president's council" composed of "the heads of twenty one [sic] leading business and civic organizations of Chicago" which included Mead in his role as head of the CCC (Hewett 1919). The presidents of Northwestern University, the University of Chicago and important business association also served. In 1919 they were called together to help in a coal crisis emerging from a strike by coal miners in Illinois. Mead's strong support of unions must have influenced his participation in a group largely organized by power brokers who called for a "law to allow volunteers to work the state mines" (Hewett 1919). Further information on Mead's participation on this council is lacking, but this one issue shows the circle in which he moved during his time as president of the CCC.

Mead's Writings and His Presidency of the CCC, 1918-1920

Mead served as President of the CCC during the last year of the war and the year immediately following. He wrote two presidential reports, one in 1919 that is reprinted in reading 9A here. The transition from wartime to peace-time Mead is apparent in this role, particularly through his debate with Senator Medill McCormick discussed in reading 9B, with four supporting documents charting the debate's progress. Reading 9C contains Mead's second report as president of the CCC in 1920, summarizing his year's work and retirement from the position.

President Mead's Message to Members, 1919

Mead summarized his busy and successful year as the leader of the CCC during the last year of the war (See reading 9A). He documented the broad range and reach of the group in 1918-1919, as well as its growth and finances. Mead's organizational acumen and politics are clear. He still hoped for a positive end to the conflict. One of the signs that he had a false hope was his public debate with Senator Medill McCormick, of the powerful Chicago family who owned the Chicago Tribune.

The Mead and Senator Medill McCormick Debate

Wilson's hope for the League of Nations, one of his few successful steps in his Fourteen Points to survive the Versailles Treaty, clashed with the political interests of the U. S. Congress. Senator Medill McCormick from Illinois was a leader in this opposition. He feared the take over of the United States by communist forces and envious nations. Mead, of course, wanted an international organization to help make the world safe for democracy and international-mindedness. This led to a significant, public, national debate. Mead and Senator McCormick argued over America's entry into the League of Nations in the following four documents.

I present first a telegram from Mead and the Chicago pragmatist and CCC member Addison W. Moore to McCormick. This message was published in the New York Times ("McCormick Attacks League Covenant" 1919; see reading 9B, #1). McCormick replied publicly, addressing only Mead and ignoring Moore (see "McCormick Tells Why He Opposes World League" 1919; see reading 9B, #2). Mead's response not only answered McCormick's points but it became an excellent example of "a national conversation of gestures." He responded to each of McCormick's objections: "Mead Answers McCormick as to Nations League." This answer was found in the [Chicago] Evening Post (7 March 1919; clipping in Mead papers, box 1, folder 16; reading 9B, #3). A full page of the New York Times continued the debate on 9 March. Eleven readers and other public citizens wrote spirited letters. One, by Professor George Burton Adams (1919) specifically endorsed Mead's position, revealing once more Mead's national audience. An unidentified article, probably an editorial, considered McCormick's points one at a time and found them wanting in logic ("Senator M'Cormick's Objections," clipping in Mead papers, box 1, folder 16).

The CCC also supported their president and published their own version of the event (see "The Lodge Resolution and the League" 1919; reading 9B, #4). The CCC wrote an official report of the controversy and this discussion revolves around Mead's support of globalization, international arbitration, and future ways to mediate international conflicts to avoid war. Mead and his club members lost this debate over American's participation in the League of Nations and Wilson's plans for social justice after the war.

Such a macro-level, politically important conversation of gestures is defined as impossible by many sociologists who call themselves symbolic interactionists and followers of Mead! They focus, instead on smaller, face-to-face interactions without public, structural consequences. Mead does not analyze why this rational and just position failed. Instead this was one of the bitter ends of a war that did not end wars but deliberately established conditions that lead to another horrific conflagration.

President Mead's Final Message to Members, 1920

In 1920 Mead wrote his last "Retiring President's Address" (see reading 9C). Mead's closing address to the City Club is vitally important because it signals his sea change towards active city leadership, his views on World War I, his return to a co-operative model, and his withdrawal from political debates. This address is striking by its absence of planning for future programs of the CCC and Mead's characteristic optimism is missing. His weariness with the war and its costs, both personally and to the club members, is striking. He is turning over his leadership to those who follow him. Mead's expertise with organizational finances and administration is displayed, too, but this is one of the last times he employs it for civic work.

He had labored for a more just end to an unjust war. He failed, and he withdrew from the urban spotlight. He restored his friendship with Addams, he continued his alliance with Dewey, and he apparently learned few positive lessons from his scalding errors on self, war, and society.

Conclusion

Mead played a major role during wartime in one of the most powerful positions in one of the most powerful city clubs in the United States. His public citizenship made him a spokesman for the club, the city, and its male elite. He participated in local crises, the club's activities during wartime, and a national conversation of gestures about establishing an international "society of nations" through the League of Nation. His activities in the CCC from 1918 to 1920 firmly supported his ideas about WWI and moral actions. They illuminate both his successes and failures as a city leader.

His commitment to peaceful and fair arbitration after the war was betrayed by an ailing President Wilson and the U. S. Congress, and he withdrew from such a major public role as he played for the CCC for the rest of his life. He turned to more abstract philosophical thought and writings, although he never completely abandoned his political commitments and he became more convinced of the need to work for peace and co-operation in the international arena.

Mead's hope for "a war to end wars" were dashed as soon as the Versailles Treaty was signed. The vindictive response of the Allies to the defeated Central Powers, especially Germany, created many of the conditions that led to WWII and the Holocaust. Mead never pursued an analysis of why Wilson's Fourteen Points generally failed. Such an analysis might have aided him to continue as an important public citizen during peacetime.

READING 9A

PRESIDENT MEAD'S MESSAGE TO MEMBERS[3]

George H. Mead, President of the City Club, in his address to the members at the annual meeting last Friday said:

"The past year of the City Club has been a war year. Our eyes have been focused for long distances, and local problems have been regarded from the standpoint of their effect upon methods of preparation, of influencing public sentiment, and upon the fighting of our forces abroad.

Club Renders War Service

"Two hundred and thirty members of the City Club have been in the service and three of them have fallen—two of them on the battle field, one of them [a] victim of disease. In the campaigns for Liberty Loans, for the Red Cross, and the other organizations that have stood behind the lines, the Club has done its part in the presentation of the needs of the service and in the subscriptions of its members. With two great camps just outside the city, the City Club with the other clubs in the community has opened its doors to the solders and sailors who have come into Chicago on leaves and furloughs.

"Perhaps the greatest single contribution the Club has been able to make has been a part of the time of our Civic Secretary, Mr. [George] Hooker, [who] has worked continuously and at high pressure on one of the Exemption Boards throughout the whole period of the war. It is unnecessary to add that Hooker contributed generously of his time and effort outside of the hours ordinarily given to Club duties.

"The War-Time Committee has continued the interests and efforts that it brought to our situation before the country itself entered the war, and joined with analogous committees of other clubs in Chicago in a Council of War-Time Committees has served to organize efforts in the community on the issues of the war.[4]

"On one occasion the Club made guests for a day of as large a number as it could accommodate of the Blackhawks,[5] as they passed through Chicago to Camp Grant.

"Those of you who were present at the Homecoming Members' Dinner will remember vividly the welcome the Club sought to give to those returned from the service and the excitement and emotional appeal of their responses.

War Affects Club Income

"But the war has affected the Club on the side of its income most seriously. From remittance of Club dues of those in the service we have lost over $6,000. But more serious still has been the resignation of some three hundred members, most of whom have felt obliged to withdraw in the interest of economy. The

City Club with its low initiation fee, and large number of members of moderate means, and the considerable number who only belong to the Club because of its value to the community, was bound to suffer more seriously than other clubs in the city. Members are back from the service, new members are coming in, in increasing numbers, and some of those who have felt the necessity of dropping out are coming back and more will return later. We will soon be back where we were before the pressure of wartime restricted our income, but in the meantime the war has left us with a deficit which must be made up as the price which we have paid to keep the City Club alive during the war and a growing factor in the life of Chicago.

House Committee Makes Record

"Thanks to the vigor and constant effort of the House Committee, seconded by the efforts of the steward and his staff, I think no administration of the Club has been able to face its membership after a lean year with a better conscience. The Club has carried on a larger business at less relative expense even in the face of rising prices than it has ever done in the past. There has been no extravagance. There has been no waste, and there has been continued, extended and wise operation of the Club's restaurant, its rooms and the whole house. Our deficit has not been due to loose or faulty management.

Membership on Up Grade

"I desire to call your attention as well to the efforts of the Membership Extension Committee. Its work is hard, continuous and absolutely essential to the continued existence of the Club. The Directors, following the decreasing membership list during the period of greatest stress, realized that the corner had been turned, when thanks to this Committee's work the additions exceeded the resignations. The work of the committee carries little if any interest in itself. The enthusiasm to carry it on must be found in the results and the consciousness that the committee has — the interest and encouragement of the Club membership behind them. It is easy to forget that the Membership Extension Committee is doing the work of all of us, for us. The justification for this building and its extensive operation is found in our confident belief that there are more than enough civic minded men in Chicago, as genuinely interested as we are in the intelligent development of the city, and willing to use the City Club for this purpose, to more than balance the Club's accounts. It is a belief that we must make good, and it can only be made good through our support of and collaboration with the Membership Extension Committee, and while we support and collaborate we can show grateful appreciation as well. Out of the work of this committee have come two notable membership dinners which have done perhaps more than anything else this year to give members a sense of fellowship and solidarity.

Club Meetings are Success

"The addresses and discussions at the Club luncheons during the year just ended have exceeded in number and have certainly equalled in excellence the discussions of any other year in the Club's history. There were seventy such meetings last year.

"The subject of the war and the international questions growing out of the war have naturally bulked largest on the Club program. There were twenty-six discussions of international questions, including six on Russia. Nine were devoted to problems of mobilization and the war, ten to personal experiences of men and women in the war zone [see Table 9. 1 here]. Our domestic problems, however, were not forgotten in the general overpowering interest in the war. There were twenty-five luncheon meetings devoted to various domestic problems, of which nine had to do with local or state matters. Attention may particularly be called to the series of four traction discussions last fall at which both sides of this most controversial question were presented to members of the Club by the leaders of public opinion on the subject.[6]

"The speakers at these meetings represented not only many parts of the United States but many foreign countries, including Russia, England, Belgium, France, India, Canada, Australia and Macedonia.

"The Civic Committees have been reorganized on the basis of 2 system[s] worked out last year by a committee appointed by the Directors. Under this system a close association has been formed between different members of the Public Affairs Committee and different Civic Committees and they will report briefly the undertakings of these committees during the past year.[7]

New Co-Operative Spirit

"Two undertakings of considerable moment deserved to be called to your attention at the end of the year. They are both expressions of a co-operative spirit in the civic organizations of the city. The Public Efficiency Bureau, which is close to the City Club, being in theory a committee of the Club, has brought before the city a program for the reorganization of Chicago City Government. It has had the approval and support of various clubs and associations, but in its complete form it has not been felt that it could be carried through this legislature. Seven civic bodies, the City Club, the Public Efficiency Bureau, the Association of Commerce, Civic Federation, Chicago Real Estate Board, Women's City Club, Citizens Association, with others that joined later, have united through their committees to push such portions of this program as might pass the Assembly in Springfield. If any part of this program is realized it will be due to this co-operative attitude on the part of these organizations.

"When the City Government asked for [an] increase in taxing power to meet its obligations, Governor Lowden asked the city government to convince much the same organizations that their request was justified. Out of this has grown up a group of representatives of these organizations which has sat in with the Finance Committee of the City Council and has presented its estimate of the requirements of the City Hall for the coming year. Representatives of this committee are at Springfield urging competently the measures they think should be passed for the relief of the city's finances.

"One finds among the influential members of these civic bodies City Club men not only in its own representatives but in the representation of other organizations.

Getting a Common Ground

"I know of nothing in the city's life of the last year that is so encouraging as the natural coming together of these groups on a common belief. That belief has been that most of the evils of city administration come back not to lack of civic morality in the community, but civic intelligence, that to cure them we need competent continuous application of intelligence with adequate publicity. There is no organization in the city that stands so definitely for this doctrine as the City Club. The City Club has reason to he gratified that what it stands for is becoming a more conscious part of the mind of the community. It is becoming clearer every day that the one incontestable moral that can be drawn from the city election that has just taken place is that the legislative program which representatives of our committees and those of other civic bodies are pushing at Springfield ought to be passed.

"We have no reason to be ashamed when we contemplate the ideas and the movements that can be traced back through men and meetings to the City Club of Chicago."

READINGS 9B

THE MEAD AND SENATOR MEDILL McCORMICK DEBATE[8]

Reading 9b (1): Mead's Telegram to McCormick[9]

"M'Cormick Attacks League Covenant." New York Times, 6 March 1919. 6, cols. 6-7. Special to The New York Times. Washington, March 5.

Senator elect Medill McCormick of Illinois, one of the thirty nine Senators who signed the Lodge resolution on the League of Nations, made public tonight a letter sent to him today by George H. Meade [sic], President of the City Club of Chicago, defending his course. The President of the City Club telegraphed to McCormick, criticizing him for opposing the constitution of the League of Nations. His telegram read:

> "Regard the action taken by Republican Senators on the constitution of the League of Nations as a fatal disaster to the party, and if it should prevail in our neighborhood it would lose the party one half to three fourths of its vote."

Reading 9b (2): McCormick Tells Why He Opposes World League

Illinois Senator Replies in Open
Letter to Head of Chicago
City Club

Washington, March 5 — Senator Medill McCormick today made public the following letter in reply to a telegram from George T. [sic] Mead, president of the Chicago City Club, criticizing him for opposing the constitution of the league of nations [sic] in its present form:

"Sir — In your capacity as president of the City Club of Chicago and A. W. Moore[11] with you telegraph [to] me that your regard the action taken by Republican senators on the constitution of the league of nations [sic] as a fatal disaster to that party and if it should prevail — that in our neighborhood it will lose the party one-half to three-fourths [of] its vote.

"You are for the constitution of the league of nations as reported in the Paris conference. I am not. Since you are for the proposed constitution, you approve of giving the British Empire six votes in the league to one vote for the United States, and in your capacity as president you commit the City Club to that project, to which I am opposed.

BRITAIN THE GAINER.

"Upon what ground do you justify giving the British Empire, in proportion to its self-governing population, twelve times the voting strength of the people of the United States? Is one Englishman twelve times as important as one American?

"The projected constitution provides that all differences upon all subjects are subject to arbitration. This includes the question of immigration to the United States. Upon that point Count Okuma, speaking in the Japanese House of Peers on Feb. 33, voiced the determination of Japan in no unmistakable terms.

"You are prepared to submit the matter of immigration to arbitration and to accept the almost certainty that Oriental labor would be permitted to enter the United States.

PERIL OF ORIENTALS

"Your are willing to see efficient and economical Japanese operating our street railways, to find Hindoo janitors in our offices and apartments, to hear busy Chinese craftsmen driving rivets, and you are willing to commit the City Club to this proposition. But I am utterly opposed to a plan which may admit Asiatic labor into America.

"Under the projected constitution of the league, the cession of territory in the American hemisphere to Asiatic or European nations is determinable by the Executive Council or arbitrable.

"The council composed of eight Asiatic and European nations and one American nation could award to Japan the right to buy Magdalena Bay or the Galapagos Islands lying off the Panama Canal. You are for that, but I am not.

GARRISONS OF AMERICANS

"An American garrison today is keeping the peace on the shores of the Adriatic between former allies, now prepared to spring at each other's throats. Under the league, the Council could require Americans to keep garrisons on the marshes of Poland, Hungary, Roumania, the new Serbia, Bulgaria and the greater Bohemia to guard disputed frontiers.

"If Russian armies were to break through the Khyber Pass into the northern plains of India, even though the Indians welcomed the Russians, the executive council could call upon America for 100,000 or 500,000 or 1,000,000 men.

"Regiments from the mines of Illinois, from the north woods of Michigan and. Wisconsin, from the prairies of Iowa and Indiana, by decree of a non American council and not by act of the American Congress, could be summoned to march out to the strains of Yankee Doodle in order to uphold, at the foot of the Himalayas, the scepter of George the Fifth.

"You would keep our men in Russia, send them to garrison the Balkans or order them to battle on the parched Sahara if the powers of Asia and Europe commanded.

"Under the projected constitution we may be forced to go to war against the wishes of our people and the judgment of our Congress. The proposed league will not prevent war, as Mr. Wilson himself said at the White House conference,[13] and in seven different ways its proposed constitution possibly provides for war, as Senator Knox (who was Mr. Taft's Secretary of State) proved in his great speech, which I gather you cannot have troubled to read.

"I am not ready to abandon the Monroe Doctrine or agree that the voices and votes of Europe and Asia shall declare war for us, decide where our armies shall go and choose their commanders for them.

"During his week's visit to the United States, Mr. Wilson gave voice to a couple of rhetorical rhapsodies, but he adduced no argument in support of any one of the disputed articles of the proposed constitution.

NOT PARTISAN ISSUE

"This is not a partisan question. Mr. Wilson and Mr. Taft, whose leadership was definitely rejected by the American people in 1912 and 1918, are for the league as planned by Gen. Smuts of the British war cabinet and accepted by Mr. Wilson.

"Tomorrow in New York two Democratic senators and one Republican senator will speak against the constitution of the league now proposed. Mr.

Wilson is not the sum of human wisdom, but he will consider no amendment to the British plan.

"I am here in a representative capacity, but I must act upon my conscience and upon my judgment to serve my country, to protect it not only from the aggressions of ambitious autocrats, but from the vagaries of autocratic internationalists.[14]

"It is a bad sign when the Chicago City Club, which was organized as a forum for civic discussion, has become under your presidency an engine of political coercion.

Respectfully yours,
"MEDILL MCCORMICK"

Reading 9b (3): Mead Answers McCormick as to Nations League[15]

Senate Resolution Is Called
Harmful by City Club
President

George H. Mead, president of the City club [sic] today answered Senator Medill McCormick's open letter to that institution concerning the senator's attitude on the league of nations [sic]. Prof. Mead said that in his judgment the resolution of the "thirty-seven senators" against the league was a mistake from the standpoint both of the country and of the Republican party, His letter follows.

"Hon. Medill McCormick, Washington, D. C.

Sir: I have read your open letter to me in reply to the telegram sent you by Mr. A.W. Moore and myself. By a clerical error, for which I was not responsible, I was made to sign the telegram as president of the City Club. As you state the City club is a forum for discussion, and no officer can speak for the club unless the club as a whole gives him the authority. My telegram was addressed to you in the role of an American citizen, who is one of your constituents and has been a member of the Republican party and wishes that party to express the sentiments and opinions of the American people.

"The telegram stated our opinion that the action of the Republican senators with reference to the proposed league of nations runs counter to the sentiments and opinions of the American people and, if made the policy of the Republican party, will lead to its defeat at the polls, though that party may defeat an undertaking of greater moment perhaps than any that have ever been within the grasp of human society.

FORM NOT ADOPTED

"Your letter implies that the acceptance or rejection of the proposed constitution of the league of nations is the issue involved in the resolutions signed by yourself and thirty six other Republican senators. This is not the issue. This form of the league has not been adopted even at Paris. It is still under discussion and should be discussed as it has been in the United States Senate and elsewhere, and as it will be with increasing interest and attention. President Wilson has expressed himself to the effect that this is the best form that can be obtained, but the final form of the league's constitution is still on the knees of the gods. The fullest and freest discussion should obtain with reference to that form, and such discussion will have its weight in the world's council that is now sitting in Paris.

"I have no question that the American people wish such discussion, because I have no question that they wish the league of nations as a means of settling international disputes. If the proposed form is the best form that can be now obtained[,] I do not doubt that America wishes this form. If a better form can be secured I have no doubt that America wishes the better form. But in any case America wishes to approach the future possible occasions of world wide wars, equipped with the civilized method of a council of nations.

RESOLUTION DOES HARM

"Now it is against this wish of America and that of the peoples of the other countries of the world that your resolutions are directed. For while they give it lip service, they call in the first place for postponement of the league till the peace is signed, while in the second place they reject this proposed constitution of the league even if it proves to be the best obtainable. These resolutions serve notice at Paris that a group of United States Republican senators stand ready to defeat a peace treaty if it includes a league of nations as a part of the peace — especially if that league has the form now before the world, even if that form be the best that can be now inaugurated.

"It should not be necessary to point out that the issues of most wars in the world's history have been formulated at earlier peace tables. If today the victorious powers settle the issues of this war without a league of nations the guarantee of that settlement can be found only in the military establishments of the victorious nations, who must then maintain the military regime of which the world so passionately wishes to rid itself.

"If anyone is so simple as to believe that after Italy, France, and England have undertaken to hold on to gains assured through victory by their own individual or collective might, the nations of the world will then come together to do what they have been unable to accomplish at the peace table, let him regard the conflicts already so bitter over the pieces of the fallen empires of Austria Hungary and Turkey. A peace which is just to the smaller nations, and to those nations just coming into existence, can by no possibility be formed without a league of nations, and such a peace can by no conceivable possibility be maintained without such a league.

BLOCKS THE PROJECT

"To resolve that America shall [meet] first in peace with her enemies, and then consider formation of [the] league, is to damn the project by insisting that at the one great world exigency, when the league is imperatively needed, it is not to be permitted because thirty seven American Republican senators are against [it]. If the league of nations cannot be formed now when the peoples of all Europe are demanding it, when the American people approve it, when it is the only thinkable means of reaching the peace that the world demands, can an occasion ever arise that will realize it?

"This, sir, was in our minds when we urged you in the interest of the party that has given you your seat, as well as in the interest of the nation whose future fortunes you and your Republican colleagues can so powerfully affect, to reconsider an attitude which will bring disaster upon the party which promises disaster to the nation. The sentiment for a league to meet the world's terrible need is growing rapidly in the consciousness of the American people. Those who have met this sentiment abroad, though they were at first opposed to a league, have bowed before the passionate popular demand that is fired by those four years of horror more terrible than ours.

HYPOTHETICAL CASES

"You present a series of hypothetical cases under the proposed constitution of the league — the danger to the Monroe Doctrine, the danger of oriental immigration and the threatened use of American troops in defense of the English empire. In my opinion none of these dangers exist under this constitution,[16] but it is not upon this proposed form of the document that the issue rests. This is subject to criticism and change. It is the impossible alternative of no league in the settlement and maintenance of the present peace that arrests attention, the impossibility of dealing with the affairs of the world, of which we have become an inextricable part, except under the conditions of the old militarism. Even our own peculiar interests, those embodied in the Monroe Doctrine, can be properly safeguarded in no other way. Without the league guaranteeing the integrity of the territory of all nations, we will find ourselves faced by a league of Latin nations in America, resentful of our assertion of supremacy in this hemisphere. Over against such a league we would be compelled to maintain a vast military establishment and our whole life would be vitiated by the very system against which we took up arms in a Prussianized Germany.

"Allow me in closing to call attention to the constant animus against England which breathes through your whole letter. Is the spirit in which we are to approach this common problem of us all to be that of hostility toward our ally? Have you already reached the attitude in which you would sow the seeds of the next war by innuendo and attack?

"If the Republican party identifies itself with the attitude which is expressed in the resolutions recited in the Senate and with the spirit and narrow vision of your letter, it will have parted company with the sentiment and upright nationalism of America that maintains no rights and seeks no ends that are not defensible before the reason and common interests of the world.

Reading 9b (4): The Lodge Resolution and the League[17]

Prof. George H. Mead, last Friday replied to the open letter on the League of Nations, addressed to him by Senator Medill McCormick. Prof. Mead and Prof. A. W. Moore had wired Senator McCormick their disapproval of the "round robin" resolution, introduced by Senator Lodge and signed among other Republican senators by Mr. McCormick, opposing the proposed constitution of the League of Nations. In their telegram they said that they "regard the action taken by the Republican senators on the Constitution of the League of Nations as a fatal disaster to the party." "In our neighborhood," they said, "it will lose the party one half to three fourths of its vote." Senator McCormick's reply to this telegram was printed in the Chicago Herald Examiner and in the New York Times.

SENATOR McCORMICK'S OBJECTIONS

Senator McCormick's criticism of the proposed Constitution of the League as outlined in his reply to Prof. Mead was, in brief:

1. That it gives the British Empire six votes in the League for one vote of the United States.

2. That the arbitration provisions would require the United States to submit the question of immigration to arbitration, thus raising the probability — nay almost the certainty — that Oriental labor would be permitted to enter the United States.

3. That the cession of territory in the American hemisphere to Asiatic or European nations is determinable by the Executive Council or arbitrable.

WOULD LOSE CONTROL OF ARMY

4. That "under the League, the Council could require Americans to keep garrisons on the marches of Poland, Hungary, Roumania, the new Serbia, Bulgaria and the greater Bohemia—to guard disputed frontiers.... Regiments from the mines of Illinois, from the north woods of Michigan and Wisconsin, from the prairies of Iowa and Indiana, by decree of a non-American Council and not by act of the American Congress, could be summoned to march out to

the strains of Yankee Doodle in order to uphold, at the foot of the Himalayas, the scepter of George the Fifth, Kaiser Mind, King of Great Britain and Ireland, Emperor of India."

5. That "we may be forced to go to war against the wishes of our people and the judgment of our Congress."

6. That it would endanger the Monroe Doctrine.

WILSON EXPLAINS NOTHING

"During his week's visit to the United States, Mr. Wilson," Mr. McCormick said, "gave voice to a couple of rhetorical rhapsodies, but he adduced no argument in support of any one of the disputed articles of the proposed Constitution.... He explained nothing, he converted nobody.... Mr. Wilson is not the sum of human wisdom, but he will consider no amendment to the British plan.... If our common hope to create some League of Nations fails, the fault will be his....

"I am here," he concluded, "in a representative capacity, but I must act upon my conscience and upon my judgment to serve my country, to protect it not only from the aggressions of ambitious autocrats, but from the vagaries of autocratic internationalists. There is no way in which I can divest myself of my responsibility, the heaviest which I have ever borne and I suppose the heaviest which I shall ever be called upon to bear. Men have died the death in this war to defend representative institutions. We in the Senate should be unworthy of them if we were to blench before the threats of those who have been carried away in an effort not to create a League of Nations which we may safely join, but to impose upon us the Constitution of a super state, an international confederacy which would extinguish our national independence and our American liberties."

Prof. Mead in his reply, to Senator McCormick said [This reply is identical *except each headline is different and this change is a more positive statement of principles than those in the newspaper. The League of Nations is also capitalized*]:

SHOULD BE FREEST DISCUSSION

"Your letter implies that the acceptance or rejection of the proposed constitution of the League of Nations is the issue involved in the resolutions signed by yourself and thirty six other Republican senators. This is not the issue. This form of the League has not been adopted even at Paris. It is still under discussion and should be discussed as it has been in the United States Senate and elsewhere, and as it will be with increasing interest and attention. President Wilson has expressed himself to the effect that this is the best form that can be obtained, but the final form of the League's constitution is still on the knees of the gods. The fullest and freest discussion should obtain with reference to that form, and such discussion will have its weight in the world's council that is now sitting in

Paris. I have no question that the American people wish such discussion, because I have no question that they wish the League of Nations as a means of settling international disputes. If the proposed form is the best form that can be now obtained I do not doubt that America wishes this form. If a better form can be secured I have no doubt that America wishes the better form. But in any case America wishes to approach the future possible occasions of world wide wars, equipped with the civilized method of a council of nations.

AGAINST AMERICA'S WISH

"Now it is against this wish of America and that of the peoples of the other countries of the world that your resolutions are directed. For while they give it lip service, they call in the first place for postponement of the League till the peace is signed, while in the second place they reject this proposed constitution of the League even if it proves to be the best obtainable. These resolutions serve notice at Paris that a group of United States Republican senators stand ready to defeat a peace treaty if it includes a League of Nations as a part of the peace — especially if that League has the form now before the world, even if that form be the best that can be now inaugurated.

LEAGUE MUST BE PART OF TREATY

"It should not be necessary to point out that the issues of most wars in the world's history have been formulated at earlier peace tables. If today the victorious powers settle the issues of this war without a League of Nations the guarantee of that settlement can be found only in the military establishments of the victorious nations, who must then maintain the military regime of which the world so passionately wishes to rid itself. If anyone is so simple as to believe that after Italy, France, and England have undertaken to hold on to gains assured through victory by their own individual or collective might, the nations of the world will then come together to do what they have been unable to accomplish at the peace table, let him regard the conflicts already so bitter over the pieces of the fallen empires of Austria Hungary and Turkey. A peace which is just to the smaller nations, and to those nations just coming into existence, can by no possibility be formed without a League of Nations, and such a peace can by no conceivable possibility be maintained without such a League.

MUST BE NOW — OR NEVER

"To resolve that America shall first make peace with her enemies, and then consider the formation of League, is to damn the project by insisting that at the one great world exigency, when the League is imperatively needed, it is not to be permitted because thirty seven American Republican senators are against

[it]. If the League of Nations cannot be formed now when the peoples of all Europe are demanding it, when the American people approve it, when it is the only thinkable means of reaching the peace that the world demands, can an occasion ever arise that will realize it?

"This, Sir, was in our minds when we urged you in the interest of the party that has given you your seat, as well as in the interest of the nation whose future fortunes you and your Republican colleagues can so powerfully affect, to reconsider an attitude which will bring disaster upon the party which promises disaster to the nation. The sentiment for a League to meet the world's terrible need is growing rapidly in the consciousness of the American people. Those who have met this sentiment abroad, though they were at first opposed to a League, have bowed before the passionate popular demand that is fired by those four years of horror more terrible than ours.

AMERICA'S INTERESTS SAFE

"You present a series of hypothetical cases under the proposed constitution of the League — the danger to the Monroe Doctrine, the danger of Oriental immigration, and the threatened, use of American troops in defense of the English empire. In all such cases you assert that the executive council of the proposed League could determine what our action must be. If you were sufficiently familiar with the document you would realize that under this proposed constitution, on the appeal of either party in the controversy the question must be referred to the delegates of all the nations of the League, excepting only the contending parties, and that no action would be binding upon them unless the action be unanimous — in other words unless the entire world be unanimously against us, a supposition that is practically inconceivable in any issue in which the United States would be involved.

"Also greater familiarity with the proposed constitution would have shown you that on the Executive Council to which you so frequently refer the United States has equal representation with Great Britain.

"However, it is not upon this proposed form of the document that the issue rests. This is subject to criticism and change. It is the impossible alternative of no League in the settlement and maintenance of the present peace that arrests attention, the impossibility of dealing with the affairs of the world, of which we have become an inextricable part, except under the conditions of the old militarism. Even our own peculiar interests, those embodied in the Monroe Doctrine, can be properly safeguarded in no other way. Without the League guaranteeing the integrity of the territory of all nations, we will find ourselves faced by a league of Latin nations in America, resentful of our assertion of supremacy in this hemisphere. Over against such a league we would be compelled to maintain a vast military establishment and our whole life would be vitiated by the very system against which we took up arms in a Prussianized Germany.

ANIMUS AGAINST ENGLAND

"Allow me in closing to call attention to the constant animus against England which breathes through your whole letter. Is the spirit in which we are to approach this common problem of us all to be that of hostility toward our ally? Have you already reached the attitude in which you would sow the seeds of the next war by innuendo and attack?

"If the Republican party identifies itself with the attitude which is expressed in the resolutions recited in the Senate and with the spirit and narrow vision of your letter, it will have parted company with the sentiment and upright nationalism of America that maintains no rights and seeks no ends that are not defensible before the reason and common interests of the world."

AMERICA NOT OUT VOTED

At the "home coming" dinner at the Club last Friday evening [7 March 1919], S. J. Duncan Clark of the Chicago Evening Post, in his address on "America and the New World Order" also took up the cudgels to defend the League constitution against Senator McCormick's attack.[18] The statement that Great Britain with her self-governing colonies would have six times the voting strength of America, he said, misrepresents the facts, for the executive council in which the real power of the League resides is constituted by one representative from each of the five great powers, including Great Britain and the United States, and of four of the smaller nations.

On the council of delegates, it is true Great Britain and her colonies would have a greater representation than America, but action by this council must be unanimous and it is inconceivable that America would ever have the entire world against her, Referring to Senator McCormick's charge that America might have to open her doors to Oriental immigration at the orders of the League, Mr. Duncan Clark while denying the jurisdiction of the League on this matter, replied that if it should ever come before the League, America would have the right to carry the case to the body of delegates. The presence of representatives, of Australia and Canada on that body, far from creating a balance of power against America, would be a positive guarantee that our immigration policy would never be interfered with.

Mr. Duncan Clark denied also Senator McCormick's statement that the proposed constitution would oblige the United States to send soldiers to fight "for the scepter of George V. at the foot of the Himalayas." The League could not move a soldier, he said, without the consent of the American government.

WARNS AGAINST PROPAGANDA

Finally, he warned his hearers against the propaganda against the League and urged them to study the proposed constitution in order that misstatements and misunderstandings about its provisions may be corrected. He expressed the conviction that, while the language in a few spots should perhaps be clarified, the principles which should govern the League are all there and, even as it is, it is a document which we can support whole heartedly.

The heart of the masses of Europe is set upon this thing, he said, and if the Senate of the United States should bring to naught the work of the Paris conference, America, which is now looked upon as a savior, would be execrated as having betrayed the hope of the world. There would be seething discontent in Europe, a fertile field for Bolshevik and Spartacan, and America could hardly hope to resist the spread of revolutionary doctrine to her own shores. Either that, or a period of nationalistic militarism would be ushered in, a regime of fear among the nations which in another generation would result in war. With the progress of science in the development of destructive warfare civilization itself would totter. Only a League of Nations, constituted to avoid wars and to help the infant nations which have succeeded the Hohenzollerns, Hapsburgs and Romanoffs to orderly self-government, can avert one or the other of these calamities.

READING 9C

RETIRING PRESIDENT'S ADDRESS[19]

George H. Mead, in retiring from the Presidency, addressed the members in detail upon the affairs of the Club. He said:

"In 1917 18 the loss of the year was $15,222. After this had been reduced by subscriptions and the appropriation of initiation fees a deficit of $5,598 was carried forward.

"The loss in 1918 19 was $21,000 and the deficit carried forward was $16,424. The loss on the operation of the Club for the last year 1919 20 has been $7,765. Subscriptions toward this deficit aggregate $4,243. 94 and the initiation fees appropriated to meet the deficit have amounted to $7,622. 50.

"We have, therefore, been able to reduce the accumulated deficited of $23,718 by $11,866, leaving a deficit to be carried forward of $11,190.

"It was the estimate of the board in the early months of the year that we would have this year a deficit to face in the neighborhood of $30,000. That this has not been the case has been due to the remarkable achievement of the House Committee and the Steward and his staff in the operation of the restaurant, cigar counter and billiard room. A club restaurant is an accepted loss, existing not for profit but for the convenience of the members. The Club restaurant during this last year has actually made a profit.

"The next great reason for the reduction of our estimated loss from some $15,000 to about $7,000 was the response of the Club membership to the drive which carried our resident membership up from 1,914 to 2,362 during the year. The Directors of the Club met here also a defeat of their anticipations. Our first undertaking was to secure from some 900 members guarantees of a new member apiece, a guarantee which called for the payment of the new member's dues until he was actually brought into the Club. But this guarantee was not to be good unless the whole number of guarantors was secured.

"Only some seven hundred of these guarantors were in evidence, and the Directors were obliged to release them from their provisionally assumed obligations. The movement which this appeal started, however, has continued steadily, bringing in over seven hundred new members and making a net addition to our membership list of over five hundred.

"We are within fifty of the limit, which must be set upon Club membership with our present facilities. The City Club has never had as large a membership as it has at present. That resignations will be proportionately reduced we may expect, since the Directors have placed the amount of the initiation fee at that of the annual dues. Many have felt in the past that they could drop out for a period and return with no loss. There will be no economy in such a procedure in the future.

"The matter of the greatest import to the Club in this great accession to our membership lies in the fact that with a modest addition to the amount of the yearly dues, the Club can leave behind it its institution of a yearly deficit to be made up by general subscriptions from the Club membership with larger ones from a few gentlemen who have been interested in the existence of the City Club in Chicago.

"If the Club can keep its membership at 2,400, with dues and initiation fees at $40 it can balance its books at the end of the year without a deficit to be carried forward. It is of vast importance to the Club that it can see its way to pay as it goes along, with minimum dues and an aggressive interest in civic affairs. This satisfaction of economic independence can be maintained only if the numbers are kept at the limit of 2,400, or the dues are further raised. The membership of the Club are invited to make its affairs far more really their own than they have in the past.

"Mr. Dwight Akers, our acting Civic Secretary during the past year, has resigned and is at present on the Atlantic to spend a vacation abroad. His place has been filled by the acceptance of the position by Mr. C. A. Dykstra.

"We know that Mr. Dykstra can successfully carry out the work which falls upon the executive officer of the City Club of Chicago, because he has done this in a similar organization in Cleveland. His history is a guarantee of his future. Mr. E. W. Lathrop, formerly connected with the Club, later in the army in France, where he carried heavy administrative responsibilities, and then in Boston with an Industrial Commission, comes back to us as Assistant Civic Secretary.

"Inevitably the Club must take up again the burden of active civic responsibility, which we have in part laid down per force during the period of the war. We have all been far sighted and have now to adjust our vision to exigencies at home. The increased membership of the Club indicates our opportunities and the interest that is awakening in the operations of corporate Chicago.

"We are confident that in the gentlemen just named the members of the City Club will find effective means of coming into intimate touch with the problems of the City, and of helping to formulate the ideas and public sentiment by which these problems must be solved. The Club needs to stretch and exercise its civic muscles, after four years of predominantly war activities and war consciousness."

Notes

1. These lectures are listed in the weekly *City Club Bulletin*. Some of the important ones here are those where she shared the platform with Mead. See their shared presentation "Labor Night," *City Club Bulletin* 5 (27 May 1912), pp. 214 15 and 222 for Mead and Addams, respectively.
2. Membership lists are found annually in the *City Club Bulletin*.
3. *City Club Bulletin* 12 (18 April 1919), 101-102.
4. Mead served on one such committee.
5. The Blackhawks are an honored and famous regiment of the U. S. Army. They were founded in May 1846 and continue to serve to this day.
6. Presumably these were talks that led to new positions and insights for Mead in his role as public citizen.
7. A review of Civic Committee work will be printed in the next issue. [Footnote in article.]
8. Clippings from Chicago newspapers are found in the Mead Papers, box 1, folder 16.
9. This copy of Mead's telegram to McCormick is found in "McCormick Attacks League Covenant." *New York Times* (6 March 1919): 6, cols. 6-7.
10. Anon. (Chicago) *Evening Post* (6 March 1919). Mead papers, box 1, file 16.
11. Addison Webster Moore was a Chicago pragmatist who had been trained by Mead and Dewey and then joined the faculty at the University of Chicago. Moore was Mead's close friend for years, see Mead's (1930) obituary on Moore delivered at the latter's memorial.
12. Mead supported the creation of arbitration to resolve labor strikes in the garment industry during the 1910 strike in Chicago. See Deegan (1988, 115-16).
13. I could not identify this White House conference, but it likely occurred between 1919 and 1920.
14. An additional passage by McCormick noted in "McCormick Attacks League Covenant." *New York Times* (6 March 1919): 2, col. 7, reads:
    There is no way in which I can divest myself of my responsibility, the heaviest which I have ever borne and I suppose the heaviest which I shall ever be called upon to bear. Men have died the death in this war to defend representative institutions. We in the Senate should be unworthy of them if we were to blench before the threats of those who have been carried away in an effort not to create a League of Nations which we may safely join, but to impose upon us the Constitution of a super state, an international confederacy which would extinguish our national independence and our American liberties.
15. Anon. *Evening Post* (7 March 1919; two pages, clipping found in box 1, folder 16, Mead Papers).
16. A large segment of the letter by Mead was included in "The League and the Community" but was not included in the newspaper article I used. This omitted portion read:

In all such cases you assert that the executive council of the proposed League could determine what our action must be. If you were sufficiently familiar with the document you would realize that under this proposed constitution, on the appeal of either party in the controversy the question must be referred to the delegates of all the nations of the League, excepting only the contending parties, and that no action would be binding upon them unless the action be unanimous — in other words unless the entire world be unanimously against us, a supposition that is practically inconceivable in any issue in the United States would be involved. "Also greater familiarity with the proposed constitution would have shown you that on the Executive Council to which you so frequently refer the United States has equal representation with Great Britain (pp. 71-72).

17. "The Lodge Resolution and the League." *City Club Bulletin* (March 10 1919): 69 71.
18. The (Chicago) *Evening Post* supported Mead in this debate as noted earlier in this chapter.
19. "Retiring President's Address." *City Club Bulletin* 13 (19 April 1920): 94 95. Mead presented other documents prepared by the CCCs former Civic Secretary, Dwight Akers, on committee activities. In Mr. Akers absence, these notes were read by Mead as part of the CCCs annual report. Mead's address is often cited as including pages 97 through 99, although the latter pages were not written by Mead. I do not include these extra pages here.

Part 6

Mead's Writings on War Post-World War I

10

Mead's Return to Co-Operative Social Thought and a Retreat From Politics Post-World War I

"I read through [A. F.] Grant and [Harold William Vazeille] Temperly's Europe in the 19th Century *[(1789-1914) 1927], finishing it only in time to read two chapters of Mrs. Wolfe's [Virginia Woolf]* To the Lighthouse *[1927/1977].*

Grant and Temperly makes a great impression when read in this fashion, for it carries through the whole period from the French Revolution to the conclusion of the Great War, making the reader feel the inevitableness of national conflicts, and the inevitableness of war as the outcome." (G. H. Mead to Irene Tufts Mead, 8 August 1927, Mead Addenda, box 3, folder 1).

A calmer, more rational, reflective, and critical Mead appeared as soon as the war ended. His doomed hopes for a new world order echoed those of Dewey, so a review of the latter's positions is appropriate here. Dewey's ideas, moreover, have been examined in-depth by scholars, while Mead's have not.

Dewey and His Post-War Ideas and Life:
A Return to Pragmatism's International Cooperation

After the war, Dewey, like Mead, returned to his pragmatic views established before the war. But seismic changes were underway. First, Dewey's formal ideas and teaching resumed their pre-war paths, but they shifted and intensified and became more radical and political. His commitment to earlier ideas and values were clearer with a renewed emphasis on human rights. Second, Dewey and his wife Alice Chipman embarked on a major international journey. Their letters from China and Japan to their daughter Evelyn documented their work overseas, commitment to international education, and family ties (Dewey and Dewey 1920). J. Dewey's romantic interests in Anzia Yezierska were ended completely. (She continued to rehash their unhappy relationship for years, however [Rosen 1989; Yezierska 1932]). Third, Dewey and Addams reestablished their friendship and painfully recalled their strained friendship. Finally, Dewey incorporated and adopted Addams' pacifism into his philosophy (Dewey 1945a, b, c).

Because Dewey abruptly returned to his prewar arguments after the war, did little immediately to integrate his ideas during the war into his earlier approach, and Addams' postwar influence on him has been largely ignored, many scholars have focused on his wartime ideas in the context of his over-all theory. Bourne was the most poignant at pointing to Dewey's failure to act on his beliefs during the war (see discussions in chapters 1 and 2).

Immediately after the Armistice, on 11 November 1918, the League of Free Nations Association (LFNA) emerged with Dewey and Addams as two of its members, with Addams on the Executive committee (Helbich 1967-1968, 569). The LFNA was more radical than the LTEP in the terms of peace-making after the war. The LFNA wanted both future security and equality in economic opportunity for all (Helbich 1967-1968, 574), while the LTEP was focused on the peace terms developed by the post-war democratic nations.

The *Nation,* usually supported by Dewey, published numerous recriminations against the Versailles Treaty and Wilson. They characterized the pact as "madness," "an international crime," and the initiation of chattel slavery for the German people (Helbich 1967-68, p. 581). Dewey ultimately split with the LFNA because he opposed the treaty and the emerging League of Nations while others in the LFNA hoped to continue to fight together for the League of Nations.

Charles F. Howlett (1976, 341) explains Dewey's "remarkable metamorphosis" from war advocacy to peace advocacy with his new view of America as not being democratic after the Red Scare of 1919. Dewey's pessimism of a just state also extended to a lack of trust in the proposed League of Nations, as noted. Dewey held this same disbelief toward the World Court (pp. 343-44). The more radical step of ending all wars was needed: thus he supported the "outlawry of war" movement. Dewey wrote two widely cited articles explaining "What the Outlawry of War is Not" and "War and a Code of Law" that brought him to the head of the debates surrounding this campaign (pp. 345). Howlett locates Dewey's interest in the movement to outlaw war to his trip to the Far East from 1919 to 1921. Howlett (1976, 338) attributes Dewey's "conversion to pacifist ideals" as a result of his "skepticism" over the Treaty of Versailles and the League of Nations. Dewey continued to believe in this cause after its demise in the late 1920s and thought it had never had a fair hearing.

Alan Cywar (1969) sees Dewey as increasingly understanding the need for more rational intelligence to understand WWI, its effects, and American's acceptance of the Treaty of Versailles. More democracy, not less, was needed, a familiar Addams' (1902) argument which Cywar does not mention. Dewey believed Americans would ultimately learn from their mistakes in WWI, as he did. Cywar argued that Dewey did learn from his mistakes and became more radical in his politics in the 1940s, a claim that is easily substantiated.

All of these analyses of Dewey's change of heart ignore the influence of Addams on this process. Howlett shared the patriarchal biases of many pragmatists and could not imagine Addams' influence on Dewey. Thus Howlett (1976, ftn 6, 353-354), considers only Bourne and not Addams as the source of Dewey's new search for peace. Again, Howlett notes Dewey's rejection of the witch-hunting Palmer Raids in 1919, but not Addams' decade-long attack by anti-communists (Davis 1973, 212-81; Deegan 1988, 309-11). Addams' cautious response to the outlawry of war movement was again more farseeing than Dewey's, but her greater wisdom was invisible to Howlett.

Charles Chatfield (1970) delineates the many groups and ideas that split liberal pacifists during WWI into different factions. He uses Dewey as one example, although Mead could have fit his argument as well. Dewey did not anticipate his wartime position and he symbolizes one type of position: the pre-war pacifist who became a war advocate. Only pacifists who had imagined a conflict of interest between pacifism and United States' militancy during the war retained their pre-war stance. This failure to conceive of divided interests between the self and group affected both Dewey and Mead.

Unlike Dewey, Mead continued to write about war immediately after the Armistice. I begin with his unpublished, postwar writings below and then follow with his small body of published work.

Mead on "Humanity, Happiness, And the Moral Order of the Universe"

After the war Mead again believed society was evolving into a more unified world. The major, world religions were a sign of this evolutionary progress and our increased understanding of morality became a new social obligation. Mead argued in "Humanity, Happiness, and the Moral Order of the Universe" that these were potent factors for social reconstruction after the war (see reading 10A). In line with his pragmatist assumptions of moving from universalist to rational/Enlightenment ideas to ultimately increased social consciousness, he saw the contemporary world propelled to analyze the interconnections of a global social order. Thus he wrote:

> In regard to what I have called the moral order of the universe — the conception of the ideal community, whose laws were understood by God alone, and whose perfection was to be experienced only in the next world, is giving way at the present time, to the recognition that the laws governing the social and economic order, can actually be worked out by the people experiencing them. They are no long thought of as arbitrarily imposed by an external being. The individual is no longer a traveller through a foreign country where he must suffer without understanding why. He is

an integral part of the world in which he finds himself. Production, commerce, and development of methods of intercommunication are bringing men together.

Mead examined sociological themes here that were studied by his contemporaries Max Weber and Émile Durkheim. Thus Weber's (1920/1957) powerful analysis of the Protestant Ethic as succeeding Catholic "other-worldliness" and the association of this newer perspective with wealth and capitalism is similar to Mead's interpretation. Mead emphasizes that moral understanding is available to all, however, and not only to the "elect." Mead linked this broad human capacity for rationality to progressive social improvement and increased democracy. It did not result in the "iron cage" that Weber predicted. Durkheim (1912/1961), like Mead, argued that the ideal community and religion were separated in the organic society. Durkheim attributed this social behavior to structural changes only while Mead also noted changes in meaning, consciousness, and the self.

Mead on "The Estime in Which Germans Will Be Held After the War"

Mead foresaw a lowering of "The Estime in Which Germans Will Be Held After the War" (reading 10B). Both Germans and Americans needed to deal with a number of heightened and hostile emotions which would not simply disappear after the war. The feelings of hatred would not stop automatically, and perhaps he was reflecting here on his own roiled and hostile emotions. Thus he views the German colonial policies as brutal and recalls wartime atrocities. He was analyzing the sociology of emotions in this essay, a common concern in his writings before 1920 (see Mead 1999, 2001), which he apparently abandoned during the later 1920s. He may also have been anticipating the disastrous anger and vindictiveness that would be fueled by the Treaty of Versailles.

Although Mead sees Germany's feudal social structure, he ignores imperialism by the United States in Cuba and the Philippines. American consciousness is favorably compared to the more feudal consciousness of the German people. Thus Mead remains enmeshed in his wartime animosity and predicts that Germany will have difficulties accepting defeat and the Allies will find it hard to forgive the Central Powers. Mead's return to international pacifism had not occurred yet.

Mead on *Thoughts of a Psychiatrist On The War And After* (N. D.)

Mead left a typed, unpublished review of *Thoughts of a Psychiatrist on the War and After* by the neo-Freudian William A. White (see reading 10C). This important essay is Mead's longest discussion of Freudian thought which challenges Mead's ideas for many reasons. Several prime differences are their contrasting view of human malleability, the role of age during the life course, the degree of openness of the human mind, and the impact of culture upon the individual. Mead finds many of White's interpretations interesting and agrees that human hostility is important, especially during wartime. Mead took issue, however, with the Freudian assumptions of "sublimations"[1] and, to a lesser degree, "repression." This review documents Mead's familiarity with Freudian thought, and it is one of the few times he directly addressed these concepts. The review also shows how Mead's writings on war made his work more compatible with that of Freudian psychologists than any of his other essays were. Mead's acceptance of the power of hostility, discussed in his newspaper articles (see readings 3A-E here), provides another set of writings with which to compare his ideas with Freud's. Mead's later rejection of the cost of the significance of hatred, national violence, and the social, institutional consequences of international conflict also reveals how he fundamentally broke with the basic epistemology of Freud and his followers by the mid-to-late 1920s.

The contrast between wartime and peacetime Mead is dramatic here. To Freud humans were pleasure seeking, selfish, and profoundly effected by early family life. To Mead humans found pleasure in others. Family life and early childhood were vital, but adults were flexible, rational, and capable of understanding new ideas and situations. Adults could and did change, create new meanings, and have a capacity to mean what they said and to do so without the influence of hidden, "unconscious" meanings. A few scholars (e.g., Berger and Luckmann 1966; Zeitlin 1973) try to integrate Mead's thought with Freudian theory and practice (as well as Marx! See Mead's criticisms of Marxist thought in chapters 3 and 7 and readings 3A to E and readings 7A and 7B here). I believe the social psychology of Mead and Freud overlap on some issues, but they differ on so many fundamental points that such an integration is bound to fail. In Mead's review of *Thoughts of a Psychiatrist on the War and After* (White 1919) he expresses my view clearly.

Mead's complex understanding of this book, therefore, is worthy of further study. White begins with an argument in favor a "The Social Perspective" (pp. 1-5) which explains the effect of war as a frustration of everyday life and expectations. Individual goals are subsumed by the needs of the state (pp. 6-41). "The Integration of Social Groups — Culture" posits a conflict between the individual, the unconscious, and society which calls for repression. These arguments are the opposite of Mead's. The latter believes the individual is only possible because of the society, and rationality — not instinctive, innate drives — guides social behavior. The two theorists are incompatible, up to this point.

White then discusses the individual's regression during wartime which is visible in a change "to lower ways of instinct expression [and] he also renounces the higher intellectual processes and drops to lower levels of emotional reaction to account for and to justify his conduct" (p. 65). In some ways, this description of the social psychology of war fits Mead's behavior during the war. He would have been most uncomfortable with this analysis because of his own internal conflicts: Ambivalent emotions yield conflict within the person. On the one hand, Mead was an internationalist who loved Germany. On the other hand, he became a patriotic American who felt repulsed by Germany, the enemy. White argued that war removed cultural repressions and allowed formerly controlled instincts to be expressed (p. 75), another observation that fit Mead's own behavior and responses. War tore down old institutions, according to both men, but White argued that this made war inevitable (e.g., 85) while Mead thought it made war irrational and unnecessary: He wanted to end all wars. Again, they both believed that democracy, women's rights, and government control over utilities were increasingly legitimate in Europe, and, therefore, society was improving (pp. 92-93).

But White held that the "new democracy" was at odds with the increasing appearance of socialism (pp. 96-98, 102). He accepted the dialectical model of change with the thesis being democracy and the antithesis being socialism. Perhaps, he argued, the dialectical struggle was between individualism versus socialism, or perhaps it was between progressivism versus conservatism. Another dialectical process occurred within the individual, according to White, with a battle between love and hate (pp. 102-106). These dialectical processes oppose Mead's pragmatism with its union of dichotomies and his perceived unity between the self, mind, and society in democracies like the United States. Mead believed that society emerged primarily from cooperation and unity between the self and other. Within the self the individual responded to and generally controlled the weak biologic impulses. Internal conversations of gestures, especially between the I and the me, responded to rational analysis and applied intelligence. Mead and White foresaw different responses to the end of the "War for democracy."

Nations operating on hate or vindictiveness towards the defeated enemy were on a path of destruction (pp. 112-113), a point White shared with Mead who believed in the lack of vindictiveness in American policy. White foretold that soldiers returning from the war would be "socially handicapped" by unemployment; injuries, physical and mental; and a return to a new society (pp. 130-137), but Mead saw a growing welfare state to protect against such ravages. Mead believed in the goodness of Americans and their postwar society. He was dismayed, therefore, with the vindictive treaty of Versailles, the rejections of Wilson's Fourteen Points by the U. S. Congress, and their vote against the League of Nations. Thus White was correct in many of his anticipated behaviors characterizing post-war America while Mead needed to reassess what he believed in and what the postwar America called out to him. This dialogue between White and Mead is reflected in Mead's review of White's book.

Mead returned to his early emphasis on democracy and education as processes to understand and improve society. He was growing more cautious, however, in his argument that war could ameliorate the social condition. Finally, he critiqued sublimation as a concept that applied to pathological, not everyday, conditions. In other words, Mead was neither a therapist nor even particularly friendly toward their goals and practices.

Mead on "National-Mindedness and International-Mindedness" in 1929

Mead published only one major post-war essay directly linked to his pre-war and wartime ideas, but it was a major essay rejecting most of his wartime thoughts. Thus in 1929 Mead wrote one of his most important articles on war. He reflected on pacifism, WWI, hostile impulses, and national unity. Here, in "National Mindedness and International Mindedness" (see reading 10C here), he developed his most mature critique of war. He takes as his subject William James' struggle with these same issues in the latter's 1906[2] speech on "The Moral Equivalent of War." James suggests a new cult be formed for youth to be conscripted into public service in order for them to become passionately attached to the public good. Although a version of his vision was enacted with the founding of both the Peace Corps, founded in 1960, and Volunteers in Service to America (VISTA), founded in 1965, Mead considered such organizations in 1929 a naive and impossible goal. Mead argued that passions and cults cannot be controlled rationally, reflecting his new view of his own patriotism and pacifism during wartime. Rather than uncritically supporting James' interpretation, by 1929 Mead aligns with a position more compatible with that of Addams.

Mead expressed one of his most powerful rejections of war in this essay when he wrote unequivocally: "Warfare is an utterly stupid method of settling differences of interest between different nations" (Mead 1929a, see reading 10D here). He also revealed his revulsion against the violent fighting in WWI, a war he had valiantly and personally defended at great cost. An extended quotation reveals Mead's (1929a, see reading 10D here) new social consciousness:

> We have learned more from the published archives of Foreign Offices than we have from the records of battlefields and atrocities. We have learned that those who controlled public policies and finally mobilized armies were utilizing fears and hatreds and cupidities and individual greeds and jealousies which were far from representing issues over which the communities themselves wished to fight or thought they were fighting. We know that even in this day a war may arise between self-governing communities, but we know also that the issues that would lead up to this war, if they could be intelligently presented to the peoples involved, would never be left to the arbitrament of the god of battles.

Thus in 1929 Mead had returned to his perspective of 1915 where he first argued that the international-mindedness of people throughout the world was creating a new social reality. He picked up the thread from his 1915 essay in *The Survey* which he wrote for the issue collected and edited by Addams (see chapter three, reading 3C here). The 1929 article revisits the ideas of a nation-state as having a psychology, a mind, and a self involved in conversations with other nations and with the citizens of those nations. The 1915 article written in conjunction with Addams and Balch, among others, is almost a flawless "Part I" to this article of fourteen years later. It is as if the wartime Mead had not existed.

Mead was sobered by the excesses of his war fever and briefly mentioned his dismay with the aftermath of such emotions.

But he substantially returns, nonetheless, to the arguments of the pre-war William James. He does not return to his prewar assessment of Addams and her analysis of James found in *The Newer Ideals of Peace* (see reading 3A here), revealing that Mead remains tied to the perspectives of a patriarchal pragmatism and not a feminist pragmatism.

Mead's Political Activities Related to War and Peace after World War I

Mead's fervor supporting WWI directly emerged from his belief that the United States was peace-loving and non-vindictive. He believed the new world order would be based on social justice, democracy, a Fabian socialist governmental *apparati*, and his ideal community. He was immediately thrust into the chaos following the war in his role as president of the CCC, as we saw in chapter nine. His influence and interests in war and peace exceeded this one organization, however, as I discuss below.

Mead's Opposition to Punishment and Its Relation to the Versailles Treaty

In 1918, during World War I, Mead wrote a powerful analysis about his opposition to punitive punishment as a response to crime (see reading 6D here). The psychology of punitive justice inflicted harm not only on those who transgressed the law, but also on the friends and relatives of the law-breaker. The community needed to help the violator return to a productive place within the everyday life of the group (a fundamental assumption in "restorative justice;" see Neeley and Deegan 2005). Following this same logic, he was committed to the integration of nation states into an international community after the armistice. Democratic, progressive thinking politicians would be necessary to deliver a just and fair verdict assessing the injury inflicted upon other national states by the aggressors, particularly the Germans. These arguments permeate his wartime writings, and are discussed in depth in chapters 6 to 9 here.

Although Mead did not write specifically on the Versailles Treaty, one can easily imagine his dismay with this punishing document, the epitome of vindictiveness and the continuation of spite after the war. Signed on 28 June 1919, the treaty restored national borders seized during the war, but also restored some earlier borders from land claimed by Germany, released Germany's colonies in Africa, and restricted the size of Germany's military. Austria was deemed an independent nation, and significant financial reparations, especially for Belgium and France, were demanded. In January 1921 an international commission settled on the sum of 269 billion gold marks for this payment, but they reduced this to 132 billion gold marks later in the year. Both amounts, however, were crushing to the German economy and spirit. In 1921 and 1924 this amount was reduced again, but the start of the Great Depression in 1929 stripped Germany

of any ability to repay these war costs and their economy collapsed. John May-
nard Keynes argued that the devastating effects of the treaty led to the rise of
Adolph Hitler who vowed to end this financial burden, as well as its military and
territorial stipulations. Although some scholars now challenge Keynes' view,
virtually no one suggests that the treaty was not vindictive. Establishing the
League of Nations was the only significant input of Wilson's Fourteen Points,
and in chapter nine we saw how Mead valiantly tried to defend this one issue
in his battle against Senator McCormick.

Mead erroneously believed that democracy and justice would be established
after the war. If Mead's view had governed the Treaty of Versailles, which determined the terms for peace and was based on punitive punishment, then the
disaster generated by punitive psychology could have been prevented. Since it
was not a just and democratic pact, Mead was severely disillusioned about the
positive outcomes of war after 1920. He turned to institutions and organizations
to help build, or rebuild, an international and peaceful world.

The League of Nations

As noted in previous chapters, Mead was a strong advocate of the League
to Enforce Peace (LTEP), which some scholars consider a precursor to the
League of Nations. All the feminist pragmatists supported the latter, but not the
former, organization while Dewey supported neither group. Thus in 1919 Mead
continued alone in his optimism about the good effects of the war.

Mead, Dewey, and the feminist pragmatists shared the assumption, nonetheless, that the discussion of post-war national differences in a context of
cooperation was the mechanism for giving a voice to all people and states.
His commitment to labor arbitration, his opposition to punitive psychology,
and faith in education and good citizenship all supported the emergence of an
international forum for national debate and conflict resolution. He vigorously
defended the League of Nations in the McCormick debate (see readings in
9B here), and he also mentions the organization in his widely read *Mind, Self,
and Society* (1934, 209, 287) that has been misinterpreted often as a "micro"
sociological text. Wilson's failure to successfully bring the United States into
the League of Nation must have been a bitter disappointment to Mead. If this
part of Wilson's program had been the final result of the war for Americans in
1919, it would have justified some of his wartime acceptance of national violence. He also believed a just and democratic and fair-minded treaty would be
established and the former enemies would be incorporated into an international,
co-operative society. Instead, the world was as disorganized and conflicted as
it was before the war, and it foreshadowed more violence in the future. Only if
an international order emerged could there be even a hope of reducing international violence. After the Versailles Treaty Mead and his colleagues knew that
future wars were inevitable.

The Fabian Socialist Welfare State

In 1918, Mead perceived the American welfare state as growing and following the model of England. The American welfare state, favoring soldiers, women, and children (Skocpol 1992), only partially followed this model after the war, and Mead's hopes for this more egalitarian future were dashed, too. Again, the feminist pragmatists were more successful in their practical goals than Mead's hopes for help for the unemployed, the elderly, and the ill. Capitalism and militarism reigned and Mead's ideal democratic society did not happen. The Treaty of Versailles was punitive, humiliating, and crippling for the economy of the Germans and their society. Every good that was intended to result from the war for democracy was not institutionalized. His patriotic enthusiasm paled in the aftermath of blood and death, and Mead drew back from his hostility and war fever.

Once again, Mead, Dewey, and Addams shared common perspectives after the war, and their remarkable friendship was restored, albeit Mead and Dewey changed considerably more than Addams. For Mead, a sign of his re-alliance with Addams was their work to supply food for Russians.

Relief for Russian Women and Children

Addams (1918, 1922) had a major role in collecting and distributing food both during and after the Great War. This was a Quaker commitment that Addams filled by working alongside the young Herbert Hoover, another Quaker who subsequently became the U. S. president at the start of the Great Depression. This wartime work was central to helping Addams handle her anguish over the violence and her ostracism from the majority of Americans, including her beloved friends and neighbors. Before the war she also had served as a member of the national committee for Friends of Russian Freedom (see letterhead on James Bronson Reynolds to Addams, 22 December 1908, SCPC, Addams papers, series 1). This group tried to help Russians seeking political freedom in the United States, a goal that the pre-world war, liberal pacifists like Mead had advanced.

After WWI and the Russian Revolution had ended, starvation, illness, and chaos stalked the land. Meanwhile, in the United States, the 1919 Red Scare initiated a hunt for "communists." Charges of being a Bolshevik could result in imprisonment and certainly a badly damaged reputation in the minds of many Americans. Addams was a target of their persecution for a decade and the WILPF offices were under government surveillance and harassment.

At this point, Mead's re-alliance with his prewar positions appeared. In 1920 Quakers in England were pleading for humanitarian relief for Russians and several Chicagoans, notably Addams, Grace Abbott, Robert Morss Lovett, and Mead supported this work ("For Russian Women and Children" 1920; "The

Status of Russian Relief" 1920). Mead and Addams, therefore, joined hands to battle for international reconciliation in a group organized by Addams and supported by Mead to help fight against the hunger facing women and children in Russia. Although Addams was a central target for red-baiting, Mead's affiliation with her was a significant political step. He braved these national zealots and capitalist bigots through his commitment to a group dedicated to providing food, medical care and supplies, disinfectants, and social services to the Russian people. Their work was coordinated with that of the Joint Committee of the American and English Societies of Friends, a group of pacifist Quakers. In 1922 Addams chaired the national organization and led Chicago events (Addams and William F. Byron to Anita McCormick Blaine, 3 June 1922, SHSW, Blaine papers). Mead's work here reflected his changed, less belligerent justification of war. Another sign of his restored international pacifism was his stance on the World Court.

The World Court

Mead and Addams, again, both argued for a world court to settle legal conflicts between nation-states. Mead suspended his belief in international justice during the war, however, and he follows her leadership once more, returning to the theory and practices he so precipitously and disastrously abandoned.

Helen Castle Mead, Her Female Relatives, and WILPF

Helen Mead, and her remarkable female relatives, especially her sister-in-law Mabel Wing Castle, actively joined WILPF after its formation in 1918. Thus M. W. Castle was another family member who built a vital relationship with Addams and the Chicago female world of love and ritual (Deegan 1996). M. W. Castle, for example, provided sculptures for the Hull-House gardens and was active for decades in WILPF (Deegan 1999, lxxxvi).

Whether the Mead women openly supported the feminist pragmatism of WILPF during wartime, like their friend Harriet Thomas, and confronted George Herbert Mead with following the wrong direction is unknown: Perhaps they quietly resisted his ideas, perhaps they supported the war hysteria, perhaps they suffered from indecision. Whatever their wartime stance, after the war they were feminist pragmatists on the front line for international peace. Thus Mead's return to global pacifism reflected a united home and professional standpoint, many years before Addams and this perspective were accepted as legitimate in the wider society.

Conclusion

Mead expected a meaningful and just end for the war to end wars: a war for democracy should have been inclusive and generous. The international mind and consciousness called out for a new expression of global justice. Instead of this dream, a disastrous and vicious treaty emerged from the "winners" who punitively punished the losers, especially Germany. By and large, Mead retreated from his wartime analyses of the nation state, conflict, and his historical location. Although he made a significant foray into an international analysis in 1929, he struggled with his own hyper-patriotic emotions, his skepticism toward a scientific response to war by experts or politicians, and a deep concern for new institutions such as the World Court or international alliances to feed women and children. Mead reverted to his global, optimistic epistemology in many ways, but he found it hard to turn away from men's "natural aggressiveness" and it was the women in his family and not he who joined WILPF. In contrast, Dewey became a pacifist and political activist, not only reverting to his pre-war internationalism but becoming more radical and fervent in his commitments to peace and world co-operation.

WWI profoundly shaped Mead's ideas and praxis after 1920, creating a more humble, less intense, and more abstract theorist. It many ways these were good changes, but he lost a vibrancy, involvement, innovativeness, and racial edge that characterized his early work. His power as a world-class analyst, a person in the midst of politics and the city declined, as we see in the next and final chapter.

READING 10A

HUMANITY, HAPPINESS, AND THE MORAL ORDER OF THE UNIVERSE[3]

There are three conceptions potent in the life of the world today, whose development I should like to sketch: the conceptions of humanity, of happiness, [and] what may be termed ["]the moral order of the universe.["]

Before the introductions of the universal religions, [and their founders] Christ, Buddha, Mohammed and Confucius, there was no conception of humanity as a whole. Each group or tribe had its own gods, usually hostile to those of other groups. Members of other groups were strangers if not enemies and were not to be treated according to the same laws and customs that prevailed within the tribe. The great contribution of Christ, Buddha, Mohammed and Confucius was the extension of the idea of the neighbor beyond the limits of the tribe or the race, to include possibly all peoples of the world. To Mohammed racial barriers were obliterated among believers. Christ said "Who is my brother and my sister?" God was a universal father. His children and all men were brothers. Mankind was set off as a whole against an external power.

With universal religion came also the idea that every one might have happiness, but in another world. Those who resigned themselves to the suffering and evils of this world and lived in accordance with God's will would attain to perfect happiness in the world to come. Sickness and poverty were in the world as necessary features of the divine plan. It was man's lot to bear them for they were punishments for his sins and the sins of mankind in general. The greatest virtue was the passive one of resignation. The universal religions, in the third place, kept before men's eyes the ideal of a perfect community, which any one might enter who had lived in accordance with God's will in the preparatory phase of this world. God's ways with nature and man were held not only to be inscrutable but beyond the right of question.

What part are these ideas playing in the present-day organizing of society? At the present time the idea of humanity as a whole, kept alive in an idealistic way through the centuries, is beginning to take a small but recognizable part in international policy. The League of Nations, feeble though it be[,] is its child; so is the compact for the limitation of armaments; so is the spirit wherever found that makes for the abolition of wars and the arbitration of international differences. Mankind has long realized its unity in art[,] and in the fields of science[,] and in the fields of economics, [it] is realizing it now. We are one common humanity.

The conception of happiness — the idea that suffering and evil are punishments for sin, and as such are to be meekly borne, is giving way to the recognition that disease is something that can be got rid of here and now. One need not wait for the New Jerusalem. The laws of medicine, which are very gradually being worked out, are the step toward the freedom of health, which [is] the precursor of happiness. It is no longer a crime to be poor or ignorant. Poverty is the result of a faulty organization of society, and the organization of society can be changed.

In regard to what I have called the moral order of the universe — the conception of the ideal community, whose laws were understood by God alone, and whose perfection was to be experienced only in the next world, is giving way at the present time, to the recognition that the laws governing the social and economic order, can actually be worked out by the people experiencing them. They are no long thought of as arbitrarily imposed by an external being. The individual is no longer a traveller through a foreign country where he must suffer without understanding why. He is an integral part of the world in which he finds himself. Production, commerce, and development of methods of intercommunication are bringing men together.

We have[,] then[,] as over against the New Jerusalem, i.e., the enjoyment of a perfect social order worked by an external being, the picture of humanity as a whole working with conscious determination to free itself from the evils arising from the ignorance of its social and economic laws, mankind beginning at last to consciously create the world. The ends of the Earth are being brought together. Growing social organization bringing with it the gradual understanding of the laws and forces of nature, and of the economic and social order, have opened men's eyes to the possibilities of a happier and fairer world.

THE ESTIME IN WHICH GERMANS WILL BE HELD AFTER THE WAR[4]

There are voices heard in Germany, occasionally reaching the world outside, that betray serious anxiety in regard to the estime in which Germany will be held after the war. It is a practical matter. Men and women cannot be forced to buy of those whom they hate nor to sell to those whom they detest. The German statesmen may assure their countrymen that in the treaties made after a German victory [that] all provisions will be made for the establishment of profitable commercial relations with all the world and their enemies[.] But those, who will stop and consider that all the world and the enemies of the Central Powers are almost synonymous, and that even a crushing victory cannot compel trading, must look with growing distrust to the future, in an age whose life is so predominantly industrial and commercial. Nor is this anxiety confined to the economic situation. It extends to the profounder experience of seeing one's self as others see him. Back of the extravaganza which the overweening pride in German *Kultur*, the arrogance springing from the assumption of victory and the intoxicating dream of world control [that] have [been] woven in the German spirit, lies the uneasy sense that they have to live in a world in which they are regarded with a sense of growing detestation not to say abhorrence.

[There is a stimulus in the fear and hatred with which your enemies regard you, while you are under the elation of success. They call out the sanguine emotions arising from the consciousness of superiority to others. Even if they call out hatred felt by the conquered the excitement of this emotion sweeps men along into vivid conduct and experience. But repulsion felt for him by others can arouse in a man none of the excitement and elation of conflict. One may bitterly resent the implication of repulsion, or clothe himself in a sense of superiority, but these attitudes are not in the long run interesting or stimulating. The effect of the sense of being repulsive to one's neighbors gives rise to unrelieved depression, a depression which is in direct proportion to the actual unavoidable intercourse, and the intercourse which is desired but is unattainable because of the abhorrence in which one is held. The attitude which we assume toward those whom we hate involves [an] active hostility of feeling if not of action, but it is an attitude that keeps the enemy constantly present in the mind. It normally reaches a climax and subsides, and as the emotion subsides, the grounds to hate tend to lose their force. In the case of fear the vivid interest in the fearful object tends to keep it also present and to lead to some solution which will free us from the emotion. In the case of repulsion, however, the instinctive tendency [is] to keep the object away or if that is not possible to keep ourselves out of its presence[. This behavior] leads to no solution of the emotional situation, and the attitude is one that may persist indefinitely. There are few that we can hate or actively fear through long periods of time, but there are an indefinite number of persons and things that throughout a lifetime may be repulsive to us. Furthermore the emotional attitude of repulsion shuts out other emotional responses, which come in to alleviate or change the attitudes of hatred or terror. It is almost impossible to pity what disgusts us, and friendliness and affection are an impossibility while the attitude persists. But even hatred may leave the door open to admiration and love, and fear combines with affection to produce reverence.

If then Germany is arousing this sentiment in the world[, its] effect may be more serious than any other which can overtake her. There are evidences of such a growing sentiment. Those who have found themselves among the French have recognized it, and recognized it as different from the attitude which was dominant earlier in the war. The German has become a repellent object, to be crushed if possible, but in any case to be got away [from] as loathsome. In England liberal minded men[,] who rejected the proposals of the Versailles Conference which prepared for an economic war after the war, are recognizing the probable wisdom of organizing the rest of the world with German peoples outside. For this policy there is presented as a ground the pressure which the prospect of such an exclusion will exercise in forcing a change of mind upon Germany herself, but back of this lies the feeling that with a nation such as Germany is today it would be impossible to keep house.

The earlier conception of Germany's position in the world called for a change of government in the interest of the German people as really as in the interest of the rest of the world. President Wilson's distinction between the German government and the German people reflects that attitude. There has arisen another feeling as to Germany, its government and its people, a feeling that the German government is an entirely natural expression of the German community, its people and its history. The medievalism of feudal loyalty is as genuine as the medievalism of the feudal control by a right that owes no responsibility to the community. The effect of four years of war has been to relieve in some sense the people and the government of Germany of responsibility for what they have done, because, being what they are, they could not well have done otherwise.

[Furst von] Lichnowshy's revelations[5] even have not left us with the same sense of distribution of responsibility for the events of the war as that with which we regarded the first letting loose of Germany's army corps. Just as Germany's government and Germany's people have never been able to understand that America is not preparing to use its force for the purpose of exploiting Mexico and the Central and South American countries, simply because our fundamental political habits do not allow us to govern other people against their wills, just so has it been next to impossible for the American to comprehend how naturally and how logically the German community conceives of the use of force as the one natural means of carrying on international intercourse. Belgium and Servia today are natural expressions of the political habit of the German people, just as the government of German Poland has been the natural expression of the

German attitude of spirit, and as German colonial policy has expressed German instinctive reactions toward those who they undertake to govern. German brutality in West Africa, German atrocities in Belgium, German devastation in Servia, are but the logical development of the attitude of the German police. The efficiency and even humanity of the German police implies its acceptance by the community.

A control which is accepted can be rendered efficient with the efficiency of a machine. A control which is not accepted and which has no principle force in its enforcement, which sees in [the] refusal to obey no problem for statesmanship, but only for the repression by a vigorous administration, must push its exercise of force to the limit which the stubbornness of the revolt demands. To a community in which the sole relation of the government to the man who refuses to accept governmental authority is that of constituting itself a terror to the wrongdoer, the terror that enveloped Belgium is as inevitable and as legitimate as the conclusion of sorties. Inside a state, even in one whose self-confessed principle is force, representative institutions may make the bare exercise of force against the criminal a procedure that is under constant revision, in which the recalcitrant gets a certain consideration. His point of view and attitude may be recognized. In the international situation where force is recognized as the essential expression of the state toward those whom it opposes, there is no possibility of such a recognition of the individuality of the enemy. As an enemy he is to be crushed, and even those measures which are not those of actual physical annihilation take on the form of the invasion of the national personality of the enemy.

The administration of Belgium under German occupation has been directed toward the disintegration of its society, especially in the effort to foster a Flemish sentiment that would affiliate itself with the protecting German state. The plans for the occupation of the French territory, called for the elimination of enough of the French population so that it could become German in its culture. The program of occupation of the border dependent states, which Germany is erecting between itself and Russia, calls for the alliance of the German government with those classes which will be dependent upon German power for their control and will spread German influence in their communities. The whole program of *Mittel Europa* contemplates the bringing about of such German organization of industry, commerce, scientific direction, finance and political orientation that the independent action of the different peoples and nations that were to fall within it would have been impossible. Direction in the essentials of life under this program would have inevitably passed into the hands of a bureaucracy sitting at some central point, presumably at Berlin. The spirit of the German state is as hostile to independence of conception and actions on the part of the communities that are their own allies as they are toward their enemies. A state whose principle is force cannot recognize the ends and purposes of other communities as worthy of achievement, for in that case force would become a mere means for the accomplishment of other things and not the essence of the state. Such action as that of the United States in Cuba has proved quite incomprehensible to the German. The existence of other states with their independent power is, from a logical German point of view, a substraction [sic] from the power which the German state might and should have. The accomplishment of the impulse, implied in the German state, is inevitably the achievement of universal domination. Every added item of efficiency and social organization in the German state has made it more formidable to the world. Wilson's pronouncement that America never again would annex by conquest another foot of the soil of another people, was not an announcement in the spirit of renunciation, but of a principle of a society which could express itself in recognizing the value to itself of the existence and independence of another community. It recognized an international society within which national self-consciousness attains its fullest expression.

Contrast with this the pronouncement of the eminent authority on international law in the University of Leipzig. Interrogated by a society in Holland, devoted to the interests of international law, on the form which international law would take after the war, his answer was the logical development of the principle of the German state[. H]e contemplated of course a victory for the Central Powers, and in that event he assured his questioners that after the war there would be no international law; that the direction of the affairs of the world would be in the hands of the Central Powers; nor need, said he, other peoples regard such an outcome with apprehension, for the justice and consideration of Germany for other peoples under her wise direction were not to be doubted.

I hasten to acknowledge the reply which must be in every reader's mind, that Germany and her allies have no monopoly of the national attitude of crushing one's enemies, with its implication of their surrender of national individuality. Every nation which has talked of "manifest destiny," which has assumed the "White man's burden"[6] of governing other peoples, as the inevitable function of superior races and nations, every nation which has been imperialistic since Virgil[7] called to his Roman Lord: —

Tu regere imperio populos, Romane, memento;[8]

has sought to gratify its ambition by the destruction of the national life of other peoples, even when the destruction of the subject nations' autonomy is regarded as the condition of governing it better than it could govern itself. America herself started along this imperialistic highway, in its conquest of the Philippines, but eventually America's own political habits let to a new orientation and government without the consent of the governed took the form of giving the subject people the means and mechanism of governing themselves. It is this new orientation which England is taking in her reforms in India.[9] It is this orientation which will force her to settle the Irish question in the manner which the Irish people themselves really demand.[10]

It has remained for Germany to create a state that rules at home as imperialistic liberal states have ruled abroad. Germany has accomplished this by the welding together of feudal institutions and feudal loyalties remaining over from the medieval period with the mechanisms of modern life, and it is this fusion which constitutes her *Kultur*. It undertakes to govern its own people better than they could govern themselves under so-called liberal institutions, such a state calls for obedience; and this obedience is not demanded because the people have made their own laws, but because its bureaucracy enforces the laws which bureaucracy has itself made. From the standpoint of the governed, the principle of such a state is force and not reason. It should be added that such a state can maintain itself at home only by success in the external mechanisms of government, and by the sense of prestige which the people draw from the fear which the state inspires abroad.

This then is the issue that in its fourth year is becoming the issue of the war: a *Kulturstaat* or a society of nations which are organized to recognize the rights of the members of the society. For there can be but one *Kulturstaat*, or if more than one exists, they can exist after some time only through a truce. A state whose principle is force can never be at peace until it is recognized as dominant or itself conquered. It can recognize only the peace of the throne or of the grave. Two circumstances have sharpened this issue; the entrance of America into the war, with that formulation of its own political attitudes which President Wilson has so successfully made, and the Brest-Litovsk treaties,[11] with their sharp assertion of force as the principle of order in international life.[12] When Lenine and Trotsky[13] referred to the formula of self-determination and no indemnity, General von Hoffmann referred to the victorious German army which stood without opposition on Russian land.

In the medieval period the assault of such a state upon the people of other communities would have aroused fear or hatred but not repulsion. Men accepted the principle of authority embodied in their ecclesiastical and feudal institutions. The political individuality of a people was determined by their dynasty. A man was a subject and not a citizen. He might resent to the point of sacrifice of life and forcible transfer of his subjection from one sovereign to another, but the warfare which undertook such transfers of subjection was[,] after all[,] on all fours with ideas embodied in their institutions and called out no abhorrence. With the gradual growth of the national states there arose something more intimate in the community consciousness and attacks upon the country brought with them a feeling of an attack upon that which made up the personality of the citizen of the country.

And yet national consciousness has never arisen in Austria-Hungary. As an empire the relationship of the individual is to a sovereign. The nationalistic consciousness that has so enlivened the history of Austria-Hungary during the last half of the nineteenth and the opening decades of this century has not been an integrating force, on [the] contrary it has been divisive. But nationalism itself since the middle of the 19th century has become a different manifestation from the earlier sentiment. It has become an expression of the life of the nation in the consciousness of the individual. Nationalism has had its romantic period as has every phase of the life of the human spirit, and this has made politics as much a part of the inner life of the individual's religion[, as] art became during the early part of the 19th century. Devotion to a country is no longer devotion to a land simply, nor its king, but to a social organization of which one feels himself an active part. In a much greater degree than ever before a man's consciousness of the society of which he is a part enters into his personality. This has been formulated in terms of natural rights — a very insufficient expression, but they indicate that in the modern man his political relations are recognized as an integral part of the man himself. The whole democratic development of the last century has given added meaning to this[,] for nationalism has expressed itself in wars of liberation, in revolutions, in reform movements, in struggles for language and the spiritual life that has gone with it.

Certainly there has never been a period in the history of the world, in which the program of intensive domination of other peoples, which is embodied in the very nature of the German autocratic and bureaucratic state could carry with it such a profound invasion into [the] very personalities of the peoples whom Germany attacks and undertakes to subdue. And it is from this fundamental assault that men turn with abhorrence. Beside the fury of anger that responds to the attack upon the citadel of one's individuality, there is a repulsion aroused by those who inaugurate the attack, that has early recorded itself in terms such as ["]Hun,["] and ["]Boche,["] and it is this repulsion which Germany has invited from all the world by what she is and by what she has undertaken to do.

Finally it remains as yet an open question to what extent the German people will continue to accept the implications of the form of their state. It is at present a hazardous undertaking to determine how far party, popular[ity,] and economic opposition to the directing forces in the state lie inside of the traditional structure[,] and to what extent they actually contemplate a different attitude of spirit, and such a different political control that Germany could enter into an international society on the basis of right instead of might.

Reading 10C

Review of *Thoughts of a Psychiatrist on the War and After*, by William A. White[14]

White, whose competence in the field of constructive psychiatry is known through his *Principles of Mental Hygiene* [1928] and *Mechanisms of Character Formation* [1916], has presented in this small compass the important comments of [a] psychiatrist both on the psychology that leads to war, and on the conditions which war superinduces and leaves behind. He presents the individual as a bundle of instincts that seem [to insure] his own preservation and that of

[the] species. He shows him existing however in a society, necessary to his own life and training him to its own larger purposes. The process by which the organization of the individual into the social organism takes place is through repression of the individual instincts, so far as these run counter to the social functions, and their sublimation into social, valuable activities. Repression takes place through the "herd critique." Sublimation through "the utilization of the energies so repressed to find satisfaction in ways that [are] progressively more and more removed from primitive types." "The force that deflect the primitive instincts of love and hate from the immediate satisfaction — is that group of necessities which arise in consequences of man's living together in groups, the so-called instinct of gregariousness, or herd instinct." To put [it] another way: The force which, in its negative aspect makes for repression — the herd critique — produces in its positive aspect the desire for the reward of social esteem. "As individuals are organized into groups, so are groups and communities organized into larger communities, nations and international groups, This takes place by a process of differentiation of function and organ. The process of this differentiation is away from primitive instincts and their immediate express[ion]. Let the organization break down [, then] the "primitive" infantile instinct reaches expression. ["] Thus war's arise in the break down of international organization, and provide the opportunity for rebuilding, *rejuvenesces*, an opportunity which has been necessary in the past.[15] It remains to be seen whether a community of nations can be built up in the future which will be able to grow without this process of destruction precedent to rebuilding.[16]

The principle or theme of the book is the display of primitive instincts as the nature which has been subject to the training of the group.

With any breakdown in this organization appears the primitive instinct, in what may be called their infantile form. This unconscious group of instincts the author considers selfish, and the dominant appearance [is seen] as in varying degrees as abnormal, and degenerative. Dr. White shows that in large degree war must, with its break down of the league social organizations, throw men back upon the primitive instinct and set free that original human mind that is free from the social restraints and group critique which makes of us civilized men. He lays stress upon hate and fear as the attitudes which predominate and which are anti-social in their influence. His comments upon the expressions of these attitudes are illuminating and will have most salutary influence where these are read.

There is one conception largely used by Dr. White upon which the reviewer cannot forbear a critical comment, and that is that of sublimation. In the necessarily summary statement in so short a treatise, sublimation appears simply as repression plus the turning of the energies of the repressed instincts into other and socially valuable channels. He thus leaves the reader with the impression, which is otherwise borne out, that man remains at bottom a primitive savage with a group of trained social habits. If these habits break down[,] the original savage appears. Is not this an inadequate psychological analysis? Does it not present the training as an entirely external affair. What the reviewer feels this psychology overlooks is the fact that all real training is the result of conflict of impulses, which leads to reconstruction and reorganization of [the] individual's own nature.

This is only in so far as this inner reorganization is quite inadequately carried through that man remains at the core a savage. Human nature does not always remain the same. What our Freudian psychology still lacks is an adequate study of the growth of the self. But this comment should in no way detract form the impression of the fundamentally sane and highly important message which Dr. White has given out of his professional experience and his experience of the war.

READING 10D

NATIONAL-MINDEDNESS AND INTERNATIONAL-MINDEDNESS[17]

In the year 1910, in an article entitled, "The Moral Equivalent of War," William James stated the anomaly of war in the following sentences:

> There is something highly paradoxical in the modern man's relation to war. Ask our millions, North and South, whether they would vote now (were such a thing possible) to have our war for the Union expunged from history, and the record of a peaceful transition to the present time substituted for that of its marches and battles, and probably hardly a handful of eccentrics would say yes. Those ancestors, those efforts, those memories and legends, are the most ideal part of what we now own together, a sacred spiritual possession worth more than all the blood poured out. Yet ask those same people whether they would be willing in cold blood to start another civil war now to gain another similar possession, and not one man or woman would vote for the proposition.

This was written for the Association for International Conciliation and was published four years before the beginning of the Great War. If the same proposition were offered to the voters of the nations who fought through that war, I doubt if there would not be as unanimous a consensus of opinion in favor of expunging that war from history and replacing it by a peaceful advance toward our present day, though there might be a tough minded group in the community who would insist that there had been gained in the awful conflict a lesson that could never have been learned in any less terrible an experience. And that lesson they would say was the duty that lies upon the society of the human race of doing away with war. We are in no mood to cover up the criminal ineptitude of warfare by the heroisms which it displays or the ideals which it may consecrate. Yet we have not become noncombatants. The country would arm to a man in a genuine war of self-defense, but the doctrine of the recently solemnized Pact of Peace,[19] that war as a legitimate measure of public policy has been forever damned, has the full hearted support of the communities of the Western world. And I do not think that it is the horror of human suffering, even on the colossal scale of the Great War, that has been the controlling sentiment in this almost unanimous consensus of the communities of the world.

We have learned more from the published archives of Foreign Offices than we have from the records of battlefields and atrocities. We have learned that those who controlled public policies and finally mobilized armies were utilizing fears and hatreds and cupidities and individual greeds and jealousies which were far from representing issues over which the communities themselves wished to fight or thought they were fighting. We know that even in this day a war may arise between self-governing communities, but we know also that the issues that would lead up to this war, if they could be intelligently presented to the peoples involved, would never be left to the arbitrament of the god of battles. Even national cupidity, if it exist, realizes that under present conditions a so called successful war will cost more than it can profit. Warfare is an utterly stupid method of settling differences of interest between different nations.

Professor James's position is this, that no people would enter upon a war for the sake of that very ideal heritage, which they would not be willing to sacrifice after the war was fought. He did not believe that in prospect any community would regard war as a spiritually profitable undertaking. The belief I have expressed is that as regards the Great War no nation in retrospect regards the spiritual results of fighting it as a sufficient price to pay for having undergone its evils. Having stated his paradox, that while a war in retrospect may have paid a spiritual dividend which renders it a great national blessing, no war in prospect can be so assessed, Professor James advances to the explanation of wars continued existence, for we do not now maintain armies and navies for the sake of "battles long ago" but in preparation for those which may be just around the corner. I am using the word spiritual as the opposite of material. It covers every value that we cannot put into economic form.

Let us be quite clear upon the issue under discussion. It is conceded by everyone that any war but a genuinely defensive war is a prospective evil which intelligent communities will avoid. We are not entering into the contentious question whether offense is not the best method of defense, nor are we, at present, undertaking to define the field which a genuinely defensive war will defend, whether this field will include national honor and peculiar interests. We will assume that these questions have been decided in a common agreement to the satisfaction of all civilized communities. It is evident that if this fortunate position were ever attained, intelligent statesmanship would without difficulty eliminate war.

And Professor James goes on to point out the spiritual losses which society will suffer if war goes. First of all come "those ancestors, those memories and legends the ideal part of what we now own together," the spiritual heritage from war. But it is not upon this that Professor James insists, for he admits that we cannot deliberately shape our conduct to reach these results. We cannot plan wars to obtain spiritual heritages. The important spiritual values that he spreads out which come to us from war are the hardihood of body and mind, the willingness to pay to the uttermost for a supreme value, the ability to get out of our lesser selves, the acceptance of a supreme discipline which consistently subordinates minor ends to an ultimate end, the sense of at oneness with all others in the community in the great enterprise, that exaltation of spirit which we all know is the loftiest experience and is so rare of attainment. For these war is in some sense a school. Professor James does not discuss the seamy side of this schooling and the immense spiritual frustrations which it involves. And indeed he is not called upon to do so, since he was a pacifist and was seeking for the moral equivalent which he thought we should provide if we abandon this schooling, however costly and unintelligent it may be. For there is in his opinion nothing in an industrial civilization, which is organized for profit and comfort, whose springs of action are competition and our efforts to get ahead of our fellows, and whose great social organizations fail to sweep the individual into emotional realization of his identity with the community — nothing indeed in such a civilization that does or can provide this schooling. We conduct our government only by the use of political partisanship. The church anxiously avoids the major issues of the community. Loyalties to family, business, or schools, the more intense they are, the more exclusive are they.

Professor James's suggestion is that the youth of the country should be conscripted for useful labor, in which they would get the hardihood of body and mind which military training gives. It would be essential to the accomplishment of the purpose which Professor James had in mind that this labor should be felt by the conscripted youth to be necessary to the life of the community. They would have to feel that they were identified with the community in what they did, if they were to reach that emotional fusion which war under favorable conditions induces.

I do not think that Professor James regarded his suggestion so much as an immediately practicable undertaking as an illustration of the type of experience which society in some fashion must bring into the lives of citizens if they are to get the qualities and training which war gives however imperfectly. What he insists upon is that the social ends and values are there and that they should enter the lives of our citizens, and that society has within its power to work out in some fashion practicable ways in which this can be accomplished. His scheme of conscription to community labor was a striking and picturesque manner of presenting what ought to be a logical part of a pacifist program.

Nearly twenty years have passed since Professor James wrote "The Moral Equivalent of War," and within those years the Great War has been fought, and has brought forth the League of Nations, the most serious undertaking to end war which international society has ever made. The attention of the pacifist is upon other things than the "moral equivalent of war." A hopeful project has been put into actual operation, and the relations of nations have been subject to a publicity and a sort of criticism which are novel in history. We have remained outside of the League of Nations because in our history we have been largely outside of the political life of Europe that led to the great catastrophe. We have been and are unwilling to enter into that complex of national, racial, and economic problems which are so foreign to us. But the outcome of the war has none the less brought us into more intimate human and economic relations with European peoples than we have occupied in the past, and the absence of imperialism in our history and our fundamental dislike of militarism inevitably arouse a sympathy with the great experiment that is being tried out at Geneva. The pacifist has a text to preach from that that he never had before and a practical program that was inconceivable twenty years ago. The somewhat embarrassing challenge which the great psychologist put up to him, he has pushed one side in the press of more practicable undertakings. Indeed, one re reads the essay today with a certain sense of unreality.

Following this essay in *Memories and Studies* (1910/1911) is an after dinner address given by Professor James at a peace banquet. There is there the same account of human nature, bred through long centuries to fight, the same emphasis upon the failure of the pacifist's program to come to terms with the exigencies of life, and there is the same sense of the strength of the enemy — the rooted bellicosity of human nature and its demand for the thrill of battle. Said Professor James, "A deadly listlessness would come over most men's imagination of the future if they could seriously be brought to believe that never again in *saecula saeculorum* [throughout the ages] would a war trouble human history. In such a stagnant summer afternoon of a world, where would be the zest or interest?" We have had a surfeit of those thrills and have counted their cost, says the pacifist. It is not necessary to see the good in fighting any longer. The task of getting rid of it is too insistent when we have seen it and lived through it on the grand scale. There is the [Kellogg-Briand] Peace Pact[20] and there is the World Court, the very inception of which was American. For us to remain out of it is a scandal. In the midst of such activities, why should the pacifist stop to consider the psychology of fighting? But the challenge is still there, and it may be that the pacifist is not wisely pushing it [to] one side, in the press of his immediately practicable undertakings. He might get a deeper insight into their import.

Let us consider the spiritual values in which war may school men and women, however costly the schooling may be. The hardihood of body and mind — the opposite of the nature of Roosevelt's "mollycoddle"[21] — can conceivably be secured without the expense of warfare. The program suggests that of Charles Lamb, burning down the house to get a roast pig,[22] but it points out sharply the criticism upon the present order of society. Our insistent motives to strenuous conduct are personal and individualistic, those of success in the competitions of business, the professions, and the social struggle. The effective public ideals are those of well being, comfort, and that condition of body and mind in which men can enjoy life. Our social programs look to the removal of evils, sickness, misery, and drudgery. As Frederick Harrison[23] said of the ideal of the utilitarians, they look toward a world in which everyone could be sure of smacking his lips over a good breakfast of ham and eggs. The strenuousness of life seizes upon the individual in the struggle for the means of living and competitive success, but it does not inexorably involve his public interests, until the existence of his society is threatened, and when a man becomes altruistically interested in public ends, these ends appear as the alleviation of suffering and attained enjoyments rather than as his own achievements — the concentrated interest in mastering and controlling his world.

The other values that war may foster — willingness to pay to the uttermost for supreme goods, the rising above our lower selves, the acceptance of a discipline which subordinates minor ends to ultimate ends, and the exaltation that rises from identification of one's self with all who are with him in the great enterprise — that we should look away from civil life to war to arouse these is but a further reflection upon the conscious motivation of that civil life. War presents common goods in an imperative mood, which they will not assume in peaceful times, and therefore gives them a hold upon us which they never secure in philanthropic undertakings.

Professor James, however, has painted a picture of men who enjoy fighting immediately and have the zest of violent adventure in their blood through a long physiological and social heritage — the immanent bellicosity of human nature which I think he has overdrawn. The average man does not want to fight for the sake of fighting. Threaten him and what is precious to him and the fighting complex is indeed ready to blaze out. His interest in violent adventure is easily satisfied by the movie, the detective tale, and the dramas of literature and history. Professor James was himself sympathetic with the revulsion to violence from drudgery and ennui. There is a story current that after a two days' session at a Chautauqua[24] he exclaimed, "O, for an Armenian massacre!" But I do not think that in the interests of peace we have to combat a fundamental instinct of bloodshed. If the bare interest in slaughtering our fellows were so immediate, the campaigns of Army and Navy Leagues would be much simpler and much less expensive. The case for war does not lie in the fighting itself, but in that for which war compels us to fight.

Professor James then calls the attention of his fellow pacifists to war as a schoolmaster that succeeds, at least on occasions, in making the public good the intense interest of the individual, in enforcing a discipline which reduces minor ends into subordination to a supreme end, and finally in arousing an exaltation of spirit that springs from identification of one's self with the community for which he is ready to make the supreme sacrifice, and points out that as long as human nature responds almost instinctively to the call to arms and as long as there is no other undertaking that accomplishes this for the whole community those who would abolish war must offer some moral equivalent for war or render a reason for the sacrifice. War on occasions makes the good of the community the supreme good of the individual. What has the pacifist who would abolish war to put in its place?

In a word we make the public good our immediate interest when it arouses the fighting spirit. Otherwise it is apt to be a philanthropic good, to reach which we must put [on] one side our private interests. To be interested in the public good we must be disinterested, that is, not interested in goods in which our personal selves are wrapped up. In wartime we identify ourselves with the nation, and its interests are the interests of our primal selves. And in the fighting mood we find that we are in sympathetic accord with all others who are fighting for the same cause. Then we experience the thrill of marching in common enthusiasm with all those who in daily life are our competitors, our possible rivals, and opponents. The barriers are down which we erect against our neighbors and business associates. In daily life they may be hostile to our interests. We proceed warily. We protect ourselves even against our partners, associates, and employees with contracts and agreements defended with penalties. Even our good manners are means of keeping possible bores at a distance. It is sound sense to regard everyone as a possible enemy. In wartime these barriers are down. We need to feel the support of our fellows in the struggle and we grapple them to ourselves. The great issue itself is hallowed by the sense of at oneness of a vast multitude.

It is easy to study this in everyday situations. Gather ten or fifteen of your acquaintances and make the subject of your conversation the admirable qualities and services of someone known to all. Then change the subject of converse to someone for whom all have a common dislike, and note how much warmer is the sense of at oneness of those who are engaged in common disparagement than in encomium. The hostile attitude is peculiarly favorable to social cohesion. The solid South is the product of common hostility to the negro [sic] as a social equal. The Ku Klux Klan is a deliberate manufacture of compact groups by the use of racial and religious antipathies. I think it is worth our while to make some inquiry into this cohesive power, which the hostile impulse in human nature exercises with such absolute authority.

We have long known that behind the spiritual exaltation of wartime patriotism and the irresponsibility of mob consciousness lies the same psychological mechanism. And this fact is a ground neither for extolling it nor for damning it. It is just a psychological mechanism which like other mechanisms has served both fine and ignoble ends. It is equally inept to define, with Dr. [Samuel] Johnson,[25] patriotism as the last refuge of the scoundrel, and to exalt Judge Lynch as the embodiment of social justice.[26] But it is both apt and obligatory upon us to examine this mechanism when we are not caught in its meshes, and are free to comprehend it; for when we are involved in it, it is next to impossible to approach it with impartial consideration. Neither the patriot in his moment of exaltation nor the member of the blind mob in his unrestrained ferocity is capable of following the dictum: Know thyself. He may conceivably get outside of his intoxication, but he is then engaged in controlling his passionate impulses. He is in no mood to understand them.

I have already indicated the character of this mechanism. The hostile impulse unites us against the common enemy, because it has force enough to break down customary social textures, by which we hold others at a distance from our inexpugnable selves. But it was this social structure by which we realized ourselves. Our rights and our privileges, our distinctions of capacity and skill, our superiorities and our inferiorities, our social positions and prestige, our manners and our foibles not only distinguish and separate us from others but they constitute [to] us what we are to ourselves. They constitute our individualities, the selves that we recognize, when we thank God that we are not as other men are, and when we determine upon what terms we can live and work with members of our families, with our neighbors and our countrymen. If these are in any degree broken down we are no longer the same individuals that we were. To join ourselves with others in the common assault upon the common foe we have become more than allies, we have joined a clan, have different souls, and have the exuberant feeling of being at one with this community.

There lie in all of us both of these attitudes. It is only in our common interests and our identities with others that there is found the stuff out of which social selves are made — and it is only in distinguishing and protecting these selves from others that we exercise the self consciousness that makes us responsible and rational beings.

But even the apparatus of this self-consciousness we have borrowed from the community. What are our rights in which we defend ourselves against all comers, but the rights which we recognize in others, that ours may be recognized by others? What are our peculiar powers and capacities but the facilities by which we perform our parts in common undertakings, and where would they be if others did not recognize them and depend upon them? The proudest assertion of independent selfhood is but the affirmation of a unique capacity to fill some social role. Even the man who haughtily withdraws himself from the crowd, thinks of himself in terms of an ideal community which is but a refinement of the world in which he lives. It is by assuming the common attitudes to each other, which an organized community makes possible, that we are able to address ourselves in the inner forum of our thoughts and private purposes. A self is a composite or interaction of these two parts of our natures — the fundamental impulses which make us co operating neighbors and friends, lovers and parents and children, and rivals, competitors, and enemies; on the other side the evocation of this self which we achieve when we address ourselves in the language which is the common speech of those about us. We talk to ourselves, ask ourselves what we will do under certain conditions, criticize and approve of our own suggestions and ideas, and in taking the organized attitudes of those engaged in common undertakings we direct our own impulses. These two parts are the matter and the form of the self, if I may use Aristotelian phraseology. The one is the stuff of social impulses and the other is the power which language has conferred upon us, of not only seeing ourselves as others see us but also of addressing ourselves in terms of the common ideas and functions which an organized society makes possible. We import the conversation of the group into our inner sessions and debate with ourselves. But the concatenated concepts which we use are ours because we are speaking in the language of the outer universe of discourse, the organized human world to which we belong.

In the sophisticated field of self-consciousness we control our conduct. We place ourselves over against other selves and determine what we want to do, what we have a right to do, and what other people may do. Here we assert ourselves and maintain ourselves by recognized rights and accorded privileges. In the field of the stuff — the matter — of personality we have no such power. We are born with our fundamental impulses. We choose our business associates and the members of our clubs and the guests at our dinner parties, but we fall in love, and whatever action we take upon this primal premise, it is not a matter of our own choice. We say that we instinctively help a child who has fallen down, and our immediate attitudes toward puppies, kittens, and little pigs are different from those we take toward dogs, cats, and hogs, and the impulse to helpfulness is just as much an endowment as the impulse of hostility. This primal stuff of which we are made up is not under our direct control. The primitive sexual, parental, hostile, and co operative impulses out of which our social selves are built up are few — but they get an almost infinite field of varied application in society, and with every development of means of intercourse, with every invention they find new opportunities of expression. Here by taking thought we can add to our social stature. But we have no direct control over our loves and our hates, our likes and our dislikes, and for this reason we are relatively helpless when a common enemy fuses us all into a common patriotic pack or stampedes us under the influence of sympathetic terror.

This, then, is the stuff out of which human social selves are made up, their primal stuff or matter of social impulses, and the form of sophisticated self consciousness. But society is the interaction of these selves and an interaction that is only possible if out of their diversity unity arises. We are indefinitely different from each other, but our differences make interaction possible. Society is unity in diversity. However there is always present the danger of its miscarriage. There are the two sources of its unity — the unity arising from the interconnection of all the different selves in their self-conscious diversity and that arising from the identity of common impulses; the unity, for example, of the members of a great highly organized industrial concern or of the faculties and the students of a great university and the unity of a crowd that rushes to save a child in danger of its life. By these two principles of unity society is maintained; but there is an ever present risk of failure. Every society has it at the back of its mind. We want security and we distrust it. Society in every period of its history has presented to itself that danger in one form or another. Today we dread the Bolsheviki. At another time it has been the "interests"; at times the mob, and at other times the arbitrary power of a monarch.

We come back to our original question, How shall we get and maintain that unity of society in which alone we can exist? The ever present method of creating cohesion from below, from the impulses, is found in the common hostile impulse. The criticisms which are exercised upon the civil motives are but illustrations of this. Government is by partisanship. We can bring the voters to the polls only through their hostility to opposite parties. A campaign for a community chest is quickened by competitive teams. The great days of the religions have been the days of hostility, between the religions, between the Church and the sects, or between different churches. The fight with the devil and all his angels united men whom a common hope of salvation left untouched. More evident still is the need of the fighting attitude when a large community with varied groups and opposing interests is to be brought into a self conscious whole. The antagonism of the Chinese to the Japanese and the English did more than anything else to awaken a Chinese national spirit. In our Civil War slavery was the issue, because it divided the nation. Men of the North fought for the Union and in fighting for it they felt it. The readiest way of arousing an emotional appreciation of a common issue is to fight together for that issue, and until we have other means of attaining it we can hardly abandon war.

It is not a question of thrills nor of satisfying a deep seated bellicosity in the human animal. It is a question of making ourselves actually feel the values that are wrapped up in the community. While war was still a possible national adventure, there was a certain rough psychological justification for the dictum, that at least one war in a generation was essential for the spiritual hygiene of the nation. The toleration of secret diplomacy, the cherishing of national honor and peculiar interests as lying outside the field of negotiation had behind it an obscure but profound feeling that in national honor and in these peculiar interests were symbolized a national unity which could be made precious by the arbitrament of war.

What better illustration of this can be found than in the Monroe Doctrine? None are agreed upon what the doctrine is. The nations of South and Central America in whose interests it was inaugurated with one voice denounce it. It is absurd to say that we can find an issue in the threatened neighborhood on this hemisphere of European powers, when our continent wide, unfortified Canadian frontier, within the century and more since it was established, is almost the only frontier in the whole wide world that has not been crossed by belligerent forces. No, it is something — no matter what it is — for which we will fight. To think of it in these terms is to feel that there is a nation back of it. The more unintelligible the issue is, the more it emphasizes the unanimity of the community. It is an issue that cannot be discussed for we cannot in cold blood find out what the issue is. We must be of one mind about it, for it is impossible to have different minds about that which no one can comprehend. The only issue involved in the Monroe Doctrine is this, are you a patriot, are you a red blooded American, or are you a mollycoddle? Let us get down to real reasons and abandon good reasons. Even when we hope that there may be no future wars, we feel that we should keep certain issues which can arouse the fighting spirit, for the sake of their effect in drawing men together in a fashion which cannot be achieved by public interests, which are after all so divisive.

I take it that this is the real question that is put up to us by Professor James's moral equivalent of war. Can we find outside of the fighting spirit that unifying power which presents a supreme issue to which all others are subordinated, which will harden us to undergo everything, and unite us in the enthusiasm of a common end?

> When I have borne in memory, what has tamed
> Great Nations, how ennobling thoughts depart
> When men change swords for ledgers, and desert
> The students bower for gold, some fears unnamed
> I had, my Country — am I to be blamed?[27]

There is nothing in the history of human society nor in present day experience which encourages us to look to the primal impulse of neighborliness for such cohesive power. The love of one's neighbor cannot be made into a common consuming passion. The great religions that have sought to embody it when they have dominated society have appeared as the Church militant. Auguste Comte (1853/1868), the great French sociologist and philosopher, sought to fashion a universal religion out of it. It gathered a handful of great souls into its communion. How widespread was its sweep of the community may be indicated by the tale that, in London, a gathering of the Comtists took place within which a schism arose. For even in this church sects appeared. A London wag reported that the members of the convention gathered in one cab and came away in two. There is, to be sure, no falling off in numbers of those who identify themselves with different Christian sects in the Western world, but there never was a time when the churches have had less power in organizing the community into common action. We can unite with common zeal to aid the victims of famines, of earthquakes, and of conflagrations, but we do not go into nor come out of such common undertakings with a sense of the supremacy of the nation or society that holds us together. The passion of love between the sexes isolates those whom it consumes, and family life segregates us. The positive social impulses exhibit no forces that bind us immediately together in conscious devotion to the complex community out of which our sophisticated selves arise. They have their place in the cults, mores, and customs that form the tissue of human society, but they do not flame out into a patriotism that can fuse men in the devotion to the fatherland.

The Great War has presented not a theory but a condition. If war were a possible measure of public policy, it might be kept for the sake of social cohesion, even if the ends for which wars are ostensibly fought were illusory and inadequate. But the Great War has made this no longer possible. Every war if allowed to go the accustomed way of wars will become a world war, and every war pursued uncompromisingly and intelligently must take as its objective the destruction not of hostile forces but of enemy nations in their entirety. It has become unthinkable as a policy for adjudicating national differences. It has become logically impossible. This is not to say that it may not arise. Another catastrophe may be necessary before we have cast off the cult of warfare, but we cannot any longer think our international life in terms of warfare. It follows that if we do think our national and international life, we can no longer depend upon war for the fusion of disparate and opposing elements in the nation. We are compelled to reach a sense of being a nation by means of rational self consciousness. We must think ourselves in terms of the great community to which we belong. We cannot depend upon feeling ourselves at one with our compatriots, because the only effective feeling of unity springs from our common response against the common enemy. No other social emotion will melt us into one. Instead of depending upon a national soul we must achieve national mindedness.

Professor James seems to have thought that we might substitute some other cult for the cult of warfare and reach the same emotional result — the cult of youth conscripted to necessary social labor. But cults are not deliberately created in this fashion. Plato admitted this. He needed a set of cults for his ideal state, but he was compelled to postulate them as already in being. Even his philosopher king could not legislate cults into existence. [Benito] Mussolini[28] refuses to recognize the logic of the situation. He is depending upon the hostile impulse to fuse his Fascist state, and he is compelled to talk in terms of wars. He has to quicken imaginations with pictures of Roman conquests, and the threat of full panoplied legions. He is undertaking to arouse an Italian soul, not to fashion an Italian mind. He is, undoubtedly, very far from wanting the wars whose threat helps to hold this society together, for nothing would more certainly shatter it than the operation of a modern war; but he can safely threaten for a while, in a Europe whose surrounding populations have had a surfeit of fighting. The task of becoming nationally minded is then that which the outcome of the Great War is imposing upon us.

We enter upon our civil conflicts with the comfortable sense of a sovereign state behind us endowed with supreme and ultimate force to compel adherence to law and order. This state can if necessary call out the national troops to enforce the unity of the community which conflicting interests may have threatened. Can we keep this sort of state unless it is endowed with an army trained to fight the country's wars? A police force, even a national police force, is not an army. The dread sovereignty of the state is evidenced in troops trained to the unthinking obedience which warfare enforces. If we are compelled to surrender war with the blind military obedience which it puts into the hands of the state, we will be compelled to think out rational solutions of our civil quarrels and think them out a good deal more quickly. It is a great deal easier to feel than it is to think. It is a great deal easier to be angry with one's enemy than to sift the grounds of one's quarrel and find the basis for a reasonable solution. And if you can find grounds for making your enemy the enemy of the community — a Bolshevik, for example — the procedure is still easier. To use the mind with which the community has endowed you to compass the common interests rather than as a means of pursuing your own interest is a strenuous affair, and this is what it means to become nationally minded.[29] Let me repeat if we surrender war there is no way of maintaining national unity except in discovering that unity in the midst of the diversity of individual concerns. There is a common good in which we are involved, and if society is still to exist we must discover it with our heads. We cannot depend upon our diaphragms and the visceral responses which a fight sets in operation.

There is something profoundly pathetic in the situation of great peoples, that have been struggling up through long centuries of fighting and its attendant miseries, coming closer and closer to each other in their daily life, fashioning unwittingly larger racial, lingual, liturgical, confessional, political, and economic communities, and realizing only intermittently the spiritual life which this larger community confers upon them, and realizing it only when they could fight for it. The pathos comes out most vividly in the nationalisms of the nineteenth and twentieth centuries. These nationalisms have meant the sudden realization that men belonged to communities that transcended their groups, families, and clans. They had attained selves through which they entered into relation with their common nationals, and the only way in which they could seize upon and enjoy this new spiritual experience was in the fight for its symbols, their common language and literature, and their common political organizations. The pathos lies in the inability to feel the new unity with the nation except in the union of arms. It is not that men love fighting for its own sake, but they undergo its rigors for the sake of conjunction with all those who are fighting in the same cause. There is only one solution for the problem and that is in finding the intelligible common objects, the objects of industry and commerce, the common values in literature, art, and science, the common human interests which political mechanisms define and protect and foster. But all these values are at first divisive. They appear at first as individual and class interests and at first one fights for them and against others who threaten them. The rational attitude is to find what common values lie back of the divisions and competitions. Within our communities the process of civilization is the discovery of these common ends which are the bases of social organizations. In social organization they come to mean not opposition but diverse occupations and activities. Difference of function takes the place of hostility of interest. The hard task is the realization of the common value in the experience of conflicting groups and individuals. It is the only substitute. In civilized communities while individuals and classes continue to contend, as they do, with each other, it is with the consciousness of common interests that are the bases both for their contentions and their solutions. The state is the guardian of these common interests, and its authority lies in the universal interest of all in their maintenance. The measure of civilization is found in the intelligence and the will of the community in making these common interests the means and the reason for converting diversities into social organization.

The Great War has posed the problem before contending nations of carrying civilization into the community of nations; that is, it has left us with the demand for international mindedness. The moral equivalent of war is found in the intelligence and the will both to discover these common interests between contending nations and to make them the basis for the solution of the existing differences and for the common life which they will make possible.

This is the moral equivalent of war if the office of war is to adjust international differences. As an adjudicator war is utterly discredited since, as I have said, if war is logically pursued it leaves nothing to be adjudicated, not even the enemy nations themselves. However, it has not been the peace treaties after hostilities have ceased that have been the valuable contributions which warfare has made to human history. Professor James has indicated them — the spiritual heritage of devotions and heroisms and the consecrations of national values which occupy the most precious pages in history, and the emotional exaltation which accompanies the merging of a crowd of discrete individuals into a living union of men with a single purpose. These are the by products of war which are in themselves invaluable, but to compass which no people would deliberately undertake war. This constitutes the paradox with which Professor James opened the discussion of his theme. It is a paradox the full depth of which he did not sound. The lying secret diplomacies, the exasperations of suppressed minorities, the profiteering of individuals and combines, the underhand conservation of selfish interests, which men have allowed in the past and still in a measure allow because they keep war as a valued possibility to hold the nation together — this is a stranger paradox. Must we simply surrender the values which we dare not directly invoke?

It is a question that concerns both ethics and psychology. The answer of ethics has already been given. The spiritual losses of war in prospect enormously outweigh any estimate we dare put upon these by products. The psychological solution Professor James sought in a somewhat fantastic cult of youth conscripted for social labor. He would substitute a harmless cult for one that is extremely hazardous. We have seen that cults cannot be manufactured to order. The willingness of the communities of the world to keep up the apparatus of fighting and the threat of war is an advertisement both of the supreme value of the larger national self and the extreme difficulty of bringing the citizen to realize it. What Professor James saw was that it was only in war that public interests do not leave men cold. The war taxes are the only taxes that are willingly paid. It is still so much easier to revert to the old dispensation and chant with the Psalmist that our God is a man of war.

What I am seeking to bring out is that the chief difficulty in attaining international mindedness does not lie in the clash of international interests but in the deep seated need which nations feel of being ready to fight, not for ostensible ends but for the sake of the sense of national unity, of self determination, of national self respect that they can achieve in no other way so easily as in the readiness to fight.

National mindedness and international mindedness are inextricably involved in each other. Stable nations do not feel the need in any such degree as those that are seeking stability. It was the militaristic fusing of the German nation out of separate German states by Bismarck's[30] policy of blood and iron and the fusion of a vast backward community of Russian peasants by a Czardom with a pan Slavic battle cry that played a great part in the origins of the Great War. When the French are convinced that the German nation no longer needs to threaten her neighbors in order that she may feel her own national self, the fears of France will subside. Bismarck's proud sentence — Germany fears God and no one else on earth — was the challenge of a nation that dared not disarm because it feared internal disintegration. Bismarck's God was a man of war, that was the reflex of an international inferiority complex.[31]

The outlawry of war[32] as proclaimed in the Peace Pact goes then only halfway toward its great goal. It will be presumably approved by the nations of the world. So far as ostensible international differences are concerned, the peoples of the Western world are agreed that they should be settled by some method of negotiation, and that war to this end is no longer a policy which civilized nations may pursue. Self-defense remains a permissible ground for fighting, but with no war of offense there would be none of defense, and wars would vanish with the development of adequate means of negotiation, but we are not willing to have the readiness to fight disappear. So we retain national honor and peculiar interests. Why cannot these be adjudicated as well? Because these touch the sense of national self respect. As long as we have these provisos, we have the proud sense of being willing to fight — to stake everything upon the assertion of national selfhood. It was this sense which President Wilson's unfortunate phrase offended — being too proud to fight. It was seemingly a phrase that contained a contradiction in terms. Pride predicates a fighting spirit.

Now, if I am not mistaken such an attitude at the present period in human history is a revelation of an uncertainty of national selfhood and a grasping after the approved means of securing it—the wartime spirit. For at this period of the world's history there is no point of national honor and peculiar interest which is not as open to reasonable negotiation in a community of self respecting nations as any of the so called justiciable and negotiable issues, if we were sure of ourselves. But we are not sure of our national selves, and a certain amount of national psychoanalysis would be very valuable if not very probable. One thing, however, is clear, that we cannot attain international mindedness until we have attained a higher degree of national mindedness than we possess at present; and a rough gauge of it will be found in the necessity of retaining national honor and peculiar interests as causae belli [causes of war].

Such a formulation seems to imply that if we were willing to get down to real reasons and abandon good reasons, if we were willing to be really reasonable we could immediately banish the threat of war from our international and our national life. I do not believe that this is the case. Civilization is not an affair of reasonableness; it is an affair of social organization. The selfhood of a community depends upon such an organization that common goods do become the ends of the individuals of the community. We know that these common goods are there, and in some considerable degree we can and do make them our individual ends and purposes, to such a degree that we have largely banished private warfare from the recognized methods of maintaining self respect in civil conflicts. But there are still great gaps in our social organization, notably between our producers and the social service which they perform. Here there are groups that have to assure themselves of their self respect by fighting on occasions. The labor unions and the employers as well preserve their solidarity, that is their sense of common selfhood, by the mechanism of hostility, that is by the threats of strikes and lockouts. Back of it lies the inability of the laborer to realize himself in the social process in which he is engaged. Where such a situation becomes acute, men, if they can, will always bind themselves together by hostile organizations to realize their common purposes and ends and thus assure themselves the selfhood which society denies them. Men will always jealously maintain and guard this mechanism to assure themselves to themselves. We will get rid of the mechanism of warfare only as our common life permits the individual to identify his own ends and purposes with those of the community of which he is a part and which has endowed him with a self.

Notes

1. See ftn. 22, p. 151.
2. Mead (1929) believed that James first gave this speech in 1910, but James delivered it first in 1906, at Stanford University.
3. Box 5, folder 5, Mead Addenda.
4. Box 3, file 15, Mead Addenda.
5. Karl Max, Furst von Lichnowsky (1860-1914) was a German ambassador to England from 1912 to 1914. He tried to prevent WWI, and was in direct conflict with his government. He wrote several essays and pamphlets that detailed how his efforts were resisted.
6. See ftn. 14, p. 238.
7. "Vergilius (70 B. C.- 19 B. C.)," or Virgil, was the noted Roman poet who wrote the epic *Aeneid* (ca. 29 B. C.).
8. This is from *The Aeneid*. "Remember, O Roman, it will be your mission to rule the world."

9. Gandhi's nonviolent resistance to colonial exploitation obviously was not foreseen by Mead although Addams (1931) was already admiring Gandhi's resistance in South Africa.
10. Although the Irish Republic soon formed, the division of Ireland continues to haunts us.
11. The Brest-Litovsk treaties, negotiated at what is now Brest, Belarus, near the Polish border, were arrangements made between Germany and the Central Powers. Russia ceded control over much of the Ukraine, Finland, and Poland and promised to make reparations to Germany. The treaties were negated after the Armistice but had a long term impact on all the partners involved.
12. See fn. 7, p. 264.
13. Dewey (1937) later investigated the murder of Trotsky.
14. Box 5, folder 5, Mead Addenda.
15. Mead not only cites White here but also indicates his familiarity with Freudian thought.
16. Mead is asking if James' (1910/1991) program for "a moral equivalent to war" is possible.
17. "National Mindedness and International Mindedness," *International Journal of Ethics* 39 (1929): 385 407.
18. James presented earlier versions, in 1906 and 1908, of this famous essay. The 1906 version inspired Addams to write her counter-argument in Newer Ideals of Peace (1907). A copy of the 1910 version is found in James (1910/1991).
19. The Kellogg-Briand Pact was signed by many nations between 1929, when the United States entered into the agreement, and 1933. The nations who joined it pledged to forego national aggression to gain land. It did not stop WWI, however.
20. See ftn. 19, above.
21. Theodore Roosevelt popularized the word "mollycoddle" in several speeches starting in 1912. It refers to being overprotective and indulgent toward a person, especially a male.
22. In 1822 Charles Lamb published Essays of Elia which included "A Dissertation on Roast Pig," concerning the fictional, accidental origin of cooked pork.
23. Frederick Harrison was a utilitarian who expanded on the ideas of Bentham.
24. This adult education program was started by Bishop John Vincent, the Baptist father of the Chicago sociologist George E. Vincent. Addams was a frequent figure in the Chautauqua reading lists and lectures. See Deegan (1988, esp. 92-98).
25. Dr. Samuel Johnson prepared *A Dictionary of the English Language* and published it in 1755. This was one of the most influential dictionaries in English and he was the first to use many literary illustrations in his definitions.
26. Judge Lynch condoned the hanging of his own son and his name became the word for immoral hanging of a victim. See Addams (1930, 335-36).
27. William Wordsworth (1770-1850), English poet. This passage is from "England, 1802."
28. Benito Mussolini was elected to the Italian Parliament in 1921 and represented the National Fascist party. In 1935 he aligned with Adolph Hitler. Mussolini was captured and shot in 1945 after the end of World War II.
29. Mead states here that national-mindedness is incompatible with Marxist's conflict theory.
30. Bismarck created the German empire out of previously disconnected small states. His rule was autocratic and earned him the name of the "Iron Chancellor."
31. See ftn. 22, p. 151.
32. This social movement wanted to end all war. See Howlett (1976) for a detailed discussion of Dewey's support of this effort.

Part 7

Conclusion

11

Bringing Mead's Theory of Self, War, and Society into the Twenty-First Century

> *"Yet it is not too much to say that between 1915*
> *and 1925 the war and its meaning for his vision*
> *of the world were constantly on Dewey's mind.*
> *Indeed, Dewey's espousal of near isolationism dur-*
> *ing the 1930s tempts one to say that the war was on*
> *his mind from 1915 until he died thirty-seven years*
> *later." (Ryan 1995, 156)*

Mead's writings on self, war, and society call out for new conversations on his theory and relationships to other theorists. I initiate this conversation in this chapter, beginning with a short analysis of the "big three" classical theorists, Karl Marx and Mead's contemporaries, Max Weber and Émile Durkheim. I then challenge the way many symbolic interactionists interpret Mead's theory. Their perspective colors the way other sociologists read Mead, since the symbolic interactionists are the major group now interpreting his work. I subsequently discuss several contemporary branches of pragmatism: feminist, native, prophetic, and general, all too frequently ignored within sociology. Next, I highlight a few of the interesting paths that intersect with Mead's macrosociology. Finally, I apply his macrosociology to global society today and assess the errors in his macrosociological view.

Mead's Macrosociology and Classical Sociological Theory

Although classical sociological theory was written in the past, connecting Mead to that body of work is nonetheless a contemporary project. I have completed such work in various publications, especially in reference to Dewey, Addams, and McDowell (e.g., Deegan 1999, 2001), and here in reference to Karl Marx. To summarize the differences between Mead and Marx, Mead employs a co-operative model, not a conflict model. Mead assumed laborers varied in their relationship to the nation-state, with democratic nations providing workers with the best voice to shape the state and the workplace. There was not, therefore, a word-wide proletariat. Mead assumed that both material and non-material resources created society, and he did not privilege the power of the material world over the non-material world. He concentrated on the ability of rational consciousness to guide the worker rather than a false consciousness generated by those in power. He opposed dichotomized notions, such as the bourgeois versus the proletariat. He established a complex, ongoing processual model based in empirical reality and the passage of time, whereas Marxists assumed that a universal, historical, dialectical process unfolds. Despite these significant differences, both Mead and Marx were committed to the processes of human liberation, social justice, and a role for social scientists to use knowledge to help generate greater human freedom. Mead, moreover, wanted a Fabian socialist state to mitigate the excesses of economic injustice and he opposed monarchies and dictatorships. He thereby supported the Marxist revolution in Russia during a time of extreme anti-Communism championed by many people who were associated with the United States government and various voluntary associations.

In the future, more extensive analysis will place Mead within the classical discourse of Weber and Durkheim. Mead's macrosociology can incorporate both the idealism and structuralism of the two respective theorists and argue against their separation into two opposing camps of theorists. This blended model avoids the rigidity found in Talcott Parson's (e.g., 1937/1949, 1951, 1971) cybernetic hierarchy, one of the few theories allowing for the combination of Weber and Durkheim. I do not provide a Meadian approach to Weber and Durkheim here, but I suggest that this is fully possible via Mead's macrosociology. Both Weber and Durkheim represent "movements of thought" based in European traditions which Mead (1936) analyzed extensively in his book of that title. Mead's analysis of the failures of German idealism, especially in the work of Immanuel Kant (see chapter 6 and reading 6A here), can be extended to critique Weber's (e.g., 1920/1957) idealism. Both Mead (1934) and Weber (1946, 1947) were committed to the role of rationality in everyday behavior and social science, but they differed on the role of politics and praxis in sociology.

Mead's analysis of "consciousness" during wartime and Durkheim's (1912/1961) analysis of "collective consciousness" arising from the group reveal striking parallels concerning the emergence of the self and the larger society. Mead's work on law and crime is another connection with the French theorist, as is Mead's analysis of the emergence of law and democracy over time. Durkheim (1983) saw his work as distinct from pragmatism, but it does not follow that all pragmatists would come to the same conclusion.

Linking the work of Marx, Weber, Durkheim, and Mead requires an alternative perspective. In a different, but interrelated, project, I connected the race relations theories developed at Hull-House and the University of Chicago to both classical and more contemporary approaches. This involved building a "third way" to racial justice, one involving both the "talented tenth" and the "masses," to enact the vision of feminist pragmatism (Deegan 2002a, b). Here, too, a "third way" is required to see the productive links between Marx, Weber, Durkheim, and Mead.

Mead's Macrosociology and Symbolic Interaction

Ironically, symbolic interactionists, who claim Mead as a founding figure, are responsible for much of his absence from both classical and contemporary sociological theory. Although symbolic interactionists helped keep Mead's work alive within the discipline, they also read his work narrowly, divorced it from its political and practical roots, and restricted the selection of resources from Mead's corpus. They have a limited public role as intellectuals and they have made Mead's work irrelevant to much intellectual discussion, analysis, and action. Herbert Blumer (1969), Mead's major supporter and self-appointed standard bearer, is largely responsible for the direction of the field he called "symbolic interactionism." Blumer's followers rarely question his reading of Mead, his outline of the approach, or the consequences of its constricted, apolitical framework.

I have puzzled for many years over Mead's early writings, which are decidedly political and macrosociological, versus the dominant contemporary interpretation of Mead as a microsociologist singularly focused on face-to-face interactions in small communities. He has been portrayed in textbooks as engaged in work opposite that done by Marx, Weber, and Durkheim. These "big and important" Europeans, so the story goes, founded sociology. They were followed by less ambitious and more limited theorists in America, such as Mead. According to this popular interpretation, American sociologists recognized in the 1930s and 1940s that they could be more accurate if they tried for less sweeping insights and concentrated on what Merton (1949) called "middle-range" theory. Mead, moreover, is assigned to "qualitative" methods for collecting data whereas Merton championed "quantitative" methods. But this "neat" Mertonian turn is fundamentally incorrect. As we clearly see from this anthology and my analysis, Mead was the contemporary of Durkheim and Weber, not Merton. Mead was a full-fledged and insightful macrosociologist who concentrated on democratic theory and its relation to society, including institutions, the community, neighborhoods, and nations.

Ellsworth Faris, one of Mead's students and later a faculty member at the same university, shared my reading of Mead as a macrosociologist. When Faris (1936, 810) reviewed *Mind, Self, and Society* for the *American Journal of Sociology*, he was confounded by the posthumous organization, imposed by Mead's former philosophy students[1] who compiled the book from their student notes:

Mind, self, and society is the reverse order to that which the structure of Mead's thought would seem to make appropriate. Not mind and then society; but society first and then minds arising within that society — such would probably have been the preference of him who spoke these words.

The sequence chosen by Mead's philosophy students colored and shaped the work of generations of later sociologists. It is the purpose of the present volume to restore Mead's intent: first macrosociology, then a mind, and then a self. Now we can assess how the "early" Mead's wartime work fits into his later corpus.

Mead's Macrosociology in the 1920s

By 1921, Mead had corrected his over-enthusiastic and patriotic response to the Great War, but he also toned down his previous, significant public role and profound commitment to applied, liberation sociology. Mead, in many ways, became more abstract in his thought and writings. Dewey and Mead had argued before the war that this form of disembodied writing was an inappropriate path for pragmatists: Pragmatists relied on experience, behavior, and concrete practices. Although Mead modified the practice of his ideas, he did not abandon them. Occasionally he returned to an applied, co-operative model of war and peace. Thus the previous chapter showed that in 1929 (see reading 10D here), *after his lectures* comprising *Mind, Self and Society,* Mead was at work analyzing international relations and the world community.

The line between eras, therefore, is more a change of emphases than the change of direction indicated by many interpretations of his posthumous books (Mead 1932, 1934, 1936, 1938), especially by symbolic interactionists. It is only if these posthumous books and the student notes on which they depend were correct, that we can conclude that Mead, during the last five years of his life, did not continue to actively pursue in the classroom what Feagin and Vera (2001) call "liberation sociology." I conclude, to the contrary, that these posthumous books must be re-evaluated, the original student notes re-read, and his published essays included in "late Meadian" thought and praxis. This re-evaluation is required before we can understand Mead's macrosociological work post-WWI.

Mead's subsequent work bore the imprint of the world conflict. This chapter was prefaced with Ryan's comment that WWI dominated Dewey's work for the rest of his life. Although Dewey changed his ideas and praxis as a result of the war, he never denied his war writings, never examined them in-depth, nor explicitly explained how they changed him. Mead followed a similar pattern. He was altered seriously by the war, and his 1929 article on international mindedness and moral equivalents to war (see reading 10D) hints at his disillusionment with his former ideas. Yet he never publicly analyzed the vindictive Versailles Treaty, the failure to create global democracies, the lack of a Fabian socialist type of government in the United States, his losing battle with Senator McCormick, or why a society of nations — as he envisioned it — did not emerge. His dream of an international, co-operative, and democratic society did not appear, even within the League of Nations and its successor the United Nations. The LTEP faded away and did not play a leading role in shaping global democracies, despite his hopes to the contrary. Mead remained silent on his disappointment.

His relationship to Addams, however, returned to its former strength. To-gether, they worked for the poor and hungry who were dislocated by the war, revealing Mead's continuing concern with global issues after the war ended. His posthumous books, moreover, discussed the need for international life and are optimistic and co-operative. Yet they are not filled with the specific details, programs, and strategies that characterized his wartime essays. His less politi-cal, less passionate, and less involved role as an organic intellectual suggests a painful withdrawal from his practices as a pragmatist. In this largely "silent" analysis of war and politics, Mead's later work was embedded in wartime experi-ences, but did not address the war explicitly. It is an open question far beyond the issues documented in this book to determine and document the extent to which the war may have "dominated" Mead's later thought.

We do know that Mead did not correct the errors in his understanding of macro-politics, violence by the state, international pacifism, or the role of eco-nomics in large-scale institutions. He did not seriously question the flaws in his understanding of democracy, a fundamental error he needed to address. In other words, in the years following the end of the war he could have articulated the mistakes in his pragmatist thought and practices, but he did not. What he could have accomplished with a stronger model of structure, social injustice, and power can only be imagined. What he did accomplish as a theorist is, nonetheless, monumental.

A Reinterpretation of Mead and Micro-Analysis

Mead's micro-analysis, the center of considerable sociological interest by symbolic interactionists (Blumer 1967; Deegan 1987b; Manis and Meltzer 1979) is not an endpoint. Rather, we must follow Meadian thought from an analysis of the self, to the nation-state, and the world. Mead established many of these connections through his concepts of "arbitration," "democracy," "education," "international-mindedness," "international pacifism," "the psychology of the nation-state," "internationalism," "anti-militarism," and "social reconstruction," and through his cooperative theory of the connections between the self and the other. His extensive work on social movements and their organization, such as progressivism, progressive education, citizenship, the labor movements, and the woman's movements are understudied, but provide important clues to his macrosociological perspective.

Work along these lines has begun. For example, Anthony Blasi (e.g., 2005), Raffaele Rauty (1997), and Luigi Tomasi (e.g., 1992, 1994, 1997) bring a significant political interpretation to symbolic interactionism. They focus on Park, not Mead, however. Rauty and Tomasi, in particular, have brought symbolic interaction and Chicago sociology to an Italian audience. Their combined work discusses contemporary issues and theories in Italy and the United States which are both macrosociological and Meadian.

There is obviously more work to do, but the way is clear. The legacy of Mead's macrosociology, his theory of self, war, and society (based on his writings compiled here) offers much to contemporary sociology, particularly the new forms of pragmatism: feminist pragmatism (including ecofeminist pragmatism), native pragmatism, prophetic pragmatism, and contemporary pragmatism.

Mead's Macrosociology and Feminist Pragmatism

The politics and practices of Addams and her cohort of Hull-House sociologists were highly compatible with Mead's general theory of society, mind, and self. The women of Hull-House, nonetheless, were also systematically more radical and politically advanced than Mead when it came to issues of economics, race, labor, politics, women, and peace.[2]

Those similarities and differences are epitomized in the relations between Addams and Mead, as I have demonstrated extensively for the subject of play (Deegan 1999), and more generally over a wide range of other topics (Deegan 1987b, 1988). Although they were friends and cooperative theorists, Addams took the more difficult roads to analyze and enact nonviolence, anti-imperialism, vocational and adult education, labor relations, cultural feminist values, and civil rights (especially for women and African Americans). This difference is most apparent in their goals and articulation of programs for the welfare state and for world peace. It is symbolized by Addams being awarded the Nobel Prize for Peace in 1931 while Mead's contributions as a significant theorist of cooperation between the state, mind, self, and international pacifism have been "discovered" only now, over seventy-five years later. The differences between the world of Chicago pragmatism and their male and female worlds of love and ritual were partially filled by the women of Mead's family, but Addams and Mead also reflected this gendered difference.

Thorstein Veblen's work has not been examined in-depth by feminist pragmatists, but it is a rich source of insight and meaning. As I discussed in the preceding chapter, Veblen's work on peace directly challenges many of the flawed ideas on war held by Mead, Dewey, and James. Veblen also trained and strongly influenced two important feminist pragmatists, Katherine Bement Davis (Deegan 2000) and Edith Abbott (Deegan 1991). Veblen also studied the history of women and many of his ideas shaped the work of Charlotte Perkins Gilman. Gilman's *Dress of Women* (1915/2002, 3) relied on Veblen's (1899) theory of the leisure class to reveal how "cloth is a social tissue."

Charlene Seigfried (1995, 1999) and her associates (see the special issue of *Hypatia*, edited by Seigfried 1996) explore feminist pragmatism from the perspective of Dewey and James, and to a lesser degree Addams. This valuable work is related to Mead, although Addams is rarely examined. As philosophers, this work privileges abstract knowledge and thus suffers where applications and practices derived from their model are required. The political consequences of such work echoes the flaws of the male pragmatists they study (for a notable exception, see Seigfried 2006). Seigfried and her colleagues are generally unreflexive about the significance of the historical context (for an exception to this statement, see Seigfried 2006). Ironically, since their intention is specifically feminist, feminist practices are nonetheless underexamined in this literature.[3] Further explorations of the relationships between men and women of the Chicago and Hull-House schools of sociology will clearly increase our understanding of their united thought.

Dewey and Feminist Pragmatism

Addams and Dewey carefully rewove their friendship after WWI, with Dewey making the largest strides toward her views. For example, they both signed a 1928 petition that was sent to President Calvin Coolidge asking for the restoration of the civil rights of Americans convicted of spying during WWI (JAMC, 20, frames 0533-0534). Dewey opened the way to bring Chicago pragmatism (as Mead perceived it) into a tightly argued school of feminist pragmatism. One occasion of their restored friendship was Dewey's seventieth birthday, a festive event celebrated by his many colleagues and allies in New York City.

Addams gave a significant tribute to Dewey. The Survey (Addams 1929q) published one version," A Toast to John Dewey," while another version is found in an anthology of the speeches delivered at that ritual event (Addams 1930c, 140-51). Although the two versions are similar, they are not identical. Addams (1930c, 140) said at the dinner, for example, that she would break "all precedents and read [her speech], which is a horrid thing to do. But I am afraid of all these philosophers." Likely, her fear was partially occasioned by the ritual importance of mending this vital friendship among Dewey's community of scholars: James Angell, Mead, and others from the faculty of the University of Chicago who shared the dais with her. Similarly revealing remarks, as well as some amusing anecdotes, were edited from the journal version.

Addams recalled their often overlapping, international efforts for education: in China, Turkey, Mexico, and Russia and she also mentioned Dewey's efforts to outlaw war. Addams (1930, 148) reflected on their painful split over WWI:

> Only once in a public crisis did I find my road taking a sharp right angle to the one he recommended. That fact in and of itself, gave me pause to think and almost threatened my confidence in the inevitability of that road. Our rough journeyings thereon often confirmed John Dewey's contention that unless truth vindicates itself in practice it easily slips into futile dogma, although advocates of peace in time of war were perforce thrust into the position of the doctrinaire. The Dewey teaching however saved

us from resorting to the ineffable solace vouchsafed to the self-righteous; and as we struggled in one country after another, for a foothold in reality, we actually found enough of it, to justify the application of the Dewey method and were grateful to him from having taught it to us.

This was a public, painful, and ultimately healing recollection by Addams of their prior disagreement.

In that same year, Dewey reciprocated when Hull-House celebrated its fortieth anniversary. Dewey was one of the special guests for this occasion, and he, too, recalled their fractured past. Much later, in 1945, Dewey (1945b) again honored Addams, this time as a professional colleague and before a conference of philosophers. *The Journal of Philosophy* later published a version that employed brief excerpts from Dewey's (1945a) introduction to Addams' (1922/1960) *Peace and Bread in Time of War*. He argued here that international political organizations which rely on force are less vibrant and successful, "less realistic," than international, socially humane organizations which operate nonviolently for the common good. Dewey had now reversed his previous ideas on pacifism and nonviolence because of Addams' persuasive worldview.

In contrast to Mead's 1907 review of *The Newer Ideals of Peace* (see reading 3A here), Dewey (1945a, xii-xiii) completely supported Addams' organization and conceptualization by 1945:

> In her book *The Newer Ideals of Peace,* published some years before the outbreak of World War I, she set forth aims and methods that are so intimately connected with *Peace and Bread* [in *Time of War* 1922] that the two books form a whole. The aims and methods set forth in both are of a kind that more than justify her in referring to them as "vital and dynamic."

Dewey's many eminent, white male colleagues — T. V. Smith, Arthur O. Lovejoy, Joseph P. Chamberlain, William Ernest Hocking, E. A. Burtt, Glen R. Morrow, Sidney Hook, and Jerome Nathanson — seriously considered, and largely rejected, the "Addams-Dewey" comparison (Dewey et al 1945c). Dewey learned much from WWI and from Addams, but his male colleagues argued for the power of fear and violence and pointed to the weaknesses and smugness associated with good intentions that result in bad consequences. Since some of these philosophers — e.g., Smith and Hook — were themselves pragmatists, this discussion points to the fundamental division between a patriarchal pragmatism (which rejects cooperation during wartime and reifies the dichotomy between "them" and "us") and the more logical and consistent views of Addams and the later Dewey. Mead's writings on self, war, and society amplify these contrasts and their significance for contemporary feminist pragmatism.

Seigfried (2001), in addition, has edited an instructive series of papers on Dewey and feminism that is extremely helpful in revealing the myriad ways in which Dewey supported a feminist agenda. This collection provides a substantial framework to connect Mead to such a project in feminist pragmatism (see also Deegan 1987b, 1988, 1999, 2001).

Mead's Macrosociology and Ecofeminist Pragmatism

Many contemporary pragmatists have turned to questions about the environment and its rapid destruction by contemporary, industrialized societies. Two important, legitimated leaders in ecopragmatism are Dewey and Mead. Their world-view is sympathetic to ecological questions and oriented to problem-solving, a point successfully argued by "environmental pragmatists" (Light and Katz 1996).

Similarly, many ecofeminists stress the interconnectedness of life, nature, and the environment, but connect this with women's worldview and reproductive capacity (e. g. Griffin 1978, Plant 1989) rather than with pragmatism. Ecofeminists also examine the relationship between women's social oppression and the exploitation of nature as two faces of patriarchal control (Gaard 1997; King 1987). Many ecofeminists trace their roots only to the 1980s and the historical convergence of feminist, environmental, labor, peace, anti-racist, and animal rights movements (Pois 1995). Joanna Macy (1989, 201) defines the "new" ecofeminism as unique in human history, calling ecofeminism a radical change from "a millennia-long amnesia as to who we really are." Christopher Podeshi and I questioned the "newness" of this ecofeminism and trace its historical legacy back to ecofeminist pragmatists writing between 1890 and 1930. We document this earlier vision of human cooperation which emerged from interaction with humans, animals, the earth, and the cosmos (Deegan and Podeshi 2001). This ecofeminist pragmatism is only now being rediscovered and reconnected (e.g., Gottlieb 1993; Pois 1995). Thus, many contemporary "ecopragmatists" are disconnected from the contemporary work of "feminist pragmatists" such as myself (Deegan 1987, 1988a, 1991, 1995), Seigfried (1991, 1995), and Mary Mahowald (1997) as well as their historical "foreshadowing" (Pois 1995) in the early writing of both ecofeminists and ecofeminist pragmatists like Gilman and Addams.

Andrew J. Weigart (1997) and J. Ronald Engel (1983) are two important practitioners of ecopragmatism. Weigart, a sociologist who considers himself a "symbolic interactionist" studying the environment and ecology, or an "ecological social psychologist" (p. 25), or a "pragmatic social constructionist" (p. 3), identified closely with Mead. Weigart developed a sophisticated extension of Mead's concept of the "self and the other" wherein "the other" becomes the physical and natural environment, land, animals, and physical resources. Instead of Mead's focus on "social interaction," Weigart focuses on "transverse interaction" between the self and the living, physical world (p. 25). Like the environmental pragmatists, however, Weigart ignores feminism, even feminist symbolic interactionism (e.g., Deegan 1987, 1988a, 1995, 1996).

Similarly, Engel traces the powerful political, social, and intellectual struggle rooted in community activism (often in conjunction with both Chicago pragmatism and Hull-House's "feminist pragmatism") that resulted in the establishment of the National Lakeshore in the Indiana Dunes. His multidisciplinary work emerges primarily from religious studies. Engel's eloquent intellectual, religious, and politically involved ecopragmatism is closely allied with ecofeminist feminism, but he, too, lacks an explicitly feminist analysis.

I closely documented elsewhere that "play" is a central concept in Mead's theory and that it ties directly to similar ideas and activities found in Dewey, Addams, and McDowell (Deegan 1999). That intellectual and activist network applied their ideas in kindergartens, progressive education, playgrounds, urban parks, and the Labor Museum in Chicago. The latter institution displayed the connections between work, play, and art in both the old and new world with an emphasis on depicting how the material world links with the industrial process, even when capitalists try to separate this intrinsic linkage. In this previous work, I analyzed pragmatism and feminist pragmatism in light of major environmental and ecological issues surrounding playgrounds, education, and the child, thus forming yet another nexus between these diverse theorists and activists.

Ecofeminist pragmatism is directly associated with the ecological epistemology and activism that is associated with the more general social thought of pragmatism, what I call "ecopragmatism" (see Deegan and Podeshi 2001). Ecofeminist pragmatism comprises a large body of work but, like ecofeminism, it usually defines itself as of recent origin in terms of female founders. Ironically, long-recognized, white, male, philosophers are acknowledged as founding figures even if they lack explicit ecological and feminist ties. Thus the extensive work of early ecofeminists and feminist pragmatists are ignored generally. This pattern applies most clearly in the case of "environmental pragmatism," discussed more later in this chapter.

Scholars in ecopragmatism, feminist pragmatism,"ecological symbolic interactionism," environmental pragmatism, and ecofeminism are sympathetic to the world and activities emergent from ecofeminist pragmatism. These groups are largely disconnected in scholarly writings and literature, however, and Mead is especially under represented. To the extent that Mead's writings on macrosociology are taken seriously, I foresee an end to this unfortunate separation in the future.

Mead's Macrosociology and Native Pragmatism

Studies of the impact of Indians upon early pragmatist thought, especially in the 1700s and 1800s, is another relatively recent movement, called "native pragmatism." This approach emphasizes the interconnectedness of the native worldview, and its lack of stereotyping and dichotomization that characterize much of European and Western thought. Scott Pratt (2002) outlined these major points in *Native Pragmatism*, as has Bruce Wilshire (2000) in *The Primal Roots of American Philosophy*. Andrea Smith (2005) extends this work to focus on "Native American Feminism, Sovereignty and Social Change." Smith picks up many of the points raised by ecofeminist pragmatists, noted above. A further extension of this thought appears in the writings of Ella Cara Deloria (e.g., 1988, 1998) on the language, society, mind, and self of the Sioux. Mead is rarely brought into these discussions, but his macrosociology could bridge these separate discussions.

Mead's Macrosociology and Prophetic Pragmatism

Cornel West (1989, 1993) insightfully analyzed the genealogy of pragmatism and updated it for the contemporary pan-African experience. In particular, he calls on the prophetic or religious underpinnings to empower pragmatism in a world fractured by colonialism, racism, and capitalism. Despite his significant intellectual accomplishment, he analyzes neither Mead nor Addams. I have partially expanded and connected his work on racism and pragmatism elsewhere, but this remains an undertaking to be fully explicated and critiqued (Deegan 2002a, b). West's deeply Christian, Marxist, and post-modernist interests are problematic for such a project, but his basis in the work of Dewey, DuBois, C. Wright Mills, Veblen, James, and Emerson provides important commonalities with the men and women of the Chicago and Hull-House schools of sociology. Adding Mead and Addams to the genealogy of prophetic pragmatism greatly enhances our understanding of the self, race, gender, religion, and social justice.

I have documented elsewhere the importance of race to the epistemology and practices of the early Chicago sociologists, especially for Addams and for Mead's student, W. I. Thomas (Deegan 2002b). Mead's work, nonetheless, still needs to be fully combined with my analysis of abolitionist thought, democracy, and the institutions of Hull-House and the University of Chicago. This effort would connect Mead with West's contemporary interest in prophetic pragmatism.

Mead's Macrosociology and General Pragmatists

There are many pragmatists, located primarily in philosophy and history, who focus on Charles Pierce, James, and Dewey, but not Mead. Richard Rorty is one of these leading pragmatists, but his language, epistemology, stance toward morality, science and realism do not align him with Mead. Hilary Putnam (e.g., 1998) and James T. Kloppenberg (e.g., 1998) discuss the flawed direction of Rorty's work in detail. Throughout this book, I have drawn on the scholarship of recent Deweyan scholars especially Westbrook (1990), Ryan (1995), Chatfield (1970), and Rockefeller (1991). In general, however, these scholars do not understand Addams' social thought or pacifism which greatly limits their usefulness here. Ryan (1991, 149-53), in particular, understands neither Addams' pacifism nor the intellectual and political relations between Addams and Dewey, despite his devoting several pages to a discussion on them. By and large, Mead is also invisible in all these books. Feminist pragmatism is discussed rarely, and this is also true for discussions of women as subjects and social objects. These scholars usually do not discuss sociological theorists, and, not surprisingly, symbolic interactionists are not integral to their perspectives or collegial networks. It is time to make Mead visible to contemporary, general pragmatists.

Hans Joas (1985), a German sociologist and pragmatist, raised many of the issues I discuss in this section, and addressed them after his own fashion. In his book *G. H. Mead: A Contemporary Re-examination of His Thought* Joas integrated Mead with many sociological theorists and issues. Joas, however, has not followed this exciting book with an equally insightful and innovative work on Mead's links to contemporary issues, such as discussions of feminism, Addams, play, and creativity. In fact, Joas (1996) wrote an entire book on creativity but did not turn to Mead as a rich theorist in this area of study.

Mead's Macrosociology and Critical Theory

Mead's disparaging perspective on German society, militarism, authoritarianism, and aggression, as noted in chapters 4 to 9 here, was continued by many critical theorists from the 1930s through the 1960s. Mead, however, evaluated the German people and state as far less belligerent than many critical theorists interpreted them. Mead's view of Germans as almost anti-authoritarian challenges a large body of critical theory written between the 1940s and 1960s. Adorno's "authoritarian personality" is particularly questionable in light of Mead's approach. But the large body of Freudian or neo-Freudian thought, especially by Erich Fromm (Schaar 1961) and Herbert Marcuse (1964), is similarly put in doubt. Mead did not see Marcuse's "surplus repression" or Fromm's problematic "egos," but rather saw German citizens who did not fully articulate and enact their liberal rights.

More recent work in critical theory, by contrast, focuses on globalization and changes within Germany. This new turn places less emphasis on Freud and Marx. New social movements, such as ecology, feminism, and the world economy, are given more priority over the labor or communist movements. Mead's social thought anticipated these and similar changes and thus makes an excellent, though untapped, intellectual resource for these newer critical theorists.

Mead and Habermas: Connecting the Lifeworld and Social System

Mead's macrosociology has potentially deep ties with contemporary critical theory. Jurgen Habermas (1985/1987), in particular, brings Mead into the theoretical matrix of contemporary critical theory, but he substantially alters Mead's ideas in this process. First, Habermas' work is less radical than Mead's and is deeply patriarchal. Second, Habermas emphasizes almost exclusively Mead's micro-analysis. Third, Habermas mistakenly converts this face-to-face micro-analysis into the study of "identity" and fails to retain the fundamentally different concept of the "self" — as Mead intended. By equating "the self" with "identity" Habermas decreases the agency inherent in the social origins of the self, its creativity, and its connection to community and society. Thus Habermas throws away a tool for understanding how the lifeworld and system become disconnected. Paradoxically, he disconnected Mead's dramatic understanding of how society creates the self and is sustained by it. Finally, Habermas did not analyze Mead's positions on peace, war, the role of the citizen, and his sharp critiques of German Kultur. The bulk of Mead's writings on these topics is now readily available in this book for the first time. Hopefully this may lead to an enhanced understanding of contemporary society and the genesis of the communicatively competent self.

Habermas relies heavily on the posthumous *Mind, Self, and Society* (Mead 1934), and he could have understood much of Mead's extensive theory of democracy by following that text in Mead's discussion of "society." Habermas could have read many of his early essays on the international self, social justice, and education, too. Habermas's approach, furthermore, would benefit from an increased understanding of the significance of play in Mead's (1934, 1999) writings. This latter aspect of Mead's thought lightens the rather depressing and grim view of life that permeates the writings of most critical theorists. But resolving these problems is minor compared to the potential to unify these approaches in a liberatory intention. Mead's vital work informs the analysis of the nation-state, feminism, democracy, education, racism, and peace. The readings in this book, therefore, are a key to understanding and reconstructing Habermas' views on the "colonized self," "communicative competence," and the connections between the Lebenswelt and the social structure.

Feminist Pragmatism and Critical Theory

Again, the work of Seigfried (1995, 1999, 2002) and her associates (see special issue of *Hypatia*, edited by Seigfried 1996; Sullivan 2001) is relevant in linking feminist pragmatism to critical theory. They usefully explore feminist pragmatism from the perspective of Dewey and Friedrich Nietzsche. They examine the post-modern assumptions often explicitly rejected by Habermas. Although I do not share their post-modern epistemology and do not agree that the pragmatists and feminist pragmatists from this early era would share this "post-modern" worldview, they have written important theoretical work that challenges the problems in contemporary critical theory.

Mead, Germanic Influences, and Reconstructing Critical Theory

Critical theorists who use Mead would do well to examine his connections to Germanic thought. For example, I have explored Mead's deep and formative ties with Wilhelm Wundt elsewhere (Deegan 1999, 2001), primarily in terms of Wundt's early influence on Mead's notions of comparative physiology; emotions; communicative and symbolic gestures; and the child. Wundt is not discussed by critical theorists, however. Similarly, Wilhelm Dilthey influenced Mead as a postgraduate student, and these ties are explored by Joas (1985), who is not a critical theorist, only briefly. Finally, the critical theorists who came to the United States during World War II shared many of Mead's interpretations of German society because, in part, they all lived through many similar experiences and advanced training. These German scholars provide a logical gateway to connect Mead to contemporary critical theorists, especially Habermas (1985/1987).

Because Mead's model of peace, war, society, democracy, internationalism, and labor can now be explored by critical theorists, this new direction must proceed with the full understanding that Mead's ideas were vulnerable to manipulation by the state during wartime. After the war, these same ideas did not advance an international, co-operative, and restorative model of world-wide democracy. These failures in his theory continue to echo in the contemporary mistakes of the recent wars waged by the United States in the Middle East, wars ostensibly fought once again in the name of "democracy." This repeated pattern of American warfare requires examination in light of Mead's misplaced optimism about the outcome of state violence and Addams' more successful fight for newer ideals of peace.

Bringing together the liberating sociology of Addams and Mead, however, requires the removal of conceptual mistakes in the theories of Mead, Addams, and contemporary critical theory. The patriarchal underpinning of the latter approach is particularly problematic, because it is linked to an authoritative model of control that is hostile to democracy emerging from community power. Critical theory privileges the power of the state.

Habermas developed a serious analysis of the disconnection between the self, the state, and the colonization of the lifeworld. His analysis depends on the work of Marx, Freud, Durkheim, and post-modernist thought, among other intellectual traditions. This elaborately complex approach, however, is filled with jargon and many loose and contradictory ends. This morass could be simplified by examining these same issues through Mead's perspective, including his macrosociology. As Mead repeatedly noted: The democratic state needs active citizens to be just and moral. Changes in the society, and liberating social reconstruction, do not require sophisticated layers of mediation, infusion of meaning, complex knowledge, expertise, bureaucratization, theories of rationality, or hopeless calls for the nostalgic past.

Mead, as well as Addams and Dewey, posit more power to the people, democracy, public education, and neighbors than any of the more "presumably sophisticated" theorists that Habermas employ in his call for increased unity between the self and the other; between the citizen and the state; and the search for human meaning. In contrast, American feminist, prophetic pragmatism offers a constructive path to a new, more just, world order.

Mead's Macrosociology and Other Contemporary Sociological Theories

Mead is included rarely in the body of contemporary theory that runs from Talcott Parsons, Alfred Schutz, Erving Goffman, Anthony Giddens, and Alan Wolfe to rational choice and exchange theorists. A thorough reading of Mead as a macro-sociological theorist with connections to and substantial differences from this huge body of work is yet to be completed. Below I briefly mention a few efforts in this direction.

Mead and Schutz

Mead and Schutz are often paired as if they are part of one approach. This is sloppy and inaccurate. Valerie Malhotra [Benz] and I (Deegan and Malhotra 1977; and Malhotra and Deegan 1978) demonstrated how Mead and Schutz are both connected and yet distinct. Our work directly criticized the fuzzy assumption that they are easily combined without making specific reservations about their often opposing positions on politics, methods for collecting data, and stances on rationality. Each of these points requires full epistemological analysis in future studies.

Mead, Goffman, Turner, and Giddens

Mead is also similar to yet distinct from the exciting, more contemporary ideas of Erving Goffman, Victor Turner, and Anthony Giddens. I have completed extensive studies of how social rules and meanings are interconnected in American rituals (Deegan 1989, 1998). In this work I emphasize the concepts of Goffman and Turner, and to a lesser degree, Giddens. I have not yet brought Mead into this discussion, however. Part of this omission arose from my own training in symbolic interaction which limited him to micro-analyses, a reading which I have been slowly correcting for decades (e.g., Burger and Deegan 1981; Deegan and Burger 1978). Mead's (1998, 2002) early work, which employs the ideas of Wilhelm Wundt on language and ritual, could be combined with the present study of his macrosociology on war and peace to forge a new interpretation of American dramas in the community and mass media.

Mead and the Theories of Exchange and Rational Choice

The lack of Meadian discussion in exchange and rational choice theories and other related approaches is puzzling. Perhaps it can be traced to the overemphasis of Mead's micro-analysis, or possibly it arises from the insularity and over-specialization of many sociological theorists, or it might be suggested, they fail to read other theories with an open mind,[4] or perhaps too many sociological theorists have divorced themselves not only from liberation sociology but also from other sociologists generally. Although exchange and rational choice theories tend to support conservative economic assumptions, broadening the concepts of exchange and rationality to include more humanistic goals would make Mead much more compatible with these bodies of thought and ameliorate their conservative biases.

In the spirit of my suggestions for applying Mead's macrosociology to contemporary thought, I provide an example below of how to use "feminist pragmatism" from Mead's macrosociological perspective to analyze globalization.

A Contemporary Interpretation of International Pacifism, the Self, and a Global Society: International-Mindedness and the Genesis of the International Self

Mead's macrosociology helps us understand today's global society: the international approach to the other emerges from the foundation of a self born within a community of interacting others. Mead noted that there are stages in the genesis of a growing and increasingly complex self. But he provided little detail on the steps in the process of the emerging "self" and he did not specifically name the different types of structures of the self emerging in the self-development that he describes. Here I specify how the national self changes to become part of other nations.

I call the initial foundation for the self "the community self" and it forms in childhood. This basic self is not a highly abstracted structure. It lacks an understanding of relative, competing values and perspectives. It is specific. It emerges from a local community and a given historical location.[5] The capacity to develop "international-mindedness" (Mead 1915, 1929b) emerges from the community self. The community self is a "substructure," a necessary first step, to an expanded consciousness of other groups and definitions of situations. "International-mindedness," then generates a new self, what I call "the international self." It emerges from the ability to take the attitude of others who are very different in their historical and group location from that of the community self. This new self has the ability to abstractly and pragmatically accept difference and to perceive common interests with others whose community self emerged from very different perspectives (Mead 1938). The international self provides a new structure with the potential to generate more complex understandings of multiple cultures and ethnicities as an individual meets and interacts with more people and cultures over time.

Both Mead and Addams assumed that achieving what I call an international self occurred through pragmatic processes (i.e., embodied, rational behavior) resulting in a changed consciousness. Mead, however, emphasized the intellectual apparatus for this new self while Addams emphasized the embodied process of generating this new self. The first step in generating an "international self," for both sociologists, was taking the attitude of the other from a different society, racial/ethnic group, or nation within the community self, my next topic for discussion.

Taking the Role of the Other

The ability to find common interests between different people or communities stems from the human capacity to "take the role of the other." Each person with a self has the skill to understand different perspectives. Although members of different nations form different selves emergent from their different communities, generating different "community selves," they can expand their social consciousness so that their generalized other incorporates the perspectives of people with different community selves. This lays the foundation for the emergence of the international self. "The genesis of the international self" includes the process of building on a community self emergent from a meaningful social order. The generation of an international self includes experiences from the combination of a new social order and with accompanying disorder cuased by new ways of thinking and acting in the world (Thomas and Znaniecki 1918-1920). This process of socialization, often occurring as an adult, may be difficult but not impossible and is as potentially rewarding as one's generalized other expands. Creating an international self requires choice and learning (what many scholars call now "agency"). The capacity to understand "others" in a context of diversity potentially involves progressive growth for the entire society, not just for the individuals who make such internal changes. The rejection of specific ideas of national/ethnic superiority; "purity" of ideas, culture, or biological inheritance; and of dichotomous categories such as "insiders" versus "outsiders" must be actively encouraged. The international self becomes a mechanism to break down the restrictions of a colonized self and to mend the disconnections between the lifeworld and society that Haberams (1985) discusses. It increases communicative competence as a result of the increasing grasp of the other who is outside one's community and nation state.

Democracy in a Global Society

Acceptance of democratic ideals, the validity and viability of different perspectives, and belief in the expansive capacity to understand others must be encouraged simultaneously to develop a global, democratic society (Mead 1934; Taft 1913). A new consciousness results but does not blur the national self. Instead, the "stir-fry" process of cultural pluralism (Kallen 1915 a, b) emerges when the international community enjoys and supports the identifiable differences within the collective selves that comprise it. This model emerges from the metaphorical unity of having a surrounding bowl that allows this symbolically complex process to occur. Such a bowl holds the various cultures together and makes possible the formation of the international self and community. This underlying unity has been frequently misunderstood as an attempt to destroy cultures. Instead, it is the means to give cultures continuity in a context of increasingly sophisticated global interactions.

Mead understood the power of nation-states to influence laborers in the generation of national and/or culturally-rooted selves. Thus, Mead explicates the contemporary global society which draws upon a wide range of workers from different nations and cultures. His model of international commonality and difference is more accurate than the Marxist's view of a world-wide proletariat.

Changing Consciousness and Structural Barriers

These changes in consciousness meet resistance on three different dimensions: economic, cultural, and political (Addams 1910, 1930; Deegan 1988). For example, the oppressed (especially women, the poor, and people of color) typically need employment, money, and resources for education, but economic assets in capitalist communities privilege the vested interests of white men with capital. Changing this fundamental distortion calls out for meaningful democratic power and the reconstruction of major social institutions. Mead's notion of "liberal institutions" calls for the end of bureaucratic, hierarchically-organized institutions that follow the values of capitalism, patriarchy, and racism at the cost of democratic values (Deegan 1989, 1998).

Political mechanisms for voting, citizenship, knowledge of the law, and administration of justice need to be articulated and enacted based on liberal values. The protection of liberal and human rights is fundamental not only in the formation of the self but also in the definition of community relations. Defining any community or its representatives as outside the rights of the populace guarantees both organized and diffuse community resistance to such injustice. In addition, social disorganization is generated quickly in specific cases of political injustice and abuse. Thus the recent institutionalization of imprisonment, torture, and restrictions on democratic processes by the United States government in Cuba, Afghanistan, and Iraq are practices diametrically opposed to increasing democratization, despite government propaganda to the contrary.

The Social Reconstruction of a Flawed Self

The most difficult area of social tolerance — because it is the most everyday and outside the mechanisms of formal institutions — is the social acceptance of others from different communities and nations. Social acceptance of the other is the bedrock for a tolerant and cooperative society. It involves changes in the way of being, thinking, and experiencing the world. The structure of the self moves beyond the known world of the home and nation and embraces the unknown, abstract world of those who are different in speech and custom. The interpersonal understanding, respect, and affection that generates everyday life is often the last arena to undergo social change. Although discrimination can be outlawed through legislation (which may or may not be enforced), the ability to like and understand the other is grounded in social interactions beyond the law and public rules. It is the most difficult area of social reconstruction and the least subject to social coercion and the most stable. The lifeworld, like the self, is simultaneously capable of both change and resistance to change. Taking the role of an other who is different from the self involves international-mindedness, a transformation in the generalized other, a stretching of one's skills in taking the role of the other, and the ability to create new ways of thinking. Symbols and emotional understanding also change in this process.

Mead's Macrosociology and Restorative Justice

Elizabeth Neeley and I explored the epistomological connections between the restorative justice movement in criminology and Mead's commitment to social justice in the early twentieth century in Chicago. There he supported the Juvenile Protective Association, the Juvenile Court, the Psychopathic Clinic, and the Institute of Juvenile Research (Neeley and Deegan 2005). Mead's arguments for these liberal institutions advocated the re-incorporation of young criminals into the larger community. Mead's commitment to education, rationality, the social impulses, and the flexible self point to the need to bring juvenile delinquents into the larger community. This re-incorporation involves a reconstructed self and breaks the cycle of repeated crimes and increasing alienation and violence.

Mead's Macrosociology and Liberation and Public Sociology

American sociologists have too often become disconnected from national leadership. Their insights into conflict resolution, their data on social injustice, and their interpretations of group processes languish in scholarly tomes unread by policy-makers and the public. Calls for a public role in shaping the nation are raised periodically, and the two most recent efforts have been led by two eminent scholars and leaders in the profession: Joe R. Feagin (2001), ASA president in 2000, and Michael Buroway (2005), ASA president in 2004. Feagin calls for "liberation sociology" and Burroway for "public sociology." Mead's macrosociology responds to both calls in the discipline for greater public citizenship and leadership for sociology. But unfortunately Mead presented a model to analyze peace and war that shared two of the biggest blind spots for many Americans and American sociologists: an unrelexive patriotism and a widespread support for war. Today, once more, Americans are responding to a militant agenda, and once again mainstream sociologists generally are failing to analyze the flaws in these arguments or taking a collective stand against military adventurism and war mongering.

In like manner, sociologists are far from the forefront in examining the underlying social problems emerging after the natural disaster of Hurricane Katrina in 2005. There are so many issues that need study: the failure of public institutions to respond with alacrity and aid, the horrendous mistakes in public housing, the blatant racism, and the egregious capitalist profit serving the interests of the elite. Mead's ideas on self, war, and society can help us understand American society, the power of democracy and liberal institutions, and the need for Americans, particularly sociologists, to take the role of the other in times of social disaster, but sociologists must make efficacious and timely use of his work.

Mead's Macrosociology and Peace and War Today

Mead's international pacifism can guide sociological investigations of America's present wars in the Middle East. President George W. Bush initiated one of the few major American invasions of another nation-state in modern times (with a historical precedent in the treatment of and wars against Indians) under the obscuring propaganda of "a pre-emptive strike." This violent assault on Iraq was unnecessary because the potential for an attack involving "weapons of mass destruction" was totally unfounded: no nuclear warheads or chemical weapons depots have been found in Iraq despite massive international efforts to find them. Many Americans ignore this fact despite voluminous data confirming it. Mead's faith in rational data to change public consciousness was not realized in this instance. Again, the voices of other nations were ignored in this century, as they were in Senator Medill McCormick's coalition against the League of Nations in 1919.

Echoing WWI, our contemporary American president today justifies great violence in the name of spreading "democracy:" If other nations would only establish voting rights, this logic asserts, then all national and international problems would disappear. Thus, the American mass media focuses on elections per se and not on the multitude of difficulties preventing fair elections: street violence; internal ethnic conflicts; multiple, problematic candidates; imposed mandates; and American interference with other nation's politics. Such sham electoral processes are heralded as progress and victories for democracy rather than charades that mock democracy. Democracy, as Mead points out, can only emerge from an educated and free citizenry.

The disastrous mire created by America's aggression in Afghanistan and Iraq is unsettling all Arab nations and potentially even wider wars may erupt. South Asia, for example, is brimming with trouble and unrest while the Israeli and Arab conflicts remain agitated. Nuclear weapons open the possibility of worldwide mass murder, death, annihilation, and ecological disaster — conditions that Mead could never have imagined. WWI was not the war to end wars and it was not a war for democracy, as Mead argued. It was violent, international chaos embedded in militarization, ethnic/racial strife, and sexism that continues in various nations and "hot spots" such as North Korea.

Terrorism remains unchecked and many Arabs in the United States and Europe are subjected to the kind of bigotry that German speakers and their descendants experienced in America during WWI. The illegal incarceration of people in Guantanamo Bay, Cuba, reveals the ugly underside of our contemporary "democracy." The wire-tapping of millions of Americans proceeded without substantial or effective resistance until the recent elections of November, 2006. A democratic government that blatantly violated civil rights and international bans on torture cannot hold the moral high ground. The United States, moreover, is pushing democracy onto other nations while failing to understand that democracy at the end of a weapon is no democracy at all. There are no mainstream discussions of how oil and the environmental destruction caused by cars, trucks and industries lurk behind the scenes of American involvement in the Middle East. "Contract workers" hired by the United States government are not explained to everyday Americans as sometimes including mercenary soldiers outside public control. The long-range health-care costs of tens of thousands of American veterans injured in the war are omitted from "war budgets" and have yet to be calculated.

Further, the connections between failing public school systems, capitalism, and war are unexamined. Mead dreamt of a public school system that educated future citizens, a system with the potential to create communicative competence for all citizens. Our loss of a viable public education system is a national tragedy. Our public schools are mired in divisions based on class, gender, and race that separate and disempower Americans. Today, these same fracturing divisions are mirrored in the government's response to Hurricane Katrina and the resulting destruction of New Orleans: with its once culturally vibrant African American community.

Many of the mistakes American diplomats made at the end of WWI are repeated today, and as a populace we may be even less informed about these diplomatic errors and their consequences. This lack of a communicatively competent public had emerged despite the rise of multiple new venues for providing news — via the internet and other mass media. These new structures of information have resulted in neither sophisticated, thoughtful interpretations nor open access to information that truly informs. The mass media reflect the problems of our larger society and are, in part, a source of international enmity: they often *create* barriers to the emergence of the international self in America. To help Americans move from a situation of confusion, fear, and anger, the mass media need to improve our understanding of Muslims, Arabs, the role of oil and national policy on energy and the environment, and the havoc caused by American violence. A few reporters and programs do provide such a service, sometimes heroically, but most of the news perversely dichotomizes the Middle East and Asia in contrast to "us," the morally just Americans. This reporting fuels suspicion and fear; exacerbates scandal; and sensationalizes "breaking news."

The liberation sociology that inspired Chicago pragmatism finds little purchase today in the profession of sociology as a whole. This professional

resistance (especially among symbolic interactionists) to pragmatist working hypotheses and other potentially rich resources for social change mirrors
American media, education, and public opinion. Such resistance, Habermas
explicates, is integral to the processes of communicative incompetence, separation from the social system, and the colonization of the self. In the classroom,
for over three decades, I have taught students about the international pacifism
of Mead, Addams, and their allies, but it remains an uphill struggle when the
overwhelming mass of symbolic interactionist literature privileges the micro
perspective with such crushing and unreflexive exclusivity. Privileging the
micro-world has serious consequences, not only in the classroom specifically
but also for pragamatists generally: the separation of Mead from his macrosociology. What became — and what is to become — of the liberation sociology
that inspired Chicago pragmatism?

Mead's Biggest Pragmatist Mistake after the War

The opaque shroud over Mead's pragmatist macrosociology today was
partially fashioned by Mead himself. As with all theorists, it is relatively easy
to find myriad minor flaws in their work many decades later, and Mead is no
exception. Nonetheless, major flaws deserve special mention. In Mead's case,
the biggest error was his personal lack of faith in his own working hypotheses
for international pacifism. Addams and Dewey, unlike Mead, continued to
elaborate their ideas on war and peace and as a result they both became world
leaders on this subject. While Mead's wife and female relatives joined WILPF
— which many men such as Robert Morss Lovett (1948) did, too — Mead did
not. Similarly Helen Castle Mead was a member of the Citizens Committee
which honored Addams for her work in the 1920s, but George Herbert Mead
was not (*The Citizens Committee,* pamphlet, SWHC, NFS, SWD 1, file 2). Some
scholars, including me, believe that this occasion signaled the end of Addams'
social ostracism, but G. H. Mead was not party to this symbolic and practical
end of Addams' governmental persecution.

Mead's failure to show the ways in which his original theory was correct
was a direct consequence of his lack of reflective intelligence on the flaws in
his social thought and behavior during wartime. Mead dichotomized the United
States versus its enemies; his patriotic emotions held sway over his rationality
for at least two years; he argued that violence would generate democracy and
freedom; and he trusted violent leaders to become strong advocates for peace
after the war. His pre-war and post-war theory demonstrates why these assumptions are mistakes, but he failed to openly analyze the peculiar situations of
war (i.e., the factors that can turn the most open of liberals into supporters of
national violence) that left his theory with a huge internal weakness: an intellectual vulnerability to irrational patriotism and unreflexivity.

Mead withdrew most of his energy, optimism, and commitments from the
struggle for world peace and a global, co-operative society. Mead's work (his

brilliant theories of the genesis of the self, of the present, the movements of thought of the nineteenth century, and the philosophy of the act) make him the most important sociological theorist in the world from 1892 to 1938. He would have made significantly greater contributions if he had continued his political struggle on the public stage.

Mead's study of emotions, the economy, aristocracy, militarization, political leaders, the nation-state, laborers, citizenship, and the global society were central to his study of war and peace. When he failed to critique his analysis of WWI, however, he also failed to further develop and strengthen his ideas in these major social arenas. His analysis of other theorists, particularly Karl Marx and Sigmund Freud, also languished. His criticism of German idealism became so invisible that many contemporary theorists wrongly interpret him as supporting that social movement.

Mead's fights for liberal institutions, his battles against punitive justice, his civic leadership, his dedication to the League of Nations, and his public and vocal support of the government-persecuted women of Hull-House (who were subjected to witch hunts for over a decade) could have (and should have) continued. Had Mead followed through, he would have been a far more important intellectual and citizen. Like many of us, he was human in his response to a public failure. His ardor cooled and he turned to more abstract ideas and teaching, and for the first time in his career he turned to the university as an ivory tower.

Mead never abandoned his political commitments entirely, as I have shown, but he did temper them. After the war, his philosophy students were treated to a very different style of teaching (which they immortalized in their editions of the four posthumous books from Mead's "late" period, *Mind, Self and Society* (1934); *Movements of Thought in the Nineteenth Century* (1936), *The Philosophy of the Act* (1938); and *The Philosophy of the Present* (1932). The monumental accomplishment embodied in Mead's later work can and should be joined to his equally significant early work. Including the book in hand, we now have four major books from the early Mead (i.e., *Essays on Social Psychology* [2001]; *The Individual and the Social Self* [1982]; and *Play, School and Society* [1999]). The ideas in these early works hold the premise for and the promise of an integrated Meadian model of behavior that reflects Mead's original vision for liberal institutions and that incorporates his initial optimism regarding the efficacy of responsible action by informed citizens. When this promise is marked "paid in full" by future thinkers, Mead will become (as did Addams and Dewey before him) a genuinely organic intellectual.

The role of the public sociologist is itself a working hypothesis. Addams and Dewey, in differing ways, made good on their professional commitments to their fellow citizens and we have much to learn from their examples. How much more could we have learned if Mead had directed his considerable brilliance toward a reflexive analysis of the errors in his macrosociology that became so painfully evident during WWI? Today, American sociologists continue to pull back from a public role and fail to analyze the social forces that make the United States a flawed democracy characterized by weak liberal institutions in education, criminal justice, and social welfare. It is my hope, and my working hypothesis, that inclusive re-examinations of Mead's work will provide an opportunity for re-thinking and re-energizing the potential public role of sociology in American society. In the interim, the American military juggernaut and the ever increasing industrialization of hyper-modern warfare rolls forward on its terrible, worldwide journey.

Conclusion

Mead's writings on self, war, and society anchor his thought in the macrosociology between the citizen, violence, and the state. They do so from an American perspective based in education and democracy and civil rights guaranteed by the U. S. Constitution, Declaration of Independence, and the Bill of Rights. Mead's elaborate theory of the emergent self, its rational capacity, and the goals of an international society and world peace through communication and democratic participation is an important new view of how to understand both our selves and the other. His critique of the conflict model fueling much political protest, terrorism, and violence is central to his sophisticated political and social theory.

His ideas emerged from a specific historical context and a world of friends, family, and intellectual life. These friends, especially the women of Hull-House, need to be considered in the forging of a more powerful and adequate understanding of world peace and cooperation. Today's new social situations, armaments, and political and economic questions call out for a reconsideration of these issues as well as our continued hope that we can understand each other and the world we have created.

Suffice it to say, in closing, that Mead's last words on the topic of self, war, and society, published after his lectures that comprise Mind, Self and Society (1934), are very much worth repeating:

Civilization is not an affair of reasonableness; it is an affair of social organization. The selfhood of a community depends upon such an organization that common goods do become the ends of the individuals of the community. We know that these common goods are there, and in some considerable degree we can and do make them our individual ends and purposes, to such a degree that we have largely banished private warfare from the recognized methods of maintaining self respect in civil conflicts. But there are still great gaps in our social organization.... We will get rid of the mechanism of warfare only as our common life permits the individual to identify his own ends and purposes with those of the community of which he is a part and which has endowed him with a self.

Notes

1. The long list of students, their notes, advice, additional manuscripts, and suggested bibliography is found in Mead 1934, pp. vi-vii.
2. Addams applied her radicalism to other, related and unrelated, areas such as ecofeminist pragmatism, African American race relations, and various forms of nonviolence and passive resistance.
3. Shannon Sullivan (2002), *Living Across and Through Skins*, brings Nietzschean analysis to feminist pragmatism; Sullivan (2003) analyzes Addams and race relations in an interesting but partially inaccurate article. Although Sullivan does note the reciprocity between Addams and cultural differences, Sullivan (2003, 48) incorrectly charges Addams as having a "hierarchical reciprocity" where whites are more civilized yet deadened than non-whites who are wild and lively. See Deegan (2002a, b).
4. Wolfe (1998), for example, suggests a lack of adequate methodology, realism, and false, untested beliefs, such as the assumption that inequality is bad, or communicative competence is good.
5. To the extent that a community self is formed in a pluralistic society, the community self could incorporate multiple communities. Many Americans believe they matured in a "melting pot" of ethnic groups, but many analysts question if this occurred or was a romantic dream of the dominant community.

Bibliography

Archival Collections

Cambridge, Massachusetts

Radcliffe College, The Arthur and Elizabeth Schlesinger Library on the History of Women in America
• Ethel Sturgess Dummer Papers

Chicago, Illinois

University of Chicago, Regenstein Library, Special Collections Research Center
• George Herbert Mead Papers
 Correspondence, box 1, folder 9; box 4, folder 4
 Anon. "McCormick Tells Why He Opposes World League" 1919. (Chicago) *Evening Post* (6 March), box 1, file 16
 Anon. "Mead Answers McCormick as to Nations League." 1919. 2pp. (Chicago) *Evening Post* (7 March), box 1, file 16
 Anon. "Senator M'Cormick's Objections," (7 March), box 1, folder 16
• George Herbert Mead Addenda
 "How Can a Sense of Citizenship Be Secured?" box 2, folder 3
 "I recognize that there are many socialist doctrines" [Socialism and the War"], box 3, folder 7
 "Immanuel Kant is the Koenigsburg philosopher" ["Immanuel Kant on Peace and Democracy"], box 2, folder 21
 "In the face of the problem of our modern industrial society" ["The Failure of Liberal Institutions in England and America"], box 2, folder 28
 "The most serious injury which can be dealt" [Germany Versus International Life], box 2, folder 32
 "Out of a situation of great confusion" ["The Completely Definite Attitude Of a Fighting Power at War"], box 2, folder 19
 Review of *Thoughts of a Psychiatrist on the War and After* by William A. White, box 5, folder 5
 "Since the middle of the nineteenth century there has been a rising tide of nationalism" ["The Rising Tide of Nationalism"], box 3, folder 2

"There are certain inheritances of an intellectualistic psychology" ["Psychology and the Moral Conduct of War"], box 3, folder 22

"There are voices heard in Germany" [The Estime in Which Germans Will Be Held After the War"], box 3, file 15

"There are three conceptions potent in the life of the world" ["Humanity, Happiness, and the Moral Order of the Universe"], box 5, folder 5

"The two sides of our emotional life" ["The Government of the State and War"], box 3, folder 26

"This change of attitude," ["The Changing Attitude Toward Militarism"], box 3, folder 1

"What are the Specific Interests of Labor in the War?" box 2, folder 29

- *Official Publication of the University of Chicago, 1917.* Chicago: University of Chicago Press.
  University Lecture Association in Cooperation with the University of Chicago, 1917-1918.
  War Courses.
- *Official Publication of the University of Chicago, 1918.* Chicago: University of Chicago Press.
  University Lecture Association in Cooperation with the University of Chicago, 1918-1919.
  Patriotic Service.
  Training of Women for National Community Service.

Swarthmore, Pennsylvania
Swarthmore College Peace Collection, Swarthmore College
- Addams Papers, series 1

Internet Resources

"The Manchester School" http://cepa.newschool.edu/het/schools/manchester. htm. Captured 13 June 2006.

References

"5 Women Sent by Chicago Will Save War Babies." 1917. *Chicago Daily Tribune* (28 October): 7.

Adams, George Burton. 1919. "To a Senator-Elect." *New York Times* (9 March): 36, cols. 4-5.

Addams, Jane. 1898. "Ethical Survival in Municipal Corruption." *International Journal of Ethics* 8 (April): 273-91.

_____. 1901. "Respect for Law." *Independent* 53 (3 January): 18-20.

_____. 1902a. *Democracy and Social Ethics.* New York: Macmillan.

_____. 1902b. "Count Tolstoy." *Chautauqua Assembly Herald* 27 (11 July): 5, 8.

_____. 1902c. "Tolstoy's Theory of Life." *Chautauqua Assembly Herald* 27 (14 July): 2.

[_____]. [1902d]. *First Report of the Labor Museum, 1901-1902.* Chicago: Privately printed pamphlet.

_____. 1907. *Newer Ideals of Peace.* New York: Macmillan.

_____. 1909. *The Spirit of Youth and the City Streets*. New York: Macmillan.

_____. 1910. *Twenty Years at Hull-House*. New York: Macmillan.

_____. 1912a. *A New Conscience and an Ancient Evil*. New York: Macmillan.

_____. 1912b. "Remarks on Labor Night." *City Club Bulletin* 5 (27 May): 222-23.

_____. 1915. "Foreword: War and Social Reconstruction." *Survey* 33 (6 March): 603.

_____. 1916. *The Long Road of Woman's Memory*. New York: Macmillan.

_____. 1917a. "Patriots and Pacifists in War Time." *City Club Bulletin* 10 (18 June): 184-90.

_____. 1917b. "Tolstoy and the Russian Soldiers." *New Republic* 12 (29 September): 240-42.

_____. 1918. "The World's Food and World Politics." *Proceedings of the National Conference of Social Workers*, 45, pp. 650-56.

_____. 1919. "Americanization." *Publications of the American Sociological Society* 14, pp. 206-14.

_____. 1920. "Nationalism — A Dogma?" *Survey* 43 (7 February): 524-26.

_____. 1922. Testimony. P. 55 in *Negroes in Chicago*, The Chicago Commission on Race Relations. Chicago: University of Chicago Press.

_____. 1922/1960. *Peace and Bread in Time of War*, intro. by John Dewey. Boston: Hall.

_____. 1928. "Tolstoy, Prophet of Righteousness." *Unity* 102 (10 September): 11-12.

_____. 1929a. "A Toast to John Dewey." *Survey* 63 (15 November): 203-4.

_____. 1929b. "Memorial." Pp. 18-23 in *Helen Castle Mead*, ed. anonymous. Privately printed pamphlet.

_____. 1930a. *The Second Twenty Years at Hull-House: With a Record of a Growing World Consciousness*, illus. by Norah Hamilton. New York: Macmillan.

_____. 1930b. "Reflections on the First Pan-Pacific Women's Conference." Pp. ix-x in *Record of Proceedings* 2.

_____. 1930c. "John Dewey and Social Welfare." Pp. 140-51 in *John Dewey and His Philosophy*, ed. by Henry W. Holmes. Cambridge, MA: Harvard University Press.

_____. 1931. "Tolstoy and Gandhi." *Christian Century* 48 (25 November): 1485-88.

_____. 1932. *The Excellent Becomes the Permanent*. New York: Macmillan.

_____. 1935. *My Friend, Julia Lathrop*. New York: Macmillan.

_____. 1976. *Jane Addams on Peace, War, and International Understanding, 1899-1932*, ed. and intro. by Allen F. Davis. New York: Garland.

Addams, Jane; Emily Greene Balch; and Alice Hamilton. 1915/2003. *Women at the Hague: The International Congress of Women and Its Results*, intro. by Mary Jo Deegan. Amherst, NY: Humanity Books.

Addams, Jane, et al. 1927. *The Child, the Clinic and the Court*, intro. by Jane Addams. New York: New Republic.

Adorno, Theodor, Else Frenkel-Brunswik, Daniel J. Levinson, and R. Nevitt Sanford. 1950. *The Authoritarian Personality*. New York: Harper.

Allard, Leola. 1920. "Rents Raised: Relief Sought; None in Sight." 1920. *Chicago Daily Tribune* (4 February): 19, col. 8.

Alonso, Harriet Hyman. 1993. *Peace as a Woman's Issue*. Syracuse, NY: Syracuse University Press.

_____. 1995. "Nobel Peace Laureates." *Journal of Women's History* 7 (Summer): 6-26.

_____. 1996. "A Response [To A Very Different Vision of Jane Addams and Emily Greene Balch.]" *Journal of Women's History* 8 (Summer): 127-29.

Anon. 1919. "The Lodge Resolution and the League." *City Club of Chicago Bulletin* (10 March): 69-71.

Balch, Emily Greene. 1910. *Our Slavic Fellow Citizen*. New York: Charities Publications Committee.

_____. 1915. "Racial Contact and Cohesions: As Factors in the Unconstrained Fabric of a World At Peace." *Survey* 33 (6 March): 610-11.

_____, ed. 1918. *Approaches to the Great Settlement*. With a bibliography by Pauline Knickerbocker Angell, introduction by Norman Angell. New York: B. W. Huebsch.

_____, ed. 1919. *Report of the International Congress of Women*. Zurich, Switzerland. Geneva: WILPF.

_____, ed. 1921. *Report of the Third International Congress of Women*. Vienna, Austria. Geneva: WILPF.

_____, ed. 1927. *Occupied Haiti*. New York: Writers Publishing Co.

_____. 1972. *Beyond Nationalism*. New York: Twayne Publishers.

"Becoming an Archbishop" 1916. *Chicago Tribune* (10 February): 5, cols. 1-5.

Bennett, Scott H. 2004. *Radical Pacifism: The War Resisters League and Gandhian Nonviolence in American, 1915-1963*. By Syracuse, NY: Syracuse University Press.

Berger, Peter and Thomas Luckmann. 1966. *The Social Construction of Reality*. Garden City, NY: Doubleday.

Blasi, Anthony, ed. 2005. *The Diverse Histories of American Sociology, 1905-2005*, ed. by Anthony J. Blasi. Sponsored by the History of Sociology Section, American Sociological Association. Leiden (The Netherlands): Brill.

Blumer, Herbert. 1969. *Symbolic Interactionism*. Englewood Cliffs, NJ: Prentice-Hall.

Bourne, Randolph S. [One of Them.] 1911. "The Handicapped." *Atlantic Monthly* 108 (September): 320-29.

_____. 1915. "John Dewey's Philosophy." *New Republic* 13 March): 154-56.

_____. 1917/1964. "Twilight of Idols." *Seven Arts* 2 (October): 688-702. Pp. 58-64 in *War and the Intellectuals*, ed. by Carl Resek. New York: Harper and Row.

_____. 1964. *War and the Intellectuals*, ed. by Carl Resek. New York: Harper and Row.

Boydston, Jo Ann. 1977. "Introduction." Pp. ix-lxvii in *The Poems of John Dewey*, ed. and intro by Jo Ann Boydston. Carbondale: Southern Illinois University Press.

Boyer, John W. 2004. "Judson's War and Hutchins's Peace: The University of Chicago and War in the Twentieth Century." *University of Chicago Record* 38 (8 January): 2-14.

Burger, John S., and Mary Jo Deegan. 1981. "George Herbert Mead on Internationalism, Democracy, and War." *Wisconsin Sociologist* 18 (Spring-Summer): 72-83.

Buroway, Michael. 2005. "For Public Sociology." *American Sociological Review* 70 (February): 4-28.

Bussy, Gertrude and Margaret Tims. 1965. *Pioneers for Peace: Women's International League for Peace and Freedom, 1915-1965*. London: Allen and Unwin.

Butler, Nicholas Murray. 1913. *The International Mind: An Argument for the Judicial Settlement of International Disputes*. New York: Charles Scribner's Sons.

Chatfield, Charles. 1970. "World War I and the Liberal Pacifist in the United States." *American Historical Review* 75 (December): 1920-1937.

"Chicago Bids Wild Welcome to Mundelein" 1916. *Chicago Tribune* (9 February): 1, col. 5.

"Children's War Work Peril to Nation." 1917. *City Club Bulletin* 10 (19 November): 268-70.

Clayton, Bruce. 1984. *Forgotten Prophet: The Life of Randolph Bourne*. Baton Rouge: University of Louisiana Press.

Comte, Auguste. 1853/1868. *The Positive Philosophy of Auguste Comte*. Tr. and ed. by Harriet Martineau. Reprinted New York: Williams Gowans.

Costin, Lela B. 1983. *Two Sisters for Social Justice: A Biography of Grace and Edith Abbott*. Urbana: University of Illinois Press.

Cywar, Alan. 1969. "John Dewey in World War I: Patriotism and International Progressivism." *American Quarterly* 21 (Autumn): 578-94.

Dante, Alighieri. 1895. *The Inferno*, tr. by Henry Francis Cary. New York: Cassell Publishing Co.

Davis, Allen F. 1973. *American Heroine*. New York: Oxford University Press.

Davis, Katharine Bement. 1918. "How the Public May Help." *Proceedings of the National Conference of Social Workers*, 45, pp. 673-74.

Deegan, Mary Jo. 1978. "Women in Sociology, 1890-1930." *Journal of the History of Sociology* 1 (Fall): 11-34.

_____. 1983. "Sociology at Wellesley College, 1900-1919." *Journal of the History of Sociology* 6 (December): 91-115.

_____. 1985. "Multiple Minority Groups." Pp. 37-55 in *Women and Disability: The Double Handicap*, ed. by Mary Jo Deegan and Nancy Brooks. New Brunswick, NJ: Transaction Publishers.

_____. 1987a. "An American Dream: The Historical Connections Between Women, Humanism, and Sociology, 1890-1920." *Humanity and Society* 11 (August): 353-65.

_____. 1987b. "Symbolic Interaction and the Study of Women" and "Working Hypotheses for Social Change." Pp. 1-15, 443-449 in *Women and Symbolic Interaction*, ed. by Mary Jo Deegan and Michael R. Hill. Boston, MA: Allen and Unwin.

_____. 1988. *Jane Addams and the Men of the Chicago School, 1892-1920*. New Brunswick, NJ: Transaction Publishers.

_____. 1989. *American Ritual Dramas: Social Rules and Cultural Meanings*. Westport, CT: Greenwood Press.

_____, ed. 1991. *Women in Sociology: A Bio-Bibliographical Sourcebook*, intro. by Mary Jo Deegan. New York: Greenwood Press.

_____. 1992. "The Genesis of the International Self." Pp. 339-53 in *Non-European Youth and the Process of Immigration*, ed. by Luigi Tomasi. Trento, Italy: University of Trento.

_____. 1995. "The Second Sex and the Chicago School: Women's Accounts, Knowledge, and Work, 1945-1960." Pp. 322-64 in *A Second Chicago School?*, ed. by Gary A. Fine. Chicago: University of Chicago Press.

_____. 1996a. "'Dear Love, Dear Love': Feminist Pragmatism and the Chicago Female World of Love and Ritual." *Gender & Society* 10 (October): 590-607.

_____. 1996b. "A Very Different Vision of Jane Addams and Emily Greene Balch." *Journal of Women's History* 8 (Summer): 121-25.

_____. 1997. "Gilman's Sociological Journey from Herland to Ourland." Pp. 1-57 in *With Her in Ourland*: Sequel to *Herland* by Charlotte Perkins Gilman, ed. by Mary Jo Deegan and Michael R. Hill. Westport, CT: Greenwood Press.

_____, ed. 1998. *The American Ritual Tapestry: Social Rules and Cultural Meanings*. New York: Greenwood Press.

_____. 1999. "Play from the Perspective of George Herbert Mead." Pp. xix-cxii in *Play, School, and Society*, ed. and intro. by Mary Jo Deegan. New York: Peter Lang.

_____. 2001a. "Introduction: George Herbert Mead's First Book." Pp. xi-xliv in *Essays in Social Psychology*, ed. and intro. by Mary Jo Deegan. New Brunswick, NJ: Transaction Publishers.

_____. 2001b. "The Chicago School of Ethnography." Pp. 11-25 in *Handbook of Ethnography*, edited by Paul Atkinson, Amanda Coffey, Sara Delamont, John Lofland, and Lyn Lofland. London, UK: Sage.

_____. 2002a. "Fannie Barrier Williams: A Chicagoan's View of the African American Experience, 1893-1926." Pp. xiii-lx in *A New Woman of Color: The Collected Writings of Fannie Barrier Williams*. DeKalb: Northeastern Illinois University.

_____. 2002b. *Race, Hull-House, and the University of Chicago: A New Conscience Against an Ancient Evil*. Westport, CT: Praeger.

_____. 2003a. "Introduction." Pp. 11-34 in *Women at the Hague: The International Congress of Women and Its Results* by Jane Addams, Emily Greene Balch; and Alice Hamilton, intro. by Mary Jo Deegan. Amherst, NY: Humanity Books, 1915/2003.

_____. 2003b. "Katharine Bement Davis: Her Theory and Praxis of Feminist Pragmatism." *Women & Criminal Justice* 14 (#2/3): 15-40.

_____. 2005a. "Women, African Americans, and the ASA, 1905-2005." Pp. 178-206 in *The Diverse Histories of American Sociology, 1905-2005*, ed. by Anthony J. Blasi. Sponsored by the History of Sociology Section, American Sociological Association. Leiden (The Netherlands): Brill.

_____. 2005b. "A Private Trouble Behind the Gendered Division of Labor in Sociology: The Curious Marriage of Robert E. Park and Clara Cahill Park." Pp. 18-39 in *The Diverse Histories of American Sociology, 1905-2005*, ed. by Anthony J. Blasi. Sponsored by the History of Sociology Section, American Sociological Association. Leiden (The Netherlands): Brill.

_____. 2005c. "Harriet Martineau and the Sociology of Health: *England and Her Soldiers (1859)* and *Health, Husbandry and Handicraft (1861)*. Presented at the Third Harriet Martineau Society Working Conference, 24 May 2005, Mammoth Cave, Kentucky.

_____. In preparation. "The University of Chicago Social Settlement and the Department of Sociology."

Deegan, Mary Jo and John S. Burger 1978. "George Herbert Mead and Social Reform: His Work and Writings." *Journal of the History of the Behavioral Sciences* 14 (October): 362-372.

Deegan, Mary Jo, and Michael R. Hill, eds. 1987. *Women and Symbolic Interaction*. Boston, MA: Allen and Unwin.

Deegan, Mary Jo, and Michael R. Hill. 1991. "Doctoral Dissertations as Liminal Journeys of the Self." *Teaching Sociology* 19 (July): 322-332.

Deegan, Mary Jo, and Valerie Malhotra [Benz]. 1977. "Symbols in the Thought of Alfred Schutz and George Herbert Mead." *International Journal of Symbology* 8 (March): 34-35.

Deegan, Mary Jo, and Christopher Podeshi. 2001. "The Ecofeminist Pragmatism of Charlotte Perkins Gilman: The Herland Sagas." *Environmental Ethics* 23 (Spring): 19-36.

Deegan, Mary Jo, and Anna-Maria Wahl. 2003. "Introduction." Pp. 1-35 in *On Art, Labor and Religion* by Ellen Gates Starr, edited and with an introductory essay by Mary Jo Deegan and Ana-Maria Wahl. New Brunswick, NJ: Transaction Publishers.

Deloria, Ella Cara. 1988. *Waterlily*, with a biographical sketch of the author by Agnes Picotte and an afterword by Raymond J. DeMallie. Lincoln: University of Nebraska Press.

_____. 1998. *Speaking of Indians*. Introduction to the Bison Books edition by Vine Deloria, Jr. Lincoln: University of Nebraska Press.

Dernby, Karl. G. 1918. "The Finnish Revolution." *City Club Bulletin* 11 (24 June): 207-208.

Dewey, John. 1915a. *School and Society*, Rev. ed. Chicago: University of Chicago Press.

_____. 1915b/1942. *German Philosophy and Politics, Rev. Ed.* New York: G. P. Putnam Sons.

_____. 1917a. "Force, Violence, and Law." *New Republic* 11. Pp. 211-15 in *John Dewey, The Middle Works*, 10 (1916-1917), 1980.

_____. 1917b. "The Future of Pacifism." *New Republic* 11: 358-60. Pp. 265-70 in *John Dewey, The Middle Works*, 10 (1916-1917), 1980.

_____. 1917c. "War's Social Results." *New York World* 29 (July): 1E. Pp. 21-25 in *John Dewey, The Later Works*, vol. 17. Miscellaneous Writings, ed. by Jo Ann Boydston, intro. by Sidney Hook. Carbondale: Southern Illinois University Press, 1991.

_____. 1918. View on "What the War Means to America." *Columbia Alumni News* 9 (17 May): 1002. P. 123 in *John Dewey, The Later Works*, vol. 17. Miscellaneous Writings, ed. by Jo Ann Boydston, intro. by Sidney Hook. Carbondale: Southern Illinois University Press, 1991.

_____. 1920. *Social Reconstruction*. New York: Hamilton Holt Co.

_____. 1925/1971. *Experience and Nature*. Rev. ed. Peru, IL: Open Court.

_____. 1931. "Memorial." Pp. 10-23 in *George Herbert Mead*. Chicago: Privately printed pamphlet.

_____. 1937. *Truth Is On the March*. New York: American Committee for the Defense of Leon Trotsky.

_____. 1945a. "Democratic Versus Coercive International Organization: The Realism of Jane Addams." Pp ix-xx in *Peace and Bread in Time of War*, by Jane Addams. Boston: G. K. Hall & Co., 1922/1960.

_____. 1945b. "The Theory of International Relations: "A Discussion of the Theory of International Relations." *Journal of Philosophy* 42 (30 August): 477-78.

_____. 1946. "Emily Greene Balch — An Appraisal." Pamphlet. New York: Women's International League of Peace and Freedom.

_____. 1977. *The Poems of John Dewey*, ed. and intro. by Jo Ann Boydston. Carbondale: Southern Illinois University Press.

Dewey, John, et al. 1945c. "A Discussion of the Theory of International Relations." *Journal of Philosophy* 42 (30 August): 477-97.

Dewey, John, and Alice Chipman Dewey. 1920. *Letters from China and Japan*, ed. by Evelyn Dewey. New York: E. P. Dutton.

Dewey, John, and Evelyn Dewey. 1915. *Schools of To-morrow*. New York: E. P. Dutton.

Diggins, John Patrick. 1981. "John Dewey in Peace and War." *American Scholar* 50 (Spring): 213-30.

_____. 1994. *The Promise of Pragmatism*. Chicago: University of Chicago Press.

Diner, Stephen. 1978. "George Herbert Mead's Ideas on Women and Careers: A Letter to His Daughter-in-Law, 1920." *Signs* 4 (Winter): 407-409.

_____. 1980. *A City and Its Universities: Public Policy in Chicago, 1892-1919*. Chapel Hill: University of North Carolina Press.

Dodd, William F. 1915. "Constitutional and Political Guarantees," *Philosophical Review* 24 (March): 193-194.

Durkheim, Émile. 1912/1961. *The Elementary Forms of the Religious Life*, translated by Joseph Ward Swain. New York: Collier Books.

_____. 1933. *The Division of Labor in Society*, translated by George Simpson. Glencoe, IL: Free Press.

_____. 1983. *Pragmatism and Sociology,* translated by J.C. Whitehouse, edited and introduced by John B. Allcock, preface by Armand Cuvillier. New York: Cambridge University Press.

Eastman, Max. 1941. "John Dewey." *Atlantic Monthly* 168 (December): 671-85.

Engel, J. Ronald. 1983. *Sacred Sands*. Middletown, CT: Wesleyan University Press.

"England and France Since the Armistice." 1918. *City Club Bulletin* 12 (10 March): 67-70.

Ekirch, Arthur A., Jr. 1974. *Progressivism in America*. New York: New Viewpoints.

Faris, Ellsworth. 1936. Review of *Mind, Self, and Society* by George H. Mead. *American Journal of Sociology* 41 (May): 809-13.

Faris, Robert E. L. 1967. *Chicago Sociology: 1920-1932*. Chicago: University of Chicago Press.

Farrell, John C. 1967. *Beloved Lady*. Baltimore, MD: Johns Hopkins Press.

_____. 1975. "John Dewey and World War I." Pp. 299-340 in *Perspectives in American History*, edited by Donald Fleming and Bernard Bailyn. Cambridge, MA: Charles Warren Center for Studies in American History, Harvard University.

Feagin, Joe R. 2001. "Social Justice and Sociology." *American Sociological Review* 66 (February): 1-20.

Feagin, Joe R. and Hernan Vera. 2001. *Liberation Sociology*. Boulder, CO: Westview.

Feagin, Joe R., Hernan Vera, and Pinar Batur. 2001. *White Racism*, 2nd edition. New York: Routledge.

Feffer, Andrew. 1993. *The Chicago Pragmatists and American Progressivism*. Chicago: University of Chicago Press.

_____. 2001. "Sociability and Social Conflict in George Herbert Mead's Interactionism." *Journal of the History of Ideas* 51 (April-June): 233-54.

Ferguson, Kathy E. 1980. *Self, Society, and Womankind*. Westport, CT: Greenwood Press.

Filene, Edward A. 1915. "The Melting Pot and the Fires of War." *Survey* 33 (6 March): 608-609.

Fine, Gary A, ed. 1995. *The Second Chicago School?* Chicago: University of Chicago Press.

"For Russian Women and Children." 1920. *Survey* 44 (26 August): 604.

Freud, Sigmund. 1991. *On Narcissism*, edited by Joseph Sandler, Ethel Spector Person and Peter Fonagy for the International Psychoanalytical Association. New York: Yale University Press.

Frey, John B. 1918. "A Menace to Morale." *City Club Bulletin* 11 (15 July): 219-20.

Gaard, Greta. 1997. "Ecofeminism and Wilderness." *Environmental Ethics* 19 (Spring): 5-25.

Galsworthy, John. 1910. *Justice: A Tragedy in Four Acts*. New York: Charles Scribner's Sons.

Garrison, William Lloyd. 1904/1924. *William Lloyd Garrison on Non-Resistance*. New York: Nation Press Printing.

Gilman, Charlotte P. "The Yellow Wall-Paper." *New England Magazine* 5 (January 1892): 647-56.

_____. 1915/2002. *The Dress of Women: An Introduction to the Symbolism and Sociology of Clothing*, edited and with an introductory essay by Michael R. Hill and Mary Jo Deegan. Westport, CT: Greenwood Press.

Glazer, Penina Migdal. 1972. "From the Old Left to the New." *American Quarterly* (December): 584-603.

Goffman, Erving. 1963. *Stigma*. Englewood Cliffs, NJ: Prentice-Hall.

_____. 1976/1979. *Gender Advertisements*. Cambridge, MA: Harvard University Press.

_____. 1977/1987. "The Arrangement Between the Sexes." Pp. 51-78 in *Women and Symbolic Interaction*, edited by Mary Jo Deegan and Michael R. Hill. Boston, MA: Allen and Unwin.

Goodwin, Joanne L. 1997. *Gender and the Politics of Welfare Reform*. Chicago: University of Chicago Press.

Gottlieb, Robert. 1993. *Forcing the Spring: The Transformation of the American Environmental Movement*. Washington, DC: Island Press.

Grant, A.J. and Harold William Vazeille Temperly. 1927. *Europe in the 19th Century (1789-1914)*. New York, London: Longmans, Green.

Griffin, Susan. 1978. *Woman and Nature*. New York: Harper Colophon.

Habermas, Jurgen. c. 1984. *The Theory of Communicative Action*, vols. I & II. tr. by Thomas McCarthy. Boston: Beacon Press.

Hamilton, Alice. 1918. "Munitions Workers Risk Death." *City Club Bulletin* 11 (18 February): 63-64.

_____. 1943. *Exploring the Dangerous Trades*. Boston: Little, Brown.

"Hanson Holds Up Shoop's Last Two Appointees." 1918. *Chicago Daily Tribune* (27 August): 15, col. 8.

Harper, Samuel N. 1918. "Munitions Workers Risk Death." *City Club Bulletin* 11 (15 April): 131-32.

Hegel, Georg Wilhelm Friedrich. 1807/1977. *Phenomenology of Spirit*, tr. A. V. Miller. Oxford: Oxford University Press.

Helbich, Wolfgang J. 1967-1968. "American Liberals in the League of Nations Controversy." *Public Opinion Quarterly* 31 (Winter): 568-96.

Hewitt, Oscar E. 1919. "City Imperils, Leaders Move in Coal Crisis." *Chicago Daily Tribune* (2 December): 2, cols. 2-3.

Hill, Michael R. and Mary Jo Deegan. "Introduction: Charlotte Perkins Gilman on the Symbolism and Sociology of Clothing." Pp. ix-xxvii in *The Dress of Women: An Introduction to the Symbolism and Sociology of Clothing*, by Charlotte Perkins Gilman, edited and with an introduction by Michael R. Hill and Mary Jo Deegan. Westport, CT: Greenwood Press.

Hobbes, Thomas. 1651/1929. *Leviathan*. With an Essay by W. G. Pogson Smith. Oxford: Clarendon Press.

Holli, Melvin G. 1981. "The Great War Sinks Chicago's German *Kultur*." Pp. 260-311 in *Ethnic Chicago*, ed. by Peter d'A. Jones and Melvin G. Holli. Grand Rapids, MI: William B. Eerdman's Publishing Co.

Holmes, John Hay. 1912/1972. *The International Mind*. New York: Garland.

_____. 1916. *New Wars for Old*. New York: Dodd, Mead.

"Housing War Workers in Chicago." 1918. *City Club Bulletin* (10 June): 195.

"How Chicago Will Profit." 1918. *Chicago Daily Tribune* (2 November):15, cols. 6-7.

Howe, Frederic C. 1915. "Reservoirs of Strife: The Distribution of Wealth in Relation to the Invisible Causes of War." *Survey* 33 (6 March): 614-15.

_____. 1917. "Financial Imperialism." *Atlantic [Monthly]* 120 (October): 477-84.

Howlett, Charles F. 1976. "John Dewey and the Crusade to Outlaw War." *American Scholar* 50 (Spring): 336-55.

"Huge Bomb Plot Exposed." 1916. *Chicago Tribune* (15 February): 1, cols. 7-8.

James, Alice. 1934. Alice James, ed. and intro. by Anna Robson Burr. New York: Dodd, Mead.

James, William. *The Principles of Psychology*. New York: Henry Holt and Co., 1890.

_____. 1904. "The Chicago School." *Psychological Bulletin* 1 (15 January): 1-5.

_____. 1910/1991. "The Moral Equivalent of War." Pp. 14-17 in *The Eagle and the Dove, 2nd Edition*, ed. and intro. by John Whiteclay Chambers, II. Syracuse, NY: Syracuse University Press.

_____. 1911. *Memories and Studies*. New York: Longmans, Green.

Janowitz, Morris. 1966. "Introduction." Pp. vii-lviii in *W. I. Thomas*, edited and introduced by Morris Janowitz. Chicago: University of Chicago Press.
Joas, Hans. 1985. *G. H. Mead: A Contemporary Re-examination of His Thought*, tr. by
Raymond Meyer. Cambridge, MA: MIT Press.
_____. 1993. *Pragmatism and Social Theory*. Chicago: University of Chicago
Press.
_____. 1996. *The Creativity of Action Design*. Chicago: University of Chicago
Press.
_____. 1998. "The Inspiration of Pragmatism." Pp. 190-98 in *The Revival of Pragma-
tism*, edited by Morris Dickstein. Durham, NC: Duke University Press.
Johnson, James Weldon. 1918. "Negro Soldier Praised." *City Club Bulletin* 11 (6 May):
160.
Kafka, Franz. 1954. *The Castle*, tr. by Willa and Edwin Muir; rev. and with add. materials
tr. by Eithne Wilkins and Ernest Kaiser. With an Homage by Thomas Mann. New
York: Alfred A. Knopf.
_____. 1956/1961. *The Trial*, tr. by Willa and Edwin Muir; rev. and with add. materials
tr. by E. M. Butler. New York: Modern Library.
Kallen, Horace. 1918. "The Jewish People and the War." *City Club Bulletin* 11 (15
April): 135-36.
Kant, Immanuel. 1992. *Lectures on Logic*, tr. and ed. by J. Michael Young. New York:
Cambridge University Press.
_____. 2002. *Theoretical Philosophy After 1781*, tr. by Gary Hatfield et al., ed. by
Henry Allison and Peter Heath. New York: Cambridge University Press.
King, Ynestra. 1987. "What is Ecofeminism?" *The Nation*. 12 December 1987. Pp.
702, 730-731.
King James Bible, translated Olga S. Opfell. 1982. Jefferson, NC: McFarland.
Kloppenberg, James T. 1998. "Pragmatism: An Old Name For Some New Ways of
Thinking?" Pp. 83-27 in *The Revival of Pragmatism*, edited by Morris Dickstein.
Durham, NC: Duke University Press.
Knock, Thomas J. 1992. *To End All Wars: Woodrow Wilson and the Quest for a New
World Order*. Princeton, NJ: Princeton University Press.
Kropotkin, Petr. 1968. *Kropotkin's Revolutionary Pamphlets: A Collection of Writings*,
ed. and intro. by Roger N. Baldwin. New York: B. Blom.
Kurtz, Lester R. 1984. *Evaluating Chicago Sociology: A Guide to the Literature, with
An Annotated Bibliography*. Chicago: University of Chicago Press.
Lagemann, Ellen Condliffe. 1983. "Introduction." Pp. 1-42 in *Jane Addams on Edu-
cation*, by Jane Addams, ed. and intro. by Ellen Condliffe Lagemann. New York:
Teachers College Press.
Lamb, Charles. 1822/1908. *Essays of Elia*. With an introduction by William Archer.
New York: Cassell.
Lengermann, Patricia Madoo and Jill Niebrugge, eds. 1998. *The Women Founders:
Sociology and Social Theory, 1830-1930*. New York: McGraw-Hill.
Levine, Daniel. 1971. *Jane Addams and the Liberal Tradition*. Madison: State Historical
Society of Wisconsin.
Lewis, J. David and Richard L. Smith. 1980. *American Sociology and Pragmatism*.
Chicago: University of Chicago Press.
Light, Andrew and Eric Katz. 1996. *Environmental Pragmatism*. New York: Rout-
ledge.
Locke, John. 1699/1967 *Treatise on Civil Government*, reprinted in *Two Treatises of
Government*, a critical ed. with an intro. and apparatus criticus by Peter Laslett.
London: Cambridge University Press.

Lovett, Robert. 1948. *All Our Years: The Autobiography of Robert Morss Lovett*. New York: Viking Press.

Lowden, Frank P. 1918 "Should We Amend Our Constitution in Wartime?" *City Club Bulletin* 11 (24 June): 211.

Lowell, James Russell. 1848. *Meliboeus-Hipponax: Bigelow Papers*, ed., intro., notes, glossary, and index by Homer Wilbur. A.M. Cambridge: George Nichols.

Lucas, W. P. "Children of the War Zone." *City Club Bulletin* 11 (17 June): 201-202.

"M'Cormick Attacks League Covenant." *New York Times* (6 March 1919): 2, cols. 6-7.

McLaughlin, A. C. 1917. "As to 'English Treachery'." *Chicago Herald* (18 July): 4, cols. 6-7.

McDowell, Mary. 1912. "Remarks on Labor Night." *City Club Bulletin* 5 (27 May): 219.

_____. 1919. "England and France Since the Armistice." *City Club Bulletin* 12 (10 March): 67-70.

Mahowald, Mary B. 1997. "What Classical American Philosophers Missed: Jane Addams, Critical Pragmatism, and Cultural Feminism." *Journal of Value Inquiry* 31: 29-54.

Malhotra [Benz], Valerie and Mary Jo Deegan. 1978. "Comment on Perinbanayagam's 'The Significance of "Others" in the Thought of Alfred Schutz, G.H. Mead, and C.H. Cooley.'" *Sociological Quarterly* 19 (Winter): 141-145.

Mallock, W. H. 1920. *Memoirs of Life and Literature*. London: Chapman and Hall, Ltd.

Manis, Jerome and Bernard Meltzer, eds. 1979. *Symbolic Interaction*, 3rd Edition. Boston: Allyn and Bacon.

Marchand, C. Roland. 1972. *The American Peace Movement and Social Reform, 1898-1918*. Princeton, NJ: Princeton University Press.

Marcuse, Herbert. 1964. *One Dimensional Man* Boston: Beacon Press.

Marx, Karl and Friedrich Engels. 1848/1932. *Manifesto of the Communist Party*, ed. and annotated by Friedrich Engels. New York: International Publishers.

Mason, Otis Tufton. 1894. *Woman's Share in Primitive Culture*. New York: D. Appleton.

Matthews, Shailer. 1917. "Why the U.S. is at War." *Chicago Herald* (16 July): 4, cols. 6-7.

Mead, Lucia Ames, ed. 1915. *The Overthrow of the War System*. Boston: Forum.

Mead, George Herbert. 1882-1883. "John Locke." *Oberlin Review* 10: 217-19.

_____. 1899a. Review of *The Psychology of Socialism* by Gustave Le Bon. *American Journal of Sociology* 5 (November): 404-12.

_____. 1899b. "The Working Hypothesis in Social Reform." *American Journal of Sociology* 5 (November): 367-71.

_____. 1907. Review of *The Newer Ideals of Peace*. *American Journal of Sociology* 13 (July): 121-28.

_____. 1908. "The Social Settlement, Its Basis and Function." *University Record* (Chicago) 12 (January): 108-110.

_____. 1912. "Remarks on Labor Night." *City Club Bulletin* 5 (27 May): 214-15.

_____. 1913. "The Social Self." *Journal of Philosophy* 10 (3 July): 374-80.

_____. 1915a. "The Psychological Bases for Internationalism." *Survey* 33 (6 March): 604-607.

_____. 1915b. "Natural Rights and the Theory of the Political Institution." *Journal of Philosophy, Psychology and Scientific Methods* 12 (March): 141-155.

_____. 1915c. "Constitutional and Political Guarantees." *Philosophical Review* 24 (18 March): 193-194.

_____. 1917a. "Patriots and Pacifists in War Time." *City Club Bulletin* 10 (18 June): 184.

_____. 1917b. "Germany's Crisis — Its Effect on Labor: Part I." *Chicago Herald* (26 July): 4, cols. 4-5.

_____. 1917c. "Germany's Crisis — Its Effect on Labor: Part II." *Chicago Herald* (27 July): 4, cols. 4-5.

_____. 1917d. "War Issue to U.S. Forced by Kaiser." *Chicago Herald* (2 August): 4, cols. 4-5.

_____. 1917e. "America's Ideals and the War." *Chicago Herald* (3 August): 4, cols. 4-5.

_____. 1917f. "Democracy's Issues in the World War." *Chicago Herald* (4 August): 4, cols. 4-5.

_____. 1917g. "Camouflage of the Conscientious Objector." 1917. *New York Times* (23 December): 56, cols. 1-4.

_____. 1918a. "Social Work, Standards of Living and the War." *Proceedings of the National Conference of Social Workers* 45 (1918): 637-44.

_____. 1918b. *The Conscientious Objector*. Pamphlet No. 33, Patriotism through Education Series. New York: The National Security League.

_____. 1918c. "The Psychology of Punitive Justice." *American Journal of Sociology* 23 (March): 577-602.

_____. 1918d. "Review of *The Nature of Peace and the Terms of Its Perpetuation* by Thorstein Veblen." *Journal of Political Economy* 26 (July): 752-763.

_____. 1919a. "A Translation of Wundt's *Folk Psychology*." *American Journal of Theology* 23 (October): 533-36.

_____. 1919b. "President Mead's Message to Members." *City Club Bulletin* 12 (18 April): 101-102.

_____. 1920. "Retiring President's Address." *City Club Bulletin* 13 (19 April): 94-95.

_____. 1929a. "Mary E. McDowell." *Neighborhood* 2 (April): 77-8.

_____. 1929b. "National-Mindedness and International-Mindedness." *International Journal of Ethics* 39 (July): 385-407.

_____. 1929c. "The Nature of the Past." Pp. 235-42 in *Essays in Honor of John Dewey*, ed. by John Cross. New York: Henry Holt.

_____. 1930. "An Address." Pp. 24-32 in *Addison Webster Moore*. Chicago: Privately printed.

_____. 1932. *The Philosophy of the Present*, ed. and intro. by Arthur E. Murphy, pref. remarks by John Dewey. Chicago: University of Chicago.

_____. 1934. *Mind, Self and Society*, ed. and intro. by Charles Morris. Chicago: University of Chicago Press.

_____. 1935. "The Philosophy of John Dewey." *International Journal of Ethics* 46 (October): 64-81.

_____. 1936. *Movements of Thought in the Nineteenth Century*, ed. and intro. by Merritt H. Moore. Chicago: University of Chicago Press.

_____. 1938. *The Philosophy of the Act*, ed. and intro. by Charles W. Morris, in collaboration with John M. Brewster, Albert M. Dunham, and David L. Miller. Chicago: University of Chicago Press.

_____. 1982. *The Individual and the Social Self*, ed. and intro. by David L. Miller. Chicago: The University of Chicago Press.

_____. 1999. *Play, School, and Society*, ed. and intro. by Mary Jo Deegan. New York: Peter Lang.

_____. 2001. *Essays in Social Psychology*, ed. and intro. by Mary Jo Deegan. New Brunswick, NJ: Transaction Publishers.

Mead, George Herbert, and Helen Castle Mead, eds. 1902. *Henry Northrup Castle: Letters*. London (UK): Privately Printed.

Mead, George Herbert, Tucker A. Wreidt, and J. Bogan. 1912. *A Report on Vocational Training in Chicago and in Other Cities*. Chicago: City Club of Chicago.

Mead, George Herbert, Ernest A. Weidt, and William J. Broggan. 1912. *A Report on Vocational Training in Chicago and in Other Cities*. Chicago: City Club of Chicago.

Mead, Henry C.A. 1915. "Berlin in War-Time." *The University of Chicago Magazine* 7 (April): 173-75.

———. 1938. "Biographical Notes." Pp. lxxv-lxxix in *The Philosophy of the Act*, ed. and intro. by Charles Morris. Chicago: University of Chicago Press.

"Mead, George Herbert." 1943. P. 825 in *Who Was Who in America*. Vol. 1 (1897-1942). Chicago: Marquis.

Merton, Robert C. 1949. *Social Theory and Social Structure*. Glencoe, IL: Free Press.

Mill, John Stuart. 1963-1991. *Collected Works of John Stuart Mill*. 33 vols. Toronto: University of Toronto Press.

Miller, David L. 1973. *George Herbert Mead: Self, Language and the World*. Chicago: University of Chicago Press.

———. 1982. "Introduction." Pp. 1-26 in *The Individual and the Social Self*, by George Herbert Mead. Chicago: University of Chicago Press.

Milton, John. 1904. *Areopagitica*, ed. and intro. by John W. Hales. Oxford: Clarendon Press.

———. 1909-14. *The Complete Poems of John Milton*. 4 vols. New York: P. F. Collier & Sons.

Muncy, Robin. 1997. *Creating a Female Dominion in American Reform, 1890-1935*. New York: Oxford University Press.

Nasmyth, George W. 1915. "Constructive Mediation: An Interpretation of the Ten Foremost Proposals." *Survey* 33 (6 March): 616-20.

Neeley, Elizabeth and Mary Jo Deegan. 2005. "George Herbert Mead on Punitive Justice: A Critical Analysis of Contemporary Practices." *Humanity & Society* 29 (February): 71-83.

"News of the Chicago Women's Clubs." 1917. *Chicago Daily Tribune* (11 November): F6.

Nietzsche, Friedrich. 1901/1924. *The Will to Power*, 2 vols., tr. Anthony M. Ludovici, edited by Peter Gast, Ernst Horneffer, and Ernst Horneffer. London: T. N. Foulis.

"New of the Chicago Women's Clubs" 1917. *Chicago Tribune* (11 November): F6.

"100 Poisoned At Banquet" 1916. *Chicago Tribune* (11 February): 1, col. 3; 4, cols. 6-7.

"Our Ambulance in France." 1918. *Chicago City Club Bulletin* (17 June): 197-98.

Parsons, Talcott. 1937/1949. *The Structure of Social Action*. Glencoe, IL: The Free Press.

———. 1951. *The Social System*. Glencoe, IL: The Free Press.

———. 1971. *The System of Modern Societies*. Englewood Cliffs, NJ: Prentice-Hall.

Patten, Simon N. 1915. "Economic Zones and the New Alignment of National Sentiment." *Survey* 33 (6 March): 612-13.

Plant, J. 1990. "Searching for Common Ground: Ecofeminism and Bioregionalism." Pp. 155-161 in *Reweaving the World: The Emergence of Ecofeminism*, edited by I. Diamond and G. Orenstein. San Francisco, CA: Sierra Club Books.

Plato. ca. 360 B.C./2003. *The Republic*, translated by Desmond Lee. New York: Penguin Classics.

Poe, Edgar Allan. 1827. *Tamerlane and Other Poems*. Privately Printed.

Pois, Anne Marie. 1995. "Foreshadowings: Jane Addams, Emily Greene Balch and the Ecofeminist/Pacifist Feminism of the 1980s." *Peace & Change* 20 (October): 439-65.

"Poisoner's Arrest Near" 1916. *Chicago Tribune* (14 February): 1, col. 8.

Putnam, Hilary. 1998. "Pragmatism and Realism." Pp. 37-53 in *The Revival of Pragmatism*, edited by Morris Dickstein. Durham, NC: Duke University Press.

Ratcliffe, S. K. 1918. "A Picture of British Politics." *City Club Bulletin* 11 (18 March): 93.

Rauty, Raffaele. 1997. *Anticipatzioni: Percorsi della Ricerca Sociale Statunitense tra il XIX ed il XX Secolo.* Salerno, Italy: Gentile Editore.

Rockefeller, Steven C. 1991. *John Dewey: Religious Faith and Democratic Humanism.* New York; Columbia University Press.

"Reports Show Tide Rising for Car Ordinance." 1918. *Chicago Daily Tribune* (1 November): 7, cols. 1-3.

Rosen, Norma. 1989. *John and Anzia.* New York: Dutton.

Rosenberg, Rosalind. 1982. *Beyond Separate Spheres.* New Haven, CT: Yale University Press.

Rousseau, Jean-Jacques. 1797/1913. *The Social Contract*, tr. and intro. by G. D. H. Cole. New York: E. P. Dutton.

Ross, Dorothy. 1990. *The Origins of American Social Science.* New York: Cambridge University Press.

Ross, E. A. 1901. *Social Control.* New York: Macmillan.

Rucker, Darnell. 1969. *The Chicago Pragmatists.* Minneapolis: University of Minnesota Press.

Ryan, Alan. 1995. *John Dewey and the High Tide of American Liberalism.* New York: W.W. Norton.

Sandeen, Eric J. 1981. *The Letters of Randolph Bourne: A Comprehensive Edition.* Troy, NY: Whitston Publishing Co.

Schaar, John H. 1961. *Escape From Authority.* New York: Basic Books.

Schott, Linda. 1993. "Jane Addams and William James on Alternatives to War." *Journal of the History of Ideas* 54 (April): 241-54.

_____. 1997. *Reconstructing Women's Thoughts: Women's International League of Peace and Freedom.* Stanford, CA: Stanford University Press.

Shvan, August. 1915. "Permanent Peace." *Survey* 33 (6 March): 621-24, 639.

Seigfried, Charlene Haddock. 1991. "Where are All the Feminist Pragmatists?" *Hypatia* 6 (Summer): 1-19.

_____. 1996. *Pragmatism and Feminism: Reweaving the Social Fabric.* Chicago, IL: University of Chicago Press.

_____. 1999. "Socializing Democracy." *Philosophy of the Social Sciences* 29 (June): 207-30.

_____, ed. 2001. *Feminist Interpretations of John Dewey.* University Park: Pennsylvania State University Press.

_____. 2002. "Shedding Skins." *Hypatia* 17 (Fall): 173-86.

_____. 2006. "The Dangers of Unilateralism." *NWSA Journal* 18 (Fall): 20-32.

Shalin, Dimitri N. 1987. "Socialism, Democracy and Reform: A Letter and an Article by George H. Mead." *Symbolic Interaction* 10 (2): 267-78.

_____. 1988. "G. H. Mead, Socialism, and the Progressive Agenda." *American Journal of Sociology* 93 (January): 913-51.

"'Show Us,' Say Civic Bodies To Suppliant City." 1917. *Chicago Daily Tribune* (16 December): 14, cols. 1-3.

Sklar, Kathryn. 1993. *Florence Kelley and Women's Political Culture.* New Haven, CT: Yale University Press.

Skocpol, Theda. 1992. *Protecting Soldiers and Mothers*. Cambridge, MA: Belknap Press of Harvard University Press.

Smith-Rosenberg, Carroll. 1975. "The Female World of Love and Ritual." *Signs* 1 (Autumn): 1-29.

Spencer, Anna Garlin. 1913. *Woman's Share in Social Culture*. New York: Mitchell Kennerley.

_____. 1920. "Constructive Pacifism." *Survey* 63 (10 January): 387.

"The Sphere of Government." 1916. *Chicago City Club Bulletin* (19 April): 67-69.

"The Status of Russian Relief." 1920. *Survey* 44 (26 June): 431.

Stone, Gregory and Harvey Farberman. 1970. *Social Psychology Through Symbolic Interaction*. Waltham, MA: Xerox College Publishing.

Strong, Anna Louise. 1908. *A Consideration of Prayer From the Standpoint of Society*. Ph.D. Dissertation, Department of Philosophy, University of Chicago.

Sullivan, Shannon. 2001. *Living Across and Through Skins*. Bloomington: Indiana University Press.

_____. 2003. "Reciprocal Relations Between Races: Jane Addams's Ambiguous Legacy." *Transactions of the Charles S. Peirce Society* 39 (Winter): 43-60.

Swift, Jonathan. 1898. *The Works of Jonathan Swift*. 2 vols. With a memoir of the author by Thomas Roscoe. London: Bell.

Taft, Jessie. 1915. *The Woman Movement from the Point of View of Social Consciousness*. Minasha, WI: Collegiate Press, George Banta Publishing Co. (Repr. No. 6 of the Philosophic Studies under the direction of the Department of Philosophy. Chicago: University of Chicago Press, 1916.)

_____. 1942. "The Function of the Personality Course in the Practice Unit." Pp. 55-74 in *Training for Skill in Social Case Work*, ed. by Virginia P. Robinson. Philadelphia: University of Pennsylvania Press.

Thomas, W. I. 1923. *The Unadjusted Girl: With Cases and Standpoint for Behavior Analysis*. Boston: Little, Brown.

_____. 1907. *Sex and Society: Studies in the Social Psychology of Sex*. Chicago: University of Chicago Press.

[Thomas, W. I.], Robert E. Park (listed erroneously as first author) and Herbert A. Miller. 1921. *Old World Traits Transplanted*. New York: Harper & Brothers. (Reprint, with the authorship of "W. I. Thomas Together with Robert E. Park and Herbert A. Miller," a new intro. by Donald R. Young. Montclair, NJ: Patterson Smith, 1971).

Thomas, W.I. and Dorothy Swaine Thomas. 1928. *The Child in America*. New York: Alfred A. Knopf.

Thomas, W. I., and Florian Znaniecki. 1918-1920. *The Polish Peasant in Europe and America*, 5 vols. Boston: Richard G. Badger. (Vols. 1 and 2 orig. pub. University of Chicago Press, 1918).

Thoreau, Henry David. 1849/1993. "Civil Disobedience." Pp. 1-18 in *Civil Disobedience and Other Essays*. New York: Dover.

Tolstoy, Leo. 1904/1924. "What I Owe to Garrison." Pp. 46-55 in *William Lloyd Garrison on Non-Resistance*. New York: Nation Press Printing.

_____. 1910/1928. "Letter Written by Tolstoy to Gandhi, Two Months Before His Death." *Unity* 102 (10 September): 21-22.

_____. 1928-1937. *The Works of Tolstoy*, 21 Vols., edited by Aylmer Maude and translated by Aylmer Maude and Louise Shanks. Oxford: Oxford University Press for the Tolstoy Society.

Tomasi, Luigi, ed. 1992. *Non-European Youth and the Process of Immigration*, ed. by Luigi Tomasi. Trento, Italy: University of Trento.

_____. 1994. *Robert E. Park and the "Melting Pot" Theory*, edited by Renzo Gubert and Luigi Tomasi. [*Sociologia*, Vol. 9]. Trento (Italy): Reverdito Edition.

_____. 1997. *La Scuola sociologica di Chicago*, Vol. 1: *La teoria implicita* by Luigi Tomasi. Milan, Italy: FrancoAngeli.

"University Club Soup to Be Tried on Guinea Pigs." 1916. *Chicago Tribune* (12 February): 1, col. 8.

Villard, Garrison, Fanny. 1924. *William Lloyd Garrison on Non-Resistance*. New York: Nation Press Printing.

Veblen, Thorstein. 1899. *The Theory of the Leisure Class*. New York: A.M. Kelley.

_____. 1914. *The Instinct of Workmanship and the State of the Industrial Arts*. New York: Macmillan.

_____. 1904. *The Theory of Business Enterprise*. New York: Charles Scribner's Sons.

_____. 1917. *The Nature of Peace and the Terms of Its Perpetuation*. New York: Macmillan.

Virgil, Publius Maro. 29 B.C.E./1909. *The Aeneid*, translated by John Dryden with introductions, notes and illustrations. New York: P. F. Collier & Son.

Voltaire [François-Marie Arouet]. 1968. *The Complete Works of Voltaire*, edited by Theodore Besterman and others. Toronto: University of Toronto Press.

Wald, Lillian D. 1933. *Windows on Henry Street*. Boston: Little, Brown.

Weber, Max. 1920/1957. *The Protestant Ethic and the Spirit of Capitalism*, edited and introduced by Talcott Parsons and tr. by A.M. Henderson and Talcott Parsons. New York: Free Press.

_____. 1946. *From Max Weber. Essays in Sociology*, edited by Hans H. Gerth and C. Wright Mills. New York: Oxford University Press.

_____. 1947. *The Theory of Social and Economic Organization*, edited and introduced by Talcott Parsons and tr. by A. M. Henderson and Talcott Parsons. New York: Free Press.

Weigart, Andrew J. 1997. *Self, Interaction, and Environment*. New York: SUNY Press.

Wells-Barnett, Ida B. 1901. "Lynching and the Excuse for It." *Independent* 53 (16 May 1901): 1133-36.

_____. 1970. *Crusade for Justice: The Autobiography of Ida B. Wells*, ed. by Alfreda M. Duster. Chicago: University of Chicago Press.

West, Cornel. 1989. *The American Evasion of Philosophy*. Madison: University of Wisconsin Press.

_____. 1993. *Keeping the Faith*. New York: Routledge.

Westbrook, Robert B. 1991. *John Dewey and American Democracy*. Ithaca, NY: Cornell University Press.

White, William A. 1916. *Mechanisms of Character Formation*. New York: Macmillan.

_____. 1919. *Thoughts of a Psychiatrist on the War and After*. P. B. Hoebler.

_____. 1928. *Principles of Mental Hygiene*, intro. by Smith Ely Jeliff. New York: Macmillan.

Wilson, Howard Eugene. 1928. *Mary McDowell: Neighbor*. Chicago: University of Chicago Press.

Wolfe, Alan. 1998. "The Missing Pragmatic Revival in American Social Science." Pp. 199-98 in *The Revival of Pragmatism*, edited by Morris Dickstein. Durham, NC: Duke University Press.

Woolf, Virginia. 1927/1988. *To the Lighthouse*, edited and introduced by Harold Bloom. New York: Chelsea House.

Yezierska, Anzia. 1932. *All I Could Never Be*. New York: Brewer, Warren, and Putnam.

Zeitlin, Irving M. 1973. *Rethinking Sociology*. New York: Appleton-Century-Crofts.

Subject Index

Name Index

Abbott, Edith, 25, 32 n. 1, 312; and Sophonisba P. Breckinridge, 242, 243
Abbott, Grace, 278
Adams, George Burton, 246
Addams, Jane, 4-5, 9, 10, 11, 12, 18 n. 4, 21-22, 25, 71 n. 1, 95 ns. 1, 2, 247, 304 n. 24, 317, 331 n. 1; and Chicago City Club, 241, 264 n. 1; cultural feminism of, 26, 28; and Hicksite Quakers, 5; and LTEP, 159; and John Dewey, 5, 13-14, 271, 278, 313-14; and Juvenile Court, 158, 237 n. 4; on peace, 23-24, 26, 28, 38, 39, 95 ns. 12, 13, 101, 150 ns. 3, 4; non-resistance of, 5; and Red Scare, 278; and Red Summer, 244-45; and Russian relief, 278-79; and Women's International League of Peace and Freedom (WILPF), 28, 278; and war slogans, 208 n. 11; and World Court, 279; and *Newer Ideals of Peace* (1907), 27, 28, 35-36, 39, 43-49, 211; and *Women at the Hague*, 28, 31. *See also* Hull-House; Liberal institutions
Adorno, Theodor, 38, 157
Alonso, Harriet Hyman, 314
Angell, James Rowland, 313. *See also* Chicago Pragmatism
Aristotle, 56
Asquith, Herbert Henry, Lord, 190, 208 n. 4
Austin, John, 56

Balch, Emily Greene, 22, 275; and cultural pluralism, 40. *See also* Addams, Jane.
Ball, John, 72 n. 22
Barnes, Alfred, 208 n. 12
Bentham, Jeremy, 56, 72 n. 24, 169
Bernstorff, Count Johann, Von, 82
Bismarck, Otto von, 182, 184 n. 18, 304 n. 30
Blasi, Anthony, 311
Blumer, Herbert, 17 n. 1

Bourne, Randolph S., 29, 99, 270, 271; "Twilight of Idols," 29
Boyer, John W., 82
Boydston, JoAnne, 31
Breckinridge, Sophonisba, 14, 25, 32 n. 1
Burawoy, Michael, 325-26
Burke, Edmund, 88, 95 n. 11
Burns, John, 71 n. 1
Bush, George W. 326
Butler, Nicholas Murray, 38-40; and "international mind," 38-39; and "practical politics," 39

Campbell-Bannerman, Henry, Sir, 109
Castle, Harriet, 9
Castle, Helen (see Mead, Helen Castle)
Castle, Henry, 7-8, 156
Castle, Mabel Wing, 9, 28, 279, 280
Chamberlain, Houston Stewart, 66, 73 n. 37
Chatfield, Charles, 271, 317
Chesterton, G. K., 71 n. 1
Cicero, 237 n. 7
Chipman, Alice. *See* Dewey, Alice Chipman
Comte, August, 298
Cooley, Charles H., 7, 18 n. 4, 36
Cywar, Alan, 30, 270-71

Dante Alighieri, 128
Davis, Katherine Bement, 101, 151 n. 20, 312
Deegan, Mary Jo, 321, 322-28; and Hill, 18 n.1; and Malhotra [Benz], Valerie, 321; and Podeshi, 315; and play, 316. *See also* Mead, early
Denby, Karl, 243
Dewey, Alice Chipman, 9, 269-70
Dewey, John, 4, 8, 9, 11, 12, 36; and Evelyn Dewey, 269; general perspec-

355

CPSIA information can be obtained at www.ICGtesting.com
Printed in the USA
LVOW122339100512

281286LV00007B/10/P